Demonic History

Demonic History

From Goethe to the Present

✦

Kirk Wetters

NORTHWESTERN UNIVERSITY PRESS
EVANSTON, ILLINOIS

Northwestern University Press
www.nupress.northwestern.edu

Printed in the United States of America

10 9 8 7 6 5 4 3 2 1

ISBN 978-0-8101-3253-5

The Library of Congress has cataloged the original, hardcover edition as follows:

Wetters, Kirk, author.
    Demonic history : from Goethe to the present / Kirk Wetters.
    pages cm
    Includes bibliographical references and index.
    ISBN 978-0-8101-2976-4 (cloth : alk. paper)
    1. Demonology in literature. 2. German literature—19th century—History
and criticism. 3. German literature—20th century—History and criticism.
4. Devil in literature. I. Goethe, Johann Wolfgang von, 1749–1832. Urworte
orphisch. II. Goethe, Johann Wolfgang von, 1749–1832. Urworte orphisch.
English. III. Title. [DNLM: 1. Goethe, Johann Wolfgang von, 1749–1832—
Criticism and interpretation.]
    PT134.D456W48 2014
    830.937—dc23
                                                              2014012468

To write the history of a thought is sometimes to write the history of a series of misinterpretations.
—Pierre Hadot, *The Veil of Isis*

The Future is wholly a Stygian Darkness, spectre-bearing.
—Diogenes Teufelsdröckh in Thomas Carlyle, *Sartor Resartus*

CONTENTS

PREFACE AND ACKNOWLEDGMENTS

In the context of intellectual or conceptual history, "the demonic" may seem relatively peripheral—and perhaps it is. It undoubtedly covers, however, an extremely varied field spanning numerous intellectual traditions without at any point landing in a single discipline or arriving at a clear consensus or even at an extensive pre-sorting of the relevant semantics. This is not to say that the demonic is absent from lexica and scholarship, but use and usage of it in the main period of the present study—roughly 1800 to 1950—is anything but uniform. Rather than producing reliable conceptual or theoretical differentiations, the demonic, starting with Goethe and following his example, is often reinvented by every author who employs it. The demonic as I understand it is thus not a concept with a single definition (or even a set of definitions) but primarily an operative term and a vehicle of various kinds of rationalization.

The specificity of this construction is most easily demonstrated in the word itself: A "demon" can be understood as a substantialized or personified force, including the possibility that it may unify a collection of heterogeneous forces. If this substantialization is not taken literally as an actually existing or imaginary entity with a given appearance, specific attributes and motivations, then it can only be understood as a substantialization or rationalization or collectivization of *another force* (or forces). The essence of all demons is displacement and dislocation: whether as a daemon or a genius or an evil demon, demons are always proxies that make it possible to imagine the operation of other unidentified forces. The specific form or figure of the demon is a placeholder for invisible and unknown activities and motives which, like computer programs, mostly run silently in the background of a given operating system. Such systems can be made manifest, visible, and nameable; their specific conditions and codes can be brought to light; as specific functions, they may be made predictable and controllable. Normally they are aspects of an unquestioned functionality, but in moments of crisis, when the function becomes problematic, a plurality of unknown causes manifest themselves as a "demonic" singularity. From the point of view of the subject who experiences it, the unknown sources of a system-crisis are singularized and metaphorized as "demons."

The prevalence of the adjective "demonic" relative to the noun "demon" (which typically belongs to fantasy, myth, religion, and imagination) offers further illustration. One may not believe in actual demons, but many nouns—objects, persons, behaviors, situations, ideas—may act as if they were possessed by demons. Virtually anything is capable of acting as if it were under the control of an unknown force. Thus the word "demon," which strives to substantialize unknown and insubstantial agencies, is adjectivally de-substantialized into an ambiguous intentionality that can be attributed to almost anything. This act of attribution itself corresponds to the verb "to demonize," which suggests that the supposedly demonic object, person, or situation is not really possessed by such a force but has only been made to appear that way by a specific and unambiguous agency.

It may be that the German language's propensity for substantialization is partly to blame for the adjectival noun, "the demonic" (*das Dämonische*), which re-substantializes the adjectival de-substantialization of the noun's originally unwarranted substantial positing. Emerging from the movements of this—inevitably ironic—play of de- and re-substantialization, *the* demonic, starting from Goethe, served as a vehicle of variable thoughts and intention. Rather than presenting a dialogically structured field of "argument" and "counter-argument," the conceptual history of the demonic after Goethe developed "mimetically" along parallel and semi-independent fault lines. The demonic delineated itself in the interplay of unknown forces and the rhetorically articulated desires associated with these forces. More concretely, however, the term was often linked to the uncertainties surrounding determining drives imagined as the source of individual biography and collective history. With maximum vagueness, the demonic is the master term for whatever needs to be explained—but cannot be explained—by known causal factors. The mimetic aspect thus lies in the demonic's limitless availability for reconfiguring underlying factors according to the needs of the moment. A purely rational theory of causation has no need of the attribute "demonic."

The intensity of the desire to compensate for the unknown or inexplicable through an ironic rhetoric of super-rationality led many to miss the irony and misunderstand the demonic as referring to a real force or substance that is only waiting to be properly defined. The rhetorical side of the demonic and its consequent underlying lack of a solid conceptual or definitional foundation can be observed in the multiple sources of the demonic in Goethe. These sources are above all: (1) the five stanzas of the "Urworte Orphisch" ("Orphic Primal Words"), (2) Goethe's autobiography, *Poetry and Truth* (*Dichtung und Wahrheit*), (3) his morphological writings and, to a lesser degree, (4) his conversations with Eckermann. Despite numerous similarities and analogies, the divergences among these four models lead me not to assume that these conceptions are mutually compatible. The morphological writings establish paradigms or "cells" that can be traced through Goethe's work, while, at the same time, the demonic may be at stake "analogically" in texts where it is not referred to by name. The demonic, furthermore, as a result of the extensive architecture of analogy within and between Goethe's works, cannot be limited a priori to any particular corpus or canon.

The reduction of this structural indefiniteness to a single understanding produces an arbitrary and appropriative privileging. This kind of univocal approach has mostly defined the reception of Goethe's term (and to a lesser degree his work in general). Following Goethe's example, the history of the term even in its most appropriative and emulative moments tends toward variation and divergence more than toward reduction and simplification. The variety of the appropriations reflects the variant possibilities intrinsic to and dormant within Goethe's conception. My approach is thus to describe and defend the complexity of the *actions and interactions* that have taken place in the field of the demonic. This complexity is, on the one hand, specific to the material presented by the demonic itself and, on the other hand, essential to my approach, which is governed by a relatively high tolerance of unresolved complexity—which may itself have contributed to my choice of this particular topic. In the interest of complexity-reduction, however, I chose to focus primarily on Goethe's "Orphic Primal Words" in order to isolate the individual moments of the demonic against which variant and divergent conceptions can be coherently developed.

In the reception as far as I reconstruct it, the most powerful moment of complexity-reduction occurred in the early twentieth century. Oswald Spengler and Friedrich Gundolf especially set the tone. Their understandings remain influential today in ways that often go unrecognized. At the same time, starting with Georg Lukács, the literary potential of the demonic for the form of the novel emerged as a dominant motif. In the 1920s, both Walter Benjamin and Heimito von Doderer developed understandings of the demonic not as a rigid conceptual schema, fixed formula, or a purely thematic element but as a variable system of transformations. My study is oriented toward this latter context: from the very beginning, Goethe's concept was at once proto-literary and proto-theoretical, contributing both to the novels and the philosophical thought of the nineteenth century. Only in the twentieth century did it take on a decisively pseudo-philosophical and pseudo-scientific character in the works of Gundolf and Spengler. At the same time, this shift toward theory seems to have tipped the balance back toward the novel with its more free-form rereading of the underlying theoretical questions.

This is a speculative account of the narrative to follow. It is speculative, in part, because there was arguably never a complete split between the theoretical and literary potentials of the demonic. The extensive treatment of Goethe's conception in Hans Blumenberg's 1979 *Work on Myth* attests to this. Also, whatever crystallized around the idea of the demonic after 1910 did not do so in isolation: it was mediated and subjected to extreme turbulence by everything else that was transpiring at the same time. For example, the first decade of the twentieth century saw major works of Wundt, Freud, and Weber, as well as a blockbuster German translation of Dostoyevsky's *Bésy* as *Die Dämonen* (*The Demons*), all of which were unpredictably absorbed into later ideas about the demonic. Such complex fabrics lead to complex questions: Is it possible that Dostoyevsky knew something about the demonic in Goethe? How did Goethe's idea of the demonic make its way into the English language and its literature—and back to Germany—through Carlyle and Melville? To what degree were later theory-traditions—especially the Frankfurt School—indebted to habits of thought associated with the demonic? How do twentieth-century appropriations of the idea of the demonic interact with the legacy of German Idealist philosophy and the philosophy of history?

Given such far-reaching questions, I do not attempt to give final answers; I find it more productive to pose these questions so that I (or others) can continue to work on them to develop more precise answers. I have no doubt that there is more to be uncovered and that a different selection of materials would produce different results. Thus much may remain to be corrected or added, but I hope that my work will at least provide a stable platform from which to conduct future research. By showing the "roughness" of the terrain while making readers aware of its very existence, perhaps this foray will contribute to the clarification of related problems (as sketched in the conclusion).

The near total neglect of the twentieth-century rhetorics and systematics of the demonic seems to be a result of the tendency of those who do not directly participate in it at the "operative" level to view it as merely ornamental or rhetorical, as an uninteresting language of crisis or amplification without any theoretical underpinnings or a specific history. This assessment is certainly partly correct, but I would argue that not all terms and concepts are created equal, and thus not all conceptual histories can be written in the same way. The prejudice toward semantic uniformity within the apparently self-evident horizons of present understandings presupposes coherent historical developments and risks imposing uniformity on heterogeneity. On the other hand, if a lack of uniformity is presupposed, then each case must be handled in detail, for itself, and not just as an example of a linear development, a general understanding, or a supposedly prevalent usage. The demonic therefore—perhaps more so than any other word—is whatever it turns out to be.

In the course of a project that has been underway for more than a decade, more thanks are owed than can be easily conveyed. First of all, I would thank Eva Geulen, who helped me to discover—and, I think, hold onto—my own voice and to navigate the labyrinth of contemporary academia. Starting from the earliest phase of this project, I would also like to thank the advisors and sponsors of my 2000–2001 German Academic Exchange (DAAD) year in Frankfurt am Main (who must have conspired to introduce me to Heimito von Doderer): Werner Hamacher and Thomas Schestag. At New York University, Eva Geulen (my dissertation advisor), Anselm Haverkamp, Paul Fleming, and Rüdiger Campe (at NYU as a visitor) have remained constant sources of inspiration and support. Rüdiger Campe especially, now my colleague at Yale, has guided and encouraged my work since its first stages. I also thank my many past and current colleagues at Yale, whose personal generosity, conversation, and critical feedback pushed my work forward: above all Carol Jacobs, as well as Rainer Nägele, Henry Sussman, Brigitte Peucker, Paul North, Howard Stern, Adam Tooze, Hindy Najman, Elke Siegel (now at Cornell), the late Cyrus Hamlin (whose conversation I greatly missed in the last years), Pat McCreless, Bentley Layton, and countless others; also, at Northwestern University, Peter Fenves and Jörg Kreienbrock. I also thank Henry Carrigan at Northwestern University Press for his unflagging support; and finally—most recently—I am grateful to Josh Alvizu, Jason Kavett, and Andrew Kirwin for helping me to complete the manuscript under tight deadlines.

I am also grateful to the Alexander von Humboldt Foundation for the fellowship at the University of Bonn in 2010–2011. There I benefited from the company, hospitality, and brilliance of Eva Geulen, Jürgen Fohrmann, Jürgen Brokoff, Lars Friedrich, Stephan Kraft, Christian Meierhofer, Eva Axer, Michael Auer, Christoph Brecht, Joachim Harst, Oliver Baron—and all of the participants in the July 2011 conference on the demonic. My work on the demonic in Heimito von Doderer also brought me into contact with the Heimito von Doderer Society and many remarkable "Heimitisten": Gerald Sommer, Rudolf Helmstetter, and Vincent Kling. I am also grateful to the Bonn *Oberseminar* which—at the instigation of Eva Geulen—spent two semesters reading Doderer.

Finally, my profound thanks go to Amy Ulrich, for her patience and perspective; also to my brother, Brent Wetters, whose musical and technological support are only the most nameable of his contributions; and above all to my parents, Carol Wetters and Richard Wetters, for their endless support.

LIST OF ABBREVIATIONS

AaM	Blumenberg, Hans. *Arbeit am Mythos*. Frankfurt am Main: Suhrkamp, 1979.
DD	Doderer, Heimito von. *Die Dämonen*. Munich: Biederstein, 1956.
FA	Goethe, J. W. von. *Sämtliche Werke. Briefe, Tagebücher, Gespräche*. 39 vols. Frankfurt am Main: Deutscher Klassiker Verlag, 1999.
GS	Benjamin, Walter. *Gesammelte Schriften*. Edited by Rolf Tiedemann. Frankfurt am Main: Suhrkamp, 1991.
HA	Goethe, J. W. von. *Werke. Hamburger Ausgabe*. 14 vols. Edited by Erich Trunz. Munich: Deutscher Taschenbuch Verlag, 1998.
HÄs	Lukács, Georg. *Heidelberger Ästhetik 1916–1918*. In *Werke* 17. Edited by György Márkus and Frank Benseler. Darmstadt: Luchterhand, 1974.
MA	Goethe, J. W. von. *Sämtliche Werke*. Edited by Karl Richter et al. Munich: Carl Hanser Verlag, 1985–1998.
R	Doderer, Heimito von. *Repertorium: Ein Begreifbuch von höheren und niederen Lebens-Sachen*. Edited by Dietrich Weber. Munich: Beck, 1996.
TB	Doderer, Heimito von. *Tagebücher 1920–1939*. Edited by Wendelin Schmidt-Dengler, Martin Loew-Cadonna & Gerald Sommer. Munich: Beck, 1996.
TdR	Lukács, Georg. *Die Theorie des Romans: Ein geschichtsphilosophischer Versuch über die Formen der großen Epik*. Neuwied: Luchterhand, 1971.
UdA	Spengler, Oswald. *Der Untergang des Abendlandes: Umrisse einer Morphologie der Weltgeschichte*. Munich: DTV, 2006.
UO	Buck, Theo. *Goethes "Urworte. Orphisch."* Frankfurt am Main: Peter Lang, 1996.
WdD	Doderer, Heimito von. *Die Wiederkehr der Drachen: Aufsätze, Traktate, Reden*. Edited by Wendelin Schmidt-Dengler. Munich: Beck, 1996.

Demonic History

Introduction

Dasein ist Besessensein. (Being is being-possessed.)
—Hans Jonas, *Gnosis und spätantiker Geist*
(*Gnosticism and the Spirit of Late Antiquity*)

The Story of a "Something" (Background and Methods)

In keeping with Goethe's famous presentation in book 20 of *Poetry and Truth* (*Dichtung und Wahrheit*), the first thing that must be said about the demonic (*das Dämonische*) is what it is not. According to Goethe's autobiographical narrative, the demonic was in the first place a "something" (an "*etwas*") that "manifested itself in contradictions and therefore could not be captured under any concept, much less in a word" (HA 10:175).[1] He proceeds to give a series of negative definitions: "It was not divine, because it seemed to lack reason, not human, because it had no understanding, not devilish, because it was benevolent, not angelic, because it frequently betrayed *Schadenfreude*" (HA 10:175). This sentence is followed by a series of tentative positive definitions, but they tend toward paradox and self-contradiction. These various "definitions" are further clouded by their reliance on a language of appearance and resemblance: "It resembled coincidence [*Zufall*], because it displayed no consequence; it looked like Providence, because it gave indications of coherence. Everything that limits us seemed permeable to it; it seemed to arbitrarily control the necessary elements of our existence; it gathered time together and made space expand. Only in the impossible did it seem to be at home, whereas it treated the possible with disdain" (HA 10:175). The riddle posed by these lines has been often cited, but never solved—probably because, taken on its own terms, it is insoluble.

According to Hans Blumenberg's *Work on Myth*, these enigmatic paragraphs about the demonic have been a perennial source and object of "interpretive desire" (*Deutungslust*).[2] In the following pages and chapters, I do not intend to give in to this desire. For now, I merely observe the deliberately enigmatic quality of Goethe's definitions, which is the precise source of unfulfillable interpretive desires. The demonic as Goethe configures it is designed to tantalize, and to the extent that the reader assumes the role of Tantalus, all that emerges is a mythic punishment, the repetition and limitless

3

extension of a futile and essentially self-serving desire. In a further tanta-
lizing concession to the apparent insolubility of the riddle, Goethe gives a
name to this "something" and thus—in a way—solves it. This name has often
been thought to provide the decisive clue to what Goethe meant, but I will
argue that this onomasiological naming only makes matters worse:[3] "This
entity, which appeared to emerge between all the others in order to separate and connect them, is what I called 'demonic' (following the example of
the ancients and of everyone else who had perceived something similar)"
(HA 10:175–76). This appellation still does not take the form of a positive
identification but continues to develop within the framework of a logic of
similarity. The title "demonic" does not definitively name the indefinite "something" it refers to. The referent remains a sheer *etwas*, which has been only
nominally and provisionally dubbed—for the lack of a better word—"the
demonic." It has not been properly named, identified, defined, determined,
clarified, contained, controlled, banished, or exorcised. Instead, "the
demonic," a substantialized adjective, performs a representation by substitution, producing a shorthand and a stopgap, at once a proxy and a powerful
personification.[4]

Goethe's introduction of the demonic thus ends: "I attempted to save
myself from this terrifying being by fleeing behind an image, as is my habit"
(HA 10:176). The "image" in question looks ahead to the next paragraph,
in which Goethe introduces his work on the play *Egmont* as a flight into
imagination and an early attempt to hide from the demonic within a literary configuration. The sentence may equally refer, however, to the "image"
created in the decision to transform an indefinite and fearful *etwas* into "a
being" and "an entity" (*ein Wesen*). The imagination of "a demonic something," even in the awareness of the inadequacy and illegitimacy of this
conception, is itself a flight from the unimaginable, unintelligible uncertainty
that gave rise to it.

This brings me back to what the demonic is and is not. It may be many
things—many contradictory things—at the same time, as Goethe's further
presentation shows. It may be, for example, "benevolent" (*wohltätig*) yet
"monstrous" (*ungeheuer*), "inconceivable" (*unfassbar*), and "terrifying"
(*furchtbar*) (HA 10:175–76). Two of these adjectives appear as nouns, "*the*
monstrous," "*the* inconceivable," which can be read, based on the general
tendency toward the substantialization of adjectives, as partially synonymous
or at least analogous with the demonic. The word *furchtbar* in particular
seems to be of special importance because it reappears in the later paragraph
on demonic characters: "The demonic appears most terrifying [*am furcht-
barsten*] when it predominates in an individual human being [*in irgend einem
Menschen*]" (HA 10:177). The repeated emphasis on the fearful and terrifying that punctuate Goethe's presentation leads me to believe—as the word
"demonic" may also imply—that *das Dämonische* is not entirely or even
primarily benevolent. However, the paradoxical juxtaposition of opposites,

together with Goethe's remark that the demonic tends "to be in play on both sides" of conflicts and oppositions (HA 10:176), might also lead one to see the demonic as *a being of contradiction*. This hypothesis in turn would have to be reconciled with the demonic's interstitial status—its *being between*—and its role as an "entity" that supposedly intervenes within and binds all things together.

It would be possible to work through such considerations at great length—and perhaps thereby give in to "the interpretive urge" (*Deutungslust*). Without going so far here, I hope to have preliminarily demonstrated that the interpreter of the passages on the demonic must decide to prioritize certain characterizations of the demonic in order to give coherence to the whole—or else allow the individual moments of the presentation to exist simultaneously, paratactically, each with its own implications, none definitively reducible to the others. I will typically follow the second approach, but either way one reads it, it is abundantly clear that the demonic is neither a classical "daemon" or "daimon" nor a "demon" or "evil spirit." It also is not a Mephistophelian "spirit that constantly negates" (*Faust*, v. 1338; HA 3:47)—even if it might be possible to find in Mephisto a further personification of the ungraspable forces that Goethe brings together under the label "demonic."[5] Thus, though it would be an oversimplification to equate Goethe's "demonic" with demons or with the idea of evil, the considerations of the various half-definitions of the demonic (for example, the reference to Providence) make it clear that residual elements of theology and theodicy are an important part of the picture.

Primarily for this reason, as well as for others that I will develop later on, I cannot follow Angus Nicholls's 2006 *Goethe's Concept of the Daemonic: After the Ancients* in its decision to read "the demonic" as "the daemonic." Nicholls's study is groundbreaking in that it represents the first systematic intellectual-historical and philological study on Goethe's *das Dämonische*. Nicholls focuses on the genesis of the conception in a trajectory stretching back to the Socratic *daimonion* and the Aristotelian idea of entelechy, and up to Leibniz, Hamann, and Herder, who lie behind Goethe's *Sturm und Drang* poetics of genius; the latter anticipated the development of the idea of the demonic in Goethe's middle and late period. This account is entirely convincing, and my own work largely presupposes it. And even though I do not follow Nicholls's orthography, I do not mean to deny his wider thesis that Goethe often articulated the demonic in a way that brought it into proximity with discourses on genius, including the Socratic *daimonion* (which is central in Nicholls's account). On this point, Hans Blumenberg's 1979 *Work on Myth* observes: "In the first instance [*zunächst*], in my view, the discourse on the demonic is only an attempt to avoid the relatively thoughtless way in which the youth of the *Sturm und Drang* applied the attribute of the 'divine' [*das Göttliche*]" (AaM 519).[6] The heroizing and highly influential tradition epitomized by Friedrich Gundolf's 1916 *Goethe* also emphatically reads the demonic in relation to Goethe's own genius. For this reason alone, the connection between the two can hardly be undone—but I approach precisely this tradition with a high degree of skepticism.

What is valid "in the first instance" (*zunächst*) is not always valid throughout. Goethe's words on the demonic from *Poetry and Truth* hardly encourage the identification of this particular "something" with some already known entity or definite idea (such as genius). On the other hand, at a certain point one may want to attribute the contradictory details of Goethe's presentation to deliberate evasiveness. The value of Nicholls's study thus lies in its attempt to pin Goethe down by tracing the genesis of the conception together with the name that Goethe gave to it. But my position is that the apparent imprecision of Goethe's definitions is not incidental or contingent, but rather systematic and essential. Goethe's claim that he named the demonic "after the example of the ancients *and others who thought something similar*" (HA 10:175–76, my emphasis) promises sources that are never named. Which "ancients" and which "others" does Goethe mean? His *Orphic* primal words (*Urworte*) begin with a stanza called "demon" (*Daimon*), but the poem itself may equally imply the Aristotelian idea of entelechy, as Nicholls argues (*Goethe's Concept of the Daemonic* 66–77). Jochen Schmidt's 2006 essay on Goethe's *Urworte* supposes Heraclitean sources (*Goethes Altersgedicht Urworte* 17).[7] Nicholls's approach leads him to summarize and generalize the demonic as the product of a certain "lineage" or "classical heritage" (230), which is further taken as a norm with respect to which Goethe can be "incorrect" (256). Such a synthetic-genetic reading, for all its value, is clearly a retrospective construct, the product of countless secondary elaborations.[8] To be sure, such constructions are often unavoidable. It is a question of the degree to which it is possible to locate the demonic within the horizons of eighteenth-century literary and conceptual history and the degree to which it represents an entirely new intellectual gambit. It may be both at once, but whereas Nicholls seeks to uncover the foundations of Goethe's conception in a comprehensive intellectual history, my work will largely pursue the demonic as something new.

In addition to Nicholls, the other relatively recent figure who has addressed the demonic at length is the great postwar philosopher Hans Blumenberg in his 1979 *Work on Myth*. Blumenberg's work is similar to Nicholls's in the sense that he also tends to trace the problem back to ancient origins—specifically to the idea of myth. The story of *Work on Myth*, however, only partly overlaps with Nicholls's account, because Blumenberg reads the demonic within the context of his own theory of "self-assertion" (*Selbstbehauptung*) and the legitimacy of the modern age. For Blumenberg, the impetus behind the demonic is radically anti-traditional and anti-classical. Also, in comparison to Nicholls, Blumenberg bases his reading on different lines from *Poetry and Truth,* leading him to identify the demonic with problems of biographical and historical representation:

In the last book of *Poetry and Truth,* published after Goethe's death, he said that the word [the demonic] encapsulated the sum of every-thing that could have been seen "at length in the course of this biographical presentation." It referred to the unresolved remainder [*der ungelöste Rest*] of his experience, to which he gave the title of the demonic. But this title and the interpretive desire [*Deutungslust*] it has awakened are not the main thing. What is crucial is this "remain-der" itself. (AaM 437)

This biographical understanding of the demonic informs an approach that is on the verge of problematic biographism: Blumenberg reads the idea of the demonic through the lens of Goethe's shifting identifications with the figure of Prometheus.[9] However, outside of the chapters on Goethe (which frequently rely on biographical reconstructions), a systematic reconstruction of Goethe's idea of the demonic can be discerned in Blumenberg's overall theory of myth. The implicit point of his treatment of the demonic is to avoid "interpreting" it (and thereby giving in to *Deutungslust*). Instead he tries to go back to square one, in order to completely retheorize *what Goethe must have had in mind.* The result of this speculative approach is that Blumenberg effectively replaces Goethe's confusing *non-concept* (and the history of its misunderstandings) with his own extensive theory. In contrast to Nicholls, whose identification of the demonic with a known and knowable lineage represents an effort of containment, Blumenberg pursues a strategy of super-saturation: he is interested in the metaphysical and anthropological questions implicit in the demonic, but he strives to develop them on his own terms.[10]

While producing a demystification with respect to *Deutungslust,* the resulting theory of myth—which may not be a theory in a strict sense at all—corresponds to only one aspect of Goethe's conception: for Blumenberg, the demonic is an attempt to name and personify the fragility of human existence in the world. This sense of a demonic contingency is reflected in an indefi-nite "something" which myth, religion, science, politics, social systems, and individual subjects have perennially tried to explain and master.[11] With clear reference to the function of myth and to the implications of his own meta-phorological method, Blumenberg invokes Goethe's idea of "fleeing [from the demonic] behind an image" (*Flucht hinter ein Bild,* AaM 437).[12] Thus myth, metaphor, and narrative, including religion, philosophy, and literature, collectively accomplish the same escapist and taming function that Goethe adopted as his own life strategy.

If Nicholls's book recently reopened the question of the demonic in Goethe, Blumenberg's implicit intent in 1979 was to close it by translating it into considerations that would allow it to be conceptually circumvented. In the denunciation of *Deutungslust* and the contextualization of the demonic in a work on myth, Blumenberg seeks to get beyond the confusions Goethe bequeathed to the tradition. According to Blumenberg, the demonic "encompasses or perhaps only names unresolved historical potency [*Potenz*] without explaining it" (AaM 559). He continues:

> This may be the fault of the weak judgment of a single fascinated individual [i.e., Goethe]. But a whole century of analytical and descriptive attempts to resolve the phenomenon [of Napoleon] through historiography (which cannot tolerate the mythic) has left something in its wake, in the form of a resistance to theorization, which is akin to that to which the poet [Goethe] at least gave a name. (AM 559)[13]

Blumenberg argues that the demonic is an improper name for "a resistance to theory"[14]—for the untheorizable remnant left over by all theories. The demonic designates the inaccessibility of first causes, especially when it comes to historical and biographical knowledge.

Angus Nicholls attempts to reconcile Blumenberg's conception with his own approach and various others (Nicholls 268–69), but I would rather see differences and even contradictions. Blumenberg's reading of the demonic as a limit of certainty and theorizability implies that the sources of genius (and of evil and earth-shattering historical events) are unknowable. While Nicholls acknowledges this, he risks overlooking the methodological implications that this "resistance" may have for intellectual history itself. Blumenberg's idea of a limit of theorizability impacts the achievability of what Nicholls calls his "central purpose," "to show that this term [the demonic] . . . springs from a rich heritage of ancient Greek philosophy, most notably embodied in the writings of Plato and especially in Plato's representation of the Socratic *daimonion*" (268). Nicholls's reading thus conflicts with Blumenberg's in a rather ironic way: Nicholls shows the historical sources of a term which, for Blumenberg, refers to the unknowability of historical sources and causes.

For me, Blumenberg's connection of *das Dämonische* to history and historiography are of decisive methodological importance. "Demonic history" is that which remains when all facts and causes, all motivations and responsibilities, lineages and descendancies, are exhausted and moot. A *demonic history* is a history that cannot be positively explained, and the history of the idea of the demonic is itself an example of the limits of historical explicability.[15] Thus, following Blumenberg—but beyond what is explicit in *Work on Myth*—my work is guided by the questions: What if the demonic is *not one thing*, but only a "something," an *etwas* called *das Dämonische*? What if it is not a term or a concept but only a metaphor, an image, a stand-in for variable unknowns and, by extension and personification, for *the* unknown? This approach leads me to focus not primarily on *the word* "demonic," but on *the thing* in its demonstrated variability, through transformations that have revealed it as a potent but problematic existential metaphor.

But, since the demonic is no thing but only a "something," it can only be pursued through what it hides behind—and what hides behind it. The demonic in this sense is a paradigmatic case for Blumenberg's method of metaphorology and non-conceptuality. His characteristic question is: what happens when a metaphor stands in for an object that cannot be (fully) known? With respect to this question, *das Dämonische*, the name that Goethe devised for the unknowable and incalculable, represents a limit case. The demonic, as a metaphor of *the* unknown, is a meta-metaphor corresponding to the lack of perfect knowledge and conceptual precision that necessitate metaphor in the first place. For this reason, I do not look for sources of "the demonic" but try to trace its possible referents and applications, overtones and undertones, uses and abuses. This means that, though I often work philologically, I do not understand philology as a search for origins. The demonic in Georg Lukács clearly "comes from" Goethe—at least in part—but it does not do so in an obvious and direct way. The reception of the demonic always involves divergences and uncertain intermediary figures, which makes a pure or linear derivation impossible. For example, it is not the case that every writer who "receives" the term *das Dämonische* from Goethe receives the same thing and adds one specific thing to it. Thus I do not presume that later appropriations conform to earlier ones—or to Goethe's understandings. My view of Goethe is constantly modulated and motivated by the specific imperatives and questions that emerge from the reception. The point for me is not to figure out "what Goethe meant" in an absolute way, but only relative to others' understandings. As a consequence, I do not treat "Goethe" as a substantial unity. He is undoubtedly a "primal father" (*Urvater*) in the sense of Freud's *Moses and Monotheism*, but I deliberately try not to approach him as an exemplar or object of identification.[16]

For this reason, the present study is not a "Goethe book" in the sense that it primarily wants to say something about Goethe. Rather than presupposing a single conception or unified paradigm of the demonic, my findings lead me to conclude that Goethe's thought was organized in a way that produced varied and divergent—but frequently inter-relatable—conceptions. The readings that follow will show that a unified concept of the demonic cannot be taken for granted in Goethe or among his readers. This reception is not organized in a linear way, and I do not claim to cover it exhaustively. For every figure I deal with extensively, there are certainly others who might have led in other directions. As I see it, the urge to "cover" everything "relevant" is based on the presumption of a linear reception that always occurs in essentially the same way. The linear approach is of course practical, in that it allows for reductions that permit simple direct comparisons. But this certainly does not work very well for the demonic. My work shows that every "reception" contains its own story; the attempt to work out these narratives in detail is of more value, I believe, than an encyclopedic or doxographic approach.[17]

This does not mean, however, that my text selections are arbitrary. The focal point of the reception—or rather its point of refraction—falls toward the end of the 1910s. Within this period, Friedrich Gundolf and the metahistorian

Oswald Spengler are responsible for popularizing the idea and giving it a burning sense of contemporariness. It is through these two figures that the underlying problems posed by the demonic reemerge with urgency. Subsequently, still in the 1910s and early 1920s, I find a "next wave" reception in Walter Benjamin and Georg Lukács, whose work proved to have a very different historical—and political—reach than that of Gundolf and Spengler. However, all of these authors included the demonic in works that shaped the later traditions that are often simply called "theory." In the run-up to long-term structurations of multiple discourse-frames leading up to the present, my work uncovers a dense and active field of discussion on the demonic in the century following Goethe's death. Such discussions sometimes occurred without direct explicit reference to Goethe, but, given the esteem in which he was widely held at the time in the German-speaking world, his ideas certainly catalyzed the sedimentation of the ancient idea of the demonic in a variety of interlocking discourses. As Nicholls shows, the roots of this can be traced back to much older sources—but it is Goethe's conception that reactivated them and made them current.

Multiple crystallizations resulted from Goethe's perception of something demonic. The relevance of this material to countless figures within the period in question is surprising enough that scholars of various backgrounds will have to confirm for themselves whether the idea of the demonic has, as I claim, an unexpected theoretical and systematic consistency.[18] One would expect such a consistency to be more evident in the German-speaking world, but the international reach of the demonic is surprisingly vast. It may not always have been directly associated with Goethe, but parallel conceptions and intermediary figures helped the idea to spread anonymously. Important examples of such figures are Thomas Carlyle, Herman Melville, Søren Kierkegaard, Sigmund Freud, Max Weber, and Carl Schmitt. What is most surprising, at least from my own perspective, is that this web of connections has been rarely noticed and never extensively studied. Given this situation, I have tried to note possible interrelations as they present themselves, in order to mark the horizons of future research and provide a basis for the critical identification of figures of thought associated with the demonic. My aim is not to produce conceptual or systematic consistency as much as to produce a sensitivity to the varied concerns that have been brought together under the title of the demonic. This is important because of the many instances when Goethe's idea of the demonic has covered over—or been covered by—or been ambiguously superimposed upon other paradigms. Such duplications allowed the specific sense of Goethe's idea of the "demonic" to all but disappear in the last fifty years. This outcome can be observed in Lukács's *Theory of the Novel*, which quite systematically superimposes the demonic upon a philosophy of history that is widely held to be Hegelian. Precisely this strategy apparently did not lead many to conclude that the demonic might be an important independent category (or even a theme) for understanding the form of the novel.

And yet the demonic never entirely disappeared, even if readers in the later twentieth century increasingly lost the awareness of precisely *which* tradition was being invoked—and even *that* a tradition was being invoked. The word "demonic" is easy to overlook as the mere symptom of an affect, and though this reading is frequently right (or partly right), my work shows that precisely in the most affectively and politically charged contexts (Spengler, Gundolf, Lukács, Benjamin), systematic aspects of Goethe's conception are implicitly or marginally retained. As a result, the relatively common word "demonic" was able to become a dominant subtext, inextricably implicated in the defining discourses of modernity as well as in the overlapping philologies of literature and theory. It at once refers to *and characterizes,* in Goethe and many others, massively prevalent conceptions (for example, the interconnectedness of "fate and character"). Precisely these aspects are often not very well understood, even in frequently read and taught "classics" of early twentieth-century theory. The demonic is thus important at least to the extent that these theories remain important, even if it is also clear that we are talking about a dated usage. To the extent that the demonic refers to things that could also be called otherwise, it will never be completely decidable what is gained or lost in the label "demonic." At the limit, it may include ideas that were conceived without the slightest awareness of it, as well as ideas that were conceived with reference to it but went on to lose the label. Thus the awareness of this odd topos may cause one to discover it where it is not, but also, more importantly, may facilitate discursively productive connections across a wide spectrum—including the whole political spectrum—of nineteenth- and twentieth-century authors.

Thus my general historical thesis is that Goethe's *metaphor* of the demonic was available, for about a hundred years, to the most diverse (and often implicit) forms of appropriation and re-articulation.[19] Moreover, this continuum, which proceeds with reference to underlying problems and implicit metaphysical questions, illustrates the interdependence of literature and theory and reveals the disadvantages of strictly differentiating them.

"Demons" or "Daemons"?

In a fragmentary chapter of André Gide's 1925 novel *The Counterfeiters* (*Les faux-monnayeurs*), entitled "Identification of the Demon" ("Identification du démon"), a character says: "Do you know what Goethe said? That a man's strength [*puissance*] and his force of predestination [*sa force de prédestination*] were recognizable by the demoniacal element he has in him [*à ce qu'il portait en lui de démoniaque*]" (*The Counterfeiters* 467). It may be that Gide "got it wrong" in presenting the demonic as a demoniacal force of character or "prédestination." But because this question is voiced in the context of a dialogue in a novel, it would be premature to attribute this conception to Gide. If anything, the question—"Do you know what Goethe *said?*"—reduces the "something" called the demonic to "something Goethe said" and thereby introduces the mechanics of reception, which tend to overlook, condense, and elide whatever is received, in order to redeploy it for its own purposes and in its own sense.

And, despite the word "démoniaque," this reading does not conjure up any literal demons. What is, after all, a "literal" demon? Gide's title, "the identification of the demon," poses this question in a way that contrasts with the staged naïveté of the question about "what Goethe said." The stated answer, that the demonic is a category of predestination, implicitly expresses doubt as to the origins and ends of the supposed predestination: A "demonic" predestination is clearly not identical with the divine one that the word "predestination" typically implies. According to this idea of the demonic, attributed to Goethe, the inherited idea of an external (divine) "predestination" is internalized within the "demonic" individual, who is not ruled by an external fate or providence but by an unidentified force—distinct from free will—which then supposedly manifests itself as personal "strength" or "power" (*puissance*).

There are no literal, physical demons here, and also no devils. The choice of the word "demonic," attributed to Goethe, only makes sense as a metaphor of demonic possession. Whether this understanding accurately reflects what Goethe "said" is not of primary importance, because Gide's presentation assumes an implicit differentiation between what Goethe actually said (which is never stated) and an attempted paraphrase. Goethe's demonic is one thing, and what it is belatedly held and claimed to be is something else. Gide's dialogue shows that whatever the demonic may or may not have been, it lends itself to misunderstanding and appropriation. This susceptibility to (intentional) misunderstanding becomes especially pivotal—a demonic ambiguity in more ways than one—precisely if one supposes that the demonic has nothing to do with devils. Gide's reliance on an implicit metaphorics of demonic possession illustrates that the exorcism of "demons" out of the demonic only works at a high level of abstraction—or to the extent that one is willing to posit that the demonic is directly and exclusively linked with the Socratic *daimonion.*[20]

I do not assume such a linkage, but rather read Goethe's *das Dämonische* as a conscious telescoping of unnamed traditions. This is explicitly the case insofar as Goethe chose the name "based on the example of the ancients and others who thought something similar" (HA 10:175–76). This reference is completely open. Gnostic or early Christian overtones, for example, may be audible. Goethe set no limits on what might be "similar" to the demonic, and later receptions—such as Jonas's *Gnosticism and the Spirit of Late Antiquity,* Lukács's *Theory of the Novel,* and Blumenberg's debates with Schmitt[21]—have often focused theological problems that begin with the end of antiquity. In this context, to a greater degree than is the case in Goethe, the demonic is a specifically modern problem. If reflections on the demonic from Kierkegaard and Dostoyevsky to Lukács, Spengler, Benjamin, Jonas, and Blumenberg are identified as the main line of the reception—which it certainly is, at least in retrospect—then the demonic is evidently coextensive with the problem of modernity.

If Goethe's *das Dämonische* was understood in this way, the decision to render it in English as "the demonic" runs the risk of overemphasizing the idea of evil. The orthography "daemonic," on the other hand, preserves ambiguity with respect to evil and avoids the implication that modernity is merely being *denounced* as a "demonic age." But what are the consequences, whether with respect to antiquity or to modernity, of supposing that *daemoniacal* forces are at work on the stage of history? Nietzsche's *Birth of Tragedy*, which Gide's dialogue may have also had in mind, conceives history as emerging from precisely such forces. On the historical stage, it may be hard to tell whether the historical force exerted by figures like Moses or Socrates or Goethe or Napoleon is demonic or daemonic, because the essence of this force is expressed in historical effects and retrospective recognitions and valuations. What makes historical individuals demonic (or daemonic) is the semi-autonomous and suprapersonal dissemination of their *daemon*. This *daemon* may, however, also be understood as *demonic* insofar as it is imagined to be capable of "possessing" countless individuals across great spans of time and space. It is in this sense that Nietzsche speaks of "the Dionysiac daemon" and "the daemonic Socrates."[22]

Given the relative ease with which the demonic and the daemonic can be pushed to the point of ambiguity, the terminological decision is by no means easy. But to the extent that theorists like Spengler and Lukács radicalize the problematic status of modernity developed by eighteenth-century thinkers such as Winckelmann and Schiller, the recourse to the demonic in the early twentieth century is directly connected with a sense of decline and a desire for renewal. The main difference with the eighteenth century—especially evident in Lukács—is that the break with a classicistic aesthetics of imitation becomes so extreme that the aesthetic itself begins to be called into question. For the young Lukács, the aesthetic no longer represents the royal road to the political but is only the siren song of an unrecoverable "Greece." In such a "fallen" modernity, the demonic can easily become a vehicle for the expression of a godforsaken state.

In Goethe, by contrast, the demonic condition is not purely negative, and this seems to have been a fact that was fairly well known in the early twentieth century. A powerful illustration of the "summary" of Goethe's conception as a reflex of early twentieth-century concerns is the theologian Paul Tillich's 1926 *Das Dämonische: Ein Beitrag zur Sinndeutung der Geschichte* (*The Demonic: A Contribution to the Question of Meaning in History*). As far as I know, this essay still represents the most important systematic theological study—with or without Goethe—on the demonic.[23] For Tillich, the demonic

refers to the endless opposition of form and formlessness, meaning and meaninglessness, which can be traced in the history of all religions, including the
Enlightenment's efforts of rationalization and secularization (Tillich 24–31).
At the limit, this conception touches on wider topics of myth and theodicy,
but, more narrowly, Tillich very clearly had "literal" demons in mind, both
in his analyses of their cross-cultural representations—as distortions of the
human form—and in the difference between the demonic and the divine.
Moreover, he supposes that a deposed god—a demon—never completely dis-
appears from the historical stage. This understanding imposes an additional
limit to the possibilities of enlightenment and secularization: vanquished
gods "never entirely lose their demonic power and always stand ready to
step into the foreground in the event that the ruling forms of divinity should
experience a crisis" (25, my translation). In conceptions like this one—indirectly traceable to Goethe by way of Rudolf Otto's 1917 *Das Heilige* (*The
Sacred*)[24]—the demonic may still play its Socratic role as "an intermediary
or hybrid entity" (*Zwischenwesen,* 25), but it does so precisely as a *demon,*
as an uncertain, ambiguous, and potentially antagonistic force outside of the
direct control of the subject. Here and in Gide, the difference between a possibly benevolent *daemon* and a supposedly evil demon can only be resolved
in view of a historical-theological horizon of ultimate ends.

The self-evident presupposition of the origins and ends of the world—and
the correlated means—was profoundly called into question and constantly
reasserted since the beginning of the Christian era. Demons, *Dämonen,* in
German as in ancient Greek can work for good or evil. Thus the German
word cannot entirely banish its ambiguous co-invocation of *evil* spirits,
whereas the English "demon" presents a tenuous claim to know the difference between good and evil. The inescapability of these ambiguities is not a
mere semantic problem but inheres in the very idea of a demon: what once
appears as a benevolent *daimonion* may later—or from a different perspective—appear as a demonic persecution. There is a plausible explanation for
the historical transformation that tilted this fundamental ambivalence in
the direction of malevolence. According to David Brakke's *Demons and the
Making of the Monk,* the meaning of the word *daimon* in the ancient world
changed decisively and irreversibly as a result of Christianity:

> Likewise, in this same period [fourth- and early fifth-century Christian
> Egypt], even non-Christian philosophers, such as Iamblichus, began
> to accept an idea that their predecessors had rejected: the *daimon* was
> not merely an intermediary divine being, filling in the gap between
> human beings and the distant gods, but could be an evil power that
> caused harm to human beings. Scholars who study ancient under-
> standings of the *daimon* often rightly use the more neutral English
> "daemon" to signal that the *daimon* is not always a negative force.
> For the Christian monk, the *daimon* became a fearsome enemy, an

agent of evil that could appear as a human being, a wild animal, or even an angel. The opponent of the monk was the unambiguously evil demon. (5)

Goethe's conception does not present the demonic as "unambiguously evil," but neither does it belong exclusively to a pre-Christian or non-Christian understanding.[25] This impasse, together with the fact that the threatening and irrational aspects are most relevant for modernity, may have motivated Giorgio Agamben and his translator to use "the demonic" even in the context of pre- and non-Christian antiquity.[26] Following Agamben, I will mostly use the word "demon" unless the context clearly refers to a "daemon" à la Socrates. Even in Goethe's "Orphic Primal Words" ("Urworte Orphisch"), in which the Greek *daimon* is glossed as "character" and "individuality," I see no immediate reason why this may not be interpreted as a kind of possession. According to the fifth line of the daemon-stanza of the "Urworte": "You cannot flee yourself" (*dir kannst du nicht entfliehen*). In this sense, the individual's daemon may be simultaneously a persecuting demon.[27] This holds, I would argue, for all instances of "demonic" self-relation, which can either be conceived, at one extreme, as a split within the subject or as a relation to an alterity (a daemon) or, at the other extreme, as a form of possession (with the self under the control of a demon). The shades of difference within this spectrum are not easy to differentiate in any given case. Socrates's fate shows how easily the suspicion of evil motives may arise when a daemon is in play. And even if it is not obviously "evil," the daemonic self-relation remains extremely suspect in the modern (Christian) world. The daemon's lack of rational basis, of logical transparency and hierarchy, of clear responsibility and accountability, mean that it can always turn out to be a demon. The post-Goethean conception, on the other hand, clearly goes beyond good and evil in that it belongs to a world in which the difference between demons and daemons is not necessarily immediately recognizable or even important. The daemon or *daimonion* is a latent demon, a demon waiting for future transvaluations; and the demon for its part is a latent god, waiting for its day.

The demonic is beyond good and evil, but as a general category of the inexplicable it is prone to mystification. Regardless of the degree to which inexplicability may be generalized into a threat or a state, the demonic in Goethe is an essentially empirical and experiential category of inexplicability, which cannot be said to occupy a specific existential or theological position (because the experience of inexplicability itself can be an aspect of numerous systems). A contemporary discourse on the demonic, a hundred years after its heyday, thus only makes sense if the term is viewed at a certain distance and from the standpoint of disillusionment with respect to whatever it may still promise in terms of "predestination." Which is to say: I do not approach the demonic as a philosophical system (except perhaps as a kind of post-metaphysical self-help) or theologically (as a term that corresponds to a specific religious idea or worldview). But to the extent that problems and fallacies associated with the demonic remain current (for example, in the discourses surrounding the idea of "political theology"), a critical archaeology may usefully show how the demonic came to represent a point of ambiguity between the attitudes of dystopian-atheistic-secular resignation and utopian-revolutionary-Gnostic hope. Rather than taking the demonic seriously as a term that conceptualizes (or theologizes) something that is genuinely characteristic of modern reality, I frequently take it as the symptom of an affect, as a metaphorical expression used to characterize a supposedly "secular" world that remains ironically haunted by "demonic" remainders. And as it turns out, I think Goethe lends himself better to this approach than to the emphatic reclamation of the demonic as a category of post- or pseudo-religious existential analysis.

Goethe's "Orphic Primal Words" as a Vehicle for the Reception of the Demonic

In comparison to Goethe's "Urworte Orphisch" ("Orphic Primal Words"), the central passage on the demonic from book 20 of *Poetry and Truth* has been the object of a more overt reception. Both Lukács and Benjamin, for example, prominently cite the key sentences from Goethe's autobiography in texts that are still canonical. Benjamin's essay on Goethe's *Elective Affinities* also spends a page contesting Gundolf's reading of Goethe's "Urworte," but the point of this is easily lost: first, because it does not pertain directly to the *Elective Affinities;* and second, and more importantly, because it cannot easily be followed unless one is familiar with both Goethe's poem and Gundolf's book. Comparably, as I will show, Lukács's architecture of the novel corresponds to the schematics of Goethe's "Urworte"—but this connection is almost entirely implicit.

These examples illustrate how the *Dämon* of the primal words,[28] though apparently well known by major thinkers of the early twentieth century, was never transmitted in an integral and coherent way. Goethe's "Urworte" (written in 1817, first published in 1820)[29] have been most often quoted without regard for their context in Goethe, for the sake of their powerful formulations; some lines became so well known that they became "winged words," cited without quotation marks or an indication of their source. This is especially true of the final line of the *Dämon*-stanza (often incorrectly identified with *das Dämonische* itself),[30] which has been deployed by diverse readers in various contexts as a compact expressive-conceptual formula: *geprägte Form, die lebend sich entwickelt* ("characteristic form, living, self-developing").[31] Especially in the absence of interpretive analysis, the powerful formulations of the "Urworte" made an impression, for example, on and through Friedrich Gundolf and Oswald Spengler (discussed in chapters 3 and 4), who used Goethe's words to amplify and distort ideas from his writings on morphology. Such reconceptualizations went on to frame later theoretical development in contexts that were often quite removed from Goethe scholarship.

The typical reception of the "Urworte" occurred in the absence or refusal of philological rigor and a full articulation of relevant contexts.[32] The primal words were, in short, more prone to be hijacked than critically interpreted. In order to begin to unfold precisely this situation, the "Urworte" are a primary focus throughout the present work. There is a lot to unravel in the early twentieth century's tendency to freely mix the "Urworte" with *Poetry and Truth* and the morphology. Given this situation, the first chapters seek to differentiate Goethe's conceptions as the basis of the last four chapters' analyses of the "blended" versions. This pragmatic division and the focus on the "Urworte" led to the following chapter-organization:

In Chapter 1, the "Urworte" are read to develop a model of the demonic separate from that of *Poetry and Truth*. The "Urworte," unlike *Poetry and Truth*, present a limited number of *positive* terms in which the demonic may be conceived. This alone represents a departure from *Poetry and Truth*, and it may be a reason why the "Urworte" were constantly in the background of discussions of the demonic: the indeterminateness of *Poetry and Truth* needed constant supplementation by the more integral and systematic articulation of the "Urworte." This does not mean that the "Urworte" are Goethe's "best" work on the demonic, only that they lend themselves to paradigmatic and schematic conceptions. The "Urworte" became central for me for the same reason: Unlike *Poetry and Truth*, they do not tend toward dispersion, ineffability, and fragmentation into seemingly unrelated topics. The terminological system of the "Urworte," with its clear developmental structure and implicit oppositions (such as fate-character, individual-society, nature-culture, etc.), compactly addresses ideas and problems common to countless theories. And in addition to the "words" themselves and their poetic paraphrases, Goethe also wrote a commentary that goes some distance in articulating this "theory." The "Urworte" thus offer a stable basis of comparison against which other conceptions can be readily contrasted.

The foundations are thus set in chapter 1, upon which all of the later chapters are progressively built: chapter 2 reexamines the schematics of the "Urworte" in the context of Goethe's writings on morphology. The morphological writings allow an increasingly rigid formalization of the structural moments of the "Urworte" while simultaneously extending and generalizing the underlying developmental parameters in the direction of nature, culture, and history. These two intersecting models are further articulated in chapter 3, which introduces the autobiographical conception of the demonic from *Poetry and Truth*. Written before the "Urworte" (but published later), *Poetry and Truth* cannot be read as an "advance" with respect to the "Urworte." However, because the autobiographical context exposes the limitations of purely structural-schematic-categorical approaches, it represents a strong contrast to the "Urworte." Thus, if a unified idea of the demonic is even desirable, it is only possible to conceive it as an oscillation between these two models. The demonic is essentially double, divided between a formal or "positive" moment and its "demonic" insufficiency whenever the attempt is made to apply it to a given history or historical individual. Formal parameters are balanced against the impossibility of their narrative formulation and final analytic application. Formal-conceptual architectures, though tempting, cannot be epistemically differentiated in the flow of life and history. In the context of historical development, concepts and their associated causal reasons constantly produce imponderables. Goethe's retrospective view of his life thus undermines the general and systematic definition of the demonic. The specific puzzle of each individual life thus emerges as a singularity that always poses itself differently.

In chapter 4, I shift to the twentieth century, in which Oswald Spengler's "morphology of world history" introduces the demonic in the context of fated decline and historical crisis.[33] He extends and amplifies Goethe's idea of morphological development into a demonic "predestination"—an inescapable fate-system that places final limits on individual destinies and collective historical developments. In chapter 5, I introduce the arguments through which Walter Benjamin opposed such "demonic" determinisms: in ways that are similar to Spengler, Gundolf conceives the demonic as a mythic fate in which Goethe plays the part of the hero. Against this reading, Benjamin interprets the "Urworte" and the *Elective Affinities* to show that Goethe was able to transcend the fatalism enthusiastically espoused by Gundolf and Spengler. Implicit in Benjamin is an alternate reading of Goethe's morphology based on the idea of metamorphosis (instead of strict determination). Thus instead of fate, Benjamin emphasizes the hope and uncertainty that lies in the possibility of unforeseen future developments.

Thus Spengler, Gundolf, and Benjamin helped to configure a highly problematic Goethean trace, which worked its way, often anonymously, into many branches of twentieth-century thought. A further profoundly influential source from the 1910s is Georg Lukács's *Theory of the Novel* (the topic of chapter 6). Through the form of the novel, the young Lukács questioned the possibilities of transcendence and revolutionary transformation. He describes the novel as a uniquely modern genre and as a system for testing the possibilities of giving meaning to individual lives in a modern world in which neither life nor world has any inherent meaning of its own. This novelistic experiment always fails, in the final fruitlessness of protagonists' "demonic" characters or in the equivocations produced by narrators' "demonic" irony. All of the novel's attempts to establish the conditions under which meaningful life might be possible thus end up attesting to the disparity, unchecked subjectivity, and incoherence of the modern world.

In order to mount this argument, Lukács reconfigured the terms of the demonic as in support of his theorizations. The demonic provides him with an infrastructure of analysis that never becomes the object of analysis. To my knowledge, the only author who may have at least partly perceived the depth of the connection between Lukács and the demonic was the Austrian novelist Heimito von Doderer (the topic of chapter 7). Doderer was born in 1896 into the generation that came after the decisive figures of German-language modernism, such as Robert Musil, Rainer Maria Rilke, Thomas Mann, and Hermann Broch. Doderer, like many in the twentieth century, had set his sights on the novel, and was profoundly influenced by the literary and artistic developments of the decades of his youth. At the same time, however, he rejected the works of these authors in order to seek what he imagined as a more fundamental and consequent modernism. After reading Lukács's *Theory of the Novel* in the early 1930s, he set out to write a massive meta-novel—a novel of the theory of the novel—to which he gave a title borrowed from Dostoyevsky: *The Demons* (*Die Dämonen*, 1956). Doderer's engagement with the demonic—and with Lukács—may also have grown, at least in part, out of his own implicit reconfiguration of the "Urworte" for a 1929 essay. He was evidently preoccupied with multiple aspects of the demonic, out of which *The Demons* emerged as a unique late modernist (post-Lukácsian) attempt at consciously writing a novel that would be as demonic—as meaningless in its excess of meanings, as limited in its avenues of transcendence—as the modern world itself. Thus a new kind of novel began to consolidate itself out of the problem of the demonic articulated in Goethe's "Urworte," Dostoyevsky's *Demons,* and Lukács's theory. I hypothetically refer to this as a "demonic" novel, which formally resembles an epically distended novella. It may be, however, that there is no great breakthrough here, insofar as the novel was always the genre of the solitary individual and the absence and artificiality of transcendence (as Benjamin argues in his essay on the storyteller). In this case, a novel entitled *Demons* only represents a more explicit and self-conscious reflection on a supposed state of the world—the limits of which always defined the form of the novel.[34]

Chapter One

✦

Urworte Goethisch

Demonic Primal Words

Goethe's "Urworte Orphisch" is a cycle of five stanzas—stanzas in the strict sense of "octave" or "ottava rime"—written in September and October 1817. In addition to the main title, each stanza has a subtitle corresponding to a different "primal word." The occasion for this work was Goethe's encounter with speculative works of ancient philology by Johann Gottfried Jakob Hermann, Georg Friedrich Creuzer, and Georg Zoëga.[1] Zoëga is Goethe's proximate source for the primal words, but the original source is Macrobius (fifth century A.D.), who uses four Greek words to name Egyptian divinities— Δαιμων (*Daemon*), Τυχη (*Tyche*), Ερως (*Eros*), and Αναγκη (*Ananke*)—that preside over birth (UO 84). The fifth *Urwort*, Ελπισ (*Elpis*), also comes from Macrobius, but he does not name her with the other four. For this reason, Benjamin will see *Elpis* as supplemental in relation to the other *Urworte* and as a transformative intervention with respect to them.

The first 1820 publication of the "Urworte" in Goethe's morphological writings only gives Greek titles, but in the second 1820 publication he added German translations: *Dämon* is rendered *Individualität, Charakter* (individuality, character); *Tyche* is *Zufälliges, das Zufällige* (chance, the accidental); *Eros* is *Liebe, Leidenschaft* (love, passion); *Ananke* is *Beschränkung, Pflicht, Nöthigung* (limitation, duty, necessity, duress); and *Elpis* is *Hoffnung* (hope) (UO 27; see also Schmidt, *Goethes Altersgedicht,* 6–9). This series means to essentialize—"quintessentialize"—"diffuse antiquity."[2] It simultaneously clarifies and modernizes the core ideas of Greek thought.[3] According to a letter to Sulpiz Boisserée from July 16, 1818, the "Urworte" represent an effort of interpretive cryogenics, which seeks to revive "dead idioms" (*abgestorbene Redensarten*) through the rejuvenating force of "one's own living experience" (*aus eigener Erfahrungs-Lebendigkeit*) (UO 72). Goethe's implicit claim, contained in the word "Orphic," is that these five words represent the earliest and most essential idea of Greek mythology and religion, abstracted to reveal its modern relevance while providing a timeless formula for (human) existence in general.

This effort of resuscitation represents an explicit engagement with the scholarly discourses that posed the question of the status of the Greek origin, its purity and endurance. In pretending to extrapolate and intuit this origin, Goethe's stanzas stage the possibility of gaining access to ancient mysteries in a way that would not be merely historical but immediately valid and relevant in the modern world. In order to understand the specific form of the Orphic "Urworte" and the means by which they establish the basis of a continuity spanning the depths of antiquity and the furthest horizons of the present age, it is helpful to know what an *Urwort* is. According to Grimm's dictionary, the word *Urwort* can be understood as a "primal word," in the sense of an "ancient, sacred, primary, creative word" (*ein uraltes, altheiliges, erstes, schöpferisches Wort*). These meanings are obviously relevant, but the additional qualification "Orphic" makes them redundant: an Orphic primal word is the same as an Orphic word. The word *Urwort* may, however, be read in a second sense (also recorded in Grimm) as "a word in an ancient language." For example, the Greek word *logos* is an *Urwort* with respect to the words *ratio,* reason, and *Grund. Urworte* in this sense are not "primal" but rather "originary" with respect to a later conceptual history.[4] This definition is reflected in the construction of Goethe's Orphic "Urworte": the "poem" is in the first instance a series of five Greek words, which are progressively and repeatedly translated: first into German equivalents, then into stanzas, and finally into Goethe's commentary. Goethe's work thus appears to be less a "poem" than the performance of a conceptual unfolding—first into German, then into verse and finally into prose.

Given this structure, it is clear that Goethe does not literally seek to go back to the Greek origin. Nor does he try to present the "original meanings" of the five *Urworte.* They are only "defined" in a foreign language as a reflex of their progressive unfolding; they are the imaginary origins of an ongoing process of translation and re-actualization. This conception contrasts starkly with both Hermann and Creuzer, whose debate inspired Goethe's conception. For Creuzer, the proto-Greek origin, prior to written records, can be deduced but not positively known. He believes that this origin must have taken the form of a religious *doxa,* which would have preceded and delimited the more "literary" myths that came later. For Hermann, this relation is reversed: the assertion of a religious-institutional-cultic origin-before-the-origin can only be entirely speculative, and even if such an Ur-dogma and Ur-religion did exist, it would have necessarily been founded upon the interpretation of an even earlier myth. Hermann thus privileged the "literary" aspect of myth over its religious or institutional codification.[5] The orthodoxies of doctrine must be derivative, because they necessarily depend on a preceding totality of myth—as overarching tradition, institution, or symbol—capable of supporting various institutions and practices over long periods of time.

Goethe preferred Hermann to Creuzer, but his approach is distinct from both. In the "Urworte" themselves and in the 1818 letter to Sulpiz Boisserée (UO 72), Goethe is not primarily concerned about what the *Urworte* meant for the Greeks. Instead, he wants to know what they can be made to mean for us. The academic dispute challenged Goethe to deduce the basic conceptual forms at the origins of Greek religion—but not as a uniquely Greek *episteme*. Instead he expands the five originary concepts in an implicit history of their translation and transformation, in order to bring their wisdom into the modern world. They are dense conceptual sketches, works of speculative philosophy, which use verse as a means of clarifying and articulating a foreign and essentially ineffable subject matter. The "Urworte" are "a series of Orphic primal words . . . clarified into stanzas" (*eine Reihe orphischer Urworte . . . in Stanzen aufgeklärt*), as Goethe wrote in a March 1818 letter to an unknown recipient (UO 72).

These "stanzas" were first published (perhaps strangely on the face of it, but with consequences that can hardly be overestimated) in the 1820 edition of his *Zur Morphologie* (*On Morphology*). Only a few months later, he republished them, with minor changes and accompanied by a commentary, in *Über Kunst und Altertum* (*On Art and Antiquity*). The decision to add a commentary may have been partly a result of the fact that Goethe's stanzas, despite their "clarifying" intent, remained cryptic. The first sentences of the commentary give precisely this explanation, but I suspect that "expandability" and "applicability" are inherent to the stanzas' design: the two 1820 publications superimpose strikingly different contexts in which the "Urworte" may be read, producing a further layering and transformation on top of the translations represented within the text itself. The aesthetic and conceptual developments that take place between the two publications may thus be read as a strategy for progressively increasing the potential complexity of the underlying "words."

This understanding of the design of the "Urworte" and the relation of the two publications breaks with a tradition of interpretation that has read the commentary only as a "prosaic" and superfluous simplification. I believe this also explains why the commentary was never translated into English. This is not to say that there are not good reasons to view the commentary as a reductive crutch. To the reader of poetry, the commentary undermines the authority of the stanzas by supplementing them with dubious and potentially inflammatory "theoretical" claims. Theo Buck and Jochen Schmidt thus treat the commentaries as secondary, in order to focus on the interpretation of the stanzas. Schmidt argues that the commentary is less authoritative than the stanzas and that readers of the stanzas are not obliged to follow the interpretations given in Goethe's commentary (Schmidt, *Goethes Altersgedicht* 14–15). This is certainly right, but the case becomes more complex if the commentary is not simply a case of a literary author trying to "explain" a difficult work. The commentary, as I read it, is a further transformation and translation of the five "primal words," which deserves to be read carefully, not as a superficial and prosaic explanation, but as a complex text with specific qualities.

Another macro-level interpretive dilemma is whether to read the relation of the five stanzas as progressive, developmental, and linear—a narrative or dialectical *sequence*—or whether they are simultaneous and conceptual in their relation.[6] These two options can be unified in Macrobius's conception of "astrological" divinities presiding over both birth and life—but these may be conceived either as constant presences or as a sequential unfolding of life and fate. In the latter case, the *Dämon* presides over birth itself; *Tyche* over childhood, education, and socialization; *Eros* over youth and awakening sexuality; *Ananke* over adulthood and the confining realities of middle age; and *Elpis* over the new perspectives of old age. In any reading, the "Urworte" can be conceived at once as narrative-sequential and as the demonstration of an analytical system that only establishes general categories of relations. On the one hand, it is a strict developmental typology; on the other, all five elements are constantly operative and interacting in all moments and events of every human life. Thus conceptual (synchronic) and developmental (diachronic) aspects are represented in the design of the "Urworte."

A further question, leading to another distinction, pertains to the level of the generality of this paradigm. More often than not—and not always wrongly—Goethe's *Dämon*-stanza has been read autobiographically as a further description of the "demonic" entity from *Poetry and Truth*. This connection is, however, only of limited validity. It neglects the speculative-historical and scholarly aspects (coming out of Hermann and Creuzer); it also conflicts with Goethe's commentary, which does not rely on anecdote or subjective accounts, but instead focuses on the stanzas' universal and objective meaning; the stanzas themselves support this, for example, in the opening astrological metaphor. The tone of universality and objectivity is a precise inversion of the presentation of the demonic in *Poetry and Truth*. These passages, written before the "Urworte," only present general paradigms at the horizons of Goethe's own experience. Both texts arguably address the same underlying problem—the basic form of human life—but the "Urworte" are more oriented toward an academic, systematic, or even dogmatic conception.

Regarding the dogmatic aspect, it is above all the formulaic intensity of the "Urworte" that distances them from the particularities of Goethe's individual life. "Urworte" may be "religious" in the sense that the stanzas formulate admonishments, sayings and "words to live by"; fundamental questions of anthropology, sociology, and psychology are just beneath the surface. Such questions, which roughly correspond to the "nature vs. nurture" dichotomy, figure prominently in the commentary. The nature-nurture opposition, however, only loosely fits Goethe's conception. Put in these terms, the "Urworte" are primarily about nature (figured in *Dämon* and *Eros*), whereas culture and society are figured in the secondary and often negative functions of *Tyche* and *Ananke*. Ultimately, the most important shared feature of the "Urworte" and the nature-nurture opposition is their degree of generality. Both paradigms are broad enough to theoretically include every outcome. At the limit, every actually existing and conceivable permutation must be representable as an interplay between determining elements. In comparison to nature-nurture,

Goethe's five-part analytic system is decidedly more complex—and aggressively unconventional. The *Dämon,* for example, is the unique identity of the individual, but it is scandalously ambivalent about the role of "nature" in the constitution of this identity. The stanza never makes it clear whether the *Dämon,* which the commentary translates as "individuality," refers to an "own nature" or to an external force that impresses itself on the individual from the outside.

The *Dämon* in question thus cannot be simply reduced to the "genie" that inspires the genius—or to a Socratic *daimonion*—or to Goethe's own "genius." In the "Urworte," *Dämon* corresponds to the character and individuality of *every* individual. The astrological metaphor of the first lines spells out the uniqueness, singularity—and fatality—of the individual destiny (as the commentary reads it). The second-person singular (*Du*) further conveys the universality of the conception:[7]

> Δαιμων, Dämon.
> Wie an dem Tag der Dich der Welt verliehen
> Die Sonne stand zum Gruße der Planeten,
> Bist alsobald und fort und fort gediehen,
> Nach dem Gesetz wonach Du angetreten.
> So mußt Du sein, Dir kannst Du nicht entfliehen,
> So sagten schon Sybillen, so Propheten,
> Und keine Zeit und keine Macht zerstückelt
> Geprägte Form die lebend sich entwickelt.

> Δαιμων, Demon.
> As on the day you were granted to the world,
> The sun stood to greet the planets,
> You likewise began to thrive, forth and forth,
> Following the law that governed your accession.
> You must be so, you cannot flee yourself,
> Thus sibyls long ago pronounced, thus prophets,
> And neither time nor any power can dismember
> Characteristic form, living, self-developing.

This first stanza gives priority to the *Dämon*—its unity, its fatefulness, its inescapability, indelibility, and ineradicability, but it still may be possible to overstate these aspects. They are balanced by an equally intense conception of growth and development that is at odds with strict fatalism. Taken a step further, the concepts of *form* and *development* may appear to be latently contradictory. "Characteristic form, living, self-developing" (*geprägte Form die lebend sich entwickelt*), to the extent that it is taken literally, can easily become an oxymoron, a paradox, or a metaphor expressing the simultaneity of synchronic and diachronic moments.[8] If this contradiction is to be avoided, the *Dämon* must be an intrinsically diachronic and temporal aspect referring to the form of development itself.[9] This principle of the developmental autonomy and elemental individuality of the *Dämon* is thereby internalized and distinguished from the merely external processes of education and socialization (*Tyche*).

In contrast with this purely developmental aspect, however, Goethe's commentary identifies the *Dämon* with an interconnection of fate and character that allows the former to be derived from the latter: "one may . . . concede that innate energy and individuality [*angeborene Kraft und Eigenheit*] determine human fate much more than anything else" (UO 13). The language used to introduce this sentence (*man möchte gestehen*) reflects a significant distance from the stanza's apodictic claims. The commentary immediately "concedes" the absolute and unquestioned status of the text it interprets. The result is a parody of the emphatic hermeneutic commentary: "Thus the stanza [*Strophe*] pronounces the invariability of the individual with repeated assurance [*mit wiederholter Beteuerung*]" (UO 13). The stanza is the source of unquestioned claims, to which the commentary self-consciously subordinates itself. Through the commentary's deference, the stanza itself becomes a *Dämon*, a fixed yet developing form: it may be paraphrased and explained (in the sense of *Auslegung*), its claims rationalized, but the truth of its formulation is not to be questioned. By imagining the stanzas as genuine Orphic utterances rather than words of a modern author, the commentary employs an obvious fiction to interpret the stanza's words without needing to doubt their claims.

The stanza, however, because it defines *Dämon* as purely developmental, is much less definitive than the commentary on the topic of fate and character: as the law of a *future* development—of uncertain duration—the *Dämon* is never given, never present, but always only "in development." Its essential role or even its existence as a part of a causal chain can never be proven as long as it is the law of an unfinished unfolding. This "fate" exhausts itself in the stanza's "repeated assurances," which amount to a promise of the individuality described. By reading the stanza as an ancient wisdom directed at every imaginable "you," the commentary avoids the question of *whether*—and *how*—this promise is ultimately believable. The acceptance or rejection of the stanza's "repeated" premise—the *belief* in the *Dämon*—may even impact the self-development of the "you." The apparent fatalism of the stanza thus subtly turns toward the possibility of freedom.

The commentary casts itself in the hermeneutic role, thereby unmasking the stanza as rhetoric and subtly undermining its claims. Once the commentator and the reader of the *Dämon* stanza are thematized, it becomes clear that individuality is not only intrinsic, but co-defined by acts of interpretation and articles of faith. The commentary proceeds to push this further, to the point of superstition. With only minimal basis in the poem, it asserts the indestructibility and indivisibility of the demon, claiming that it is not just the prime element of the individual identity, but also defines the transgenerational genetic identity of peoples and nations: "That which is most decisively individual, insofar as it is finite, can certainly be destroyed, but, as long as its core remains intact [*so lange sein Kern zusammenhält*], it can never become fragmented or torn apart, even across generations" (UO 13). The latent contradiction between form and development is thus magnified and extended across historical time: the *Dämon*, which seemed to define absolute individuality within the human life span, is recast as a potentially transferable characteristic (*das Charakteristische*, UO 13). This "characteristic" refers to the utter singularity of the individual and at the same time introduces a more fluid space of identities that are communicated beyond the limits of an individual life.

The concept of individual character can be read as a category of singularity and autonomy, but the idea of a supra-individual "characteristic" tends toward determinism. This collectivization of the individual *Dämon* is troubling, but it may also be variously interpreted. On the side of the most extreme generality, the "demon" would be the lowest term of a universal anthropomorphology that supposes the possibility of absolute generalization, of an all-encompassing genetic rule capable of mediating and subsuming every single particularity that appears in all of time. Under this rule, everything would have a *Dämon* that defines what it is and how it develops. The demon thus mediates general and particular, delimiting the difference between form and forms. Everything has a demon as the underlying principle of its being and development; everything—both as an individual and as a species—is possessed of a "form" (a nature, concept, or essence). The demon defines the plurality of diachronic forms in their temporal orientation and organization. In the Aristotelian lingo that underwrites the morphological discourse from Leibniz to Goethe and Spengler and beyond: the demon is entelechy.[10] This morphological understanding, however, ruins the stanzas' more narrowly biographical schematics of the human life span. The commentary's morphological extension and generalization breaks the promise of the *Dämon*, which "repeatedly assures" the absolute—astrological—singularity of character. In view of transgenerational and genetic continuities, the stanza's promise of a fixed and enduring individuality is dissolved into abstract formal play: *Tyche* rules as soon as individuality is viewed as a combinatorics of inherited elements that are not more than the sum of their parts.

In the terms of *Dämon*-stanza itself, the question is: where does self-development (*Entwicklung*) end and where do dispersion, disintegration (*Zerstückelung*), and entropy begin? From the standpoint of form defined in the fixed individuality of a single life, inevitable mortality contradicts the stanza's proclaimed indestructibility of the demon. From the standpoint of disintegration, "demonic" form ensures continuity in the transmission of discrete "characteristics." But such a limited continuity is still notably at odds with the indestructible, constantly developing individuality expressed as "imprinted form" (*geprägte Form*). Mortality thus limits demonic self-development, and

the inheritability of specific characteristics only (rather conventionally) com-
pensates for it at a different level. The problem is simple: if the *Dämon* does
not include a doctrine of the immortality of the soul (which would cross the
line from empirical morphology into metaphysics), then there must be limits.
But death is downplayed to the extent that it would conflict with the stanza's
pronouncement of the empirical endurance of demonically structured forms.
The deliberately overstated assurance of stability and continuity thus reflects
the unacceptability of the alternative. To prove the proclaimed indestructibility of the demon—despite certain evidence to the contrary—the commentary
introduces this-worldly genetic continuity, which provides the demon with a
means of surviving its mortal vessel. Goethe imagines the long-term survival
of the demon in the bloodlines. But this turns individuality—like the snow-
flake that always crystallizes differently—into a mere effect of an indifferent
structural determination.

If the idea of a "genetic inheritance" is meant to allay doubts about
the indestructibility of the individual demon, then this effort is—perhaps
intentionally—not very successful. The demon, which was supposed to be
indivisible and integral, ends up tragically divided and finally dissolved in
the pantheistic generality of the gene pool. The commentary's words "as long
as its core remains intact" may be a slip or a deliberate contradiction with
respect to the stanza's "neither time nor any power can dismember," but it
in any case reveals the demon as something other than the immortal and
indestructible essence. If the demon were to exist in the form pronounced in
the stanza, it does so only as an aspect of the faith in the words of the stanza
itself; because the commentary, which apparently proselytizes on behalf of
this faith, subtly undermines it.

The question of the destructibility of the *Dämon* is addressed again in the
Tyche-stanza and its associated commentary. The remarks that introduce this
Urwort proclaim its powerlessness against the perfectly resilient and autono-
mous demon:

> Of course [*freylich*], even this entity [the *Dämon*], though fixed [*fest*]
> and tough [*zäh*] and developing only out of itself [*dieses nur aus sich
> selbst zu entwickelnde Wesen*], must enter into many relations that
> may impede the effects of its first and original character or hinder it
> in its affections. (UO 13)

However, despite the reemphasis of the durability of the demon, the admission that it "enters into many relations" signals the beginning of a reversal.
At first these relations are only defined negatively, as mere externalities,
which, though they may "impede" and "hinder," do not decisively impact
the demon's characteristic form. *Tyche* is thus a more benign form of what
the fourth stanza will call *Ananke*. As a sheer impediment, she lacks positive
formative influence on the demonic development.

The *Tyche*-stanza is concerned with education and socialization, which are described as mutable and variable, ephemeral and fluid, reflecting the essential contingency of human social and institutional forms. *Tyche*'s forms are extrinsic shells, lifeless structures against and within which the demon asserts itself, while awaiting *Eros,* whose spark is anticipated in the stanza's final line:

> Τυχη, das Zufällige.
> Die strenge Gränze doch umgeht gefällig
> Ein Wandelndes, das mit und um uns wandelt;
> Nicht einsam bleibst Du, bildest Dich gesellig,
> Und handelt wohl so wie ein anderer handelt.
> Im Leben ists bald hin- bald wiederfällig,
> Es ist ein Tand und wird so durchgetandelt.
> Schon hat sich still der Jahre Kreis geründet,
> Die Lampe harrt der Flamme die entzündet.

> Τυχη, the Accidental.
> Yet this strict limit is gently circumscribed
> By a fluctuation that flows around and with us;
> You are not alone, but shape yourself socially,
> And must certainly act just as another acts.
> In life things are often due, overdue, redone,
> It is a trinket, passed in makeshift thrift.
> The circle of the years is already silently closed,
> The lamp awaits the flame that will ignite it.

Tyche here is not "chance" or "luck" (German *Glück*), fortune or *Fortuna* (the standard Latin translation), which refer to the hazards and opportunities that appear in the course of life. In Goethe's source, Zoëga, *Tyche* is a moon goddess akin to Isis; she is to the collective what the *Dämon* is to the individual; she is perhaps the most primal divinity, whose name and concept can contain all others (UO 83–84). Goethe's "Urworte" clearly oppose Zoëga: *Tyche* is not a kind of *Dämon,* but subordinate and secondary. The *Tyche* stanza never calls her by a feminine pronoun, depersonifying and implicitly de-potentiating her. In the commentary, the male *Dämon* is also conceptually neutered into "the characteristic" (*das Charakteristische*), but already in the title of the stanza, female *Tyche* is translated neutrally as "the accidental" (*das Zufällige*). Unlike the demon, which, as the principle of character and identity, is the very precondition for personification, *Tyche* is amorphous and devoid of positive characteristics; in this the *Urworte* follow Zoëga, who calls *Tyche* "a word invented to confuse, not to differentiate and determine" (UO 83).[11] In Goethe's stanza, she is "something that transforms" (*ein Wandelndes*), which lacks the demon's formal law of development.

Where the *Tyche* stanza emphasizes socialization, the commentary often reads her as the contingency of historical and cultural flux. Despite her secondariness to *Dämon,* she motivates the commentary to revise its position on the demon's transgenerational, genetic durability: "It is not accidental that one derives one's descendence from this or that nation, tribe or family" (UO 14). Natality, nativity, and nationality are not mere accidents of birth or attributes of nature but aspects of the continuity of the demon. The commentary's interpretation here goes against the grain of the stanza, because it re-naturalizes and nationalizes the contingency of culture by reading it as a demonic inheritance. This is confirmed in the commentary's sentence on *Erziehung* (education, child rearing), which is governed by *Tyche* "as long as it is not public and national" (UO 14). The qualification indicates that education may be removed from the maternal private sphere and subjected to the paternal national-cultural legacy of the demon.

Various arguments are possible when it comes to assessing the real virulence of this conception, but if it is understood as a spurious racial or proto-nationalist theory, then it is unfortunate that it appeared under Goethe's name.[12] The commentary's reading of the *Dämon-Tyche* relation comes close to naturalizing national identity, culture, and character by making them into a biological inheritance. The prime example of this is the endurance of the Jewish people (*die Judenschaft*) across the generations. The Jewish *Dämon* particularly stands out, according to the commentary, because the essence of Jewish national character—*Hartnäckigkeit,* stubbornness—reflects and redoubles the "tough" and "resilient" nature of the idea of *Dämon* itself.[13] The commentary contends that not only the Jewish people but also European nationalities will retain their national characteristics even after centuries of exile, emigration, or diaspora. Such claims have almost no relation to the *Tyche* stanza, which focuses on sociability and inevitable conformity. In the commentary, *Tyche*'s "mutable rights" (*wandelbare Rechte*) come into play through miscegenation (*Vermischung und Durchkreuzung*). Such "mixing" or "crossing"—diluting—of the national "demon" is presented, not as the *rule* of procreation, but as an *exception* to the ongoing paternity of the *Dämon.* This is an undoubtedly racist conception: rather than interpreting *Tyche* as the lawless law of *Dämon*'s transgenerational permutations, the commentary implies that the originary "demon" survives best in endogamous bloodlines.

The patriarchal and patrilineal typology already observed in the ideal of "national" education stands in opposition to "maternal" *Tyche.* She is a negligent mother who leaves the education of the demon up to chance. Biological mothers are never mentioned in the commentary's enumeration of "tychic" influences on the baby demon. Instead, maternal surrogates, such as wet nurse and nanny (*Säugamme und Wärterin*), exemplify *Tyche.* This strict gender typology only begins to dissolve when paternal figures, such as "father or guardian," are identified as agents of *Tyche.*[14] But this is merely because all "father figures" can only be illegitimate in comparison to the natural paternity of the demon itself. Just as the child is said to be the father of the man, in the commentary, the demon is the ultimate *Urvater,* the "old Adam" (*der alte Adam*) and "proper nature" (*die eigentliche Natur*). It is absolutely resistant to *Tyche*'s negative and positive reinforcements. In the context of "national and public education"—combined with the demon's supposed invincibility—the implicit point is that because the demon cannot be driven out of the child, the maternal *Tyche* should be replaced by public education specifically designed for the advancement of the demon.

Against the conformism (or even, at the limit, fascism) of this ideal of national education, a more promising educational model can be developed out of the very same premises. The universalization of the nonconformist premise of *Dämon*'s individualistic aspect could be the basis of innovative education. Though still "public and national," such an educational system would be individually tailored to the talents and proclivities of each "demon." Because the commentary does not differentiate between the various possibilities, it is difficult not to imagine the worst—but I would still see it as typical of the tendency of the "Urworte" to address problems only in terms of a general framework.

Prior to the *Eros* stanza, the commentary ceases its ambiguous reflections on education and reasserts the power of *Tyche:* "But *Tyche* does not relent . . . [*Allein Tyche läßt nicht nach*]" (UO 14). Up to this point, the commentary on *Tyche* had remained preoccupied with *Dämon;* but now she is reread in a way that fits better with the stanza, as a figure of inauthenticity, as the sum of the forces that can distract, mislead, divert, or seduce the demon from his proper nature. Conformism and inauthenticity would seem impossible based on the *Dämon* stanza and its commentary, but a decisive line of the *Tyche* stanza indicates otherwise: "and acts just like any other acts" (*und handelt wohl so wie ein anderer handelt*). The theme becomes increasingly central in the *Eros* and *Ananke* stanzas, which causes the strong initial emphasis of *Dämon* to become gradually eclipsed. The power of the demon is progressively overshadowed because it proves unable to stay true to itself in the unconditional way proclaimed by the first stanza. Confronted with a reality that it is not cut out for, the twilight of the demon gives lie to the proclaimed ineffectuality of *Tyche.* The shifting and contradictory claims of the stanzas and commentary cannot be unequivocally resolved; and no individual sentence or line is valid in isolation, but only in the context of the whole system. To the extent that the commentary's exegesis is a constantly self-modifying disunity, none of its individual claims can be taken at face value. Even taken as a whole, its ability to represent a coherent synthesis may be questionable. It certainly cannot reflect a unified authorial standpoint, because it is self-consciously rhetorical in its mediation of the stanzas to their imagined reader. Rather than anticipating, dictating, defining, or even tracing the conceptual possibilities of the "Urworte," the commentary is dependent and reactive in its relation to their contradictory impulses. At the same time, it drastically departs from the letter of the stanzas in order to explore speculative possibilities.

Against this equivocal backdrop, *Eros*' entry occurs androgynously, in masculine and feminine nouns and pronouns, breaking the static opposition of *Tyche* and *Dämon:*

> Ερως, Liebe.
> Die bleibt nicht aus!—Er stürzt vom Himmel nieder,
> Wohin er sich aus alter Oede schwang,
> Er schwebt heran auf luftigem Gefieder
> Um Stirn und Brust den Frühlingstag entlang,
> Scheint jetzt zu fliehn, vom Fliehen kehrt er wieder,
> Da wird ein Wohl im Weh, so süß und bang.
> Gar manches Herz verschwebt im Allgemeinen,
> Doch widmet sich das Edelste dem Einen.

> Ερως, Love.
> And there she is!—He hurtles down from the heaven,
> Where he had lifted himself out of ancient chaos,
> He soars and surges forward on airy wings
> Surrounding brow and breast across the vernal day,
> Seems now to flee, but in flight he turns about,
> Creating pleasure in the pain, so happy and forlorn.
> Many a heart drifts away in generality,
> But the noblest devotes itself to the One.

The *Eros* commentary begins: "Here the individual *Dämon* and the seducing *Tyche* join together" (UO 15). *Eros* is the spark that ignites two incompatible elements, *Dämon* and *Tyche*. Despite the initially proclaimed indestructibility of the demon, the collusion of *Tyche* and *Eros* proves that it is not infallible. To the contrary, under the spell of *Eros* it is virtually defined by errancy. Love's intervention seals the rule of *Tyche*. Within the sphere of *Eros,* the individual only *seems* "to belong to himself, to allow his own desire to reign, to indulge his own instinct" (UO 15). The *objects* of a seemingly innate desire are relegated to the status of "coincidences" (*Zufälligkeiten*) and "foreign nature" (*Fremdartiges*). Even in the most intimate aspects of desire, *Tyche* rules: "Errancy has no limit here, because the path itself is error" (UO 15).

The pre-erotic demon had sought to actualize itself, but it can only do so in the alien and "accidental" medium of *Tyche*. *Eros* thus appears as the divinity of the demon's renewed self-actualization and simultaneous self-forgetting. Love activates the demon by giving it a more intensive connection to the "tychic" world. But because this *self*-actualization cannot eliminate *Tyche*, it is not an event of sheerest authenticity but always co-actualizes *something other than itself*. This dynamic of externalization causes innate properties to be alienated in a foreign element. The commentary does not mince words about this problem, whereas the stanza resolves it in an idea of monogamy that implies the demon's need to devote itself, to focus its *Eros* on a single coherent development instead of floating around in the generality and promiscuity of *Tyche*. The stanza's "One" thus *not only* represents a sanctimonious sermon on morality,[15] but also indirectly thematizes the demonic role of talent, calling, or discipline, which may transcend the repeated disappointments of *Tyche* and *Eros*.

The impasse of *Dämon* and *Tyche*, made dynamic by the intervention of *Eros*, retrospectively rereads *Tyche* as powerless, as long as she is conceived as a force of purely normative socialization. Her real power is demonically exerted through *Eros*, in each individual's uniquely auto-affective relation to the world. *Eros* then, as is known from other contexts, is at once a normative force (constrainable within the collective legitimacy of *Ananke*) and a counter-normative force that drives individuals away from the collective law—into the "labyrinths" of the self (UO 15).[16] Such errancy itself has normative effects: as a merely relative or apparent aberrance (under the rule of *Tyche*), every *Eros* has the potential to formalize itself into a "path" (*Weg*), which will "dissolve" "the particular and specific ... within the realm of generality" (UO 15). *Eros*'s elective affinities are constantly producing new norms, new generalities and collectivities. *Tyche*, whose power is that of crossing and mixing, reveals herself as not only an occasional obstacle to the demon: she *always* "crosses" him, mixes up and confuses him, not by destroying him, but by diverting him, drawing on his power for her labyrinthine ends. Crossing and discontinuity are not exceptional, as they appeared to be in the *Tyche* commentary—because *Eros* cements the confusion of self and other, while, as it now appears, the demon develops only by "crossing."

According to the commentary, "frustration" (*Verdruß*)—the negative experience of *Tyche* and *Eros*, which constantly interrupt the demon's self-actualization—causes the demon to feel "that he is not only determined and stamped by nature" (UO 16). In other words, the individual loses faith in the claims of the first stanza: he becomes aware of his demon's limitations, and seeks a way out of the inauthenticity of the conspiracy of *Eros* and *Tyche*. To make this point, the commentary calls on the authority of the final lines of the *Eros* stanza and asserts that they provide a clue to how *Eros* may be something other than a fatal and impulsive "grasping" (*ergreifen*). In the negative model, *Eros* generalizes and thereby destroys the particularity of whatever it grasped. The only alternative, according to the commentary, is a more free and measured "assimilation" (*aneignen*) of that which the demon encounters through *Eros*. Shifting away from the *what*—the contingency of object-choice—the commentary emphasizes the *how*. This idea of authenticity, as the possibility of escape from deterministic nature and culture, admonishes the individual to forego a possessive, proprietary and identificatory mode of appropriation in favor of a differentiated reflective process.[17]

By the end of *Eros*, the stanzas have shifted away from an extremely negative characterization of *Tyche* and toward a more positively valued conception of education (*Bildung*) that is neither merely instinctual nor forcefully imposed from the outside. This new conception instead envisions a reflective and quasi-autonomous process that the demon initiates under the auspices and inspiration of *Eros*. The form of this education is self-education. It is not primarily concerned with "contents" or "objects" (which are essentially contingent), but defines a specific (quasi-Kantian) perceptual form based on the awareness that all "objects" are also forms, "demons," entities whose diachronic nature and inside-outside structure make full comprehension impossible.

Where *Dämon* and *Tyche* emphasize gender difference as a conflict between essentialized masculine and feminine principles, *Eros* dissolves this opposition: first, because the recognition of the other as an "other self," an *other demon,* implies that this model may apply universally—not only intersubjectively but also with respect to "inanimate" objects. The sexes are equal insofar as both are born with an innate identity or "demon." Also homosexuality—perhaps influenced by the "Orphic" legacy and the weak gender differentiation of the *Dämon* paradigm, which, though figured as masculine, can be read as a birthright of all humans—would not be stigmatized, since the interaction of nature (*Dämon*) and object-choice (*Tyche*) allow for more than one "way." The expansiveness of Goethe's idea of nature in *Eros* means that anything is possible. If the idea of monogamy is granted conceptual preeminence in the end, it is as a model of how the demonically inspired individual can learn, interdemonically, to "embrace a second being like itself with eternal, indestructible affection" (UO 16). The ideal of monogamy here stands for a form of self-reflection that is the precondition for autonomy as deliberate faithfulness to oneself—as opposed to merely enforced, accidental, instinctual, or otherwise unreflected conformism.

The commentary does not stop with the "happy ending," but interprets its more devotional form of *Eros* as a relation of *Dämon* and *Tyche* that sublates the latter within the former, "demonically" animating the "tychic" neutrality of the world. This new configuration, however, recasts each individual as a mere demon among demons, giving rise to much more binding collective forms.[18] *Ananke*—compulsion or necessity—begins as a natural law originating in the erotic bond between individuals and ends up in the general forms of collective necessity: positive law, society, and government. According to the commentary, "freedom is given up through free decision," in a seemingly inevitable devil's bargain. Here the commentary shifts again, away from the situation of the individual "demon" and toward collective, societal, and transgenerational considerations, resulting in a mini-theory of the genesis of civil society: "Family follows family, tribe follows tribe; a people has discovered itself and perceives that the individual's decision is also proper for the whole, and it makes this verdict irrevocable in law" (UO 16). Thus monogamy, *chosen* by the will of the individual and seconded by law and custom, gives rise to matrimony.

Any desire to read Goethe's text as a triumph of rationalization or progress or civilization—*or* as the affirmation of a categorical imperative in the style of Kant—*or* as an "education of mankind"—*or* as a blossoming of the private demon into the public good—will be disappointed by the pessimistic sentence that precedes the *Ananke* stanza: "And so that everything is resolved for all of time and eternity, neither state nor church nor tradition will permit any lack of ceremonies" (UO 16). As the stanza itself gloomily affirms, there is nothing good about the intersection of individual and collective wills:

> Αναγκη, Nöthigung.
> Da ist's denn wieder wie die Sterne wollten:
> Bedingung und Gesetz und aller Wille
> Ist nur ein Wollen, weil wir eben sollten,
> Und vor dem Willen schweigt die Willkühr stille;
> Das Liebste wird vom Herzen weggescholten,
> Dem harten Muß bequemt sich Will und Grille.
> So sind wir scheinfrey denn, nach manchen Jahren,
> Nur enger dran als wir am Anfang waren.

> Αναγκη, Necessity.
> Now all follows once again the stars' will:
> The terms and laws and the wills of all
> Are but a single will, just because we have to,
> And before the will all choice is silenced;
> The most beloved is exiled from the heart,
> Desire and fancy submit to hard compulsion.
> Thus apparently then, after many years, we are
> Only more tightly bound than in the beginning.

The necessity of self-discipline and ultimately of self-sacrifice—the modes of renunciation (*Entsagung*) demanded by collectively and intersubjectively instituted forms—is not given a positive face, rationalized, or purified of resentment. The individual—the vehicle of *Dämon* and *Tyche*, of will (*der Wille*) as well as arbitrary desire (*Willkühr, Grille*)—is silenced before the authoritarian and catholic rule of *Ananke*. Even *Eros,* "the most loved" (*das Liebste,* gender neutral), is banished "from the heart" and "sent away with harsh words." The experience is self-explanatory: there is "no one who has not felt himself painfully compelled when he even so much as recalls such situations in his memory, and there are even quite a few who would want to despair, when the present moment holds him captive in this way" (UO 17).

As was also the case in the preceding stanzas, the last two lines of *Ananke* point forward, toward the last word, *Elpis,* which, according to the commentary, needs no commentary. The fateful tone of the *Dämon* stanza, which presided over the beginning, is pure freedom in comparison with the social constraints of *Ananke*. She allows not even the appearance or simulation of freedom, causing the many years of growth, development, and maturation to seem futile. The only freedom that emerges from *Ananke* is the "freedom from illusion"—disillusionment of the illusion of freedom—producing the unerotic affects of realism, conservatism, and pessimism. This leaves "us" (first-person plural, object-case) more "tightly bound"—*enger dran*—than ever, but at the same time "closer," "nearer" (*enger dran*) to something else. At this limit of a different beyond, the uncertain quality of *Elpis* is reflected in the cessation of the commentary. Confronted with unyielding *Ananke,* the reader is instructed to "rush to the final lines, where every gentle spirit will gladly take over the task of creating their own ethical and religious commentary" (UO 17). *Elpis* thus introduces a moment of hermeneutic freedom—the freedom to make one's own commentary—which extends beyond the last word of the "Urworte" and beyond the interpretive authority of the commentary:

> Ελπισ, Hoffnung.
> Doch solcher Grenze, solcher ehrnen Mauer
> Höchst widerwärtge Pforte wird entriegelt,
> Sie stehe nur mit alter Felsendauer!
> Ein Wesen regt sich leicht und ungezügelt,
> Aus Wolkendecke, Nebel, Regenschauer
> Erhebt sie uns, mit ihr, durch sie beflügelt,
> Ihr kennt sie wohl, sie schwärmt nach allen Zonen;
> Ein Flügelschlag! und hinter uns Aeonen.

> Ελπισ, Hope.
> But such a limit, such a steely wall,
> Its most revolting portal is unlatched,
> Though it may stand with a mountain's age!
> A being arises lightly, without reins,
> Out of the clouds' cover, fog and rainfall,
> It lifts us up, with her, by her wings,
> You know her well, she swarms toward every zone;
> A wing flap! and behind us lie the eons.

Hope, characterized by liminality, ubiquity, and a subtly transgressive nature, rescues the individual from the strictures of *Ananke*. Theo Buck reads *Elpis* as a Pegasus figure (UO 60), invoking the power of the imagination—poetry and literature—to transcend the determinateness of the worldly here and now.[19] Without being able to destroy constraints, *Elpis* rises above them, perhaps momentarily, but constantly, all of the time and everywhere, unfettering the fixed forms of time and fate.[20]

   The possibility of freedom at the limit of constraint is finally reflected in the relation of text and commentary. In the end, the fixed authority of the stanzas, the "demonic" development of originary "Urworte" and the commentary's dubious pedantic interpretations, relax to admit the possibility that each demon, every individual reader, will continue the reading in his or her own way. The "Urworte" thus come full circle in an allegory of reading opening up multiple conflicting truth-claims, which are set into relation without allowing any to dominate. At first, interpretive freedom emerges from the space between them and out of their contradictions, and in the end, this freedom is itself allegorized in *Elpis*. Hope can be read as a displaced return to the demon: she is the demon in a state of alterity and self-forgetting. Hope reincarnates the self in its freedom from *itself*, from the "eons" of its own past and present identity, which now appear as a distant landscape, the frozen remainders of unfinished diachronic beginnings. Neither synchronic nor diachronic, *Elpis* is *achronic* in her ability to leave worldly time with its "ancient mountain's age" behind her; she is *polychronic* in her ability to "rise above the eons" and view them from a distance, not as a unified and accumulated tradition, but as if from above, with the subjective selectivity of hindsight.

At the beginning and at the end, the commentary characterizes the "Urworte" as a semi-religious cognitive model, akin to self-help or astrology. In between, the "Urworte" are developed in various iterations and translations, in order to represent *a* truth—the truth of which remains to be proven by its effectiveness. The truth of "Urworte" depends on their usefulness for life, on whether they are believed and how they are implemented. Each individual stanza and *Urwort* is possessed by its own *Dämon*—indelible imprint and demonic potential—its own *Tyche*—historical contingencies of understanding—its own *Eros*—productive and reproductive passion—its own *Ananke*—force and dogmatic authority—and its own *Elpis*—the rereading and eventual transgression of everything fixed and inescapable. This five-part rhetorical-hermeneutic model reflects a delicate balance. Within these parameters, the risk of overemphasizing any of the five moments is clear: the composite balance and dynamic five-part quintessence will revert to a static and dogmatic essentialism if any element is allowed to rule over the others. The possibilities of such reductions can be assessed as (politically and ethically) desirable or regrettable, but the composition of the "Urworte" as a text is a deliberate balancing act. It can conceive the lack of balance within its system of counterweights, but as long as none of the weights are removed, the balance is preserved.

Chapter Two

✦

Demons of Morphology

Aber das Erdenleben ist doch ein Prozeß der Umgeburt (Umgestaltung). Wer ist schuld daran, daß man sich in einen Teufel umwandelt? [But if life on earth is undoubtedly a process of transformation through rebirth, whose fault is it if someone transforms himself into a devil?]
— Stavrogin in Dostoyevsky's *Demons*, from an extra dialogue published in the 1918 German Piper edition

Given the size and importance of Goethe's natural scientific writings, my analysis of his theory of morphology will be relatively brief. Impossible to definitively categorize, Goethe's work as a natural scientist and his thinking about nature can be read as philosophical reflections—whether in the direction of ontology, Kantian critique, or an aesthetic theory—or as a strange milestone in the history of science, somewhere between Linnaeus and Darwin, or as a figural-symbolic system that informs Goethe's literary work, or perhaps even as a literary work in its own right. Though these considerations inform my approach, I will not explore them in detail. Despite their complexity, Goethe's morphological writings are crucial for the demonic, and not only because his most schematic conception of it, the Orphic "Urworte," was first published in the *Morphology*. Twentieth-century readings of the demonic tended to freely mix the demonic with morphology. With these later developments in mind, the present chapter seeks in a preliminary way to establish connections and differences between morphology and the demonic. This is first of all a question of how Goethe's "Urworte" may be read in the context of their first 1820 publication in the *Morphology*. Though Gundolf exploited it in his Goethe biography, the connection to natural science may be at odds with strictly autobiographical or anthropological readings of the demonic.

In comparison to the "Urworte" commentary in their second 1820 publication in *On Art and Antiquity,* the context of morphology focuses on even more primal and general forms. In a manuscript from the mid-1790s,[1] Goethe defined morphology in opposition to the specialized disciplines of "natural history, natural science, anatomy, chemistry, animal physiology, and psychology" as the master-term of the life sciences. Morphology is the "observation of the organic whole through the consideration of all of the separate aspects and their connection through the power of the mind" (HA 13:123; FA 364). According to Dorothea Kuhn, the editor of the Frankfurt edition of the morphology, Goethe was the first to use the term "morphology" in the context of the natural sciences. He first conceived it, according to Kuhn, as "a doctrine of forms [Gestaltenlehre] . . . meant to comprise all phenomena of natural history, the organic as well as the inorganic" (FA 1015). This idea of form focuses on phenomena *as they appear*. A fragment titled "Morphology," perhaps also from the 1790s, states that morphology "rests on the conviction that everything that is must also show and indicate itself" (FA 349).

One motivation of this conception, especially in its later and more developed form, was Goethe's concern that the sciences were becoming too analytical and specialized. His 1829 "Analysis and Synthesis" emphasizes that analyses are only possible on the basis of preexisting syntheses (HA 13:51). Against science's expansion into an increasing number of partial disciplines, morphology is the science of the whole. From this perspective, analytic interventions can only be meaningful in light of their possible derivation from a presupposed totality and continuity of being—a "harmonia mundi" as Kuhn calls it (FA 1013). Morphology in this sense is not a branch of the sciences but science itself as the science of science—transcendental meta-science—based on the ontological assumption of the primacy of the whole.[2]

How does the morphological scientific method work in practice? Somewhat contrary to what the name "morphology" might suggest, it is not a formalism (in the sense of a taxonomic approach), but rather a "trans-formalism":

> Form [*die Gestalt*] is something that moves, develops, passes away [*ist ein bewegliches, ein werdendes, ein vergehendes*]. The theory of forms is a theory of transformation. [*Gestaltenlehre ist Verwandlungslehre.*] The theory of metamorphosis is the key to all of Nature's signs. [*Die Lehre der Metamorphose ist der Schlüssel zu allen Zeichen der Natur*]. (FA 349)

This subordination of form to time and transformation breaks with the taxonomic thought of the eighteenth century. Metamorphosis, for example, more readily includes problems of function as a reason or motive of transformation.[3] Morphology does not view natural forms in static isolation, nor does it seek to tabulate systems of identity and difference between different forms. Instead it traces the identity and transformation of forms in time.

The implications of this focus on transformation are clearest in Goethe's botanical writings. A note he made in Italy, for example, summarizes ideas that he later developed more systematically: "Hypothesis. Everything is leaf. and through this simplicity the greatest multiplicity becomes possible [*Hypothese. Alles ist Blat. und durch diese Einfachheit wird die größte Mannigfaltigkeit möglich*]" (HA 13:582).[4] The point of this hypothesis is that the various parts of a plant are not *parts of a whole* but *transformations of a single underlying unit.* Goethe calls this unit "leaf."[5] Form here is not defined as a (Platonic) conceptual unity—as a "tree"—but as the metamorphic continuity of the smallest (visually) identifiable unit. Goethe sees the leaf as the basis of the visible transformations that define the plant over time throughout its life cycle. The leaf, isolated in this way, may be, as Goethe realized, only an arbitrary and nominal unit within a chain or cycle of transformations, but it can still figure as an allegory or metonymy for morphology's idea of *the continuity of forms.* Form, rather than a static shape or Gestalt, is conceived as a *cycle of cycles,* a developing variation capable, at the limit, of encompassing all living beings.

From the earliest inklings and fragmentary texts of the 1780s to the published writings on morphology, metamorphosis is the main idea of morphology. In "History of His Botanical Studies" ("Der Verfasser teilt die Geschichte seiner botanischen Studien mit"), first published in 1818 in the *Morphology* and revised at the end of the 1820s, Goethe reflects on Italy and the primal plant (*Urpflanze*):

> I pursued all forms [*Gestalten*] as they presented themselves to me in their variations and thus achieved complete illumination at the final stop of my journey, in Sicily, regarding the *original identity* [*ursprüngliche Identität*, emphasis Goethe's] of all parts of the plant—and then I sought to pursue and perceive this insight everywhere. (HA 13:164; FA 748).

Implicit in the idea of metamorphosis is the possibility of deriving all (botanical) forms from an ideal primal form, an Ur-type at the base of all visible forms. Rather than drawing analytic distinctions, metamorphosis makes them fluid to such a degree that conceptual and terminological differentiations begin to appear arbitrary.

This idea is expressed in paragraph 120 of Goethe's "On the Metamorphosis of Plants" ("Zur Metamorphose der Pflanzen"), which was published first in 1790 and republished in 1818 in the first volume of the *Morphology.* "The leaf" (*das Blatt*) may appear to be the basic unit of transformation, but Goethe emphasizes how metonymically inapt it is to name the whole continuum after it:

> It goes without saying that we would need to have a general term [*ein allgemeines Wort*] with which to refer to this organ that is metamorphosed into such varied forms [*dieses in so verschiedene Gestalten metamorphosierte Organ*], in order to compare all of the appearances

of its form to one another ... [We] can just as well say that a stamen [*Staubwerkzeug*] is a contracted petal as that a petal is a stamen
[*Staubgefäß*] in a state of expansion. (HA 13:101; FA 150–51; MA
12:67)

Goethe's use of two different words for "stamen" illustrates the general point
that human language is unable to definitively name the "parts" of naturally
occurring wholes. The "basic unit" is always nominal in that it refers neither
to "building blocks" that *compose* organic beings, nor to an abstract whole.
It only symbolizes a continuum of forms, a cycle of cycles that allows a continuous "part" to transform itself within itself.

The Goethe's idea of the *Urpflanze* has become entirely emblematic of this
idea, and his uncertainty as to its empirical or rather ideal status parallels
the contradictions developed in the five "Urworte." The "primal plant" may
have been conceived in ways that caused it to resemble a Platonic form or
Kantian a priori,[6] but in the *Italian Journey*, before these more philosophical articulations, Goethe seemed to expect that it might exist in reality. On
June 9, 1787, he wrote to Charlotte von Stein: "The *Urpflanze* will be the
most amazing creature [*das wunderlichste Geschöpf*] in the world, for which
Nature herself shall envy me. With this model [*Modell*] and its key [*Schlüs-
sel*] one then would be able to invent additional plants into infinity [*ins
Unendliche*]" (HA 13:579).[7] One could discount such a remark, which is
clearly non-scientific and apparently expresses its author's enthusiasm for
his topic—but with respect to the demonic, the affective investment may be
more significant than objective scientific validity. The superimposition of a
morphological schema with a genetic derivation makes it seem that the original ancestor might actually exist, which would exhibit all of the traits of its
offspring. And through this original "model"—real or imaginary—it should
be possible through an act of imagination to prospectively design infinite—
real or imaginary—plants. The process can work in either direction, but in
the letter the perception of an *Urpflanze* is primarily an act of intuition: the
Urpflanze is above all the possession of a subject—a possession that is the
envy of Nature herself. Because the *Urpflanze* is supposed to be based on real
forms, its real existence seems like a possibility, either as an ancient origin (an
Urpflanze) or as a speculative end (in the infinity of subjective "inventions" to
which the *Urpflanze* is the "model" and "key").

The *Urpflanze* thus resembles the "old Adam" of the "Urworte." It is
the primogenitor, *Urvater*, and *Dämon* of the botanical world; it is also the
Urmutter Tyche, encompassing every possible combination of the original
material. It is the primal imprint from which both extant forms and possible
forms are derived. As an *Urphänomen*, it is the variable "key" that permits
the development, metamorphosis, derivation, and interrelation of forms. Like
the Orphic *Dämon* and the originary "Urworte," the *Urpflanze* is defined
by the tension between infinite potentiality and determinate inheritance,

between lawless metamorphosis and a natural "law" that dictates development. This morphological development may also clarify some apparently contradictory aspects of the idea of "characteristic form" (*geprägte Form die lebend sich entwickelt*) in the "Urworte". At the limit, these words define the *Dämon*'s relation to its own development, which is to say: form's relation to metamorphosis—its relation to *Tyche*.

This question of developmental form and its correlation to organic metamorphosis is the main focus of morphology. In a late essay, "Principes de Philosophie Zoologique" (1830–32), Goethe uses the idea of developmental transformation to unify the synthetic and analytic approaches of Étienne Geoffroy Saint-Hilaire and Georges Cuvier. As part of a terminological critique, Goethe introduces words that he considers fundamentally unsuited to the natural sciences. The term "composition," with constructivist implications and transparently analytic conception, is the object of sharp criticism. The idea of composition is a misnomer, Goethe argues, in the arts as well as in the sciences:

> Composition is yet another infelicitous word that is mechanically related to the preceding mechanical term [materials]. The French introduced just such a word into our theories when they began to think and write about the arts. According to them, the painter composes his paintings, and especially the musician is nothing but a composer; and yet, if either wishes to earn the true name of the artist, then they should not compose their works [*so setzen sie ihre Werke nicht zusammen*], but instead develop a kind of an indwelling image [*sie entwickeln irgend ein inwohnendes Bild*], a higher resonance [*einen höhern Anklang*] in accord with the principles of nature and art [*natur- und kunstgemäß*].
>
> Just as in art, the idea of composition has a debasing effect whenever it is used to speak of nature. Prefabricated organs do not assemble and compose themselves. They develop themselves from and through each other to produce a necessary existence that reaches toward the whole [*zu einem notwendigen ins Ganze greifenden Dasein*]. In this context it may be possible to speak of function, form, color, measure, matter, weight and of other determinations, however they may be called—because everything is admissible to observation and research. But through it all, the living organism makes its way undisturbed [*das Lebendige geht ungestört seinen Gang*], propagates and reproduces itself [*pflanzt sich weiter*], hovering and fluctuating [*schwebt, schwankt*] until it at last achieves its final form [*Vollendung*]. (HA 13:245–46; FA 838)

The living organism goes its own way. This is a translation of the *Dämon* paradigm from the "Urworte": everything that lives—which truly deserves the name of life or art—makes its way as if according to its own internal program, undisturbed by outside influences and interventions. It moves and advances in a kind of perpetual motion that removes it from the sphere of static composites and human analytic perceptions. In the context of the opposition between analysis and synthesis, between mechanical and organic forms, development (*Entwicklung*) is Goethe's preferred terminology for living forms (*das Lebendige*), which include not only organic nature, art, and literature, but also biographical life.[8] In light of this morphological premise, "characteristic form" (*geprägte Form die lebend sich entwickelt*) is the formula of life as such, the key to the metamorphic destiny of everything lifelike, and everything that develops.

Without denying the problematic organological basis of this ideal of universal development, Goethe's morphological conception of *geprägte Form* envisions only a limited determinism and a very flexible idea of nature. The sheer existence of forms is an ontological given, but they do not automatically constitute a destiny or predetermination. The form of forms can only be known in their metamorphoses, and, since metamorphosis can only happen over time, morphology can only be a retrospective science. The past history of accomplished metamorphoses may be taken as possibly predictive of a "fate" (as Spengler would say), but morphology's idea of metamorphosis includes a plurality of metamorphoses, each of which may be unforeseeable in itself, and each of which, based on possible interactions and under the ongoing influence of changing external conditions, may be exposed to unpredictable shifts in both function and form. This guarantees that, as long as metamorphosis is the master-category of morphology, no development can ever be decisively finished, closed off, or entirely predictable. The organological basis of morphology is thus not a problem insofar as it is purely descriptive: it allows nature to *be* whatever nature *does*. More troubling issues arise, however, if descriptive morphology becomes normative morphology. The latter would propose a future telos on the horizon of past transformations. Such an implicit teleology is represented in Goethe's word "*Vollendung*" (perfection, culmination). Even provisional or "empirical" teleologies can easily be interpreted as symbols that can then replicate themselves in implicit or explicit analogies. Thus the mere perception of teleologies in the organic life cycle easily acquires normative or idealizing significance.

In this way, morphology's forms are able to provide and even impose their models on art and life. The analogical extension of purely descriptive morphology allows it to approach natural and human history as one continuous "development." Spengler's later conception especially, which envisions a cyclical "blossoming and fading" of all life, reveals the twofold risk of morphological symbolic modeling: it either reduces human history and the history of human creations to natural determinism, or it sees natural and human history, including art history, as a single process of culmination.[9] In the latter case, which leans toward historical optimism, a series of familiar ideological fallacies, up to and including eugenics, comes into play; it is a question of the degree to which humans can or should try to supplement the supposed ends of morphological nature. The former case of historical pessimism functions similarly, except that instead of using morphological reason to further nature's ends, it is invoked to justify measures intended to prevent, mitigate, or rationalize an impending end.

Morphology's conception of nature is inescapably Janus-faced, ambivalent in its dependence on the human perspective, which focuses either on inevitable mortality or infinite fecundity. In the writings on morphology and in the "Urworte," the underlying problem of morphology emerges as a specific polarity, a relation of the individual and the universal in which the former is finite and determinate, with strict ("demonic") limits that are offset by the boundless universal ("tychic") flow of time and infinity. In comparison to the "Urworte," morphology thus arguably places greater emphasis on *Tyche* and on the *Dämon-Tyche* couplet. Their relation is shown to be infinitely modifiable, projectable into other polar oppositions such as individual/totality, individual/society, part/whole, synthesis/analysis. In the context of morphology, the "Urworte" paradigm is capable of encompassing the forms of nature and history. It is also more than just a conceptual apparatus: it is apparently motivated to perceive a world that is animated and alive with development. Behind all vocabularies of life, the "Urworte" represent a medium through which all terminological systems can be translated back to an original, "natural" unity.

The "Urworte" raise the meta-science of morphology to the level of a universal system, which Goethe also expressed in the "pulsing" symbol of *systole and diastole*.[10] This generalized image of morphology extends the "demonic" conflict between the discrete *Dämon* and its world (*Tyche*) into a metaphor of universal dualism. From this elevated perspective, no single terminological grid—analysis/synthesis, *Dämon/Tyche/Eros/Ananke/Elpis*, systole/diastole—can be the referent of such a meta-metaphorical polarity. According to the rules of morphology, this polarity can have no ontological or linguistic ground that would not be a false metonymy (such as "everything is leaf"). The falseness of the metonymy means that no language can refer to "form-in-development"; it can only be represented by metaphors, which are arbitrary and improper in the sense that the relation in question can always be expressed otherwise. Such a metaphorical-analogical continuum, unlike a conceptual or definitional base, allows forms of continuity to be perceived, which are constantly implicit in empirical forms. But this continuity itself can only be nominally expressed. Even the "Orphic" terminology is arbitrary in the same way as the word "leaf": it can only refer to a single moment of the continual metamorphosis of a form that is normally—just as arbitrarily— called a "tree" (or "life" in the case of the "Urworte").

The extended consequence of morphology's emphasis on transition and transformation over identity and identifiability is the complete deconstruction of the conceptual edifice of science (to the extent that it is dependent on

nomenclature) and of language in general (to the extent that a morphologically conceived universe permits metaphors but not referents).[11] "Systole and
diastole" is an emphatic name for something that can also be called "analysis and synthesis," but which is only knowable in its constant figuration in
life, art, and nature. Constantly reconfigured, but literally unspeakable, the
demonic duality reflects underlying unity. If it did not, it would be not only
unspeakable but unthinkable: metamorphosis, unchecked by a unifying sense
of form, would be only chaos and entropy. Confronted by an inconceivable
referent—"the inconceivable" (*das Unfassliche*), as Goethe calls it in *Poetry
and Truth* (HA 10:175)—the only alternative to conceiving nothing is to
impose a temporary stopgap, a word that names the unnameable. Goethe
discusses form in this sense as the precondition of knowledge and reference
in an 1823 essay, which is aptly called "Probleme":

> The idea of metamorphosis is a very noble but at the same time very
> dangerous gift from above [*eine höchst gefährliche Gabe von oben*].
> It leads into formlessness [*ins Formlose*] and destroys knowledge by
> dissolving it. It is like the *vis centrifuga* and would lose itself in infin-
> ity [*ins Unendliche*], if an opposing drive were not granted to it. I am
> thinking of the drive toward specification [*Spezifikationstrieb*], the
> tough tendency to persist [*das zähe Beharrlichkeitsvermögen*] that is
> possessed by everything that has once come into reality. It is a *vis cen-
> tripeta*, which at its deepest level [*in ihrem tiefsten Grunde*] cannot
> be touched by anything external [*welcher keine Äußerlichkeit etwas
> anhaben kann*]. (HA 13:35; FA 582–83)

Forms are never static, but the forms of their metamorphoses also cannot
be completely random. The form of forms, however, the condition of the
possibility of knowledge, can only be known through the forms of their
metamorphosis. In the terms of the "Urworte," the *Dämon* here is the anchor
of form, defining the boundary of Being and Nothingness. The demon is the
identity and durability—*Spezifikationstrieb* and *Beharrlichkeitsvermögen*—
of developmental form, the centripetal force that prevents metamorphic
Tyche from entirely dissolving everything.

Within the horizons of morphology's diachronic conception of form, the
form of metamorphosis is itself subject to the metamorphoses produced by
metaphorical shifts, which make forms into much broader developmental
models. The *Dämon-Tyche* opposition, like all of the others, is only an arbitrary "key" or nominal reduction within a field of possible metamorphoses
and metaphorical extensions. Because morphology is implicitly a science of
conceptual metamorphosis—of the conceptual acrobatics necessary to name
and describe metamorphoses—it is a meta-metaphorology that finds "the
same" basic forms metaphorized everywhere. But it remains aware of its own
reliance on metaphor, which means that the "forms" thus "identified" only

actually exist in a differential state. Underlying and overarching unities can only be provisionally posited, and their serial "forms"—synthetic/analytic, systolic/diastolic, centrifugal/centripetal, tropic/entropic, *Dämon/Tyche*[12]—are based on a network of fragile analogies.

The transposition of "Urworte" into alternate terms exposes the insufficiency of all of these terms. The polarities posited in these words *do not refer*, except perhaps subliminally—below the level of what they actually mean—and this means, in effect, that they risk becoming mere words, arbitrary signs that fail to name a deeper system of relations (and do not even try to do so). "Urworte" thus emerge as mere signs, extending, propagating, and unifying the supposedly "primal" opposition of and between all forms. The nature of this nature itself can never be *uniquely* specified, however, because the oppositional pairs only parallel the *Dämon-Tyche* relation without ever being identical with it. Such is the "danger" of metamorphosis, which corresponds to the negational structure of the demonic from *Poetry and Truth*: short of conceptual or referential precision, negation and circumlocution are all that remain—but these means are only suggestive of an underlying mystery.

In all cases, this suggestion is the source of fascination. Morphology's suggestiveness lies in its insinuation of overarching unities that *apparently* prevail in the analogical interlacing of countless transformational paradigms. In an essay from 1831, for example, "On the Spiral Tendency of Vegetation" ("Zur Spiraltendenz der Vegetation"), the development of plants is theorized in an opposition between "spiral" and "vertical" tendencies or drives. These forces are clearly legible as a further illustration of the relation of *Tyche* and *Dämon*:

> In the growth of vegetation, the vertically ascending system effectuates the continually existent aspect [*das Bestehende*], which is simultaneously that which tends toward solidity and persistence [*das Solideszierende, Verharrende*]; it refers to the fibers in short-lived plants and to the majority of the wood in long-lived plants.
>
> The spiral system is the constantly expanding, reproducing, and nourishing part, and as such it is short-lived, which accordingly isolates it from the vertical system. If it extends its effects too excessively, it very quickly becomes weakened and subject to blight. When attached to a vertical system, both grow together to produce a lasting unity [*eine dauernde Einheit*], either as wood or some other solid.
>
> Neither of the two systems can be conceived on its own. They are always and eternally [*immer und ewig*] together, but when they are in perfect balance [*im völligen Gleichgewicht*], they produce the most perfect vegetable growth [*das Vollkommenste der Vegetation*]. (HA 13:133; FA 787)

In another passage, Goethe describes the spiral tendency (diachronically) as the "basic law of life" (*Grundgesetz des Lebens*, HA 13:134; FA 788), whereas the more timeless vertical system is "powerful but simple" (*mächtig aber einfach*, HA 13:135; FA 795). The superimposition of the *Dämon-Tyche* and these two "tendencies" or "systems" innate to plant life may produce reciprocal illumination. The two interdependent but inherently conflictual "tendencies" formalize life as a dualism, not in a Manichean sense, but rather in the interest of establishing relational limit-parameters of development.

Having observed such an opposition of forces, Goethe pursues even broader analogical conclusions by expanding the two "tendencies" into much more general polarities. He tends, therefore, to read the tendencies of plants as a symbol for the general tendency of tendencies. This exemplifies the morphological temptation to see parallelism everywhere. This is not just my own interpretive tendency—because I hope to have shown that Goethe himself thinks this way. It may be difficult, though, to tell what is mine and what is Goethe's, because morphology's perception of ubiquitous analogous forms makes it unclear when to stop. But without denying the optics of my own reading—which views morphology through the "Urworte"—I would observe that morphology, as Goethe himself reads it, produces an open system of analogies and potentially also symbols. This infinite analogical expanse— which becomes truly persuasive if one believes that there is *something* at the base of it—seeks to compensate for morphology's epistemic deficiency.

At the end of his notes on the "spiral tendency," Goethe interprets the tendencies in a way that might seem anthropomorphic, except that the *-morphic* here, rigorously understood, excludes prefixes. The two plant tendencies are construed as masculine and feminine principles, which drastically ties them to the gendered binary of *Dämon* and *Tyche:*

> The vertically as well as the spirally striving system [*das vertikal- so wie das spiralstrebende System*] are connected in the living plant in the most intimate way imaginable. If we see the former proving itself to be decidedly masculine and the latter to be decidedly feminine, then we can imagine all vegetation [*die ganze Vegetation*], starting from its very roots [*von der Wurzel auf*], to be secretly androgynously interconnected. Upon which basis, therefore, in the course of the transformations of growth [*in Verfolg der Wandlungen des Wachstums*], both systems differentiate themselves into open opposition [*sich im offenbaren Gegesenatz auseinander sondern*] and decisively separate themselves from each other [*entschieden gegen einander überstellen*], in order to reunite themselves again in a higher sense [*um sich in einem höhern Sinne wieder zu vereinigen*]. (HA 13:148; FA 805)

One may be amazed or horrified at Goethe's ability to discover a consistent symbolic system writ large in nature. This passage leaves little doubt that Goethe's thinking about synthesis implies the possibility of moving analogically from particular to general in a way that elevates every empirical detail and every experimental outcome to a symbol of the general relation of things. The well-known analogy of human chemistry and actual chemical reactions in the *Elective Affinities* depends on this kind of thinking, which is condensed to a formula at the end of *Faust II:* "Everything transitory is only a parable" (*Alles Vergängliche ist nur ein Gleichnis*). Everything transitory—that is: everything is only an analogy, a metaphor that transcends finite limits and converts into the universal and general. Everything "empirical"—limited and temporal—constantly transcends itself symbolically as non-empirical meaning. The primary and *only* function of the "real" world—the one that changes and passes away—is the symbolization of the transcendent. Science in this conception can never do more than create new allegories of universal relations, supplementary models of the way of the world.[13]

Despite the obvious grandeur of Goethe's symbolic syntheses, points of concern noted in chapter 1 may be again registered here. For morphology, that which is specifically individual, singular, and "transitory," though granted a kind of indirect immortality by virtue of its symbolic potential, can only realize itself by relinquishing its singularity, by its ability to be representative with respect to a more primal (or "higher") totality. As in the *Dämon* commentary, morphology reduces unconditional uniqueness to a definite set of representative and transferable characteristics, which at best produce highly inclusive formulae. Such a master concept cannot provide a single general rule or a norm for all life, nor does it appear to offer adequate support for the individual autonomy (as formulated in the *Dämon* stanza). Given these options, morphology's saving grace lies in its normative weakness: the lack of a truly binding or dogmatic form in the "Urworte" allows individualized recognitions and interpretations to develop within the matrix of transforming meanings provided by the grand design of the "Urworte." In comparison with morphology's more dualistic and synthetic model, however, the five-part "quintessence" of the "Urworte" looks like a more sophisticated formalization, insofar as its universal symbol contains more internal differentiation and is—one would have thought—less prone to misunderstanding. Through the lens of the "Urworte," morphology fluctuates between anthropomorphism (and anthropocentrism) and "morphocentrism." The latter sees animating tendencies, drives, and "forms" coursing through animate and inanimate nature.

Either way, morphology ends up as more religion than science or as a religion of science. The "Urworte" at least do not hide this aspect, but overtly address it. Occasionally this is also the case with morphology. The biographical origins of morpho-ontology and its worldviews are casually discussed in the essay "The Fate of the Manuscript" ("Schicksal der Handschrift"), in which Goethe reflects upon the genesis of his "Metamorphosis of Plants." This autobiographical sketch was first published in 1817 in the first volume of the *Morphology.* The text's very first sentence emphasizes

the decisive importance of Italy for Goethe's plant morphology: "Sent back
from form-filled Italy to formless Germany [*Aus Italien dem formreichen
in das gestaltlose Deutschland zurückgewiesen*], I was forced to exchange
a bright sky for a gloomy one" (HA 13:102; FA 414). Reflecting the difference between Italy and Germany in their wealth vs. poverty of forms, Goethe
explains that his perceptions of Italy were the result of a simultaneous study
of Italian nature and Greek art. The latter was especially germinal for his
idea of form:

> Little by little, I was able to get an overview of the whole [*das Ganze
> zu überschauen*], so as to prepare myself a pure artistic enjoyment
> free of all prejudice. Further, I believed I had noted how nature works
> through laws to produce a living image [*ein lebendiges Bild*] that is
> the model [*Muster*] of everything artistic [*alles künstlichen*]. The third
> thing [*das dritte*] that occupied me was the customs of the people [*die
> Sitten der Völker*], in order to learn from them how the convergence
> of necessity and arbitrariness [*Notwendigkeit und Willkür*], impulse
> and will, motion and resistance, leads to something else [*ein Drittes*]
> that is neither art nor nature but both at once, necessary and acciden-
> tal [*notwendig und zufällig*], intentional and blind. I am speaking of
> human society [*die menschliche Gesellschaft*]. (HA 13:102; FA 415)

Vocabulary associated with the "Urworte" is coupled with familiar (if somewhat displaced) dualities, which give rise to third terms. Here, however, unlike
the other examples from the morphology, the movement is not synthetic in
its tendency toward symbolic "elevation." Two "third terms" are mentioned
(*das dritte, ein Drittes*), but in the first case, Goethe implies that human culture and custom, rather than being a synthesis of art and nature, are *neither
art nor nature*—or ambiguously both at once. Such an understanding gives
human culture an exceptional and excluded status with respect to the universal symbols of morphology. Whenever human artificiality and artifice are not
representative of a true second nature that can be perceived (or imagined) as
a transparent analogue of Nature, they fit poorly within the general forms of
morphology. The Greeks alone fulfilled the ideal—but human culture usually
gets lost in *Tyche* and *Ananke*.

Within the excluded sphere of "culture," a series of oppositions describe
conflicted and potentially dualistic forms similar to both the "Urworte"
and morphology. As in the "Urworte," the conflict is mediated (but much
less systematically) by a synthetic moment, a "third" that is "neither art
nor nature," but both together, which Goethe calls "human society." Corresponding to the *Ananke* portions of the "Urworte," human society exhibits
all of the characteristics of *Dämon* and *Tyche*—and perhaps also of *Eros:*
"necessary *and* contingent," "intentional *and* blind." Despite the fact that
it may first appear as a synthetic progression, this vision of human society

produces a monster: in the difference between *diverse* "customs" (*Sitten*) and an idealized analogy of nature and art, "society" is only an exponentially greater version of culture. It is contingency incarnate, pure non-being, excluded from the morphological *analogia entis*.[14] Thus, in this limited philosophy of history that introduces the *Morphology*, human culture and society are mostly excluded from the representative syntheses of nature and art. Morphology traces an analogical stream out of nature into life and art, producing a standard with which the variable norms of human existence cannot compete. Ad hoc, non-morphological forms of human existence correspond to the possibility of inauthenticity that first arises in the *Tyche* stanza of the "Urworte." Both not only confirm the likelihood of human errancy, but conceive it as essential. Humanity has a special status with respect to morphologically derived norms: only humans are capable of forsaking their proper and innate self, their *Dämon*. The "Urworte" make this point from the perspective of the individual, whereas morphology posits it for human society. Far from any idealism, the "tychic" quality of human culture leaves it cut off from any meaningful idea of progress (dialectical or otherwise). Like the *Ananke* stanza, this passage of the morphology indicates that it is absolutely normal for societies to exist in a state of endemic delusion and loss of self.

The "synthetic" track of nature and the "tychic" variability of society thus seem to be mutually exclusive—but a final synthesis of the two remains conceivable. This synthesis would raise morphology to the level of a mythology. Such an ultimate synthesis manifests itself, according to Goethe's description in the extended reflection on religion at the end of book 8 of *Poetry and Truth* (probably written in 1811 or 1812), as a "pulsation" of being and non-being, self and non-self, identity and non-identity.

Unlike the 1817 remarks on society, book 8 depicts Goethe's religious ideas in their earliest development (at the end of the 1760s). Goethe attributes his later religious ideas (what I am calling "morpho-theology") to the study of "Arnold's history of the Church and of heresy." This reading led him to sympathize with many heretical ideas: "The spirit of contradiction and the enjoyment of paradox exists in all of us" (*Der Geist des Widerspruchs und die Lust zum Paradoxen steckt in uns allen*) (HA 9:350; MA 16:376). Gottfried Arnold's Pietism (see MA 16:985) may perhaps be traced in a sentence in which Goethe writes that he "had often heard that every man must have his own religion in the end" (HA 9:350; MA 16:376). According to the autobiography, this idea inspired him to design his own religion based on his reading in the history of heresy: "And thus I built for myself a world that was certainly rather strange in appearance [*die seltsam genug aussah*]" (HA 9:350; MA 16:379). Such qualifications, as well as the use of the past tense, allow Goethe to distance himself from this early construction—and his early "heresy." But by the time he reaches the end of the chapter, he is making general pronouncements in the present tense, one of which indicates the possible breadth of the sources of his idea of the demonic: "The history of all religions and philosophies teaches us that the great truths that are indispensable to man have been passed down by diverse nations and in diverse times and in various ways, indeed in strange fables and images dictated by the limitations of each" (HA 9:353; MA 16:381).

The demonic in book 20 of *Poetry and Truth* is similarly introduced in the context of religion. It is said to have emerged from "the interstices" (*die Zwischenräume*, HA 10:175) of religious knowledge and individual experience. The demonic is also characterized as a religious self-design, conceived "after the example of the ancients and others who thought something similar" (HA 10:175–76). Reading book 8 and book 20 together, Goethe's mature conception may include pre- and non-Christian layers in addition to the "heretical" tradition—but this does not mean that he forgot the "Neoplatonism," "Hermeticism," "Mysticism," and "Cabbalism" that inspired him in his youth (HA 10:350; MA 16:376–79).

The homemade religion that Goethe presents at the end of book 8 looks very much like what book 20 calls the demonic—combined with elements of morphology. The story begins: "I liked to imagine [*vorstellen*] for myself a divinity that produces itself out of eternity [*von Ewigkeit her*]" (HA 9:351; MA 16:379). In morphology, nature constantly transcends itself in the symbolic surplus value of metamorphosis. In book 8 as well, the cosmic principle is self-production through self-transcendence. The "synthetic" trinity here is an extension and multiplication of an originary self-producing divinity:

> But because production cannot be conceived without multiplicity, this divinity immediately had to appear to itself as a second figure [*ein Zweites*], which we recognize under the name of the Son. These two then also had to continue the act of production [*den Akt des Hervorbringens*] and appeared to themselves in turn in the third [*im Dritten*], which was now just as existent, living and eternal as the whole that preceded it [*als das Ganze war*]. (HA 9:351; MA 16:379)

Continual production of difference within identity, the act and the drive of production as (apparently) asexual reproduction, leads from a third to a fourth: to Lucifer, who is a figure of resistance, of the interruption of harmonious self-production. He, "who already cultivated a contradiction within him [*schon in sich einen Widerspruch hegte*]," is the representative of everything "that does not appear [*scheinen*] to us to agree with the idea and the intents of divinity [*mit dem Sinne und den Absichten der Gottheit*]" (HA 9:351). This division into different competencies is pragmatic theodicy, which imagines a separate office for whatever does not fit "our" expectations about divinity. For readers familiar with the paragraphs about the demonic in book 20, as well as for readers of *Faust*, the verb *scheinen* ("to appear" or "seems") stands out: like the demonic, which book 20 presents in terms of "seeming," and like Mephisto, Lucifer only *appears* (from "our" perspective) to be a force of negation, an obstacle to continual self-production. Lucifer is the moment of non-being that apparently inhabits all being. He blocks the way back to the origin and primal phenomena; his shadow inhabits everything material, and the Creation is thus a dark (or at least darkened) creation, because of its obstructed relation to transcendence. Lucifer means that the world is not a transparent communion with self-producing transcendence, but instead—in the terms of morphology—the former only symbolizes the latter. Lucifer is the difference that cannot be eliminated from the analogy. He does not entirely erase the connection to originary Being, but he makes Being's merely analogical continuity into an interrupted filiation, which only *shows signs* of derivation from an original unity.

Next Goethe develops a polar (morphological) opposition between *Konzentration* (= Lucifer, the power of materialization, determination, and singularization) and *Expansion* (= continuity, time, metamorphosis, freedom, God). This polarity results in a static impasse, favoring static and lifeless "concentration," had the Elohim—like *Eros* in the "Urworte"—not intervened:

> They [the Elohim, the divinity in plural] granted to the infinite Being the ability to extend itself, to move itself toward them. The proper pulse of life [*der eigentliche Puls des Lebens*] was reestablished, and Lucifer himself could not escape from this intervention [*Einwirkung*]. This is the epoch when everything emerged that we know as light, and everything began, which we tend to refer to in the word Creation [*Schöpfung*]. (HA 9:352; MA 16:382)[15]

The ability to constantly find (or invent) the same forms of relation—the same stories and narratives—shifts morphology from science (as empirical-analogical modeling) to religion and mythmaking. Based on a morphological infrastructure reflecting his idea of existence, Goethe retells the story of Creation with emphasis on the need for a Being that can restore the connection to divinity. But being continually finds itself under Lucifer's power, trapped in the contradictory state of being "at once absolute and limited" (*zugleich unbedingt und beschränkt*, HA 9:352; MA 16:382). Lucifer's problem, which man inherits, is—to use Blumenberg's word—"self-assertion" (*Selbstbehauptung*), self-separation and the forgetting of the Creator. Man, who was supposed to restore and maintain the connection to divinity, ends up excluded from it like Lucifer: "Separation from the Benefactor is the real ingratitude, and thus Lucifer's fall was for a second time eminent, even though the Creation itself is nothing but—and never was anything but—a falling away from and a returning to that which originated it [*zum Ursprünglichen*]" (HA 9:352–53; MA 16:380–81). A mythic fall and salvation history is re-internalized, distributed—perhaps secularized, perhaps remythologized—within the human condition:

It is easy to see how redemption is here not decided from eternity
[*von Ewigkeit her*], but rather is conceived as eternally necessary. . . .
This recognition alone suffices: that we find ourselves in a condition [*daß wir uns in einem Zustande befinden*], which, though it may
appear to draw us downward and to press upon us, nevertheless
gives us the opportunity—and indeed makes it our duty—to raise
ourselves up and to fulfill the intents of the divinity [*die Absichten der
Gottheit*], by which we are compelled [*genötigt*], from one side, to
selfify ourselves [*uns zu verselbsten*], while, from the other, we do not
neglect [*nicht versäumen*] to de-selfify ourselves [*uns zu entselbstigen*]
in regular pulses [*in regelmäßigen Pulsen*]. (HA 9:353; MA 16:381)

The Luciferian drive to concentration, specification, and individuation is
identical with the self's inherent drive to become a self. This arrangement,
which separates each self from other selves and turns them against cosmos
and Creator, was instituted in the Creation. But on the other side, in language
reminiscent of the *Elpis*-stanza of the "Urworte," the chapter ends with an
image of release from constraint, of a continual redemption from the concen-
trations and specifications of *Dämon* and *Ananke*.[16] Especially the figure of
rhythmic pulsation—as opposed to a redemption that happens once and for
all—corresponds to the wing beat of Hope. *Ananke* is the "imprisonment by
the present," whereas *Elpis* is a winged being that rises above the present and
"leaves the eons behind it" (UO 17). In the end, the saving demons are forces
of "de-determination," *Tyche* and *Elpis,* which constantly transcend limits
and relativize everything that appears absolute.

On the basis of the end of book 8, it is possible to imagine "human society" as Goethe presents it at the beginning of his *Morphology* in 1817 as
"tychic" in a more positive sense. Human society, culture, and history may
be negative, amorphous, and excluded with respect to nature and morphological symbolism, but this is precisely in keeping with man's Luciferian and
contra-divine tendency to self-specify. Humanity tends to reach false (or at
least relative) generalizations and to believe and institute them in ways that
cause human social constructions to fall short of the absolute. Man typically
exists at a distance from the divine norm that morphology can faintly perceive in its symbolic reading of nature. In *Poetry and Truth*, however, Goethe
does not reach his conclusions by directly contrasting human society and
nature but by attempting to retell the story of Creation in a way that would
adequately explain the situation of man in the world. He wants to reread
and reinterpret material excavated from the history of religion (especially its
heretical strands) in order to imagine how we came to "the state in which
we find ourselves" (*der Zustand, in dem wir uns befinden,* HA 9:353; MA
16:381).

This story is clearly not meant as the basis for a real religion but is presented as a theoretical construction of a possible religion, which, at the limit,

may have been Goethe's own. The Creation story at the end of book 8 may have been Goethe's religion, at least at a certain moment in his youth, and perhaps also later in a different way, at the moment when he wrote it down in his autobiography.[17] Though this "religion" is universal in its intents and could conceivably be believed, it lacks institutional and ritual foundation. And its content, like that of "morphology"—which may be only another name for "Goethe's religion"—is relatively undogmatic. It makes no emphatic truth- or faith-claims to further its propagation. What Goethe presents in books 8 and 20 is at best a private religion, designed on the premise that "everyone may have their own religion in the end" (HA 9:350). The reader is not enjoined to *believe* the story except as a literary creation and perhaps as a parable of the subjectivity of mythmaking and religion-founding. Goethe presents this "religion" as something he once thought and does not directly state whether he stills believes something similar. If anything, the point of telling the story of the genesis of his religious ideas may be to incite others to conceive and interpret religious ideas more freely. Like the "Urworte," which suppose an active collaboration on the part of the reader, book 8's reworking of religious ideas remains marked by "demonic" (individual) particularity. This demonic trace limits and at the same time preserves the universality of Goethe's meta-myth. It ensures that *this* claim to universality is itself morphologically *specific*—intrinsically perspectival and temporal—and follows the specific conditions of reading articulated in the "Urworte."

The universal science-religion of morphology produces an infinity of private religions, in which each individual retells inherited myths in the terms of his or her own singularity *and* universality. This is a generous reading, which allows Goethe to find his way out of the mirror-maze of morphology. He was at least partially able to retrace the patterns of his own private mythmaking, to draw them out of their latency and, at least at the highest levels of self-reflection, to resist the persuasiveness of his own insights through the recognition of his own finitude and particularity as the one who uniquely and subjectively perceived and disseminated a particular symbolic network. "Enlightenment" here is no longer a strict alternative to "myth." The former can consist only in the constant self-reflective articulation of one's own symbolic order. This "work on myth" at least has a chance of preventing the everyday unconscious and often violent self-assertion of such symbols in uncritical mythologies of the self. As a work of self-analysis, the textual weaving of symbolic fabrics may be only marginally more disillusioned than the expression of such symbols in the media of psychology, motivation, or desire. Such unreflected conceptions require conscious symbolic deciphering. And the lack of self-woven systems promotes the adoption of the finished systems of others: the failure to design one's own religion means dogmatically ascribing someone else's. Book 8 is thus implicitly critical of religion in its public, prescriptive, and collective dimensions. Submission to the collective— *Ananke*—is the typical human condition because, without massive efforts of autobiographical *analysis,* private understandings are never extensively mediated in their relation to public surrogates.

It may seem somewhat shocking to assimilate Goethe's scientific thought to problems of religion and autobiography to the degree that I am proposing, but the only other option would be to take morphology seriously as a scientific, artistic, or critical method. Though I would not automatically disparage the attempt to rehabilitate morphology, I observe that morphological paradigms can easily become reductively schematic and overgeneralized. Morphology in this sense is already too widespread. In this regard, I am arguing against taking morphology too seriously: it should be taken in the same way as the Creation-story sketched at the end of book 8 of *Poetry and Truth* and in the same way as Goethe's Orphic "Urworte," the point of which is to create a medium for reflecting on the unknown, a system that can be infinitely reread, retranslated, and transformed. This is precisely what the best readers of Goethe often did, even if they did so more in the context of their own theories than in that of Goethe's. As Lukács saw it in his *Theory of the Novel,* the true tradition of morphology lies not in science but in literature. The novel is, for Lukács, more scientific than science, due to its ability to coordinate every "truth" with a specific place, time, and perspective. This means, at the limit, that the tradition—at least a certain tradition—of the novel represents the methodologically most advanced edge of the "human sciences." The novel can think experimentally about the "morphological" significance of scientific and other developments without being tempted to believe unconditionally in insights that always depend on artificial and transitory formalizations.

Walter Benjamin's idea of "demonic ambiguity" (*dämonische Zweideutigkeit*) similarly warns of the limitations of morphology as a true science of forms. It can never get past its perspectival-temporal ("subjective") aspect. In Goethe, it does not even attempt to do so: I can find no claim to strict objectivity. In these terms, it can never produce a truly universal synthesis able to transcend the limits of language. In other words, it remains subjective. For Benjamin, morphology becomes "demonic" in the moment when it becomes convinced that such a synthesis really exists—somewhere beyond the limits of representability. The presupposition of the priority of the whole over its (supposedly) infinitely analogous parts does not permit any sub-spheres (such as nature/culture) to be even minimally differentiated. At this limit, morphology's endless systole and diastole make it impossible to draw distinctions. Morphology thus may be taken either as a merely "literary" symbolic mode or as a latently normative hypothesis. The latter, based on the spurious evidence of analogies, may offer support to countless arguments and assertions. The later reception broke this alternative into a spectrum of possibilities that (roughly) followed one or the other of these two courses. The more convincing results, however, as I will show, tended to be based on an at least implicit retention of the "literary" understanding of morphology.

Finally, to avoid confusion: what I am calling "literary" or a "medium of reflection" does not simply mean "aesthetic." The problem of the aesthetic is addressed in chapters 5 and 6, but what I mean by "medium of reflection" in the present context implies the possibility of something like a discursive formatting. Contrary to what one might expect of morphology, the visual is only important here insofar as "images" (in nature, art, or language) stand in relation to thoughts.[18] To illustrate the point, I would invoke the "Urworte," which begin with a certain Ur-phenomenon—four Greek words representing divinities of supposedly Egyptian origin—that are progressively transcribed into increasingly wider contexts. The difference lies in development over time. Whether in the arabesques of the "spiral tendency" or the linear striving of the "vertical system," the specificity of a given image-form or word-image is neither purely conceptual nor purely visual. The "proof" of an *Urphänomen* does not lie in its truth or supposed universal validity but in its potential seriality, its ongoing shifts and unforeseeable reconfigurations.

Chapter Three

✦

Biographical Demons
(Goethe's *Poetry and Truth*)

"Orphic Urworte" =/≠ "The Demonic"

In Friedrich Gundolf's reading of Goethe's "Urworte," he rather surprisingly asserts that the "primal words" represent a simple series rather than a unified conception: they do not represent a narrative progression nor do they articulate a system. Where virtually all readers have seen the "Urworte" as "cyclical" (to use Jochen Schmidt's term), for Gundolf they represent neither a process nor a cycle, but are essentially just a list. He only briefly discusses the "Urworte" in his chapter on Goethe's late poetry (*Alterslyrik*). In this passage, he asserts—casually but convincingly—that each *Urwort* represents an allegorical power; they are five "demons"—as he less convincingly argues—selected from a potentially limitless pantheon. This reading ignores the systematic and narrative coherence of the "Urworte." One could argue that this was only fully recognized later, except that Goethe's own commentary is clearly premised on the relation of the five words. It seems unlikely that Gundolf would not have known this, and I cannot imagine that he simply overlooked the obvious interconnectedness of Goethe's stanzas. Given that Gundolf emphatically appropriates—and conflates—the *Dämon* and the demonic within his own discourse, it is hard to imagine that he did not carefully study the "Urworte." Thus, without speculating on intents, it is difficult to explain his reading except as an intentional misreading. At the least, he must have been blind to data that did not fit his preconceptions. Regardless, if he had read the "Urworte" as systematically balanced powers (as I have argued), this would have invalidated his interpretation of Goethe's life as a demonic providence.

One might question whether the refutation of Gundolf's *Goethe* is of pressing importance almost a hundred years after its publication, at a time when it is infrequently read and would be considered barely reputable.[1] My claim, however, will be that Gundolf still needs to be refuted, at least in his reading of the demonic. Even if one were to hold that Walter Benjamin had the last word (which he clearly did), his arguments are much more coherent if one is familiar with his antagonist. And, more importantly, if Benjamin's refutation is not recognized precisely as a refutation of *Gundolf's reading*

59

of the demonic, then the point of Benjamin's argument is effectively missed. Goethe's life was guided, according to Gundolf, by a demonic providence; he invokes the demonic to support this idea of fate in terms derived from the *Dämon* stanza of the "Urworte." In order for this to work, the *Dämon* must be detachable from the "Urworte." Only on this basis is it possible for Gundolf to read the demonic as a predestination unchecked by chance (*Tyche*), love (*Eros*), or necessity (*Ananke*), and without any need of hope (*Elpis*). Gundolf, like Spengler, reads the demonic as equivalent to the Orphic *Dämon*. Regardless of whether one sees Gundolf and Spengler as especially influential in this regard, they are exemplary of this reading and its implications; and to the extent that the unity of fate and character is still understood as "demonic," Gundolf's reading is still alive. I hope to show that the erroneous conflation of the "Urworte" and *Poetry and Truth* made this reading possible, and that Goethe's autobiography primarily understands the demonic, not as fate, but in terms of what the "Urworte" call "the accidental" (*Tyche*).

It would be wrong, however, to say that Gundolf's (most likely deliberate) distortions prevent him from achieving important insights. His short presentation on the "Urworte" is typical in this regard:

> The Orphic *Urworte* treat suprapersonal powers [*überpersönliche Mächte*] that determine life; they are cosmic divinities of the human soul. . . . *Dämon, Tyche, Eros, Anangke*[2] and *Elpis* are neither pure ideas [*reine Ideen*] from Goethe's philosophy, nor are they pure gods [*reine Götter*] taken from his fantasy. They are allegorical demons [*allegorische Dämonen*]. . . . *Daimon* was Goethe's simple name for the law of fate [*das Schicksalsgesetz*] according to which entelechy exists and develops its essence [*west und wird*]; it is akin to the Indian idea of karma, the essence of a man [*das Wesen eines Menschen*] that creates and is itself his fate. The sum of the events that are not given as a part of ourself [*nicht mit uns selbst gegeben*], which do not bind and condition us [*die uns nicht binden und bedingen*], he called *Tyche*. And the fateful passion that transcends and goes beyond us [*die über uns selbst hinausreichende schicksalshafte Leidenschaft*] he called *Eros*. The sum of the external ties that determine our being [*die Summe der äußeren Bindungen die unser Sein bestimmen*] he called *Anangke*. And the anticipation [*Vorwegnahme*] of a possible fate, simultaneously capable of suspending and overcoming the present moment [*zugleich Aufhebung und Überwindung des Gegenwärtigen*], he called *Elpis*. He could have added more demonic powers to this series of five. To them belongs also "Fear" from the carnival procession in "Faust," as well as the grey sisters, Lack, Worry, Guilt, Necessity, and Woe [*die grauen Schwestern Mangel, Sorge, Schuld, Not*] as well as their brother, Death himself. (Gundolf, *Goethe* 675–77)

Gundolf's fleeting mention of the allegorical "impurity" of the "Urworte" deserves special attention: the Orphic "demons" are neither *pure* divinities nor *purely philosophical* ideas. Gundolf does not further illuminate the significance of this observation, but it directly points to the impurity and hybridity of the "Urworte," as well as to their susceptibility to being pushed—purified—in various directions. Gundolf himself goes too far, for example, when he declares them to be only "allegories." Just as they are neither *purely conceptual* nor *literally divine*, they also are not arbitrary personifications. Many allegorical possibilities may be uncovered in a close reading of the "Urworte," but the stanzas also present the five demons in a highly formalized and conceptual way. One could not easily say exactly what these divinities look like, and, with some exceptions—such as the wings of *Eros* and *Elpis*—their physical attributes are unmarked. What makes the five "divinities" into "demons" is precisely their ambiguity with respect to various ways of being and meaning. They are not concepts, metaphors, allegories, or gods—but they can be read as any of these; they are a variable medium representing an ensemble of interconnected forces.

Gundolf's paraphrases of the individual *Urworte* are not bad in themselves, and they come close to revealing the disavowed systematic coherence of the stanzas. By reading the "Urworte" as a loose connection of "allegories," Gundolf destroys their five-part unity. To my knowledge, Gundolf is the only reader of the "Urworte" to suggest that Goethe could have extended the series of demons. Without giving reasons, Gundolf declares the five terms of the "Urworte" to be essentially unrelated, and he further muddies the waters by naming allegorical figures from other works.[3] Rather than reading the "Urworte" as a constellation of "suprapersonal powers" that may harmonize or conflict with one another in the course of a given development, Gundolf believes that they can be extracted from their five-part context and viewed as independent figurations. Of course, the "Urworte" do not contain Goethe's only allegories, but this hardly suffices as evidence that this particular grouping is not meant restrictively. In "Pandora," Elpore, the divinity of Hope, contrasts herself with unnamed "other demons" (*die anderen Dämonen*, HA 5:343, 355), which implies a non-restrictive grouping. The "demons" of the "Urworte" can also be read allegorically, but the relatively conceptual orientation of the stanzas and especially of the commentary make it impossible to definitively opt for either the allegorical or the conceptual mode.

Gundolf's reading may have problems, but there is also a shortage of detailed and reliable evidence regarding the relation of the "Urworte" to the other allegorical figures introduced by Gundolf.[4] Though the connection of the "Urworte" to the demonic is in some sense evident, Goethe himself never articulated it. It is clear that there must be a connection, but it is unclear precisely *what* the connection is. Goethe's commentary on the "Urworte," as well as the ease with which the poems can be read in terms of morphological systematics, refutes Gundolf's reading of the "Urworte" and his conflation of

Daimon and the demonic. But an alternate theory of the connection of the "Urworte" to the demonic is still lacking.[5]

The most helpful source in clarifying this question is a letter Goethe wrote on March 31, 1818, to an unknown recipient (UO 72). In this letter, the "Urworte" are presented as an integral conception of the demonic (and not an open series of allegories). This letter may raise more questions than it answers, but it clearly refers to the Orphic "Urworte" sequence (and not the *Dämon* stanza by itself) as a "concept of the demonic." According to the letter, however, the Orphic "Urworte" are not *the only* concept of the demonic, but only "*one more* concept of the demonic":

> I especially still want to tell you how much it delighted me that, through the great *Urworte*, we are so easily and reasonably able to rise above the present moment [*daß wir durch die großen Urworte so leicht und leidlich über den Augenblick hinaus kommen*]. The absolute, the moral order of the world, systole and diastole! [*Das Absolute, die moralische Weltordnung, Systole und Diastole!*] After that, not much is necessary to reach an agreement [*sich zu verständigen*]. The next time we see each other, I have to give you one more concept of the demonic [*noch einen Begriff vom Dämonischen*], and nothing more will be necessary. A series of Orphic *Urworte* clarified into stanzas [*eine Reihe orphischer Urworte in Stanzen aufgeklärt*], which you will soon receive, are only a supplement and paraphrases [*Zugabe und Umschreibungen*]. (UO 72)

Striking at first glance is the fact that Goethe here reads "the great primal words" (*die großen Urworte*) under the sign of *Elpis*, the figure of the transcendence of time, who, in the words of Goethe's commentary (echoed by Gundolf in the passage cited above), "allows us to move easily beyond the present moment." In the letter, the idea of "rising above the present moment" seems to refer to the possibility of *Urworte* to raise the level of conversation. "Primal words" allow speakers who might otherwise disagree to distance themselves from their own "momentary"—particular and individual—understandings; *Urworte* are concepts of all-encompassing scope that can contain vast differences in perspective.

This functional-rhetorical understanding—of how to do things with *Urworte*—and the comments on the demonic directly following, do not refer to the "Urworte Orphisch." "The great *Urworte*" (*die großen Urworte*) named in the first sentence are apparently not the same as the "series of Orphic *Urworte*" mentioned at the end. Not only are the "great *Urworte*" not qualified as "Orphic." Rather, the three abstract concepts followed by an exclamation point seem to be introduced as examples of "great *Urworte*."[6] The first sentences thus explain the unifying effects of "great Ur-words" like "the absolute, the moral order of the world, systole and diastole[!]." If these three terms are examples of non-Orphic *Urworte*, then the next sentence promises the letter's recipient that, the next time Goethe sees him or her in person, he will impart "*one more* concept of the demonic" (*noch einen Begriff vom Dämonischen*). This *additional* conception is also not necessarily the same as the "Urworte Orphisch." The latter are being sent, according to the letter, as a written supplement to past and future conversations (about the demonic).

The Orphic *Urworte* are thus far from exclusively equated with the demonic: they are only "one more" in what is apparently a long onomasiological series; the "Urworte Orphisch" are *a concept* of the demonic, but they are not the only one. The letter describes them dismissively—as "supplement" (*Zugabe*) and "circumlocutions" (*Umschreibungen*)—in comparison with more effective oral transmissions, but given the widely recognized excellence of the stanzas and the fact that Goethe published them twice in 1820, this lukewarm characterization hardly seems definitive. The words *Zugabe* and *Umschreibungen* may also be suggestive beyond the immediate context of the letter: a *Zugabe* may be an "encore" as well as a supplement; and "circumlocution" (*Umschreibung*) describes the relation of stanzas and commentary to the Greek *Urworte*.

Different *Urworte* produce different concepts of the demonic. A different demonic is reflected by every *Urwort* (or system of *Urworte*); the specific concept of the demonic depends on specific word choice. The common "nature-nurture" opposition, for example, may provide *a concept* of approximately the same problem as the Orphic "Urworte," but it expresses the relation in question differently. Goethe never systematically clarifies the relation of different sets of *Urworte* to their correlated concepts of the demonic: the only way to do so is either endless terminological negotiation or a definitive decision for a single system. Either option would have required an extensive philosophical discourse, which is obviously antithetical to Goethe's way of thinking. What ultimately matters most for the demonic, however, is that he never articulated or even imagined the demonic in a single term or set of terms. Thus there is no "the" concept of the demonic or "Goethe's" concept of the demonic.

This peculiar understanding of terminology and system-building finds a parallel in morphology. Unlike philosophy and science, morphology contests the possibility of reference, viewing words—including "the demonic"—onomasiologically, as essentially inadequate and substitutable terms. This gives rise to chains of analogies and multiple names for the same unnameable thing. Morphology relies on metaphors and master-concepts (*Urworte*) to provisionally refer to indefinite *relations* whose essentially temporal and metamorphic aspect does not allow them to be definitely named. Similarly, in the 1818 letter, *Urworte* seem more like private "keywords," not concepts in a strict sense, but variable lingo. "The demonic" is apparently also an *Urwort* in this sense, perhaps even "the" *Urwort*, the master category for the unnameable "something" behind all *Urworte*. It is the most general word for that which other *Urworte*—across numerous places, times and cultures—have tried to name. The demonic is not specifiable, because it is infinitely specifiable. Goethe never directly states what makes some *Urworte* better than others in their representation of the demonic, but he does indicate that some work better than others. *Poetry and Truth* also has much to say about *Urworte* as the basis of *private* philosophies and religions. Human lives are governed by specific understandings of the demonic, which is to say: by the choice of *Urworte* and what is done with them.

The Demonic as a Theological Limit-Concept

The passage on the demonic in *Poetry and Truth* could hardly state more clearly that there is no single definition and no single concept of the demonic. Goethe explains that he became aware of the demonic through his experience with various religions—plural—that are peculiarly characterized as "regions." The young Goethe "wandered back and forth in the empty spaces between these regions" (*in den Zwischenräumen dieser Regionen hin und wider wanderte*, HA 10:175), where he encountered a force that could not be localized in any of them. The demonic thus belongs to the no man's land between religions; Goethe continues to explain—quite systematically—that the demonic refers to that which religions have always sought to contain or banish:

> There are countless names for the phenomena that are brought forth in this way [by wandering between religions]: all philosophies and religions have tried, prosaically and poetically, to solve the riddle and finally to get rid of the whole thing [*die Sache schließlich abzutun gesucht*], and they remain at liberty to continue to do so [*welches ihnen noch fernerhin unbenommen bleibe*]. (HA 10:177)

The demonic is the "problem" that religions and philosophies try to "solve," but which they may only repress or temporarily explain away. Given this definition, it makes sense that Goethe himself does not try to resolve the enigma (*Rätsel*), but only speaks of it in riddles.

This first introduction of the demonic is decidedly unenigmatic. It directly circumscribes a field that could also be called "metaphysics": the demonic is the sublime object of all philosophies and religions. It defines them *as* philosophies and religions and yet essentially exceeds their means. Especially once they achieve systematic coherence and authority, the result with respect to the demonic is either an overstated claim (to know the unknowable) or a myth. Such forms and formalizations may liberate thinkers and believers from the demonic—but only temporarily, and the demonic itself is excluded in the claim to exclusively define it. The tendency of (explanatory) systems is to cover over the enigma that necessitated their existence in the first place. Religion and philosophy are singled out as the most extreme attempts to explain the world—to explain the demonic and come to terms with what Blumenberg calls "the absolutism of reality."[7]

Such containment efforts produce words—including magic words—and *Urworte* together with signs, systems, symptoms, and effects. The demonic names the unnameable "something" at the origin of philosophy, religion, and science, but it is not identical with the history of its religious formations, representations, and explanations. The sheer number of such systems is itself a symptom of the underlying problem—which is especially problematic from the perspective of definitive codifications, orthodoxies, absolutisms, and fundamentalisms. No system for banishing "the demonic," no philosophical or religious exorcism, can succeed in the long term, because the world, to the degree that it is a demonic world, will always stretch or exceed—as in the famous example of the Lisbon earthquake of 1755—the philosophical and religious parameters (science, law, custom, society, morality, culture, history, tradition, life, nature, etc.) through which this world is supposed to be defined.

This demonic world may be monstrous, darkened—but it can never come to an end as long as the demonic holds sway. The demonic is, as my first two chapters show, above all a productive power and a power of continuation. Goethe refers to it as "the monstrous, the incomprehensible" (*das Ungeheuere, das Unfaßliche*, HA 10:175) behind all forms of comprehension. This is especially the case for religious and philosophical comprehensions, which relate to the demonic as the element of their genesis and the medium of their inevitable failure—from which something new emerges, which was not a part of the original calculation. The demonic produces "failures" in this sense whenever a theory fails to correspond to its practice, whenever a perception does not correspond to its reality, whenever explanations become threadbare and unconvincing. The story of Job, which exemplifies religion's possibility of testing its own limits, is paradigmatic here. Of course, strictly religious and other interpretations of the world constantly reassert themselves against such "failures," either dogmatically or through a process of qualification and revision. But from the standpoint of the demonic, this looks like an extension of the original denial, a misrecognition of the essential inexplicability and incomprehensibility.

Against such radicality, however, the introduction to the passage on the demonic pays lip service to the idea of a turn toward the shelter provided by religion: "he [Goethe's younger self] came more and more to see that it is better to turn his thoughts away from the monstrous and incomprehensible" (HA 10:175). Perhaps this would have been a good idea, but it is contradicted by extensive reflections on the demonic that immediately follow it. Goethe may have increasingly recognized the utility of fixed beliefs and institutions in comparison to an endless grappling with the incomprehensible, but his thoughts continued to be dictated by the latter: "I called this entity [*Wesen*] ... demonic [*dämonisch*], following the example of the ancients and others who perceived something similar" (HA 10:175–76). This sentence raises many questions: When was this "entity" first called "demonic"? And by whom? Who are the exemplary "ancients," and who are "the others who perceived something similar"? How can Goethe guarantee the similarity of these conceptions, if the word bears such a tenuous or over-inclusive connection to what it names? The casualness of this naming—the mere substantialization of the adjective "demonic"—could not be more evident. Ultimately, it is only the specificity of the word itself that suggests that it was chosen for a specific reason. The fascination that this word choice exerted on readers attests to its rhetorical success—despite and because of terminological or conceptual unclarity. Precisely the ambiguous resonance of the word may have led Goethe to it—and many others followed him.

The allusion to the origins of the idea only masks the fact that its main motivation was personal crisis. This applies to Goethe as well as to his readers. After introducing the demonic in *Poetry and Truth,* he struggles to produce a kind of minimal "face value" and keep the rhetorical upper hand against his own coinage. The term was precisely calculated to send readers looking for sources—for ways of explaining (away) the demonic—and Goethe himself was not immune to this temptation. Therefore the demonic may be defined more by its context—by what is not said about it—than by its enigmatic descriptions. Blumenberg emphasizes that Goethe identified the demonic with the entire "biographical presentation" of *Poetry and Truth,* which means that it should be understandable through the biographical motivation that led Goethe to it in the first place. Philosophical, religious, or theoretical conceptions of the demonic produce "paraphrases" (*Umschreibungen*)—more and more concepts of the demonic. Such concepts may be convincing in themselves, but they are not concepts *of the demonic* if they cannot account for its biographical dimension.

The demonic is introduced in a synoptic moment at the end of an extensive autobiography. Goethe wants to explain what he *understood* by the demonic. This is not the same as defining the demonic or saying what it *is*. He found this word for something he encountered in his experience by appropriating an inherited idea, a relatively common term of mixed or uncertain genealogy. It refers to something in his life and his narration of it that he could not otherwise pin down. The choice of the word "demonic" in this sense refers to an inner experience that is not strictly definable. Goethe admits that he is not the first to experience "something like this," thereby indirectly alluding to the ubiquity of the experience in question. Both the thing and the word are common: what he calls "demonic" may have been known at other times and places under other different names, and it is not limited to that which Goethe (or others) have *called* demonic.

The word "demonic" (*dämonisch*) and that to which it refers are conventional, but the use of the substantialized form, "the demonic" (*das Dämonische*), gives Goethe's conception unprecedented weight. The strategy of this naming is to keep a shadowy and ubiquitous *signified* constantly in play (yet absent and unspecified), while the choice of *signifier* ("the demonic") tends to eclipse its own referent (the indefinite "something" that is Goethe's stated focus). Only in view of this referent as it is developed throughout *Poetry and Truth* can "the demonic" be more than a semiological ruse. It is possible, though, to specify *what Goethe understood* without fixating on the word he gave to it; the result is something quite different from the numerous *possible* "concepts" that Goethe and others have devised.

Urworte as Self-Help in the Individual's Confrontation with the Demonic

A question Goethe does not directly ask, but which could have been answered in *Poetry and Truth,* is: when and how did he first come to call this "entity" demonic? It did not occur at the time of the events recounted in book 20, which tell the story, among other things, of how Goethe came to the court in Weimar. The long passage on the demonic is a non-chronological interpolation, motived by Goethe's uncertainty about whether he will have the chance to address the demonic in its proper place:

> And thus I will here again, for the sake of many dear readers, get ahead of myself [*mir selbst vorgreifen*]. Because I do not know if I will be able to soon resume this account [*ob ich bald wieder zur Rede gelange*], I shall here pronounce something [*etwas aussprechen*] of which I only much later convinced myself [*wovon ich mich erst viel später überzeugte*]. (HA 10:177)

This disclaimer, along with the obscurity of the connection between the demonic and the events of book 20, have led many—starting with Eckermann—to treat the demonic as a separate topic. This is understandable, because the connections to Goethe's life story are not systematically developed in book 20. The passage on the demonic is complex by itself, and it is not obvious how it relates to the autobiography; though some connections are drawn, they are mostly associative or motivic. By tracing such patterns, contexts emerge that allow the demonic to be perceived even when Goethe does not refer to it by name.

In the 1818 letter on *Urworte* and the demonic, Goethe implies that, like the name "demonic" itself, individual "words," including *Urworte,* are always subordinated to a larger (unfinished and unknowable) conception of the demonic. *Urworte,* concepts, and names thus are subordinated to a master-term, the *Ur-Urwort*, "the demonic." Both the letter and the 1820 commentary suggest that primal words, including the word "demonic," may have the status of pedagogical rubrics or heuristic devices. Thought-provoking "words to live by" correspond to diverse concepts of the demonic. *Urworte* in this sense define each individual's private religion: everyone has their own concept of the demonic, the meaning of which would remain private to the extent that it is tied to individual biography and psychology. This does not mean that such private concepts—which by definition are also defenses against the demonic—are incommunicable. Precisely the generality and variability of *Urworte* make it possible to give a voice to one's own specific life system.

Insights induced by such keywords tend, Goethe emphasizes, to "transcend the present moment" by placing individual experience in the proverbial "big picture" (and vice versa). This act of hermeneutic and rhetorical mediation renders "a lot of discussion" unnecessary. No longer necessary and no longer possible: the mediation between the big picture and the individual situation occurs as a momentary insight, which can either be left as it is or endlessly reflected. *Urworte* are thus uniquely able to grant cognitive access to an imagined totality; they are the beginning and the end of all reflections. Released from the confines of the self and the present moment, *Urworte* pull in opposing directions: as private concepts "of the demonic," they are highly nebulous, whereas their clarifying paraphrases (such as those of the "Urworte Orphisch") tend toward prosaic conceptualization. Thus to the extent that the demonic becomes communicable, it becomes general, collective, normative—and not particularly demonic.

With the exception of Gundolf, most interpreters have agreed that the "Urworte Orphisch" represent a quasi-conceptual utterance of premises that Goethe was rarely if ever able to express so compactly. My readings support this hypothesis, but they do so not with respect to the *content* of the "Urworte" but in view of a problem of their *form*. The specific content is arbitrary, or at least variable, whereas the form has implications for function. It is a fine line between consciously experimenting with the formal-functional possibilities of *Urworte* and getting carried away by them. Especially if a given set of *Urworte* is "one's own," the ability to perceive their function objectively may be impaired by their rhetorical operativity (on oneself and others). Thus the sophistication of Goethe's reflections do not exclude inconsistencies or even self-mystifications at the operative level. For example, one may be discomforted by Goethe's enthusiasm for linguistic ephemera like "the demonic" or "systole and diastole" (with exclamation point!), but such discomfort simply reflects the possibility of *Urworte*, as provisional private understandings, to become vehicles for affect and identification. Especially the rejection of a merely operative or vehicular use of *Urworte*—as a "transport" beyond the present moment—reveals a crucial aspect of their function. Even in Goethe's most differentiated understanding of *Urworte* as a medium of reflection, they risk revealing the empty functionality of transforming nothing into nothing. Any given *Urwort*-system may reflect a Weltanschauung, but it can only do so in a tautological and solipsistic way, especially if individuals primarily relate to it operatively. The challenge of *Urworte,* therefore, is to get out of the operative level, to reflect and delineate such words according to their possible functions and meanings.

Thus, neither in the "Urworte" nor *Poetry and Truth* is it a matter of articulating something that Goethe supposedly believed or of saying what the demonic is; it is rather a question of how one comes to such an idea in the first place. The demonic "as it appears in the course of this biographical presentation" is not a definite result or communicable conclusion, but precisely that which only the autobiography itself can illuminate. Only the life-context allows the role, function, and limitations of *Urworte* to be concretely determined. The point of *Poetry and Truth* is not to convey "one more idea of the demonic"; the *Urwort* "the demonic" is not a vehicle for the propagation of a private worldview. It stands instead for the impossibility and limits of such mediations. The pursuit of an *Urwort* in its biographical genesis, combined with the opaqueness of the term "demonic" itself, imply that even the mediation of the impossibility of mediation still takes place within an individual life. Thus, compared to the "Urworte Orphisch," the demonic in *Poetry and Truth* is more limited in its collective-normative implications and implicitly renounces this kind of generalizability. The material of autobiography—the meanings of an individual's own experiences—is inherently non-conceptual and incommunicable. This applies especially to the passages in which the demonic is explicitly thematized: clues are given, but these clues only make sense as a reflection of Goethe's life story. By making his life the only proper home of the demonic, its presentation in his autobiography touches the limit of what autobiography can and cannot communicate. This rigor with respect to the question of communicability sets *Poetry and Truth* apart from the more "clarifying" approach of the "Urworte Orphisch" and the 1818 letter's assurances of limitless communicability.

In the "Urworte" stanzas, it will never be possible to perfectly separate the "Orphisch" from the "Goethisch." These condensed and clarified formulations, for all their power, belong to the traditions of religion and philosophy that Goethe seeks to precisely sidestep in book 20. Even and especially flawless poetic compositions can only disavow the demonic in their coming to terms with it. This implies a radical fidelity to a certain idea of prose, but not in a definitive or exclusive way. The passages on the demonic in *Poetry and Truth* were drafted before the "Urworte Orphisch," but Goethe did not prepare the last books of *Poetry and Truth* for publication until the final years of his life. Goethe never rejected either approach but was able to think in both ways; "clarification" and "paradox" are not mutually exclusive but supplemental. The limits of clarification can be tested only in the process of clarification, or in the attempt to isolate that which cannot be sufficiently clarified. Book 20, therefore, for all its opaqueness, is decisive because it tries to directly confront that which cannot be confronted directly; but, as I will show, the autobiographical narrative itself contains significantly more direct illustrations.

Gundolf's Morphological Misreading of the Demonic

Goethe's 1818 letter on *Urworte* connects his "Urworte Orphisch" (whose first stanza is called *Dämon*) to the demonic. Without this letter, the connection would not have existed—but the desire to draw it would have proved irresistible, as the common conflation of the *Dämon* and the demonic shows. No one is more exemplary for this misreading than Friedrich Gundolf, who uses figures of thought taken from morphology to unite the *Dämon* and the demonic. The result is a reading of the demonic as the productive force of Goethe's life and genius.

In the 1818 letter, Goethe identifies "the demonic" not with the *Dämon* stanza alone but with the entire "series of Orphic *Urworte.*" One could argue, though, that the first of the "Urworte," *Dämon,* is in fact the master term in the attempt of the "Urworte" to design a general terminology to explain an originally private and intuitive conception. *Dämon* is only the title of a stanza, but it is echoed in *das Dämonische,* to which the "Urworte" as a whole refer. The Orphic demon thus cannot be rigorously distinguished from the demonic. This tendency toward self-reflexivity can also be seen in a strange doubling: for Gundolf (following Macrobius), the "Urworte" all represent "demons"—but the first is actually called "demon." This suggests that the first stanza represents a meta-principle: *Dämon* is the common name of all five forces that comprise this conception of the demonic; *Dämon* is the identity principle that defines all of the demons as intermediaries between human and divine—as semi-divine forces with distinct forms and functions.

How does this general aspect, the meta-demon that underlies all five of the Orphic demons, relate to *the* demonic? For Gundolf, what is common to both conceptions is their representation of "supra-personal powers" (*überpersön-liche Mächte*). This allows him to include numerous forces in the concept of the demonic. In Goethe, however—in his "Orphic" and "morphic" conceptions—such forces, drives, or tendencies are consistently bipolar. If the demonic is a "suprapersonal power," it is an oscillating, pulsing power of "determination *and* indeterminacy," of "individuation *and* generalization." The bidirectional "and" is crucial in its correspondence to morphological *Urworte* such as "systole *and* diastole." In *Poetry and Truth,* however, the demonic (which "manifests itself in contradictions and oppositions," HA 10:175) is not an "impersonal power"—or the quintessence of several—but the product of a highly personal affect. In other words, rather than being "suprapersonal," it is at least partly subjective in origin. This dimension further relates to the hermeneutic dilemmas of *apparently* suprapersonal "forces" that may not actually exist. Language's power of substantialization allows things that are not immediately explicable to be attributed supposed powers: just as one might ironically attribute bad luck to gremlins, "the demonic" is an implausible name for such a force; it plays with the attribution of causes in a way that is simultaneously mystifying and demystifying. The Orphic "Urworte," on the other hand, start from positive metaphysical premises—a specific set of names—and tests their possibilities and limitations.

The demonic in this sense is a problem of the animation, personification, and allegoresis of "powers" that cannot be strictly identified. *Unambiguous* powers are not demonic; causation by a delimited power like gravity is not "demonic." This essential ambiguity can also be seen in the uncertainty as to whether the demonic pertains to (personified) effects or (unknowable) causes—or if it is the result of an inability to differentiate the two. The ambiguous relation or hypostasized unity of three registers—empirical-transcendental-allegorical—may thus define the sphere of the demonic. The relation of religion and philosophy to the demonic—clarification, interpretation, and rationalization—is thus mirrored in the cognitive processes of individuals. Religion may provide something like a fixed repertoire of explanations (whose effectiveness may vary greatly), but such a function could never be strictly limited to any particular tradition or genre of discourse. Goethe's obvious awareness of a diversity of religious traditions is certainly a factor, but in any conceivable cultural constellation, the demonic would by definition push the limits of the system. One could try to imagine a completely exhaustive and absolutely authoritative practice of confession (or the totalitarian system of Orwell's *1984*), which would free the individual from the burden of independent rationalization, but even here there would be limitations of what can be told or explained (from the side of the individual) and coherently rationalized (by authority). This question is not crucial, however—because Goethe's autobiography is not called *Confessions* but *Poetry and Truth*: this title choice clearly indicates that for him it is the individual who makes sense of his or her own life—or who, failing to do so, perceives the demonic.

This functional aspect exposes the risks of reading the demonic as real power or concept. The desire to see it as something more than the subjective by-product of a rationalization-problem is blatant in the case of Gundolf, whose reading is implicitly based more on the Orphic "Urworte" than on *Poetry and Truth*. He also includes elements from morphology, which help him to read the demonic as Goethe's daemon, his genius. The demonic in this sense is the morphological-developmental force that governed Goethe's entire being, his fate, and his life; it is the force that dictated the diachronic unity and totality called "Goethe." Like the morphological "leaf," which is the lowest term of a plant's life cycle, the demonic is the total synthetic unity of life and work:

Goethe's fate was governed by that which he himself called the demonic. Seen or interpreted from God's view, this is perhaps the same thing as, from the human perspective, the very secretly formative power [*eben jene heimlich bildende Gewalt*] and creative force [*jene Bildnerkraft*] that first creates form [*Gestalt*] as well as the space and the law of this form: this space and this law of form is for the greatest of men [*die größten Menschen*] nothing other than their fate. Fate is the atmosphere of their nature, and the creative power of great men [*der großen Menschen*] does not belong to them alone and is not enclosed within them, but reaches beyond them [*reicht über sie hinaus*]. The feeling that this is so, that he was the center of a suprapersonal force, that of God or Fate or Nature, and that his essence [*Wesen*] was not to *have* a fate but to *be* a fate, all of this Goethe expresses in the ominous [*ahnungsvoll*] word "the demonic" (just as Caesar speaks of his Fortune and Napoleon of his star). The demonic is not a power that intervenes from the outside; it is inseparably bound to the character of man, similar to the related concept of genius. In this word as well, a kind of grace is expressed, granted by something suprapersonal. But the demonic appears more to be an aspect of fate, which is that which one suffers and does; genius belongs more to nature, to that which one lives and is [*dem was er lebt und ist*]. But the higher he stands, the less a man's fate and his nature can be separated: fate belongs to character, just as the character is indeed itself already a fate, the most inescapable of all fates. (Gundolf, *Goethe* 3)

Gundolf's lengthy study contains more nuanced passages than this one, but as a symptomatic utterance, none are more telling, and, it should be added, despite the patent falseness of the conception, he shows great facility in expressing ideas from Goethe's thought. The passage assembles ideas in a passionately eloquent way that is almost completely opposed to Goethe's ideas.

The differences between Gundolf's reading and mine hardly need to be further underscored at this point, but the stereotypical plausibility of this image of Goethe is remarkable and indirectly shows Gundolf's great influence. Thus a few quick corrections are in order: the suggestion that Goethe believed that the demonic was the *guiding* principle of his life is in flat contradiction with *Poetry and Truth*. At the end of the excursus on the demonic, Goethe writes: "I now return from these more elevated considerations [*von diesen höheren Betrachtungen*] to my little life, which was also about to experience some strange events [*seltsame Ereignisse*], which at least reflected a sheen of the demonic [*wenigstens mit einem dämonischen Schein bekleidet*]" (HA 10:177). Goethe here connects the demonic with the narrative of book 20 and at the same time denies that the demonic was the guiding principle of his destiny. The language of appearance endemic to Goethe's idea of the demonic strikes a further cautionary note; the very question of whether the demonic was real strongly indicates that it was not (just as "maybe I saw a ghost" means "probably I did not"). The events in question *seemed* demonic—but only as strange events. And when one analyzes the events themselves, there is nothing obviously supernatural about them. The fact that they occurred at a decisive juncture in Goethe's life is what made them seem fateful in ret-rospect, but the title "demonic" presents them, at the most, as a mystery but certainly not as fateful.

Gundolf, however, would still have certain arguments at his disposal. He could claim that the ambiguities of Goethe's depiction were motivated by modesty (a virtue he is rarely accused of) or by the desire not to appear super-stitious (in which case the demonic would have been entirely left out); or perhaps the various forms of reticence and equivocation are only a sign of the difficulty of identifying the demonic in one's own life. In this case, Gundolf can claim to know better than Goethe, because he is an outsider with retro-spective historical knowledge. This view is capable of investing past events with a morphological-developmental and teleological-totalizing form; it can posit the decisive role of the demonic with confidence. From Gundolf's per-spective, Goethe could never have known he was the medium of a destiny. He could only vaguely sense it, whereas Gundolf, who possesses the com-plete testament of Goethe's life and work, is convinced that the demonic was real. Goethe's "fate" thus only reveals itself postmortem, with morphology providing the interpretive model for reading Goethe's life as evidence of a formal-developmental law at work in history.[8]

Goethe largely excludes history and society from morphology; for him the human world is an exclusion with respect to a morphological state of nature. Gundolf might see this similarly, except that for him Goethe belongs to nature. Like ancient Greece for classicism, Goethe's life and work have a privileged connection to nature. Gundolf retrospectively reads Goethe—the man more than the work—as a totality (a "genius" and a "great man"). For Gundolf, Goethe even more than the Greeks stands as an exception to the general amorphousness of human development. Goethe is thus the morpho-logical carrier of the universal destiny of man.[9] There would be no end of good reasons to be suspicious of this claim—but perhaps the most impor-tant one is its utter triviality. I would recall Goethe's words "my little life," which—false modesty or not—stand in stark contrast to the immodesty of "the greatest men" (Caesar and Napoleon). Most telling, however—putting Goethe's "greatness" aside—is Gundolf's blindness to the negative moments, to *Tyche* and *Ananke* and the pain of *Entsagung* (or *Trauer,* as Benjamin would say), as well as to everything that one might associate with the Werther complex.

Perhaps none of these criticisms entirely suffice for those who want to believe in Goethe's greatness. My point, however, would be that Gundolf, at his worst, is only performing a kind of image management, which, even in his own time, was widely read as a provocation: to produce a *better* literary-critical morphology and a better critical foundation for Goethe's "greatness." Especially for Benjamin, it is not just a matter of refuting Gundolf but of coming up with a better morphology of the relation of life and work. Much still depends on paradigms established in and around the Stefan George school, and thus I do not think Gundolf should be written off too quickly. He is also capable of powerful insights: even in his introduction, from which I have mostly cited the most dubious claims, I take seriously his arguments against purely empirical and positivistic literary scholarship and biography.[10] He argues that biographical minutiae are meaningless except with reference to the life or work that has already been judged (or prejudged) "great." And because the traces left by lives—especially "works"—seem to somehow depend on those who originated them, it does not make sense to treat works as facts among others. Such an approach overlooks the fact that works are often the reason why the biography is of interest. It also does not make sense to view works as purely autonomous relics of intrinsic "greatness"; they must be "great"—or just meaningful—in relation to something. In relation to unknown and uncertain origins and ends, literature and art may thus have a "demonic" character, which may correspond to deficiencies of meaning in life. Goethe thus describes his *Egmont* as a "flight" from the demonic, "behind an image" (*hinter ein Bild,* HA 10:176). But even as works compensate for deficiencies in meaning, they reproduce them by extending the uncertainty. Art and literature may on these grounds be deemed a failure in comparison with religion's and philosophy's anti-demonic programs. Gundolf argues that the relation of life and work is not merely *factual*—but he goes too far in the other direction in his sweeping and obviously rhetorical assertion of Goethe's importance. This kind of over-reading of the demonic (of which Gundolf is an extreme example) seeks to banish deficiency of meaning by the violent reassertion of utter coherence; Gundolf reverses the demonic, reading it not as *a lack of meaning,* but as the ultimate meaning of both life and work.

The Absent Totality of Life

Gundolf's substitution of a unified "morphological" totality for Goethe's "demonic" intransparency and incoherence inverts the demonic into a system of the utter coherence of life and work. This system, which allows life, work, and history to feed seamlessly into one another, may have some precedent in Goethe—for example his March 11, 1828, conversation with Eckermann[11]—but in either case it is possible only on the basis of huge presuppositions. In order to read as Gundolf does, the role of chance (*Tyche*) must be ruled out a priori; if life is to become fate, everything must happen for a reason. History is thus also conceived as the result of an inscrutable morphological decree—a form of providence that may be anything but providential. In the terms of the "Urworte," Gundolf postulates a *Dämon*, unchecked and unmodified by *Tyche, Eros, Ananke,* and *Elpis.* The result is a truly "demonic" cosmology that shares little with Goethe's. In much the same way as Spengler, Gundolf postulates a morphological conception that retrospectively views whatever happened as "fate." This perspective corresponds more to *Ananke* (as sheer necessity) than to the prospectively oriented *Dämon* of the "Urworte" (which presides over birth) and eliminates familiar elements of literary narration, such as chance, unrealized possibilities, unresolved significances, and regrets.

In *Poetry and Truth,* the demonic is not a fateful power that made Goethe who he was, but instead refers to the strange indirectness of this path and the uncertainties he encountered along the way. In this sense, the demonic corresponds to a generalized helplessness in the face of life or "fate" and to the retrospective inconclusiveness of the relation of *Dämon, Tyche, Ananke,* and *Elpis* in any given life. These "Orphic" terms may make it possible to tell a story, a history, of one's own life, but such limit-terms also make it impossible to narrate it in a way that is complete, exhaustive, and unambiguous. The circumstances of Goethe's life in the final chapters of *Poetry and Truth* challenge both the possibility of a morphological reduction (in Gundolf's sense) as well as the possibility of assigning delimited and unambiguous roles to the various Orphic deities. Life's inability to be summed up, even in the micro-analysis of a specific turning point, is the narrative context into which the demonic is introduced. To establish this context, I will not cover every pertinent detail of the last five books of Goethe's autobiography (to say nothing of the first fifteen).[12] What follows is a selective reading intended to sketch an understanding of the demonic that is not based on Goethe's cryptic presentation of it in book 20.

The demonic names the unreadability of Goethe's life for Goethe. Given that it reflects what he himself could not understand about himself, it is hardly surprising that he portrayed it enigmatically. I will attempt to set the scene: where does Goethe find himself at the end of the last published installment (books 16 through 20) of *Poetry and Truth?* The complexity of the narrative strategies and the segmentation of these last five books mask the conventionality of the events. In book 20, Goethe's state of mind is defined by the indecision caused by the breakup of a romantic relationship (with Lili). The breakup has been outwardly decided but Goethe cannot internalize it. Confronted with diverging visions of his future, Goethe is unable to grasp hold of or identify himself with any of them. At the beginning of book 20, he imagines himself as the object of multiple alien wills.[13] These foreign influences may be very general—like "chance" (*Zufall*) or "providence" (*Vorsehung,* HA 10:175)—but they express themselves through specific individuals: Goethe's father wants him to finish writing *Egmont* and to follow in his footsteps by visiting Italy; he *does not* want Goethe to accept the invitations of the various courts, which are, he thinks, only toying with his son. Miscommunication, the misinterpretation of ambiguous signals, and a delayed stagecoach make things worse, and Goethe ends up a virtual prisoner in his own house. Having already said his goodbyes, he shuts himself in and works frantically on *Egmont* (under his father's watchful eye), while waiting for a coach that may never come. He goes out only at night, to look in Lili's window, tormenting himself with an unrealizable future.

In book 20, Goethe stands ambiguously between past and future, lacking both an externally dictated fate and the grounds of his own decision. *Poetry and Truth* underscores this purgatorial condition. Johann Caspar Lavater's sharply outlined but semantically ambiguous silhouettes provide a haunting background and allude to Goethe's deficiency as an artist, that he is unable to bring his drawings to life:

> I was lacking the genuine plastic power [*die eigentliche plastische Kraft*], the forthright will [*das tüchtige Bestreben*], that is required to give body to a shape [*dem Umriß Körper zu verleihen*]. . . . My reproductions [*Nachbildungen*] were more like distant premonitions [*ferne Ahnungen*] of an indefinite form [*irgend einer Gestalt*], and my figures were like the airy spirits [*leichte Luftwesen*] of Dante's *Purgatorio*, which, casting no shadows, were horrified by the shadows of real bodies. (HA 10:173)

The shadowy existence of his figures is evidently a symptom of larger problems. A few pages later, describing his return from travels that were supposed to consummate the breakup, he writes: "Now I came back, and just as the reunion of free and happy lovers is a heaven, the reunion of two persons who are kept apart only by rational arguments [*Vernunftgründe*] is an intolerable purgatory [*Fegefeuer*], an antechamber of hell [*ein Vorhof der Hölle*]" (HA 10:178). This spectral irreality also inflects the description of what he felt when he peeked at Lili through closed curtains: "she went back and forth, but in vain I sought to grasp the outline of her dear being [*den Umriß ihres lieblichen Wesens*] through the thick fabric [*durch das dichte Gewebe*]" (HA 10:182). The imagery is reflected again in troubling visions: "Lili's image hovered before me, waking and dreaming, and it mixed itself together with everything else that might have been able to please or distract me" (HA 10:185). This motivic network may have little bearing on the demonic at the conceptual level, but at the technical and emotional level, it establishes a very troubled state of mind, which is apparently related to the demonic. In this context, the demonic partly serves to deepen and deflect a superficial or trivializing reading of Goethe's love life. He describes his emotional state in concrete and uncompromising terms; he writes of "the horrible void" (*die fürchterliche Lücke*, HA 10:170), "my passionate state" (*mein leidenschaftliche[r] Zustand*, HA 10:171), "inner agitation" (*innere Agitation*, HA 10:181), "impatience" (*Ungeduld*, HA 10:181), "uneasiness, that was eating me up internally" (*Unruhe, von der ich innerlich zerarbeitet war,* HA 10:182), and characterizes himself as "doubting and hesitant" (*zweifelnd und zaudernd,* HA 10:182). This condition lends itself to demonic apparitions and could not be more distant from the triumphant certainty of self and fate.

The experience of the demonic is related to indecisiveness and the torture of waiting; at the same time, it is important to underscore *what it is not related to.* Goethe does not try to give the impression that he *deserved* one fate or another, but, to the contrary, states that the outcome of the events of book 20 occurred despite his own recalcitrance. Along with this absent sense of deserving—which one might expect in the autobiography of a "great man"—strength of character and a sense of narrative inevitability are lacking. In recounting the relation of his character and his fate, Goethe avoids any sense that the factual outcome was the only one possible. The events are mostly explained in terms of chance and by Goethe's inability to manage the situation. Rather than prioritizing character (*Dämon*), book 20 presents *Tyche* (chance) as the medium of the demonic. She is not identical with it any more than *Dämon* is, but "the demonic" aspect of Goethe's life is most apparent in (almost) missed chances and (ultimately) fortuitous coincidences. Of course, in the slippery interpretive grid of "demonic" influence, coincidences may be easily reinterpreted as fate. But Goethe never does so, thereby leaving his reader to ponder the unspoken interpretive dilemmas.

The entry point of the demonic, the place where all of the uncertainties began, can perhaps be located in the "planlessness" (*Planlosigkeit*) of the young Goethe. His irresoluteness is what allowed him to become the object of others' plans. This is seen in his relation not only to his father, but also to his father's opponent, Demoiselle Delph, whose scheming nature contrasts with Goethe's indecisiveness. Delph was the matchmaker who made his engagement to Lili possible in the first place, and he remains caught between her expectations and his father's. Neither is blamed for meddling or directly named as agents of the demonic. Delph relates to the demonic only as a limit figure of other-determination (as opposed to self-determination). If Goethe blames anything, it is his own planlessness—which tempts fate by deliberately placing him at the mercy of chance. He describes this mindset in detail:

It must be admitted that amazing things transpire [*Wunderbare Dinge müssen freilich entstehn*] when a planless Youth, which so easily misleads itself, is also driven down a false path by a passionate error of Age [of Goethe's father or Delph]. But that is what makes it Youth and Life per se [*Doch darum ist es Jugend und Leben überhaupt*]: we usually learn to perceive the strategy only after the campaign is over [*wir [lernen] die Strategie gewöhnlich erst einsehen, wenn der Feldzug vorbei ist*]. In the simple course of things [*im reinen Geschäftsgang,* i.e.,

if Goethe had worked to manage his situation], such a coincidence
[*ein solches Zufälliges*, i.e., the unexplained absence of the coach]
would have been easy to explain [*wäre leicht aufzuklären gewesen*],
but we conspire far too gladly with Error against that which is naturally true [*wir verschwören uns gar zu gern mit dem Irrtum gegen das
Natürlichwahre*]. It is the same as with cards that we shuffle before
we deal them, precisely so that chance's part in the deed should not be
diminished [*damit ja dem Zufall sein Anteil an der Tat nicht verküm-
mert werde*]. And thus the element comes into being through and
upon which the demonic so gladly operates [*und so entsteht gerade
das Element, worin und worauf das Dämonische so gern wirkt*]; and
plays with us all the worse, the more we sense its nearness [*uns nur
desto schlimmer mitspielt, je mehr wir Ahndung von seiner Nähe
haben*]. (HA 10:183)

The more we think we perceive the demonic, the more it seems to toy with
us. Feedback loops and figures of reciprocity characterize the subjective "element" *within which and upon which* the demonic exerts its influence. This
"element" is the individual whose indecisiveness deliberately or accidentally
gives the demonic its space—a space that increases "the more we are aware
of it." Through a conjuring effect of self-consciousness, the subject becomes
the object of something beyond its control—and loses control of itself in
its apprehension of the demonic. The individual experiences it, falsely, as a
quasi-autonomous rival, an apparently external volition or counterforce that
exceeds that which is willed or intended.[14]

This interpretation of the demonic, the last one of *Poetry and Truth*, is
especially noteworthy for its unmistakable demystification of the earlier
passages. From the perspective of old age, the demonic is a youthful vanity—which may be a problem not only of youth but of "life per se" (*Leben
überhaupt*). The errors of age, combined with the residual identification with
the ideals of youth, give the demonic a chance of surviving its own demystification. As little as this aspect has been the object of an overt reception, it
resurfaces—in Lukács—as novelistic irony (as the knowing relation to what
one used to think one knew).

At the very end of the story, Goethe gives the impression that he was able
to break the spell and take the reins of his life. This effect is produced by a
drastically altered tone: "It fell away from me like scales from my eyes" (*es
fiel mir wie Schuppen von den Augen*, HA 10:186). Goethe is now "decided"
(*entschieden*), "resolved" (*entschlossen*), and describes his new state as "passionate and enthused" (*leidenschaftlich und begeistert*, HA 10:186–87). This
reversal does not indicate that he was instantly able to permanently exorcise
the demonic and return to his "intended" destiny. He does not break the
spell of the demonic to become Gundolf's "great man." The absence of the
demonic may only be a reversal of its current, as fleeting as its presence; and

the decision that freed Goethe from entanglements only led to new and different ones. This can be seen in the second part of his autobiography, the *Italian Journey*, which resumes the narrative approximately a decade later. The fugitive impulses upon which *Poetry and Truth* closed are now the motivation of a flight *from* Weimar.[15]

As a narrative-biographical device, the demonic represents the confining and determining forces of life—as well as their limitations and the anguish they cause. One of its aspects is *Ananke*, but its other side is *Tyche*, which manifests as the indeterminacy in conflicting pressures and possibilities. *Dämon* and *Eros* play a lesser role here because they are subordinated to the reality principles of *Tyche* and *Ananke*. According to Goethe, his actions and behavior put him at the mercy of the latter forces, and he aggravated the situation by his misinterpretation of their nature. The result was a conflagration—more dramatic for Goethe than anyone else—that illustrates the demonic, while simultaneously downplaying it in a very everyday story of "the follies of youth." At the time of writing, in his old age, he knows that the demonic was not a real force, but a force of his own making. What he once called "the demonic" is presented with the ironic awareness that it was mostly a product of his own blindness. It was his approach to things that exposed him to determinations and indeterminacies which—if he had known then what he knows now—he could have subjected to his own will.

Despite this "downplaying," he makes it clear that the demonic represented a specific trial and a specific turning point. The demonic in this sense is a passage, a juncture—representable even as a public architectural feature like Heimito von Doderer's "Strudlhof Steps" (*Studlhofstiege*)—which, regardless of the numerous internal and external forces in play, apparently could only turn out as it did. This "fact," however, is not unambiguously "proven" by the irrevocability of its outcome. The tenuous strand of everything that could have happened differently—but did not—always remains demonically inflected, even retrospectively. At the end of a life, even after the end, the demonic continues to thrive on the sense of the *impossibility*—"only in the impossible did it seem to be content" (HA 10:175)—of changing that which once appeared possible but is now inalterable: what makes it life in the first place is that we only learn the strategy when the campaign is over. "Strategic" mastery of the demonic flies in the face of life, whose chances—the infinite divisions upon which the coherence of individual identity depends—will always be beyond the individual's ability, by force of character, strategy, or cunning, to conquer from the inside out.

The lines from *Egmont* upon which *Poetry and Truth* closes—which in context seem to say that the best one can do in life is to hold onto the reins—make peace with "fate" through an exaggerated optimism that contradicts the previous idealization of "effective management" (what Goethe calls *der Geschäftsgang*) as a way of avoiding the demonic. The lines from *Egmont* are also a citation: the young Goethe quotes them to Delph as a parting shot.

Thus even in a small moment, multiple voices are audible. The young Goethe speaks from the past, citing a literary character of his own creation, in the same words with which old Goethe closes his autobiography. The union and difference of the two—self and other, then and now, *Dämon* and *Tyche*—is the essence of the demonic. Demonic characters like Egmont, by contrast, experience their lives only in the now; they achieve self-realization without remainder or admixture—or at least present the appearance of such undiluted being. In Doderer's punctual formulation: "Anyone who only realizes his own character is demonic" (*Jeder Mensch, der nur seinen Charakter realisiert, ist dämonisch*). Demonic characters never experience anything demonic in their own lives, because they are themselves demonic (in the eyes of others).

The end of *Poetry and Truth* is Goethe's confession that he was not—or at least is no longer—a demonic figure. It may have come to him from the outside, and he may have harbored it as an ideal on the inside, but his autobiography is not capable of unifying the two. This does not mean that it would be impossible to deliberately produce the appearance of a seamless demonic identity of fate and character; this is virtually the formula of the genre of memoir. Fate is ultimately viewed from the outside, thereby giving the impression that the life in question was an intended whole. Fates, like demonic characters, can be faked. Perhaps they can *only* be faked. But Goethe did not pursue this strategy, at least not in his autobiography, except perhaps in very indirect and convoluted ways.

It almost goes without saying that Goethe's autobiography is highly staged and constructed, but for the reasons outlined above, I see it as essentially honest. Goethe does not present the self-vindication of his life but tries to narrate and analyze the mechanics of his development. The aporias of precisely this approach give rise to the demonic. In a strictly formal sense, the demonic is a deliberately staged rupture in the fabric of the autobiographical narrative. This poses a problem, not only for Gundolf, but for biography and autobiography in general. To what ends does the retrospective rereading of a life strive to memorialize and totalize something that never presented itself that way at the time? To avoid the appearance of instrumentalization and aggrandizement inherent to all biography, the demonic is a strategic refusal of the heroic supremacy of the whole based on an *apparently* successful outcome. Goethe thus works against narrative paradigms that still dominate biographical prose, to say nothing of historical narratives.

The Story of Jung-Stilling

The limited degree to which Goethe's autobiography reflects *belief* in "the demonic" is evident in *Poetry and Truth*'s extended analyses, especially in its final chapters, of the characters of others, who—unlike Goethe—acted systematically as if their lives were governed by "suprapersonal powers." Goethe is not completely dismissive of such individuals. He does not, for example, use the word "vanity" (HA 10:89, 91) and move on. To the contrary, figures like Heinrich Jung-Stilling (in book 16) and especially Johann Caspar Lavater (in books 18 and 19) are intensely scrutinized. The resulting portraits have an undeniable affinity with the demonic in book 20, but these versions of it differ in that they represent it as a specifically religious (and unironic) affect. Two extremes must be ruled out, in order to make room for the demonic: the affectation of piety and the individualistic creed, complementary mystifications that may double for and mask one another. The demonic, outside of the paradoxical and enigmatic rigor of book 20, can easily revert to a completely conventional self-mystification. Goethe may have lapsed in his own self-interpretation—relapsed to aberrant perspectives of his youth—but within the pages of *Poetry and Truth,* he clearly does not believe in the demonic as a suprapersonal force of personal predestination.

For the sake of brevity, I will not analyze both Lavater and Jung-Stilling, but will focus on the more compact case of Jung-Stilling. The budding physician Jung (or Stilling), a friend of Goethe's in the late 1760s and 1770s, became known for performing cataract operations. Unlike Goethe, Jung believed that the events of his life were providential in the sense that they could be directly understood as encouragements or admonishments from God. Beyond this obvious connection of subject matter, the Jung-Stilling episode is placed symmetrically in relation to the demonic: the last five books of *Poetry and Truth* were published after Goethe's death as a single installment, and the story of Jung appears at the end of book 16 (HA 10:87–93); the demonic is introduced in the middle of book 20, thus closing the bracket opened by the Jung story. In Goethe's account, Jung is a well-intentioned and sincere person with questionable ability as an ocular surgeon. Jung's good reputation depends at least as much on his personal qualities as on his skills, but Goethe does not go so far as to say that he is incompetent. The surgeries work sometimes, but Stilling's real problem is his reaction to failure, which leads Goethe to draw conclusions about "this kind of a psychology" (*eine solche Sinnesart,* HA 10:88). In this context, Goethe makes a remark relevant to the demonic:

> Often in such cases there is an underlying obscure mentality modified by individuality [*eine dunkle Geistesform . . . durch Individualität modifiziert*]; such persons, accidentally encouraged [*zufällig angeregt*], invest great importance in their empirical career [*auf ihre empirische Laufbahn*]. Everything is held to be a supernatural purpose [*übernatürliche Bestimmung*] based on the conviction of God's direct intervention. (HA 10:89)

The mention of "an obscure mentality" with "individual modifications" reframes the demonic as an interpretive dilemma on the border of religion

and psychology. Goethe extensively criticizes Jung's worldview and the pitfalls of his way of rationalizing life: regardless of whether well-laid plans go
awry or whether good luck leads to a positive outcome, Jung's logic results
in a deficient sense of his role, "a certain irresoluteness when it comes to
his own actions [*eine gewisse Unentschlossenheit, selbst zu handeln*]" (HA
10:89). If an individual's assessment of possible courses of action becomes
too dependent on the outcome, he or she becomes indecisive, unstable, and
begins to make bad decisions; if experiences are subjected to retrospective
theological rationalization, the ongoing interpretive recoil erodes the grounds
of subsequent actions, producing extremes of self-doubt and overcompensa-
tory self-justification.

Goethe analyzes Jung's psychological hygiene as a thoughtless application
of aperçus. Jung takes recourse to knee-jerk formulaic insights that help him
to minimally (and temporarily) maintain mental equilibrium. Using almost
the identical terms to those of his 1818 letter on *Urworte,* Goethe defines
an aperçu as a principle that "needs no temporal sequence in order to produce conviction [*bedarf keiner Zeitfolge zur Überzeugung*]; it emerges totally
and completely in the present moment [*es entspringt ganz und vollendet im
Augenblick*]" (HA 10:90).[16] But here, unlike in the letter, Goethe recognizes
that such insights, though they may work as coping mechanisms, can lead to
error, dogmatism, and interpersonal conflict.

The conclusion of the tale of Jung-Stilling is ambivalent: he emerges as
a pathetic figure, but Goethe's last words (the last of book 16) are perhaps
inflected by the fact that he did go on to "become someone." Goethe concedes
that Jung's natural energy and abilities, "supported by his belief in supernatural assistance" (*gestützt auf den Glauben an übernatürliche Hilfe*), prevented
him from becoming "entirely hopeless" (*ganz ohne Hoffnung,* HA 10:93).
Stilling's life strategy may not be completely dysfunctional, but it is a far cry
from Goethe's "worldly attitude" (HA 10:90). And despite Goethe's attempt
at tolerance, he betrays irritation in his descriptions of Jung. Goethe claims
he has nothing against the pious affect: "Certainly I am happy to let everyone
decide for themselves how to deal with and cultivate [*zurechtlegen und aus-
bilden*] the riddle of their own days [*das Rätsel seiner Tage*]" (HA 10:90). But
the explanation of the source of his anger at Stilling—the "Job drama" that
ensued in the wake of a failed operation (HA 10:91)—seems to reflect some
of the original frustration. His anger may well be justified, but its intensity
is seen in the generalization of Stilling's behavior into a "mentality" (*Sinnesart*). Goethe never completely condemns this mentality, but he clearly had
no patience for Jung's self-absorbed attempts to discern "a divine pedagogy"
(*eine göttliche Pädagogik*) in everything (HA 10:90–91). All Goethe could do
against it was to try to lead his friend to "the rational and necessary result"
(*das vernünftig-notwendige Resultat*), "that God's decisions are inscrutable"
(*daß Gottes Ratschlüsse unerforschlich seien,* HA 10:91). This platitudinous
point can be taken in at least two different directions: for Jung it means

making an exception in a universal order presupposed as comprehensible—but for Goethe the incomprehensibility of divine providence may be essential, because at the limit, the incoherence of providence implies a world more demonic than divine.

Whatever Goethe may have understood as demonic, it was not "God" or "providence" under a different name. "It *resembled* Providence" (HA 10:175) because it shows signs of coherence, but such resemblances are only the raw material of *partial* intelligibility. I am not arguing that Goethe was above superstition, but his idea of the demonic is deliberately contrasted with Jung's more conventional piety. Jung's belief in providence represents a specific coping strategy, which contrasts both with Goethe's and with the idea of a "demonic character": as an outward representation, the supernatural guidance that Stilling incessantly invokes is not convincing to others. He is unable to convincingly perform his belief in life's meaningfulness and thus fails to manifest any demonic force of character. He is blind to the demonic, because his system of aperçus leaves no room for ambiguity or interpretive uncertainty. The demonic, unlike Jung's closed aperçu-system, emerges between the lines of life's actual and possible outcomes; the demonic challenges interpretive-narrative rationalization in ways that erode the difference between truth (*Wahrheit*) and fiction (*Dichtung*). Stilling's belief in providence is fictive (for Goethe), but Jung takes it for truth—and its effects are real. Jung cannot see beyond the necessary applicability of a theological micro-narrative (or aperçu) to question the rationales of narrativity itself. For Goethe the demonic is a failure or ambiguity of biographical induction (the inability to narratively generalize), whereas Stilling's problem results from a failure of deduction (of empirical outcomes to conform to self-serving premises about the way of the world). The result for Jung is psychological crisis, a compulsive search for interpretations that can bring given outcomes in line with expectations. "True" demonic characters, however, like Napoleon, Egmont, or Alba—to the extent that they are conceivable—would neither deduce nor induce. Demonic characters would not experience the demonic or related phenomena, because they experience no dissonance between self and world, premises and experiences. Jung tended to drive himself (and others) mad, but the demonic character is only conceivable as another kind of madness: the experience of such a (purely hypothetical) character only reconfirms what it already believes. No interpretation is necessary: initial premises about life's rules never have occasion to be questioned, and processes of rationalization are never initiated because there is nothing to rationalize.

Such a character is not just unlikely but impossible: the "demonic character" can only exist in the eye of the beholder.[17] The demonic character is only as good as its ability to represent itself as such. Such self-representations, following Goethe's "monster motto" (*der ungeheuere Spruch*)—*Nemo contra deum nisi deus ipse* ("None but a god may go against a god," HA 10:177)—strive compulsively to discover the limits of their own fraudulence. The fraud of the demonic character emerges whenever he or she is tripped up by the demonic as an external force, causing the narrative of "suprapersonal" fate to collapse. The sheer desire to have or to be a demonic character is not enough. And if one did have one, the first impulse might be to try to break out of it. In the end, the *apparently* demonic character can only be referred back to the *Dämon* (in the sense of *Anlage* or disposition, before and beyond all intention) or to *Tyche* (the externalities that allowed pseudo-demons to produce convincing deceptions such as those of Goethe's contemporary Cagliostro). Consciousness and self-consciousness are thus not part of the psychological profile of—fictional—demonic characters, which are always naive or unself-conscious. At the extreme, demonic characters would be mere automatons, entirely without character (for example, Olympia in E. T. A. Hoffmann's "The Sandman").[18]

Elements of the Demonic Novel

The demonic in *Poetry and Truth* is more than a systematic matrix for fate, character, and development. It looks behind Orphic and other *Urworte* for a system of social-psychological analysis capable of revealing the experiential parameters and limitations of "character." *Poetry and Truth* conceives this system inductively on the basis of Goethe's life and the lives of others in their concrete situations. The result can be read as a repertoire or scenario-system for the design of novels. Lukács certainly realized this when he introduced the demonic in his *Theory of the Novel*. In the early nineteenth century, when the novel—a genre to which Goethe also contributed—was entering into its decisive phase, *Poetry and Truth* formalized the relation of individual and incident into a system of combinatoric potentials. This proto-typology allows numerous scenarios, especially those involving coincidences, to be classified as demonic. Dostoyevsky's *Demons,* for example, constantly shows how expectations and plans (including those of the "villains") fall apart due to unforeseen events and accidents. At the beginning of part 3, chapter 5, for example, the narrator refers to an incident that saved the villains' plans (at least for a while) as "a completely unexpected circumstance to which they did not contribute" (Dostoyevsky, *Die Dämonen,* 1985, 832, my translation).

The demonic also manifests itself when a plan or intent fails to unambiguously correspond with its result. Again in *Demons,* Pyotr Stepanovich tells Liputin that he will kill Fedka (827–28), but when Fedka is found dead the next morning, it appears that Pyotr had nothing to do with it (830). The narrator never gives an answer to this puzzle. Such are the devices of demonic uncertainty, which, multiplied in the course of a long novel, may justify the title of *Demons.* Rather than defining the novel, as Lukács did, as an experimental effort to find significance in life, the "demonic" novel overtly reverses this expectation. The demonic novel is based on the expectation of a general lack of significance, which causes even the smallest correspondences and coincidences to become loaded with meaning. The demonic novel expects to see only incomprehensible causations without resolution, and this expectation is not entirely disappointed. Formally, therefore, the demonic novel falls under Goethe's definition of the novella as an "unheard-of event" (*unerhörtes Ereignis*). The difference of scale matters, however: the narrator strives to unify a complex chain of events and interconnected plotlines into a single event, the singularity and "unheard-of" quality of which is progressively undermined and buried—under a mountain of prose. (Sterne's *Tristram Shandy* is perhaps archetypical here.) One unheard-of event is an interesting exception to the order of things, but the demonic novel views such exceptions as the norm, which produces, if not a new cosmology of the novel, then at least a specific approach, which initiates the experimental inquiry into the meaning of life from a presupposition of meaninglessness. This atheistic presumption of meaninglessness is a narrative innovation insofar as it endows coincidences and random correspondences with an enticing ("demonic") ambiguity, which is able to simulate the problems caused by such events when they occur in "real life."

Chapter Four

The Unhappy Endings of Morphology

Oswald Spengler's Demonic History

> Kyklisches so gut wie eschatologisches Denken kann sich der
> großen Parallele bedienen. [Cyclical as well as eschatological
> thought can make use of grand parallels.]
> —Carl Schmitt, "Drei Möglichkeiten eines christlichen
> Geschichtsbildes" (Blumenberg and Schmitt,
> *Briefwechsel 1971–1978*)

The Problem of "Realization-Recoil"

The Austrian novelist Heimito von Doderer used the term "Erfüllungs-Rückstoß"—"the recoil of fulfillment"—to refer to a wide range of phenomena associated with the idea of realization in its various senses. The term appears in Doderer's diary as a part of the important 1933 "thematic" list (discussed in chapter 7), which conceives it as a political allegory, specifically as a mode of reflecting on new problems that inevitably arise when an idea or plan is realized. The "realization" in question in 1933 was the end of the Weimar Republic and the Nazi rise to power in Germany. Doderer, an Austrian, had been a supporter of the Austrian National Socialist movement since before 1933. This context is clear in his diary, according to which *Erfüllungs-Rückstoß* defines the situation of artists in the new political landscape: "The condition in which a spiritual worker [*ein spiritueller Arbeiter*] now finds himself, in the first period after the birth of the new *Reich*, stands under the psychological law of *Erfüllungs-Rückstoß*" (*Tagebücher 1920–1939*, 1:651, my translation).[1]

Doderer's support of Nazism and his reactionary politics at this time pose questions that may never be completely answerable.[2] Biographical issues aside, however, the problem of realization and fulfillment undoubtedly reflects a more general experience. Georg Lukács, for example, may have confronted similar uncertainties following the Russian Revolution of 1917. A more contemporary example of such a "recoil" scenario is the post-1989 fall of communism, which led to speculation about "the end of history,"[3] while the citizens of affected nations did not experience an immediate realization of all of their hopes and dreams. On the political stage, the "recoil" of a "realization" includes renewed conflict, disappointment, and despair (which may undermine the proclaimed "realization"). Doderer's case is trivial, one might say, because he mostly seems to understand the problem with respect to his own chances as a writer. Even this triviality, however, reveals the conception's wide applicability to countless large and small events; and this in turn makes it viable as a literary theme capable of surviving Doderer's involvement with fascism.[4]

The psychological law of "fulfillment recoil" is psychological because it applies to everyone differently; it would state that once a particular sweeping change has taken effect—such as a military victory or "the birth of an empire" or the election of a certain president—this does not mean that every individual hope (or fear) is automatically realized. To the contrary, *Erfüllungs-Rückstoß* is only the first wave of future backlash, the first moment of disillusionment. Thus the Nazis' rise to power was ironically inauspicious for Doderer, because his pro-Nazi epic *The Demons* (begun around 1930) was supposed to end with a vision of the "new empire." History got there first, realizing his hopes before he could programmatically espouse them in writing. This odd case of timing provided the basis for his postwar literary success: if he had actually completed and published a pro-Nazi novel (before or after the *Anschluss*), it would have been exceedingly difficult for him to convincingly backtrack his ideological commitments in time to save his reputation.

"Fulfillment recoil" is not one theme among others—for Doderer or in general. It recurs throughout his work as a figure of the demonic, starting with early texts predating his turn toward fascist politics.[5] This idea—of "being taken aback by an unexpected realization"—is most compactly and systematically articulated in Doderer's diary (May 5, 1933) in a "microscopic comparison":

> It is this *Erfüllungs-Rückstoß* which still always takes one's breath away [*den Atem versetzt*]. Allow me a small, even microscopic comparison [*Vergleich*]. If I am thinking of someone as I walk down the street, and then he is suddenly and "accidentally" ['*zufällig*'] standing in front of me in the flesh: this means that something has jumped from the inside into the outside [*etwas von innen nach aussen gesprungen*] and a thought has become flesh [*ein Gedanke Fleisch geworden*]. After that, to put it mildly, one is left gasping for air. . . . The irrational has once again staged one of its great eruptions [*Einbrüche*] into history (and maybe history essentially consists only of such eruptions). (TB 1:591)

This kind of scenario, in which a thought, fantasy, or desire is unexpectedly realized externally—ambiguously *as if* from the outside—is an ordering principle in the final published version of Doderer's *The Demons*. Chance encounters are made to coincide with concerns welling up from the inside. This phenomenon bears an affinity with what Freud called "the uncanny" (*das Unheimliche*), and thus it is not without precedent in fiction. The difficulty of knowing or deciding what to do when something appears to realize itself can also be conceived as a morphological problem: "Fulfillment recoil" arises whenever one wants to discern a culmination or declare that a particular developmental (or historical) cycle is finished and has run its course. But not all endings are of the same quality, and, depending on one's perspective, an end may be a new beginning. A finished cycle may produce a restart—or an ending may endure in a more or less stable way, giving rise to a new (but perhaps only apparent) continuity.

Especially in biographical analyses and plot mechanics, the unworkability of the morphological format becomes apparent. Goethe's conception of morphology supposes open and potentially endless cycles; but from the perspective of an individual life, thought and action are often conceived in terms of ends. Morphology causes limited ends and "realizations" to appear subjective in a way that blocks their interpretation as the realization of a supposedly objective morphological providence. The only perspectives from which realizations can be judged are the intents and the desires of individuals. But, as Doderer knew, especially unwilled events (or those that are only wished for) are not *fulfillments* but demonically charged *wish fulfillments*, disorienting coincidences that leave one "gasping for air" in the face of an irrational eruption.

Goethe's mood on the very last page of book 20 of *Poetry and Truth* can also be taken as an example of "fulfillment shock." At first glance, it might appear that there is no sense of disillusionment here, but readers of the *Italian Journey* may still see this euphoria as a partial precondition of a future disappointment. The initial reaction may be shock—a forward-looking emptiness, in which past cares echo away in the desired outcome—but disappointment may be the only way forward: what can follow such a profound (but perhaps partly retrospective) fulfillment? The conflict is resolved, the desired outcome achieved, but how should things now proceed? Unlike the end of *Poetry and Truth*, the treatment of the problem of historical and artistic fulfillment in Goethe's conversation with Eckermann on March 11, 1828, is ironically fatalistic. "Fulfillment" here is not identical with death, but it is related to it:

> —*The only way out is to keep ruining oneself!* [*Der Mensch muß wieder ruiniert werden!*]—Every exceptional individual has a certain mission [*Sendung*], which he is called [*berufen*] to bring about. Once he has accomplished it, he has no purpose on earth in this form [*in dieser Gestalt*], and Providence will reuse him for something else. But because everything down here happens in the course of nature,

the demons try to trip him up, over and over until he finally falls. This is what happened to Napoleon and many others. Mozart died in his thirty-sixth year, Raphael at almost the same age, and Byron was only a little older. But all had fulfilled their mission [*Mission*] perfectly, and then it was simply time for them to go [*es war wohl Zeit daß sie gingen*], so that something is left to do for others in this world, which was set up to be long-lasting. (Eckermann, *Gespräche mit Goethe*, 660)

The morphological point of *Erfüllungs-Rückstoß* is that once "form" (*Gestalt*) has been achieved (as the result of a development or culmination), there is nowhere to go but down. The productive energies that went into the blossoming of form cease and become static following their realization, and death (or at least "ruin") is the precondition of continued individual contributions to a greater whole.

Goethe's explanation here differs, at least in part, from his Orphic "Urworte," *Poetry and Truth*, and the morphological writings; to Eckermann he asserts a comprehensive analogy between human life, history, and the forms and cycles of nature. Regardless of the cause of such deaths, the "morphological" or "demonic" cause was the fact that these geniuses had fulfilled their intended purpose. This "mission" was also not exclusively their own but was facilitated by "demons," as well as the higher powers of "nature" and "providence." The main topic of the conversation is the source of Goethe's own creativity, and thus his own long life stands in implicit contrast to Byron, Mozart, and Raphael. Goethe does not die, and he avoids the demons by "ruining" and subsequently reinventing himself.

Doderer presents history as *essentially* consisting of irrational breaks and false fulfillments. Goethe's remark to Eckermann, on the other hand, understands history like Gundolf, who allows contingency to be subsumed by overarching morphological necessity. In book 20 of *Poetry and Truth*, Goethe characterizes life more like Doderer as a permanent failure of learning: "we usually only learn the strategy after the campaign is over" (HA 10:183)—but he tells Eckermann that the lives of "great men" are overseen by a suprapersonal providence. History is a cosmic drama and the exclusive result of the productive energy of exemplary individuals. This is Gundolf's thesis, but it does not conform to the more systematic and less conventional narratives of the Orphic "Urworte," *Poetry and Truth*, and the morphology.

However, the naturalization of the "untimely" deaths of heroes and geniuses—rationalized so as to make them precisely *timely*—may be partly ironical. He tells this story to Eckermann in a rather unserious way (which Eckermann is likely to take seriously). Goethe ignores empirical-historical causation, for example, in favor of a legend about the "mission" of geniuses whom "demons will try to trip up." His final words offer an especially implausible justification: the productivity of geniuses must come to an end "so that, in the course of the world, which is conceived on the long term, there's something left for the rest of us to do." Such a witty explanation may work in a conversation, but there is no reason to think that Goethe actually believed it.

With respect to Goethe's own longevity, the line about "leaving something for others to do" implicitly gives voice to younger writers (who may have wished Goethe had a shorter career). With respect to history, the ironies of Goethe's story take the form of latent counter-narratives and myths. They are ironic because in our time one is supposed to know better. However, many philosophies of history arguably have a similarly ironic structure. Goethe's story of fulfillment dynamics, for all of its unseriousness, betrays an awareness of epistemological problems common to both morphology and the philosophy of history. Morphology's diachronic idea of form can, so to speak, never decide if it is cyclical or teleological. Form-in-transformation can only be represented as an arbitrary point on a continuum, and any given moment of a cycle can only represent the underlying process metonymically. The metonymic shift from transformation to enduring form (*Gestalt*) freezes metamorphosis and hypostasizes morphology's diachronic-teleological intent. A "form" in transformation, retrospectively isolated as an apparent culmination, fruition, or fulfillment, can only be a metaphor, the coloration of which always reflects value judgment and anthropomorphism. Goethe's reading of the lives of geniuses is thus not only a "naturalization" of human history through the analogy with natural forms: the morphological conception of nature itself includes the human perspective that makes the analogy possible in the first place.

Introducing Oswald Spengler

The pitfalls of this kind of philosophy of history are most apparent in Oswald Spengler's *Decline of the West* (*Der Untergang des Abendlandes: Umrisse einer Morphologie der Weltgeschichte*, 1918 and 1922). This notorious work, more often mentioned on account of its influence than actually read, is a valuable source for ideas about the demonic, because, like Gundolf, Spengler tries to fuse the demonic and morphology. Spengler, more drastically even than Gundolf, places morphology's method of retrospective analogization in the service of a sweeping historical hypothesis. Goethe's remarks to Eckermann indicate that an approach like Spengler's was always a possibility of morphology, but Goethe himself never pursued it. And he never would have, because for him morphology was a way of thinking—a medium of reflection—and not a descriptive or predictive theoretical system.

Many of Spengler's self-proclaimed "innovations" are easily unmasked as morphological rejuvenations of the clichés of a quasi-philosophical philosophy of history. In this category is the language of "rise and fall," "development and decay," "blossoming and fading." If one wanted to see an innovation here, it would lie in the interdependence and ambiguity of opposing terms: for Spengler, "recoil" is an immanent part of the formal-developmental structure of "fulfillment," "culmination" (*Vollendung*), and cannot be differentiated from "decline" (*Untergang*). "The history of a culture is the progressive realization of its possibilities [*die fortschreitende Verwirklichung ihres Möglichen*]. Culmination is synonymous with the end [*Die Vollendung ist gleichbedeutend mit dem Ende*]" (UdA 141).[6] These sentences give compact expression to Spengler's idea that every culture harbors the possibility of developing its own unique civilization; its "culmination" terminates this potential and at the same time fully realizes it (to the retrospective viewer).

For Spengler, the telos is only a passing phase, the beginning of the end. This stands in contrast with a retrospective view of history focusing on unrealized potentials or felicitous historical correspondences. This is not Spengler's approach. For him, each cultural-historical monad has only one unique realization and its only possible outcomes are success or failure. A culture may fail to realize its potential for numerous contingent reasons, but this is irrelevant for the success stories, such as the West, which succeeded but have already passed their zenith. According to Spengler, cultures blossom into civilizations, and the latter are, by definition, in a state of decline with respect to the culture that gave rise to them. To illustrate this conception, Spengler makes a literary-historical hypothesis: "Goethe could—perhaps—have died in his younger years, but not his 'idea.' *Faust* and *Tasso* would not have been written, but even without this poetic manifestation, in a very mysterious sense they would nevertheless have 'been'" (UdA 189). What applies here on the small scale is valid for history itself. All historical events are functionally "substitutable" (*vertretbar*) for other historical events within a morphologically predetermined system of inevitable realization:

> The French Revolution could have been substituted [*vertreten*] by an event of a different form [*von anderer Gestalt*] and in a different place [*an anderer Stelle*], maybe in England or Germany. Its "idea," ... the transition from culture to civilization, the victory of the anorganic cosmopolis over the organic countryside, ... was necessary, and indeed precisely at this moment [*in diesem Augenblick*]. ...When an event is epoch-making, this means: it marks a necessary, fateful turning point [*eine notwendige, schicksalshafte Wendung*] in the course [*Ablauf*] of a culture. (UdA, 193)

Unlike Doderer's "fulfillment recoil," Spengler's idea of "culmination" (*Vollendung*), though synonymous with "the end," pretends indifference toward the effects and affects of beginnings and endings. In the big picture there is only one possible outcome, he argues; accidents or coincidences only affect the specific way in which the end is achieved. Spengler's philosophy of history is thus the exact opposite of Doderer's: the latter sees history as an endless series of irrational, merely apparent fulfillments. For Doderer, no historical (or biographical) "culmination" can be the *verifiable* result of "demonic" entelechy. In Spengler, on the other hand, a preordained morphological superstructure provides certainty and stability, which allow contingencies to be cancelled in the process of culmination.

By positing that there is only one possible end, Spengler's theory of substitution (*Vertretung*) negates the sphere of means. The point of the end itself is thereby also negated: a *Vollendung* from which nothing can proceed, from which nothing begins, is precisely contrary to Goethe's morphology, which sought to imagine not only the analogical but the *generative* interconnection of all things ad infinitum. Rather than concentrating on *forms* and their genesis, Spengler's morphology focuses on the determination of a discrete, closed, and repeatable, *cyclical* form of history. To the extent that history is the predetermined form of all forms, the forms themselves are only the superfluous evidence of the "morphology of world history." For Spengler, events and actions are also morphologically structured, occurring for the sake of an unavoidable but ultimately senseless "culmination," which is to say: for no reason at all.

This reading of cyclical form in terms of inevitable mortality gives the impression of an overelaborate nihilism, which may make sense at a cosmic scale, which makes earthly life seem diminishingly small and insignificant. But there is little reason to think, as Spengler does, that cyclical forms could be generalized in a way that would allow for prognostication. He does not argue that "everything passes away" or "all life is mortal," but argues for a universal etiology of rise and fall. He refuses to call this fated cycle "teleology," because this conception instrumentalizes and "rationalizes" heroic-tragic destiny (UdA 157); the idea of inevitable decline explicitly opposes both eschatological and progressive understandings of history. But these disclaimers do not mean that his morphology of history is not teleological.[7] In Goethe's morphology, the form of the cycle itself must be teleological in order to be identified as a cycle. In part 2 of *Decline of the West*, Spengler seeks to clarify this point by arguing for "local" teleologies ("culminations") against a single unifying teleology:

> I protest . . . against two assumptions that have corrupted all historical thought up to the present: against the assumption of an ultimate goal [*Endziel*] of all of humanity and against the denial of the existence of any kind of goals [*Endziele*]. Life *has* a purpose [*Ziel*]. It is the fulfillment of that which was posited [*gesetzt*] in its conception [*Zeugung*]. (UdA 613)

The beginning always already includes the end and eliminates everything between.

One could speak in Spengler's sense of "limited" and "general" teleologies. The larger problem, however, lies in the dubious significance or meaningfulness of the *Ziele* and *Endziele:* ultimately, the secularized and naturalized providence of Spengler's theory is meaningless insofar as it lacks an external guarantee or reference. The discernment of "limited" teleological cycles endows life and history with a purely (but merely) immanent purpose within the morphological system. A further problem is the way that *perceived* cyclical "forms" are immediately identified with *real* cyclical, iterative, and developmental cycles; analogies are easily constructed if the points of comparison are general enough. The existence and meaning of iterative-cyclical form is a genuine question, but if it is approached in a very general way (as "nature"), then everything seems to fit.

Key arguments from the first pages of Spengler's introduction illustrate the approach and its drawbacks. One might imagine that he is focused on classic questions of the philosophy of history, for example, the "old questions" of Kant's 1798 "The Conflict of the Faculties": Does history reflect a general progress of mankind? Is it possible to conceive of history a priori? According to Kant, only a transcendental a priori would allow the form and ends of history to be known. Historical or economic trends in the small scale—the perception of busts and booms, advances and setbacks—are ambiguous with respect to the question of ultimate ends, and the relevant time scales for measuring cycles are never completely certain. Only if the condition of the possibility of history can be established can its direction and telos be guaranteed (even if the precise path is unforeseeable).[8] Kant treats this question with strategic irony, whereas Spengler offers a relatively prosaic answer: the a priori of history can only be perceived empirically, a posteriori. Hindsight and comparative analysis—after the end of many histories, cultures, and civilizations—make it possible to perceive the general form of history.

Beyond the systematic and theoretical aspects of this question, however, Spengler is pragmatically motivated. He wants to know how to *make history at the end of history.* To act historically, he argues, one must know what history will do and what outcomes it will favor. Lacking this knowledge, historical ends are not directly pursued by individual actors but indirectly through the "cunning of reason." It has been argued (for example, by Nietzsche and Reinhart Koselleck) that it is detrimental to human agency if history is viewed as a suprapersonal "spirit." Spengler, however, explicitly rejects human freedom as a guiding force in history. He claims, in effect, to have discovered the system of "the cunning of reason." Those who know the system will have a competitive advantage over those who do not. This peculiar "freedom" thus claims competitive advantage, motivation, and rhetorical leverage for those who pursue it. History, in Spengler's morphological conception, is a force of nature to which humans must relate in much the same way as they relate to death. And since the outcome is the same no matter what, Spengler advocates an ethics of maximizing self-interest within the preset limits of history.

Spengler, unlike other philosophers of history (and despite his claim to use a comparative historical method), claims that European modernity offers an

ultimate historical standpoint. But the problem of retrospectivity is a problem for all philosophies of history. For Kant, for example, the human *Anlage*
("predisposition" as a universal-transcendental preset) cannot be known
unless it betrays itself in a historical sign. Such a sign allows the a priori of the
human *Anlage* to be determined, and on this basis the course of history can be
known (but not predicted in individual cases). Spengler, rather than looking
for a singular sign or event, claims to use a comparative method to discover
the underlying form of human nature in a comprehensive system of analogies between nature and all recorded histories. This approach is conditioned
by his lateness with respect to his own culture and other civilizations—and
by the sheer volume of cross-cultural data available in the early twentieth
century. Spengler's relativist historicism includes non-European histories and
developing ethnographic ideas,[9] but he aims to produce a monolithic idea of
History. By pretending to use the taxonomic and tabulative methods of the
natural sciences, his idea of the human *Anlage* reflects the natural diversity
of human fauna as reflected in the variety of human history and culture.
He produces parallel analogical currents to show consistent direction and
development—but the story always ends with decline. To the extent one can
speak of a moral to the story, it emerges from a fabric of historical parallels, which are totalized into a supposedly inescapable pattern. The scope
of this systematization is apparent in Spengler's tabulation of the "simultaneous" epochs of art and spirit (UdA 71–72), which break down various
historical cultures according to rubrics such as "Spring, Summer, Fall, and
Winter" and "Prehistory, Culture, Civilization." Spengler claims that these
analogical patterns, which are presented as evidence of an inescapable cosmic
destiny, are the result of inductive analysis, but his approach is transparently
deductive.

Spengler insists that his non-Eurocentric approach represents a "Copernican" revolution in the concept of history (UdA 24), but his terminology
is conventional. His system is a hyper-historicism that imagines the development of man in a multiplicity of possibilities that are inevitably defined
by death and decline. "Culture" blossoms into unique symbolic forms that
define the historical identity of a people, but once these forms are fully articulated, there is (as Goethe said to Eckermann) "nothing left to do," and "old"
civilizations fall to the vitality of "young" cultures. Histories end in civilization, and civilization is defined by empty repetition, expansion, and eventual
self-destruction. Artistically epigonal and politically imperialist, civilizations
assert themselves mechanically until they collapse under the imbalance of
internal and external forces.

The developmental paradigm that Spengler attempts to establish in cross-
cultural and comparative historical analogies is at best debatable and at worst
disingenuous. The length of his book is the result of the overstated ambition
of its central thesis, which is relentlessly recuperated in more than a thousand
pages. This fundamental imbalance between Spengler's thesis and its proof

causes the latter to outweigh the former. This overabundance of material is only supportable to the extent his specific narratives and interpretations offer something different from his repetitive metanarratives. Also, because the theory, though influential, has been the object of decisive refutations,[10] I will now turn my attention to the methodological sections of part 1 of *The Decline of the West,* in which the demonic often merely amplifies the pathos of the conception. At the same time, however, key elements of Goethe's more systematic articulations are implicitly retained.

Fate in Spengler's Morphology of History

The "morphological" basis of Spengler's fatalistic philosophy of history grants a specific access to the problem of mortality and finitude. I take this partly from Adorno, who implies that Spengler was a lesser, more pop-philosophical Heidegger.[11] For Adorno, Spengler was the *better* Heidegger, precisely because he was a more transparent historical symptom, and his motivations were more transparent and taken less seriously by professional philosophers. The coauthor of *The Dialectic of Enlightenment* does not treat Spengler as a taboo figure because he is a symptom of Enlightenment's regressive possibilities. One might even argue that Spengler, Heidegger, and Adorno himself tried to historicize the drawbacks of instrumental reason and positivism in the absence of metaphysics. Thus in Spengler's sense, all three may be seen as "substitutable" (*vertretbar*) at the level of functional equivalence. To be clear, the point of this substitution is not guilt by association, but rather, following Adorno, to read Spengler in the context of recognized problems of modernity.

In this context, Goethe's idea of morphology gives voice and authority to Spengler's prototypically anti-rationalist discourse. Like Gundolf, Spengler reads Goethe neither as a philologist nor as a critic—not as any kind of professional—but as a disciple. Spengler presents himself as a mouthpiece, identifying himself with Goethe so intensely as to eliminate critical distance. Goethe's words, which often lack quotation marks or a reference to their source, only say what Spengler thinks. His use of Goethe is often clearly deceptive or wrong—but he may be a deceived deceiver. And even if morphology is only a legitimating discourse for ends that are both highly suspect and completely conventional, Spengler's ability to ventriloquize Goethe may also be a precondition for his work's strange persuasiveness and popular success.

When it comes to specific differences between Spengler and Goethe, the question of morphology and "fate" is answered very differently. Spengler, like Gundolf, would see his difference with Goethe on this account not as a mistake on his part but as the result of the changed perspectives of the new century. This *historical* difference in turn depends on morphology's inherent ambiguity with respect to questions of "optimism" or "pessimism." Goethe's morphology does not emphasize decline, mortality, and death but instead implicitly focuses on birth and rebirth. Spengler, on the other hand, absolutizes mortality in the discrete finitude of cultural monads. This combination of mortality and relativism may also recall Herder (one of Goethe's most important sources).[12] Spengler's morphology might also be taken as a variant of Nietzsche's idea of eternal return, except that Spengler's exposed "de-" prefixes (*unter* prefixes in German) such as *de*-mise or *de*-cline conspicuously replace Nietzsche's trans- and super- (*über*-) compounds.

Such comparisons, when articulated, make Spengler's shortcomings clear. But without such differentiations, his theory appears close enough to Goethe and to other philosophies of history to produce borrowed plausibility. Spengler lends authority to assertive theorizations by claiming inspiration from Goethe, Nietzsche, and others. Nietzsche is a possible source of Spengler's thesis that it is characteristic of the West to think historically and imagine itself upon a historical stage. He claims that the modern Occident is uniquely possessed of an acute awareness of time and history that is only haphazardly articulated in other cultures. Spengler's own system is presented as the culmination of this awareness. *The Decline of the West* proclaims itself a comprehensive and objective science that will allow "*the* form" of world history to be "known" (UdA 21).

The analogical deep structure of all known history is supposed to allow accurate predictions, but this aspect of Spengler's method is more than a little contradictory. His conception is split between "future" and "fate."[13] He claims that his methods are retrospective and inductive—and that the fate he predicts is unavoidable—but this does not stop him from invoking an ideal of futurity which, by his argument, should not exist. He wants to do more than impotently confirm the inevitable; thus he predicts inevitable decline in order to incite individuals to action—but he avoids the activist model of an "inconvenient truth" (which invokes a looming "fate" in order to avert it). Spengler paradoxically combines extreme fatalism with activism: decline is unavoidable, but the dominant affect of his book is not resignation but passion. The latter is expressed above all in the prophetic status he attributes to his own work. *The Decline of the West* will give rise to a "philosophy of the future" (UdA 6), a philosophy that depends on the certainty of decline. The case is terminal, death is inevitable, but this knowledge is, for Spengler, the basis for rational action: culture's fall into civilization (and subsequent collapse) cannot be avoided, but individuals, including individual nations, can choose their own roles. The idea of "substitutability" (*Vertretbarkeit*) means that, though the big picture cannot be changed, knowledge of it will give a comparative advantage in competition with others. In this phase of the argument, Spengler's "philosophy of the future" emerges as esoteric opportunism— hedonism and nationalism—more focused on going down heroically[14] than on resisting the inevitable. Spengler's relativist method is thus negated by his chauvinist conclusion that, though the fate is unavoidable, the knowledge of it will help Germany to assume a leading role in the West's final march toward the abyss. Thus Spengler—following a critique that can be traced from Hermann Heller to Adorno and beyond—gives a theoretical alibi to the practice of domination.

Spengler acts as if acceptance of his oracle necessarily means accepting his interpretation of it. But it may be, as Adorno implies, that the relation of the prophecy to Spengler's politics and ethics is not coherent. The political message of *The Decline of the West* can be easily set aside. Without denying that Spengler's message may do damage through those who seek the rationale he provides, his theory's politics was not essentially more convincing in the 1910s and 1920s than it is today. He believed that human and historical possibilities could be rethought on the basis of morphological "knowledge," and this idea, combined with his pessimism, certainly resonated in his time, but it presumably mostly did so in ways that reinforced existing behaviors and opinions.

Thus I would claim that nothing revolutionary came from Spengler, either in opposition to his thesis or through attempts to follow it. But much may have been activated and channeled through his work, and if a systematic point is to be rescued here, it pertains to the role that Spengler assigned to his own theoretical claims. The implicit dynamics are similar to those of the "end of man" thesis from Foucault's *The Order of Things:* in claiming the ability to perceive the approaching end of a specific, deterministically conceived epistemic constellation, the *episteme* in question—ultimately the present one—is made visible, as if from the outside, and thereby implicitly destabilized. Or, the other way around, such an "end" is performatively pronounced in the hope of producing the described epistemic break. The inherent contradiction between these two options is a productive one: it rests upon the performative bracketing of epistemic determinants, which, assuming they exist at all, may continue to do their own thing in spite of every attempt to distance them into a hypothetical "meta."[15]

Such exercises in speculative defamiliarization may have a momentum of their own, even in a case such as Spengler's. The perspectives introduced in the juxtaposition of Spengler and Foucault make it possible to define morphology in a way that is at once more general and more precise: morphology is the "science," after the end of philosophy, of accurately reading the clock of history—or of persuasively claiming to do so. This kind of speculation is never purely theoretical; there is always an oracular implication. Morphology in this sense is the art of timeliness—the *pseudoscience* of claiming to know what is auspicious. This function would traditionally fall to artists and writers, rhetoricians and politicians, but Spengler's idea is to try to formalize it and put his insight at everyone's disposal. Science is only a veneer, however—and Spengler in any case denies that morphology is a modern (positivist) science. The *art* of morphology can only be informal divinatory cultural analysis based on intuition, which may produce—with the help of good luck and eloquence—the appearance of success.

To put it in the terms of the demonic in Goethe's *Poetry and Truth*: even in very small events, the difference between chance and agency often cannot be resolved, and the final grounds of even one timely occurrence or act often cannot be recounted in a way that would control for all variables. Thus by Goethe's standard, Spengler's claims for historical morphology are either mistaken or disingenuous. But the question of the basis and motivation of action has precedents in the demonic: knowledge and desire influence action, and can be used to influence them. This much is a commonplace, but the demonic, for Goethe, exerts itself through *impossibility*, through the blockage and obstruction of knowledge and desire, and he posits that this is the typical situation of historical actors most of the time. Perhaps Spengler understood this action theory well enough to try to manipulate his readers at the level of knowledge and desire, despite the fact that the schematics of his theory can be read as contradicting it. What Spengler appears to believe—what his theory extensively *shows*—is that the era of the blossoming of culture and art is over for the West; the noxious forms of "civilization"—empire and expansion, money and bureaucracy—will henceforth be the rule. The clock cannot be turned back. Spengler thus passes himself off as a futurist and not a conservative, but his "philosophy of the future" remains conservative in its claim to differentiate the possible from the impossible in order to pick the morphologically preordained winners. And the assumption that the possible is intrinsically more desirable than the impossible is psychologically naive compared with Goethe's conception.

Inescapability with respect to the spirit of the age is "demonic" for Spengler, and the capitalist industrialist Cecil Rhodes is the emblem of the possibilities that remain in modernity. But the lure of the demonic impossibility in Goethe's sense may also have been cast by this thesis. Spengler overtly politicizes his own theory, but its fatalism can be interpreted differently—*against* the spirit of the modern age, which Spengler himself depicts as odious. His work's ambivalent "futurism" must have been discarded or modified by all but the most docile readers, whereas his analysis of history and modernity could have energized opposition (from right or left) to "modern civilization."[16] His bleak outlook on the modern world is ultimately more persuasive than his political agenda. The "fate" he perceives may be written in stone, but it remains open to interpretation and the correlated freedom of action. The provisional acceptance of Spengler's "fate," rather than producing fatalism or resignation, can just as easily produce unexpected forms of inspiration. Worried that readers will get the wrong message, Spengler emphasizes the futility of striving against fate. Resistance, he claims, only leads to the repetition of the exhausted possibilities of past eras. The epigonal strivings of modern artists are condemned as inauthentic and eclectic, classicist and romantic, yearning for a state of past wholeness. Ironically, this is what Schiller meant

by the word "sentimental" more than a century earlier.[17] Spengler's dismissal
of all attempts to go against the spirit of one's own age—even though these
efforts are themselves inevitable—raises the question: is Spengler's idea of
fate adequately paradoxical? The foreknowledge of fate can produce action,
despair, or acceptance. If a fate is truly a fate, then the attempt to thwart
it only helps bring it about. Spengler's brand of fatalism—of collaborating
with fate—thus exhibits a lack of irony with respect to the possible reactions to "impossibility." This lack of irony about his work's utility subjects
Spengler himself to a dramatic irony that makes his work appear primarily
autobiographical. *The Decline of the West* produces an unintentional self-
caricature: Spengler casts himself as "a prophet of gloom and doom," and
his performance in this role undoubtedly contributed to his book's popular-
ity. Later authors of pop philosophy, pseudoscience, and punditry perceived
the marketing strategy. Successful popularization did not completely cancel
out *Decline*'s specific claims and messages, but it made it into a vehicle of
divergent motivations that cannot be reduced to a single ideology or line of
reception.[18]

Demons of Warp and Weft (Goethe in Spengler)

I see no reason to doubt the words of the foreword to *Decline*'s 1922 republication: "I take my method from Goethe and my questions from Nietzsche"
(UdA IX). "Method" here certainly refers to "morphology," following
Decline's subtitle, "Outline of a Morphology of World History." As I have
shown, Spengler's morphology drastically departs from Goethe's—but this
does not mean that it has no basis in Goethe. And, setting aside theoretical
systematics, Goethe's sheer ubiquity in Spengler is astonishing. The name
undoubtedly occurs with more frequency than any other; citations and allusions also abound. In addition, "the Faustian" (*das Faustische,* adjective
faustisch) characterizes the modern Occidental epoch; this equation of the
Faustian and the "modern," though not entirely unprecedented, is extreme in
its scope and systematic intention.[19]

Goethe's ubiquity in itself does not mean much. Spengler's appropriations,
in the language of his own theory, are cases of "pseudomorphosis"—a form
of appropriation that syncretically distorts what it appropriates to fit its own
terms.[20] Like Gundolf, who skews Goethe's morphology toward "fate" by an
overemphasis of the Orphic *Dämon,* Spengler dismantles Goethe's architecture and puts the various concepts contained by the demonic to his own uses.
Goethe viewed the demonic as a private (sub-conceptual) and only indirectly
communicable medium of reflection, whereas Spengler makes it a part of his
universal morpho-history. He implicitly recognizes the not fully rationalizable
and communicable aspects, but this does not stop him from schematically
reducing Goethe's conception. For Goethe, *Urworte* and aperçus allow

countless individual understandings and half communications, which may produce illuminating effects in private conversation, but the demonic is not a fixed system, structure, or terminology. It is a semi-medium for talking about the ineffable. Spengler was aware of this unsystematic, dialogical aspect,[21] but he uses it in the service of his most extravagant claims—for example, that Goethe was the Socrates of our era, whereas Kant is our Aristotle. This is typical of Spengler's use of historical typologies that often prefer *placement* in a framework over specificity. He sees himself as an inheritor of the intuitive, uninstitutionalized philosophies of Socrates and Goethe (UdA 68), but, contradicting this rejection of logic and systematics, his own theory is hyper-schematic.

In Spengler's system of historical *epistemes*, Goethe's way of writing about the demonic might be categorized as an example of the "magical" un- or anti-form of the arabesque, an indefinite spiraling figure that Spengler associates with the imageless relation of text and script in early Christian and Islamic culture. For Spengler, however, the demonic corresponds to a "Faustian" idea of the infinite—of the effortful striving of the individual *Dämon* against the limits of time, knowledge, and mortality. This drive manifests itself in the unachievable will to freeze, close off, grasp, and *represent* infinite "becoming" (*Werden*) in a single moment. This conception evokes key lines of *Faust I* and *Faust II* (HA 3:57, 3:348), but Spengler never reflects on the potential problems of basing his theory of modernity on a character in a literary work, who is further identified with Goethe's own beliefs and ideas.[22]

In Spengler's typology of cultural styles and characteristics, Goethe may belong to more than one category, whereas Spengler, despite identifying with Goethe, strives to be as Faustian as possible in his theorization of the West's inevitable end. The words of the Earth-spirit (*Erdgeist*) to Faust apply to Spengler's reading of Goethe: "You are like the spirit that you can grasp, but not like me" (*Du gleichst dem Geist, den du begreifst, nicht mir*, HA 3:24). Spengler sees Goethe as purely "Faustian," "Western," and "modern" and views his own "morphology" as an equally Occidental product. Self-critical potentials that might have emerged from Goethe are thus repressed in the interest of *Decline*'s central dogmas.

Goethe is the avowed source of Spengler's mythology of the "Faustian," but this is relatively unrelated to Spengler's theory; "Goethe" merely swirls arabesque-like in the background. A methodological centerpiece can be located, however, in section 9 of the introduction (Intro. 9) and in the parallel section (I.ii.19) from the second long chapter of *Decline*'s first part, entitled "The Problem of World History";[23] section I.ii.19 is part of this chapter's second half, subtitled "The Idea of Fate and the Principle of Causality" ("Schicksals-idee und Kausalitätsprinzip"). Another signpost unites Intro.9 and I.ii.19: the *Dämon* stanza of the Orphic "Urworte" (UdA 35, 206); Intro. 9 only cites "characteristic form, living and self-developing" (*geprägte Form, die lebend sich entwickelt*, UdA 35), whereas I.ii.19 quotes the stanza at greater length.

This double invocation of Goethe's *Dämon* as the source of Spengler's idea of developmental entelechy localizes the demonic in *Decline*'s methodological sections.[24] In Intro. 9, Spengler criticizes the causal-narrative and Euro-anthropocentric biases of nineteenth-century conceptions of history. He opposes their approach to his own "Copernican" attempt to show the "natural form" (*Gestalt*) of "the total happening of the world" (*das Weltgeschehen*); the epistemic object of morphology "resid[es] within the depths," in deep structures that become "evident to the unprejudiced gaze" (UdA 34). Spengler's morphology is declaredly "developmental" and diachronic, but it is not concerned with the "substitutable" epiphenomena of events, which are contingent in comparison to the "total happening of the world." Spengler's "seasonal" schema for historical development further structures and organizes time in a way that spatially conceives historical *individuals*— including individual cultures—as substitutable elements in a grid. Both the outcome—the "fate"—and the development that produces it are static and fixed. History is divided up in analogy with the natural life cycle or the ages of man: "youth, ascent, blossoming, and decline" (*Jugend, Aufstieg, Blütezeit, Verfall*, UdA 36). This sequence reflects temporal progression, which Spengler recognizes as metaphorical, but argues that his concrete application of it will transform it into a strict terminology (UdA 36). This categorical impulse conceives time timelessly and maps the form of finite biological individuality onto history and culture, which are perceived as comparably regular, predictable, and finite.

In Spengler, the individuality of *geprägte Form* is conceived as a state of endless transfer to and from suprapersonal symbolic forms that delimit cultural monads in contrast to one another. Individuals realize the development of cultural totalities, the individuality of which expresses itself through individuals. This approach presupposes the morphological identity of individual and totality without dialectical mediation. The result is an aesthetization of world history (which is reduced to the history of cultural formations), and the comparative history of cultural forms is magnified into universal history.[25] The basis and result of this broad synthesis is the presupposition of parallelism in all spheres of a given culture: art, architecture, custom, society, government, and even the forms of language, math, and science all correspond to the same underlying symbolic-archetypal-epistemic paradigm.[26]

"I recall Goethe" (UdA 35). This evocative sentence from Intro. 9 does not lead one to expect a systematic methodology, and what follows is in fact a whirlwind of paraphrases and allusions. *Wilhelm Meister* is the only work referred to by name, but it apparently stands for the idea of the Bildungsroman. Spengler claims that Goethe "always, constantly, drew out the life, the development, of his figures, their becoming and not their being" (UdA 35). This introduces the opposition between "becoming" (*Werden*) and "that which has finished becoming" (*das Gewordene*), which is a persistent systematic differentiation in part 1 of the *Decline*, in which Spengler uses the idea of developmental *Werden* as a weapon against positivist historiography's exclusive focus on facts and causation. Spengler claims that the *representation* of becoming—of organic development (*Entwicklung*) as opposed to "process" (UdA 203)—is the specific characteristic of Occidental art and of the modern *episteme*: whereas the art of antiquity (supposedly) valued the Apollonian beauty of closed forms, Faustian art autobiographically, self-referentially, and symbolically depicts the development out of which the work emerged. Like Goethe in his comments on the debate between Cuvier and Saint-Hilaire, Spengler prefers organological development to "construction":

> Here [in Goethe] the world as mechanism did not stand in opposition to the world as organism, nor did he oppose dead and living nature, nor law [*Gesetz*] and form [*Gestalt*]. Every line he wrote as a natural scientist was meant to illustrate the shape of things in transformation [*sollte die Gestalt des Werdenden vor Augen Stellen*], to illuminate "characteristic form, living, self-developing" [*geprägte Form, die lebend sich entwickelt*]. (UdA 35)

In a quasi-Pauline language, Spengler sets the future above the past, developing form over fixed law, the living over the dead—but his own theory posits development in terms of an iron law: *Decline* tells the story of inevitable rise and fall in the exhaustion of cultural paradigms and characteristic forms. Goethe's *geprägte Form, die lebend sich entwickelt*, however, makes no such claims. Insofar as Spengler's invocation of *geprägte Form* contradicts both Goethe and Spengler's own theory, it would appear to be primarily rhetorical. There is, however, an additional systematic claim, according to which the morphological "demon" becomes a figure of typology. The type in Spengler's sense (*das Typische*, UdA 36) does not correspond to *Dämon* (as individuality) but to Goethe's fourth *Urwort*: reductive-generalizing *Ananke* who overshadows "life" with the narrative closures that are typically necessary. Spengler introduces this generalizing moment together with his idea of contingency (*Tyche*) as "substitutability" (*Vertretbarkeit*). *Tyche* with her "fickle fortunes" (*wechselnden Geschicke*, UdA 36) is *mere* contingency; she is that which could have happened differently without making an essential difference. Spengler, as he says, seeks "the necessary in the unruly surplus of the contingent [*das Notwendige in der unbändigen Fülle des Zufälligen*]" (UdA 36).

Thus an idea of development that purportedly comes from Goethe is made synonymous with Spengler's idea of fate. The "tychical" surplus that manifests itself in the time of development only adds aesthetic value and the appearance of singularity to the typical fate that necessarily befalls all life:

> And just as he [Goethe] traced the development of the form of the plant from the leaf, as well as the rise of the vertebrate type, and

> the transformations of geological layers—*the fate of nature, not its causality* [*das Schicksal der Natur, nicht ihre Kausalität*]—I will likewise trace the language of forms in human history [*die Formensprache der menschlichen Geschichte*], their periodic structure, their *organic logic,* which develops out of the abundance of sensible details. (UdA 35)

Spengler wants to "develop" his system in analogy with Goethe's "development" of the forms of nature (*so wie . . . soll hier*). He thus circularly supposes the form of development both in his object (human history) and in his own method (which will proceed by developing). "Just like" Goethe who hypothesized that "everything is leaf" (*Alles ist Blatt*), Spengler sees a universal form underlying all development. Just as the leaf is supposed as the base unit of the plant, and the plant is "pure leaf" in transformation, so human development and history are also supposed to display "organic logic" and cyclical periodicity.

However, as in Goethe's morphology, differences of scale and time scale as well as the perspectival variability of historical beginnings and endings impede the application of this method to human society, culture, and history. Kant and Nietzsche, Weber and Foucault, Koselleck and Blumenberg, all take this kind of question seriously: How can a philosophy of history identify with certainty the singular beginnings of "cycles" or epochs? How can the cyclical vs. developmental forms be unambiguously determined? What motivates and necessitates historical cycles? How does this conception relate to history conceived in layers, as a web or fabric? Are these only metaphors, and if so, can one choose between them? Is the recourse to metaphor an index of human intents and anthropocentric perspectives? In light of such questions, Spengler's shortcomings are evident—but that does not mean that his work can entirely ignore these considerations.

His preference for thetic overstatement and exaggerated univocality thus produces rhetorical benefits at the expense of internal coherence. Self-critique is not Spengler's style, but this does not stop him from aggressively attacking ideas he opposes. He argues, for example, that his morpho-developmental idea of history avoids the misconceptions of words like "process," "causation," and "motivation." This critique is brought to bear against Marx and Darwin, who only perceive causation in the lowest terms of sheer material survival, "hunger and love" (UdA 202–4). Against this, Spengler points to the varied forms of human culture, which reflect a morpho-anthropological base comprised of complex form-drives. The mechanisms of these drives are morphologically determined fates that express themselves through the "inner certitude" (*innere Gewissheit*) of individuals (UdA 198). This "feeling" (*Gefühl,* UdA 201) corresponds to a talent for the forms through which individual and collective destinies come to fruition. According to this model, individuals and cultures are possessed by predetermined culminations. The "inner certitude" of being in touch with one's self and one's time is *felt* in individual experience and "demonically" dictated in view of collective ends:

> Whoever lives in streaming ardor [*in strömendem Überschwang*] toward an unknown "something" [*einem Etwas*] does not need to know anything about purpose or usefulness [*von Zweck und Nutzen*]. He feels himself as the meaning of that which will happen [*als Sinn dessen, was geschehen wird*]. This was the belief in the star, which never forsook Caesar and Napoleon as little as it did other doers of great deeds [*die großen Täter anderer Art*]. (UdA 199)

Ironically, the more the individual experiences itself as an end in itself, the more it is instrumentalized—the more it falls under the "demonic" control of "the total happening of the world." The subjective feeling of demonic self-certainty is the medium through which morphologically predetermined forms and cosmic patterns are realized *through* (not by) geniuses, heroes, and leaders and dictators.[27]

The preestablished harmony of morphological reason (which reads all actions within a given cultural paradigm as symbolic and productive of that paradigm) combined with Spengler's refusal of the principle of sufficient reason (which is blind to "the mystery of becoming" [UdA 203]), more than earns him his reputation as an irrationalist. He is also not alone in this, however: elements of his "irrationalism" are common to much more reputable conceptions.[28] Pointing this out does not mean rehabilitating Spengler—nor is it an attempt to discredit others by associating them with him. Rather, the idea is to establish a fine line between Spengler and the many others who have offered critiques of instrumental reason. Instead of posing historical causation as a problem, he exploits its fragility through a tendentious "theory," whose greatest harm—and asset—may be that it reveals the risks associated with the critique of reason.

Spengler is, however, occasionally more than just a negative example of the risks inherent to the twentieth century's attempts to come to terms with positivism and rationalization. Other possibilities emerge whenever Spengler fails to reproduce his main thesis and unintentionally allows "tychic" surpluses to emerge. This occurs, for example, in a passage on Michelangelo, whom Spengler imagines standing before an unshaped block of marble. This image, Spengler declares, expresses "the cosmic fear of that which has already come into being [*die Weltangst vor dem Gewordenen*], the fear of death that art seeks to banish [*bannen*] into a shifting form [*durch eine bewegte Form*]" (UdA 354). This echoes Goethe's "flight behind an image" (*Flucht hinter ein Bild*, HA 10:176), and the identification of "that which has already become" (*das Gewordene*) with death thus coherently reflects another aspect of Goethe's idea of the demonic: the refugee from "*what has become* (impossible)" flees into *what might be* and *what might have been.*

Here, in opposition to Spengler's main thesis, art's attempt to banish "what was" is conceived as an allegory of the overcoming of death. Art reanimates the dead positivity of an ended historical world. "Morphology" in this sense differs significantly from Spengler's official understanding. The latter urges an attitude of *amor fati* with respect to decline, whereas the confrontation of artist and raw material is poised between metamorphosis (rebirth) and finitude (death). This is the demonic uncertainty that provokes a flight into images. Such a flight may not permanently solve or even stabilize the underlying crisis, but the uncut stone reflects sheer potentiality and a lack of predetermination. Spengler here recognizes the ambivalence of the demonic, which implicitly contradicts his schematic version of morphology. Art's transformative drive to sublimate death corresponds to Spengler's theoretical instrumentalization of death, but whereas Spengler presents a one-way street, Michelangelo's artistic-morphological decision reflects ongoing indeterminateness: the uncut stone stands for each individual's attempt to symbolically answer morphology's life-or-death question of the possibility of future developments. In Spengler's theory, the dead facticity of the uncut stone is all that matters,[29] whereas Michelangelo's "demonic" nature constantly sought to shape the dead matter of the past (UdA 354). The demonic character in this sense is not possessed by a morphologically preordained fate or a feeling of "inner certitude," but by an *inner conflict* generated by the attempt to come to terms with the demonic (in Goethe's sense) as a placeholder for death and the unknown—for the questions to which religion and philosophy have perennially sought answers.

The Michelangelo sentence reflects an accurate understanding that can be traced to Goethe; it also shows that the *appearance* of a "demonic character" is the by-product of *a given character's* confrontation with *the demonic ambiguity of morphology's lowest terms*, which push toward forms of sublimation and overcoming that are declared impossible in Spengler's philosophy of history. This may be only a small lapse, an instance of evidence that subtly undercuts the argument it is meant to support, but it is not difficult to find larger systematic contradictions, motivated by the evident obstacles to interpreting history as pure morpho-demonic fate. In particular, Spengler's strict historicism contradicts his meta-history: he is forced to admit that there is not always a direct connection between the personal and the suprapersonal, between the individual *Dämon* and the demonic force of morphology. Demonic historicism is thus supplemented by a theory of pseudomorphosis that supposes the existence of cross-cultural influences capable of obstructing the pure development of cultural monads; individuals can likewise interfere with their own development if they strive to produce forms that are not proper to their own culture and demonically dictated *episteme*.

"Non-demonic" impersonal, intrapersonal, or trans-historical epistemic cross-currents may be relegated to the status of contingencies, but they cannot be completely denied. Thus at the end of I.ii.19, Spengler presents a kind of secularization thesis based on Goethe's idea of the demonic from book 20 of *Poetry and Truth:*

> In the [modern] reality [*Wirklichkeit*] of conscious being [*des wachen Daseins*], two worlds are woven together, that of observation [*Beobachtung* = the modern way of distanced seeing] and that of abandonment [*Hingebung* = the original experience of life as pure unprecedented happening], just as in a Brabant tapestry warp and weft come together to "knit" [*wirken*] the image. In order to *be available* [*vorhanden*] to understanding in any way, every law must have once been discovered—and that means *experienced* [*erlebt*]—within the history of spirit [*Geistesgeschichte*] as something that was brought about by fate [*eine Schicksalsfügung*]. Every fate appears in a sensible costume—persons, deeds, scenes, gestures—through which natural laws are at work [*am Werke*]. The life of primitive man was abandoned to the demonic unity of fate [*die dämonische Einheit des Schicksalhaften*], but in the consciousness of individuals in mature cultures [*im Bewußtsein reifer Kulturmenschen*], the contradiction [*der Widerspruch*] between this early and their own late image of the world [*jenes frühen und dieses späten Weltbildes*] can never be silenced. (UdA 207)

This passage contrasts the modern perspective of retrospectivity, which includes Spengler's own morphological vision, with the "demonic" omnipresence and intensity of reality for pre-cultural man.[30] Spengler opposes a primitive state characterized by "certainty" and "unity" to a developed state characterized by consciousness and doubt. The self-doubt expresses itself, at least partly, in modernity's inability to authentically identify with its fate in the way that primitive man supposedly did.

In the context of fate, the loom metaphor may seem predictable, but there are no Norns or Parcae here, only a fixed fabric that presumably bears an image—of the world. This figure of a world image (*Weltbild*) defined by ambivalence implicitly cites *Poetry and Truth*'s reflections on the demonic. The wovenness of the image stands for a perpetual effect of perceptual ambiguity, defined by the retrospective idealization of primitive life and, on the other hand, by the realization that the "rational" modern era is ruled by fates that are already finished. Out of this split between absent primal unity and the awareness of an established rational world order (to which one is subjected but with which one cannot identify), a woven image appears; its unity is composite, artificial, figural, oscillating like a *Vexierbild* between an imagined picture of the whole and the partially obstructed imagination of oneself as a part of this same image.

In *Poetry and Truth,* the loom image of "warp and weft" (*Zettel und Einschlag*, Spengler's *Kette und Einschlag*) configures the irreducibility of the demonic in every conceivable world order:

Although this demonic [*jenes Dämonische*] can manifest itself in everything that is corporeal and incorporeal [*in allem Körperlichen und Unkörperlichen*]—and indeed expresses itself most notably in animals—it nevertheless stands, above all, in the most astonishing relationship [*im wunderbarsten Zusammenhang*] with man and comprises a power [*Macht*] which, though not opposed [*entgegengesetzt*] to the moral order of the world [*die moralische Weltordnung*], crosses through and cancels it [*sie durchkreuzt*] in a way that could allow the one to count as the warp [*Zettel*] and the other as the weft [*Einschlag*]. (HA 10:177)

Unlike Spengler's loom, Goethe—more like Max Weber's "iron cage" (*stahlhartes Gehäuse*)—depicts the ongoing relation of idea and realization, predictability and unpredictability, rationality and irrationality, norm and exception, in the (modern) world. What holds the extremes together and brings them into focus is the idea of an interweaving or "crossing" of opposed yet interlocking views, which join to "knit themselves into an image." The tapestry fuses perspectives which, taken separately, would either represent a totally rationalized causality or a completely unreflected natural order. The extremes belong to an omniscient God and, on the other hand, to animals. Such limit-attitudes are inaccessible to Spengler's "civilized" humans, who experience this double perspective as a fabricated unity whose illusionary quality, though perhaps occasionally evident in moments of unraveling, is habitually overlooked.[31] According to the logic of this metaphor, the perception of a morphologically predetermined fate can only be the result of an artificial synthetic unity. The supposed "demonic" unity experienced by primitive man, by contrast, only perceives *itself* as a fate and thereby derealizes all other orders for as long as this perspective is intact. In humans, this is a formula of megalomania: if I *am* a fate and I *know* it and I *affirm* it (rather than questioning it), then I imagine that I am in no way subject to the world because it is entirely subject to me.

In *Poetry and Truth*, the demonic manifests itself as the appearance of reason in beings (such as animals) or circumstances (such as coincidences) that are either ambiguously devoid of reason or possessed by unknown reasons. For Goethe as for Spengler, individuals are regularly but unpredictably confronted with such crossroads that force a decision between the fundamentally retrospective (and often unfulfillable) demands of *sufficient reason* and the much more immediate competing claims of highly mobile *reasons and rationalizations*. Thus, even if the "moral order of the world" (whether in a theological or merely sociological sense)[32] is in fact an airtight system—of laws, determination, causes and effects, fates and providences—this is not the aspect it shows to humans, who are left to interpret it ex post facto. Spengler clearly prefers the attitude of subjection (*Hingebung*), of giving one's self uncritically to the force of one's own representations, which are, according to his theory, never really "one's own" but are dictated by the morphological force of history. Retrospective critical reason, on the other hand, only impedes us in being and becoming ourselves. Spengler thus envies "the life of primitive man" for its "demonic unity," its idealized primal ability, like that of Napoleon or Caesar, to live its own representations—to just live life—free of the reason and doubt (*Sorge*) that cloud the Faustian sense of self.[33]

This leads me, in conclusion, to suggest that the demonic, and not morphology, is the more essential Goethean inheritance in Spengler's classic meta-history. *Decline* flattens the idea of morphology to such an extent that it only shares the name with Goethe's conception. The latter, though available to a dogmatic reading, was not itself doctrinaire, whereas the demonic more obviously inflects Spengler's sub-systematic thinking. Especially *Tyche* is that which Spengler most seeks to eliminate or contain. Spengler's partial adoption of Goethe's idea of demonically inspired character also produces an exemplary mystification that he is unable to theoretically sustain. "Demonic" heroes like Caesar or Cecil Rhodes are supposed to have a direct connection with the universe (in keeping with Goethe's motto *Nemo contra deum nisi deus ipse*), but Spengler is forced to interpret them as epigones, as ideals of *pre-modern* life. The psychology of the demonic character supposedly corresponds with the prehistoric unity of being, but this contradicts morphology's deterministic historicism. The word "demonic" in Spengler thus refers to the sheer appearance of an undivided being, but, in drawing on Goethe's conception, it unintentionally introduces a problem of the optics through which such "demonic" appearances are produced in the first place. Spengler tries to suppress this problem, but his reflections on the demonic (and the related idea of pseudomorphosis) reveal modernity's divided, layered, historical—*geschichtetes* and *geschichtliches*—consciousness to be demonic (in its *lack of unity*) and at the same time productive of the demonic (in idealized *unities*).

To the extent that Goethe's idea of the demonic is conceived as open and endlessly theorizable in religions, philosophies, and individual lives, Spengler's *Decline* qualifies as "one more" concept of the demonic, which further reflects the antinomies and the sense of crisis that always lie behind the demonic. These contradictions were growing during the nineteenth century, while the will to harmonize them was diminishing.[34] The popular and to some extent enduring success of Spengler's work lies not only in its expression of an underlying crisis and the consolations it offers with respect to this crisis—it also shows how the formulae, affects, and questions associated with the demonic in Goethe's "Urworte" and *Poetry and Truth* can be simultaneously foundational and destabilizing for (pseudo)theoretical discourses. If, as Blumenberg argues, the demonic marks a limit of theorizability, then it also reflects the theoretical limitations and questionable sources of theoretical power.

Chapter Five

✦

Demonic Ambivalences

Walter Benjamin's Counter-Morphology

Demonic Unity, Demonic Ambiguity

One of the most likely places where the contemporary reader may have encountered the idea of the demonic is the work of Walter Benjamin. Other candidates would be Kierkegaard or Georg Lukács, who, though certainly aware of Goethe's use of the term, do not so directly establish their understandings through readings of Goethe. The deliberate lack of clarity about the demonic and its conceptual origins causes it to be simultaneously exposed and hidden. This is the case in Benjamin as well, but to a lesser degree, because he more extensively and philologically articulates the connections to Goethe. The demonic, however, also appears without reference to Goethe as a part of Benjamin's own lexicon. But neither at the systematic nor at the philological level has Benjamin's use of the term been a frequent subject of detailed explorations.[1] In addition to Goethe, whose work Benjamin knew well, he was certainly familiar with many important later thinkers on the demonic.

Benjamin's polemic against Gundolf in his 1924 "Goethe's Elective Affinities" hinges on the details of Goethe's conceptions of the demonic in the "Urworte" and *Poetry and Truth*. Benjamin's familiarity with Goethe's morphological writings can be observed in the encyclopedia article "Goethe," from the end of the 1920s. Benjamin's readings from the 1910s and 1920s also reflect a focus on Goethe (GS 7:437–449).[2] Lukács's *Theory of the Novel*, which introduces the demonic in the context of a thesis on modernity, also occupied Benjamin during this period;[3] he probably first read Lukács's theory after its 1920 republication (GS 7:448), and his essay "The Storyteller," from the late 1930s, still substantially engages with Lukács's theses.

Regarding Spengler, Benjamin could hardly have missed *The Decline of the West* (1918 and 1922), but I find no evidence that he knew the work in detail.[4] However, given the notoriety of Spengler's work in the late 1910s, Benjamin must have been familiar with its main theses and its use of morphology. Unlike Adorno, for whom Spengler seems to have been a touchstone over a long period, Benjamin's reading of *The Decline of the West* left almost no traces. His distaste for Spengler's work is mostly documented in the frequently adduced "sow-dog" (*Sauhund*) remark,[5] but even lacking an extensive record, it is plausible to imagine that Benjamin would have identified Spengler, the prophet of decline, with the most dubious ideological currents of the period. For instance, Spengler's idea of "fate"—his equation of history, nature, and destiny—is clearly an instance of what Benjamin calls "mythic" thought.

One further source that may have contributed to both Spengler's and Benjamin's understanding of Goethe's idea of the demonic is ethnography.[6] For example, Spengler's idea of the "demonic unity" of primitive man's reality may resonate with ethnographic understandings which were apparently able to coexist and interact with more overtly Goethean conceptions. In the 1920s, Freud's *Totem and Taboo* (originally 1912–13) could also have been a source for the idea that primitive man's world is ruled by demons.[7] In chapter 2, "Taboo and the Ambivalence of the Affects," Freud cites Wilhelm Wundt on the role of demons for primitive man: "The general commandment . . . that lies behind the numerous variable and unspoken interdictions of taboo . . . is originally *a single rule:* Guard yourself from the wrath of the demons" (Freud, *Totem und Tabu* 73, my translation). Freud, of course, does not believe in demons except as manifestations of the human psyche. Unlike Goethe, Freud also does not present demons and the demonic in a way that might leave some doubts about what he meant by them. He explicitly places his hypothesis under the heading of "the omnipotence of thoughts" (*die Allmacht der Gedanken,* 136–37). This understanding fits with Spengler's equation of the "demonic unity" of the life of primitive man and of the equally atavistic nature of "great men" in the modern world. Freud, however, unlike Spengler, questions whether there is an essential difference between modern and primitive man. Primitive superstitions are the analogues of modern neuroses. Freud's "modern man" constantly recidivates to superstition, while in Spengler modern consciousness is typically unable to achieve the unconscious "unity" of primitive man or the rational transparency of full consciousness.

Such anthropological and anthropogenic considerations also seem to sometimes inform Benjamin's idea of the demonic. According to Scholem, for example, Benjamin differentiated two ages of human prehistory, "the spectral" (*das Gespenstische*) and "the demonic" (*das Dämonische*) and understood "myth" (*Mythos*) and especially tragedy as a polemic directed at prior phases of human existence (GS 2.3:955).[8] It is difficult, however, to entirely accept Scholem's explanation, which seems more schematic than what one finds in Benjamin's writings. In "Toward the Critique of Violence," for example, he calls the police "spectral" (*gespenstisch*, GS 2:189) and argues that law is a continuation of "mythic" violence—but does not say that the demonic and the spectral refer to distinct phases of human development. This claim is misleading to the extent that Benjamin's arguments assume a high degree of continuity between developmental epochs (however they may be called or conceived).[9] Nevertheless, Scholem's clarification is helpful as long as it is not allowed to obscure the fact that the demonic in Benjamin is associated with myth and the mythic, and—even more narrowly—with "ambiguity."[10]

In the "Critique of Violence," for example, the compound adjective *dämonisch-zweideutig* ("demonically ambiguous") characterizes the concept of "equal" rights (GS 2.1:198). Without attempting an extensive interpretation, the words "demonically ambiguous" can be explained with reference to the essay's central argument that positive law represents a continuation of "the ambiguous sphere of fate" (GS 2.1:197). Law belongs with myth (and mythic violence), which is opposed to justice (and divine violence). Benjamin conceives myth as the retrospective rationalization of a primal precedent and original infraction that gives rise to law as a future preventive. Myth and law are the system of rationalizing and ultimately of prolonging and repeating the originary violence that lies at the foundation of all legal systems. Mythic violence is always law-making and law-maintaining violence that institutes and upholds a cyclical-retributive system that can never escape from itself. When Benjamin speaks of the "demonically ambiguous" quality of the idea of equal rights, it is because legal "equality" (which he sets in quotation marks) is implicated in a system of violence maintained by and through the rule of law. The claim of "equality" is only a pretext for preserving an *existing* system of rights and privileges. "Equal" rights support systems of *privileges,* and the language of "equality" is thus unmasked as an aspect of the self-justificatory discourse of systems that are per se defined by inequality and solely motivated by their own continuity and self-preservation. The "mythical ambiguity of the laws that may not be broken" (GS 2.1:198) inheres in the law's blindness to the reasons, histories, and motives that lie behind law-breaking. Benjamin illustrates this with an idea from Anatole France, who said that the law equally forbids rich and poor from sleeping under bridges.[11] The point of the example is that human laws only play into (and reinforce) preexisting determinations (in this case: socioeconomic), which, even in the modern world, appear to the individual as something resembling fate. The law which claims to be "equal" only maintains *preexisting unequal* material conditions (in this case: poverty). In "Fate and Character," Benjamin establishes a similar idea by way of Goethe: "You [gods] let the poor one become guilty" (*Ihr laßt den Armen schuldig werden,* GS 2.1:175).

Even with this contextualization, "demonic ambiguity" remains open to divergent readings. The demonic (or "mythic") state may itself be characterized by ambiguity: following Wundt and Freud, the ambiguity of the demonic age would lie in the uncertainty as to whether actions will provoke the anger of demons. From the perspective of individual humans—who cannot always perceive the apparent or sufficient reasons of the orders that rule them—demons are unpredictable. If demons are conjured up to manage or rationalize unpredictability, then their function in the modern world is effectively the same as it always was.[12] If the only difference between modern and primitive humanity is the distance implied in the word "superstition," then demonic ambiguity is not only characteristic of primitive existence but is the result of a fundamentally unchanged structure. When Benjamin calls equal rights "demonically ambiguous," this means that modern laws remain ambiguous in essentially the same way as transgressions against the demons were for primitive man.

The equality of the law that forbids everyone from sleeping under bridges is literally *zwei-deutig* in that it can be interpreted (*gedeutet*) in one of two ways: either it is mythic (which means that fate remains the highest category and law is only a medium through which modern fates are expressed) or it is rational and equitable (in which case it always acts justly in response to the free will of individuals who decide to sleep under bridges). Benjamin clearly favors the former interpretation, but he also indirectly addresses the seductive force of the latter's rationalization. Law's "ambiguity" is a problem of appearances, conflicting perspectives, and interpretive claims. The ambiguity of law and myth may thus refer not only to an ambiguity inherent in myth, but to the ambiguous superimposition of the "ages" of mankind, of the mythic-demonic (in which laws only reveal themselves after their transgression) and the modern (in which laws are man-made but similarly prophylactic in their function). This means, according to Benjamin, that the mythic era continues unabated or even intensified under the cover of law. Recalling Goethe's loom metaphor of "warp and weft" from chapter 4, this superimposition can be further interpreted as a split between rational, positive, man-made, transcendental—"modern"—social orders and the "demonic" cross-currents of "superstitious" rationales that still interpret these orders in terms of fate. It all depends on the perspective. "Demonic ambiguity" resides in the uncertainty about whether humanity has fully overcome the "demonic age" and in the fear that the transformations implied in ideas like enlightenment, secularization, and democracy are a sham.

Benjamin's "Critique of Violence" thus presents a two-tiered system of ambiguity: the first level is the "primitive" ambiguity of taboo, a mostly arbitrary code of conduct that constantly confronts individuals with the uncontrollable risk of transgression and "demonic" retribution. The second level is produced by a fusion of the spheres of myth and law. As I will show in more detail, the latter sense of demonic ambiguity is connected to a general inability to draw conceptual distinctions and make effective decisions. In Benjamin, however, such a lack of differentiation between spheres often expresses itself in the ambiguity of competing interpretive claims: the mythic thinking of the individual for whom law is only a medium of fate conflicts with positive law's claims to equity, equality, rationality, transparency, and deterrence. Such a contradiction may seem acceptable in the abstract, but it also ensures that there will never be an end to crime, because the law's claims will always be doubtful if I am the one who is violating it. Demonic ambiguity comes into play most tellingly in modern systems, in which all actors (not

only the subjects of the law, but also police, lawyers, judges and juries, jour-
nalists and pundits) have interpretations at their disposal that derive from
both spheres. There is no way to conclusively decide between them, even in a
single given case, and the force of law is thus always guaranteed by the violence through which justice is done—carried out in a sentence that can never
entirely shake the suspicion that it only additionally punishes those who are
already "poor." The problem of "demonic ambiguity" reveals itself, therefore,
not as an eccentric or novel critique of law, but as the primary reading of law
in literature, in works—to name only a few well-known examples—such as
Kleist's "The Broken Jug," Dostoyevsky's *The Brothers Karamazov,* Kafka's
The Trial, and Musil's *The Man Without Qualities.*

Benjamin would see Spengler's ideas of primal unity and organic cultural
development as characteristically mythic. Spengler's desire for "demonic
unity" is only the flip side of "demonic ambiguity." False epistemic unities,
invariant in every age, are produced by the inability to draw adequate distinctions and perceive true reasons. The idea of ambiguity, however, demonic
or otherwise, is common to the present era, regardless of whether it is contrasted with an idealized past.[13] Goethe's metaphor of the demonic as a
"warp and weft" (*Kette und Einschlag*) captures this ambiguity in the uncertainty about the status of historical forces in a supposedly rational world.
Spengler, on the other hand, though he invokes Goethe's loom, overlooks
the ambiguity of the demonic already in its prehistorical form. Benjamin's
"demonic-ambiguous," by contrast, turns out to be a pleonasm, because
Goethe's loom metaphor already includes the idea of historical ambiguity.
Benjamin improves upon the models he inherits, however, by his more decisive rejection of a fundamental difference between the demonic age and our
own. The former continues unabated, redoubled in the doubt introduced by
the rule of law. Our time is more demonic to the extent that law and reason
are an ambiguous overlay to an already ambiguous situation. Spengler saw
the difference between primitive and modern man as a difference of kind,
and Benjamin sees it as a difference of degree, but history's vector is the same
in both: Spengler differentiates a simple ("demonic") and a complex ("modern") historical situation, whereas Benjamin reads the relation of myth and
law as a movement of increasing ambiguity.

Benjamin's Anti-Morphology

Like the "Critique of Violence," Benjamin's "Fate and Character" will not
be analyzed extensively here. This is because, perhaps even more than in the
later essay, "Fate and Character" is at the center of Benjamin's concerns in
the late 1910s and early 1920s. In support of this claim, I note that this six-
paragraph essay was included in Benjamin's *Trauerspielbuch*[14] and that it is
also virtually indispensable to understanding the "Critique of Violence" and

"Goethe's Elective Affinities." Benjamin himself noted the connection to the latter essay in a 1924 letter to Hugo von Hofmannsthal, the first publisher of the Goethe essay; this letter characterizes the work as a return to problems addressed in "Fate and Character." Benjamin calls his 1919 essay a "frontal assault," whereas the "Elective Affinities" will be more circumspect. The context is a justification of his later essay's general approach, which seeks to break up terminological encrustations in order to discover the "linguistic life" (*sprachliches Leben*) beneath them:

> Thus I worked years ago [in 1919] to free the words fate and character from their terminological servitude [*Fron*], in order to newly get a hold of their original life in the spirit of the German language [*im deutschen Sprachgeiste*]. It is precisely this attempt that today betrays to me in the clearest possible way what unmastered difficulties remain as an obstacle to any effort of this kind. At the point where insight proves itself inadequate to the task of actually penetrating the frozen conceptual armor, it finds itself tempted—in order to avoid falling back into the barbarism of formulaic language—to try to achieve the depth of language and thought that lies in the intention of such investigations, not so much by excavation [*ausschachten*] as by drilling [*erbohren*]. The forcing of insights [*die Forcierung von Einsichten*]—the brute pedantry of which is admittedly preferable to the sovereign allure of their falsification (which is now the almost universally widespread practice)—absolutely pertains to the essay in question, and I beg you to take me seriously when I say that the reason for certain obscurities in my work should be taken in this sense. . . . If I were to return to the problem of this earlier essay in the same way, I would hardly dare attempt a frontal assault [*Frontalangriff*] anymore, but would rather, as in the presentation on "fate" in the essay on *The Elective Affinities,* attempt to confront such things in excurses. (GS 2.3:941–42)

Benjamin here explains and justifies his methods to his editor. Such reflections rarely appear in a comparably direct way in the works themselves, which makes this self-analysis helpful despite and because of its defensive tone.

The letter claims that "Fate and Character" represented the leading edge in Benjamin's developing self-understanding of his intellectual project, and—though it is possible to share some of the author's reservations about pedantry, on the one hand, and obscurantism on the other—the earlier essay's "forced insights" make it relatively easier to establish the common problem that ties Benjamin's work together. "Fate and Character" attempts to fundamentally reconceive the two terms of its title, a double focus which is still reflected in Benjamin's later work, even if the terminological considerations themselves are confined to "excurses." The letter only mentions the word "fate," but the essay on the *Elective Affinities* plausibly stands as a second attempt to get behind both of the two terms treated in the 1919 essay.

In the 1924 letter, Benjamin defends his approach by polemically opposing it to the conventional and widespread "barbarism of formulaic language" (*die Barbarei der Formelsprache*). Because the "Elective Affinities" contains an extended attack on Gundolf's *Goethe,* Gundolf may be an example of the "formulaic" approach. The wording of the letter, however, also suggests that Benjamin has a much wider trend in mind, further characterized by the "falsification of its insights." Falsification is the common practice in comparison to which Benjamin's "forcing" of insights is the lesser evil. The idea of falsification suggests an approach that could also apply to Gundolf. Insights are "falsified" to become authoritative claims and general conceptualizations. Benjamin, on the other hand, wants the real complexity of the problems to which the terms "fate" and "character" refer to be brought into language.

Though Benjamin does not name Spengler, he would certainly be another example of the trend toward "falsification." What makes Spengler crucial, even though he is not named, is the sheer monumentality of his work's "falsification" of "fate and character." In the background of Spengler, as the most authoritative source for his claims, is Goethe. Thus it is possible to imagine that Benjamin's attack on Gundolf is also an attack on a more general trend of Goethe appropriation and an associated style of thought. Goethe's "Urworte" themselves, as I have shown, are precisely *about* the power of "formulaic" thought, and their topic is also, at least in part, the relation between fate and character. Thus I would suggest: "formulaic" insights (such as Goethe's) are one thing, but adopting them as authoritative support for authoritative claims is a "falsification."

Benjamin's attack on the language in which fate and character have often been discussed is thus not a wholesale attack on formulaic thought or on the correlated idea of morphology. In the letter, Benjamin himself uses semi-morphological metaphorics to argue against the conflation of fate and character with the developmental form of all individuals and collectivities. Leading up to the previous quotation, he writes of the

> bountiful productivity of an order whose insights powerfully strive in the direction of completely definite words, the encrusted conceptual surfaces of which dissolve magnetically upon contact [with the insights] and betray the forms of linguistic life that were locked away inside of them [the concepts]. For the writer ... this relationship means the good fortune of language that unfolds before his eyes in a way that allows it to become the touchstone of his powers of thought. (GS 2.3:941)

It is clear from this sentence that Benjamin's approach is not only antiformalist and non-conceptual (in the sense of Hans Blumenberg),[15] but actually anti-conceptual in that it seeks to dissolve the falsified and formulaic rigidity of inherited terms. The repeated word "Einsichten" ("*in*sights") propounds a *penetrative* stylistic and linguistic ideal. The "encrusted surface of the concept" is its "formulaic language," while "terminological socage" (*terminologische Fron*) is a metaphor illustrating the ease with which thought can become indentured to conceptual pre-determinations. Insight must penetrate or dissolve "the frozen conceptual armor" (*der erstarrte Begriffspanzer*) rather than merely perpetuate it. This passage's metaphors of the hollow and frozen inheritances of tradition correspond to what Spengler calls "that which has already come into being" (*das Gewordene*). Benjamin thus denounces the fatal "barbarism" of self-reproducing and merely *received* concepts that rely on the authority of inherited formulae rather than "developing living forms in language."

This argument shifts the register of morphology: instead of going with the flow of language, Benjamin uses morphological metaphorics to advocate a way of thinking and writing that would "develop" (*entfalten*) the "linguistic life" (*sprachliches Leben*) that is pent up (*verschlossen*) in clearly defined words (*bestimmte Worte*, GS 2.3:941). Such "definite terms" would include both concepts and *Urworte* (in the sense of keywords or aperçus), but for Benjamin it is not a question of avoiding conceptual sedimentations and conventionalized metaphors. The "encrustations" contain "linguistic life," waiting to be released. The most intransigent formulae are the most linguistically productive. According to Benjamin's metaphorics, the writer must side with anti-conceptual "life" against the "death" of formal ossification. In context, this means siding with the metamorphosis as expressed in the idea of "living forms." Benjamin thus opposes Goethe's morphological conception of *form as metamorphosis* to the schematism of morphology as practiced by Gundolf (or Spengler).

Instead of focusing on analogy as a system of *non-identity*, Spenglerian morphology uses analogies to formulaically reproduce identities within the wider architectonics of his theory. In a 1919 fragment entitled "Analogy and Affinity" ("Analogie und Verwandtschaft"), Benjamin also addresses the possibility of unifying subsumptive-conceptual and ana/morphological thought (fr. 24, GS 6:43–45). The fragment also introduces a third term, "similitude" (*Ähnlichkeit*); thus it is a predecessor to Benjamin's "The Doctrine of Similitude" ("Die Lehre vom Ähnlichen") and "The Mimetic Capacity" ("Das mimetische Vermögen"). The systematic point of the fragment is sketched in a preliminary note (*Vorbemerkung*), which can be easily summarized. *Similarity* is a substantial relation, which as such is meaningless and incidental unless superficial resemblance is the sign of a deeper (logical) relation, which might, for example, show that *similar* things are in fact *the same*. Similitude expresses a relation that is "literal" and "unmetaphorical" (*im eigentlichen Sinne* [*unmetaphorisch*]), whereas analogy represents a relation of "metaphorical similarity," a relation of the "similarity of relations." Analogy is abstract because it is based on a (metaphorical) third term that expresses and interprets the relation. Of the three words under consideration, however, it is affinity (*Verwandtschaft*) that is the most ineffable, because affinities can exist without ever being expressed or signified. Benjamin notes the "expressionlessness of affinity" (*Ausdrucksloses der Verwandtschaft*, GS 6:43) and states that affinity can only be "immediately perceived" (*unmittelbar vernommen*) within a sphere beyond both visibility and rationality (*weder in der Anschauung noch in der ratio*, GS 6:45). This sphere of affinity is characterized in terms of "feeling" or "emotion" (*Gefühl*), which is metaphorically connected (as the verb *vernehmen* suggests) to audibility and music: "it is the pure feeling that has an affinity to music" (*es ist das reine Gefühl, welches verwandt der Musik ist*, GS 6:44).

Regardless of whether Benjamin had Spengler in mind when he wrote this fragment, the relevance to Spengler's method of perceiving analogical "simultaneities" between eras and cultures is evident. Benjamin's harsh critique of such a method also easily applies to Spengler: "The confusion of analogy and affinity is a total perversion" (*Die Verwechslung von Analogie und Verwandtschaft ist eine totale Perversion*, GS 6:44). This is only a more drastic version of the common criticism that analogical correspondences are forced if they cannot be justified by deeper connections.[16] In light of this common criticism, it is significant that Benjamin does not condemn analogy or affinity in general. Their irrationality is a part of their objective being, but it is only their (subjective) confusion that is "totally perverse." Affinity, as Spengler also believes, is primarily a matter of "feeling." According to Benjamin, such "sensed" affinities are not purely irrational: they are perceived but not yet understood; their mode of irrationality makes them the raw material of rational analysis. For example, the reasons for music's affinity with emotion can be systematically investigated. Spengler, on the other hand, does not pursue the substantial connections that give rise to the sense of affinity, but confuses them by using affinity to found an analogical architecture (for example, in his equation of cultural-historical development with natural forms and cycles).

Benjamin's analysis of analogy and affinity, combined with the arguments of his 1924 letter, allow the reconstruction of an anti-Spenglerian morphology: against the rigid formalism and uncontrolled analogical identifications typical of Spengler, Benjamin grants the possibility of sub-rational insights based on affinities—but he denies that such insights can be translated directly into the equally sub-rational forms of analogy and resemblance. Morphology, as the study of emergent forms and forms in transformation, thus has a right to exist, but its insights should not be mistaken for other kinds of more positive and substantial relation. Benjamin further (explicitly) claims that the concept and the forms of language are also to be read morphologically, as unfinished, transforming, and "afformative."[17] Whatever transformations may be occurring in life and history, language may not be able to name or identify them; it also cannot be presumed exempt from them. Morphology thus puts language under pressure to raise itself to the level of morphology's key insight (presented in chapter 2) that there are no static forms—and no fixed referents—only unnameable transformations.

The arguments at the end of Benjamin's "analogy" fragment, even if they were not directed at Spengler, pertain directly to the problems of morphological thought. The penultimate paragraph argues that reading affinities as analogies (and ultimately as identities) serves authoritarian ends. In support of this, Benjamin refers to the goals of uniform education (*Erziehung*) and the modern idea of familial authority. The latter presupposes the intangible "affinity" (*Verwandtschaft*) of "relatives" (*Verwandten*), which gives rise to falsified authority based on similarity and analogy. "True authority," Benjamin states, comes not from any authoritative claim that one *should be like* one's relatives, but rather from affinity itself, which produces "an immediate relation at the level of feeling, which does not rediscover its object in the analogies of behavior, choice of profession, or obedience" (GS 6:45).

The last paragraph of the 1919 fragment speaks of "the type" (*der Typus*)—the kind of character—who confuses analogy and affinity. This person is "sentimental"; for him or her affinities only produce the recognition of already familiar patterns. He or she only sees the familiar (*das Anheimelnde*) but cannot navigate the "broad waves of analogy." What makes this character sentimental, as Benjamin shows in an example from Schiller's *Wallenstein,* is the refusal to accept the immediacy of affinity without the rhetorical-rational stabilization of analogy. "The flower is gone from my life," Wallenstein declares after Max's death. The representation of affinity through analogy overcompensates and misrepresents, leaving an arbitrary sign in place of a feeling.

In his later *Arcades Project* (*Passagenwerk*), Benjamin looks back at his work's development and interprets it in morphological terms. After reading Simmel on Goethe's conception of truth, it became clear to him that "my concept of origin in the *Trauerspielbuch* is a strict and compelling transposition of Goethe's fundamental concept from the realm of nature and into that of history" (GS 5.1:577). The transposition of nature into history is the "Copernican" revolution that Spengler claimed for his morphology. Benjamin continues: "Origin—the concept of the *Urphänomen*—is imported from the heathen context of nature into the Jewish context of history." The point of such an "importation," in the *Passagenwerk* and in general, is not to posit a *causal connection* but rather to "allow the emergence" of the Paris arcades to proceed "in the development proper to them [*in ihrer selbsteigenen Entwicklung*]—or better put, in their inherent unwrapping [*Auswicklung*]—like the leaf from which unfolds the whole wealth of the empirical vegetable world" (GS 5.1:577). If the paradigms of Goethe's morphology seem to be invoked here in a rather vague way, this may be contrasted with closely related reflections in which Benjamin's distance from Spengler's morphology is represented as an explicit break with the dualism of progress and decline. Benjamin argues for a method of "materialist" morphology, which would not turn parallels and structural analogies into ontological identities, but which focuses on the singularity of individual moments from which the historical totality constantly emerges anew. I will not go into detail here, but the idea is familiar: it is the dialectical image,[18] which causes far-flung historical moments to become "simultaneous" in a "flash" of insight. Unlike Spengler's systematic architecture of simultaneity (*Gleichzeitigkeit*) that connects historical epochs, Benjamin's is a free-floating and contingent illumination—a lightning strike—that does not resolve itself into a continuum of endless analogical parallels but instead discovers "the crystalline structure of the totality of events in the analysis of the smallest individual moment" (GS 5.1:575). The emphasis on the "autonomous unfolding" (*selbsteigene Ent- bzw. Auswicklung*) of manifold forms,[19] each with its own integrity as a moment within a totality, moves decisively away from conceptions based on the genealogically transmitted identity of original-indelible forms (*geprägte Formen*). The genealogical reading of the "primal plant" (*Urpflanze*), "primal phenomenon" (*Urphänomen*), and "primal word" (*Urwort*) is mistaken because it makes the fatal error of interpreting the open relation of *affinity* (*Verwandtschaft*) and perpetual circumlocution as an *identity* produced by analogically falsified insight. In the natural world, of course, genealogical continuities may exist. But historical morphology must be conceived differently, as exempt from "natural" continuities. Manifold relations of affinity do not produce analogies but dialectical images, which, though they may give rise to formalizations, are originally expressionless. Benjamin's morphology focuses on the emergence of the new—of the new *from* the old, *from within* it and *simultaneous* to it—instead of on the endless reproduction of the same. His morphology thus follows Goethe in breaking with the latent Platonism of the philosophical tradition, which is simultaneously overinvested in a priori ideas and in their utopian fulfillments.[20]

When history is interpreted by an analogical schematism like Spengler's, Benjamin calls it "vulgar naturalism," "heathen," and "mythical." This is not only due to the use of a natural analogue to define the form of human history, but because such mirroring of nature, culture, and history makes them equivalent. Benjamin makes this point emphatically in the *Passagenwerk* in a critique of Nietzsche's eternal return. In comparison to Nietzsche, however, Spengler's attempt to literally trace the "eternal return" (as a fate that endlessly repeats itself in human history) makes him even more vulnerable to Benjamin's argument against Nietzsche: "The 'eternal return' is the *basic* form of prehistorical, mythic consciousness" (GS 5.1:177); and, even more drastically: "The essence of mythic happening is return. In it the hidden figure of futility is inscribed, which inscribes several heroes of the underworld (Tantalus, Sisyphus, or the Danaids)" (GS 5.1:178). Though the way of addressing the problem changed between 1919 and the *Passagenwerk,* the goal is the same: Benjamin seeks to establish a historical morphology based on Goethe's idea of metamorphosis in order to escape the futile "mythic" repetitions that otherwise define concepts such as fate, character, and law.

"Fate and Character"

So far I hope to have shown that the problems surrounding Goethe's ideas of the demonic and morphology are central in Benjamin's work. This does not mean, however, that his discourse *originates* in morphology or in the problem of the "demonic" connection of fate and character. But morphology was at least compatible with Benjamin's thought in a way that makes it possible to draw contrasts with Spengler's morphology of history without presuming that Benjamin intentionally developed his thought in opposition to Spengler. The difference with Spengler, however, provides a general framework for Benjamin's understanding of the demonic in "Fate and Character" and "Goethe's Elective Affinities."

The difficulty of both essays, addressed in the 1924 letter to Hofmannsthal, arguably lies more in their dense and digressive "proofs" than in their argumentation. The "forced insights" of "Fate and Character" are relatively schematic, but these insights are supported by Benjamin's entire thinking on myth, history, and tragedy. "Goethe's Elective Affinities" is similar in this respect, but its much greater length leads Benjamin to develop a dense fabric of motifs and "excurses." The Goethe essay is made up of "cells," which recursively build on material already presented. Formally, there is nothing so unusual about this, but the essay's network of internal references is particularly dense and fine. This formal-compositional ambitiousness as well as the topical connections to "Fate and Character" and the *Trauerspielbuch* have led many to see the Goethe essay as a culmination of Benjamin's early work.[21] This does not necessarily mean that his later thinking was drastically different—only that the work of the late 1910s and early 1920s provided an intellectual platform for what came after.[22]

The first sentence of "Fate and Character" implicitly neutralizes the "common" and "traditional" understanding of fate and character by flatly stating that they are "typically [*gemeinhin*] taken to be causally connected and that character is determined as a cause of fate" (GS 2.1:171). This causal relation, Benjamin observes, can also be inverted. He explains this in the second paragraph,[23] which concludes that "if one has a character," then it will be definitive of fate, making the latter "essentially constant" (GS 2.1:173). Benjamin introduces Stoicism as a limit case of an ethical system that seeks to minimize the variable of fate by holding character constant. The conventional or "inherited" (*herkömmlich*, GS 2.1:172) connection of fate and character also (roughly) defines the terrain of the demonic in Goethe's Orphic "Urworte" and *Poetry and Truth*. To be sure, none of Goethe's versions of the demonic directly claim a "causal connection," but all of them (especially the "Urworte") operate with inherited conceptions of the problem of fate and character and thus clearly fall within the tradition to which Benjamin refers. And the reception of the demonic in the 1910s gives an even stronger impression of a fate-like entity that expresses itself in "demonic characters." The Orphic "Urworte" themselves, to the extent that they suggest causation, imagine *Dämon* ("character") as the primary factor; if this primacy is read as implying causality, this still would not mean that the details of causation are *knowable*. And this lack of demonstrable causation makes the claim of causation itself seem questionable.

Benjamin also dismisses the "inherited" causal connection between fate and character on epistemic grounds. It is terminologically unsustainable, because it can only lead to ambiguity: "It is in no case possible to show what ultimately counts as a function of character and what as a function of fate in human life" (GS 2.1:173). On the basis of this crux, Benjamin claims that the goal of his essay is not to show the interconnection or even the dialectical interrelation of fate and character, but rather to develop them as distinct concepts. This does not mean that they are necessarily unrelated, only that a two-way causal connection is incoherent and thus should not be presupposed. In the remainder of his essay, Benjamin uses the difference between tragedy and comedy to show how fate and character can be *represented* distinctly and still exhibit specific structural parallels. The result of this analysis is that tragedy is *the genre of the representation of the transcendence of fate* and comedy is *the genre of the representation of the transcendence of character.* In themselves, both fate and character are natural; fate is "natural guilt" and character is "natural innocence." As natural categories, Benjamin seeks to free both from their illegitimate encroachment upon the "higher spheres" of ethics (in the case of character) and religion (in the case of fate) (GS 2.1:173).

These higher spheres are implicitly contrasted with the lower of myth and law. Tragedy transcends the "demonic" sphere of mythic fate, whose ambiguities are captured in the "paradoxical" representations of tragedy;[24] comedy does the same for character by showing the natural constraints of character as a sphere of freedom and not of subjection. Fate and character are both "demonic" not only in that they represent an earlier, "mythic" epoch of unfreedom, but because they display parallel ambiguities: fate, as a category of law (*Recht*), becomes ambiguous and potentially unjust whenever it is viewed as preordained and inescapable. This ambiguity paradoxically shows that both the retribution and the transgression were fated and thus that fate's "legal system" (*Ordnung des Rechts,* GS 2.1:174) is an interminable "guilt system" (*Schuldzusammenhang,* GS 2.1:175). If everything is fated anyway, the idea of fate cancels itself out: "At base, man is not the one who has a fate; rather, the subject of fate is indeterminate" (GS 2.1:175). If fate is a "suprapersonal" determination motivating both transgression and retribution, then the system becomes arbitrary and passes entirely beyond human ends and means. Tragedy thus represents the *injustice* of the gods, even if this conclusion is unspeakable (only indirectly representable):

> It was not law [*Recht*] but tragedy in which the head of the genius
> first raised itself above the haze of guilt—because in tragedy the
> demonic fate is broken ... Heathen man realizes that he is better
> than his gods, but this knowledge deprives him of language and he
> remains mute. (GS 2.1:174–75)

This understanding need not deny the existence of suprapersonal forces like
fate or nature, but if such forces are essentially arbitrary and unjust, then
they are ethically and religiously irrelevant. In contrast with Spengler, for
example, who believes that "the laws of nature are the only laws" (UdA
127), Benjamin refuses to engage with the question of nature's ultimate ends,
the ambiguity of which plagues both Goethe's and Spengler's morphology.
Spenglerian morphology perceives individuals as merely relative means to
whichever ends, whereas Benjamin finds the ambiguity of unquestionable yet
supposedly absolute ends to be symptomatic of a "mythic" and "demonic"
system, which is by definition unable to provide individuals with justice or
ethical orientation.

   In the case of character, the inherited ambiguity lies in the tendency not to
view it as natural (and hence morally neutral) but to express it in judgmen-
tal or ambivalent terms. Examples of such words "that appear to designate
character-traits that cannot be abstracted from moral valuation" (GS 2.1:177)
are "self-sacrificing," "deceitful," "vengeful," and "envious" (*aufopfernd,
tückisch, rachsüchtig, neidisch,* GS 2.1:177). To understand what character
is in itself, "abstraction" from morality is "necessary"; Benjamin thus poses
"smart" and "stupid" as examples of character-adjectives whose moral significance is either neutral or depends on the individual context and case.
Comedies of character transform protagonists who would be called "scoun-
drels" (*Schurken*) in real life into objects of identification. Onstage, instead
of seeing morally condemnable behavior, all we see is "character." Comedy
represents character as the vicarious enjoyment of one's own nature through
a protagonist who is able to live out his or her character without regard
for moral norms or codes of conduct. "It is incumbent upon morality to
prove that traits [*Eigenschaften*] can never be morally relevant [*erheblich*],
only actions [*Handlungen*]" (GS 2.1:177). While tragedy presents fate as an
arbitrary subjection, character analogously presents the individual's specific
"genius" (*Genius*) "as the answer to the individual's mythic enslavement to
character" (GS 2.1:178). Comedy transforms the inescapable demon of character from "the determinist's puppet" into "the light under whose beam the
freedom of action becomes visible" (GS 2.1:178). The *Dämon* that Benjamin
calls *Genius* is character viewed from the perspective of "the natural innocence of man." Character thus is not a form of fate but a representation of
individual nature from the standpoint of freedom. This freedom characterizes
all actions that transcend the sphere of moral consequence—and art "symbolizes" this transcendence.[25]

"Goethe's Elective Affinities"

The double concept of fate and character figures prominently in Benjamin's "Elective Affinities." The earlier essay's more schematic presentation provides an invaluable terminological foundation for the later Goethe essay, which deals much more extensively with the demonic. And "demonic ambiguities" are also ubiquitous even where they are not labeled as such. The most prominent example of this is the relation of "material content" (*Sachgehalt*) and "truth content" (*Wahrheitsgehalt*). According to Benjamin, the objective of criticism (*Kritik*) is to differentiate them, but all of the metaphors he employs to illustrate their relation—seal and wax, fire and logs—show them to be inseparable. Especially when Benjamin uses these terms to characterize institutions (like matrimony) and non-textual productions (like a life), they are clearly interdependent. In Benjamin's refutation of Gundolf's interpretation, "truth content" and "material content" are used to argue that the "mythic" subtexts of the plot are not identical with the work's truth content (or meaning) but are only a hidden aspect of the material content.[26] Critics, content with only uncovering a layer of mythic meaning *in the novel*, affirm it as the meaning *of the novel*. To counter this reading, Benjamin isolates an antimythic layer ignored by Gundolf. This layer is comprised primarily of the novella *The Strange Neighbor-Children* (*Die wunderlichen Nachbarskinder*) and the perspective of the semi-omniscient narrator who mourns the fate of the characters in an image of a "star of hope that shoots above their heads" (above their heads and out of their view, Benjamin emphasizes). The methodological differentiation of commentary and critique thus works in service of an interpretation meant to show that the uncovering of a mythic dimension may make the novel appear (partly) as a drama of fate (transgression and retribution), but that this by itself proves neither that it is completely mythic nor that it is tragic. Using the distinctions of the *Trauerspielbuch*, Benjamin reads the novel as a mourning play, as "sad" (*traurig*) rather than tragic. The latter category belongs exclusively to the Greek battle to escape the demonic age. This historically unique situation was founded on the *institution* of tragedy, whereas modernity is ruled by history, which is always explicitly or implicitly a history of salvation (*Heilsgeschichte*) whose horizon is redemption (*Erlösung*). History's problem is the mythic holdover, its return to a guilt economy of myth, for example, in the Christian of idea of original sin (GS 2.1:308). Ideas like "nature," "law," "fate," and "character" reintroduce the demonic ambiguity of myth in doubly ambiguous forms.

The different subjects of the Goethe essay and the *Trauerspielbuch*, as well as the complexity of both works, make it difficult to establish whether they reflect the same conception. It is safe to say, however, that Benjamin's "Elective Affinities" can be more easily followed if one knows the *Trauerspielbuch*, while, on the other hand, the *Trauerspielbuch* may be clarified by the Goethe essay's concrete focus on a single work of modern literature. In the

Trauerspielbuch, Benjamin argues that modernity and Greek antiquity confront the same basic problem (the overcoming of myth), but in modernity the configuration of problem and solution are incomparably different, not only in the difference between myth and history, but in the corresponding changes in the economy of representation. The *Trauerspielbuch* contends that modern theater ("from Calderon to Strindberg," GS 1.1:292) is the result of a Christological reformatting which replaced the tragic hero's "defiance" (*Trotz,* GS 1.1:294) with the exemplary fate of the martyr. Where Greek tragedy was an act of ritual witnessing and purging that silently raised the question of justice at the end of fate, "the mourning play" is named after the affect of "sadness," which is produced when the desolation of history and infinite *injustice* are pushed to the limit of utter hopelessness (*Hoffnungsleere,* GS 1.1:406). At this limit, the affect of mourning (*Trauer*) does not imply mythic ambiguity anymore, because it is based on a univocal and irreversible historical state, but the affect of *Trauer* is subject to a specific "bipolarity" (*Umschwung,* GS 1.1:406) in the switch from "death" to "resurrection" (*Auferstehung,* GS 1.1:406). This is not an eschatological telos, because history per se can only be represented "sadly," but is, as Benjamin puts it in the Goethe essay, a "critical" force *within* history, whose function is to differentiate ambiguities into insights. Critical insight puts myth in its place, and history, by this definition, is not only "sad" but also an unfolding of truth content within material content. This does not occur in view of a final separation, but in flashes of insight that only represent a momentary disruption of modernity's constant recidivism to the pre-ethical world of myth. Even a "modern" world at no point ceases to be defined by demonic ambiguities, and the continuing existence of such ambiguities is actually guaranteed by the "demonic" interdependence of material and truth content, of myth and redemption, *within* history. As hopeless as this may sound, the pseudomorphosis of myth in the tragic and the *traurig* becomes literally fatal when it overcompensates for the primary affect of the modern age (*Trauer*) in order to revel in the pre-tragic idea of fate that tragedy tried to put an end to.

Benjamin's "Elective Affinities" presents the idea of "demonic ambiguity" toward the end of his essay's first part in direct connection with Goethe's conception from *Poetry and Truth.* For Benjamin, the sheer appearance of the demonic in Goethe's autobiography is the symptom of a massive problem for the worldview attributed to him by Gundolf. Benjamin reads the demonic as an overt desublimation, an "unpolished monolith" (*eine unabgeschliffener Monolith*) towering over the flat landscape of the autobiography (GS 1.1:149). This dark side of Goethe's Olympian striving results from his "idolatry of nature" (GS 1.1:149) and especially from the "ambiguity of his concept of nature" (*Doppelsinn im Naturbegriff,* GS 1.1:147). Here Benjamin refers to his own preceding paragraph, in which Goethe's susceptibility to mythic thinking is highlighted; the ambiguity of his idea of nature is that it "simultaneously refers to . . . the spheres of perceptible phenomena [*der wahrnehmbaren Erscheinungen*] and to those of intuited primal forms [*die der anschaubaren Urbilder*]" (GS 1.1:147). The lack of hierarchy and distinction between "perceptible appearances" and "intuited primal forms" produces the undifferentiated *Urphänomen* as a "chaos of symbols" (*Chaos der Symbole*, GS 1.1:147). As an explanation of the biographical sources of the demonic, this may sound rather obtuse, but the lawless analogizations of morphology reveal the same tendency to intuit a unifying "primal" order, which becomes highly unstable and ununified whenever it is hermeneutically or analytically deployed in life.

Benjamin uses Goethe's own words to show the risks of such a totalized idea of nature. Like Spengler's claim that the only source of law is nature, Goethe also makes everything—culture, reason, history, or language—a part of nature:

> Just shut your eyes, open your ears and listen: from the most quiet breath to the wildest noise, from the simplest tone to the most supreme harmony, from the most keen and passionate cry to the most tender words of reason—it is only nature that speaks and reveals its being, its power, its life and its relations. (GS 1.1:148)

When there is nothing that is not nature, the result is a compound—limitless—ambiguity, in which nature is the "demonic" root cause of all phenomena. The effect of this, as Benjamin will argue, is the moral muteness of the characters and world of *Elective Affinities*. The unspoken alternative would be an individual moral autonomy that allows decisions to be uttered that are not merely—fatally—governed by nature or which use nature as their excuse.[27]

In contrast to the more elevated and thorny style in which Benjamin introduces this Goethe quotation, he reacts to it in a more informal way:

> If in this most extreme sense "the words of reason" themselves are made into possessions of nature, what wonder that for Goethe thought was never able to completely illuminate the realm of the *Urphenomena*. He had robbed himself of the possibility of making distinctions. Without any differentiation whatsoever, being falls to a conception of nature that grows and extends itself toward monstrosity. (GS 1.1:148)

This is not just an isolated terminological ambiguity like that of fate or character, and it is also not an individual or historical fate that could be "mourned." It represents *total ambiguity* through the deliberate production of an epistemic foundation upon which it is impossible to make distinctions of any kind. Dimensions of hidden meaning are everywhere. Nothing is itself or what it seems to be, because everything substitutes symbolically for everything else. Every boundary is lifted and made fluid. Instead of provoking sadness, this conception gives an excuse not to mourn, but it is not a happy pantheism or "pan-erotism." Absolute morphological continuity "monstrously" dissolves all foundations and deprives language of its ability to name.

Benjamin introduces Hölderlin in opposition to the pandemonium of Goethe's conception. This non-demonic morphology proceeds on the basis of the priority of the individual above the whole. This crucial contrast between Goethe and Hölderlin culminates (GS 1.1:182) in an excursus on "the expressionless" (das Ausdruckslose). As I will show below, "the expressionless" presents an idea of form as irreducible to formulaic, nominal, or Platonic conceptions. Benjamin's version of morphology grants primacy to metamorphosis, while Hölderlinian expressionlessness seeks to reconceive artistic form as the freezing of a material whose natural state is one of motion and flux.

Morphological formalism in the style of Spengler and Gundolf demonically reduces both life and art to universal schemata, which restrict metamorphosis to an a priori canon. For the sake of universality, such forms are as general as possible, and their subsumptive typology strives toward a homogeneous continuum of always the same predetermined forms. This is the essence of what Benjamin calls myth. He diagnoses a struggle against this conception as the definitive "truth content" of Goethe's life, work, and autobiography. This reading of the idea of morphology as part of a biographic dynamic lends it a plausibility that is lacking in Gundolf and Spengler, who only exploit morphology for the sake of glorification and mythmaking. For Benjamin, Gundolf's selective appropriation of morphological mythologemes shows that he has given up the critical task of using insight to access truth content. Rather than breaking the hopelessness of the mythic paradigm, Gundolf's work mechanically reproduces idealized archetypes.

To show the damage done by such an ideologically motivated reading, Benjamin focuses on Gundolf's reading of Goethe's Orphic "Urworte." Benjamin introduces the "Urworte" in response to Gundolf's hypostasized unification of the artist's "life, essence and work" (Leben, Wesen und Werk, GS 1.1:157).[28] Such a unity, which makes the life into a work of art and the works into direct expressions of the essence of the life, allows limitless transactions between three spheres. Without actually citing Goethe's stanzas, Benjamin first shows how the model for Gundolf's style of criticism can be found in the Orphic terms. The first four Urworte define the life of an idealized hero, whose exemplary and normative functions connect him to Benjamin's concept of myth:

> If in the traditional point of view, work, essence and life carelessly mixed together in an indefinite way, then he [Gundolf] explicitly understands these three aspects as a unity. He thereby construes them into the appearance of a mythic hero. Because in the realm of myth, essence, work and life indeed form the unity that they otherwise only achieve in the minds of careless literary critics. In myth, the essence

is called "demon" [*Dämon*], life is called "fate" and the work that only these two express [*das nur die beiden ausprägt*] is "living form" [*lebende Gestalt*]. (GS 1.1:157)

Benjamin here loosely varies the specific terms of Goethe's *Dämon* stanza to characterize Gundolf's understanding of the *Dämon* and its "characteristic form, living and self-developing" (*geprägte Form, die lebend sich entwickelt*). Such a unity of existence, Benjamin argues, can only be *represented* in the superhuman ideal of the hero, a representative of mankind before the gods who fails to reflect the "moral uniqueness" (*moralische Einzigkeit*) of individual responsibility (*Verantwortung*, GS 1.1:158). Gundolf uses this model of pre-tragic heroes such as Hercules and Orpheus to typify the poet's life and vocation. Benjamin passes a harsh sentence on such idolization: "All representation by proxy [*Stellvertretung*] in the sphere of morality is mythical in nature, from the patriotic 'one for all' to the sacrificial death of the Redeemer [*der Opfertod des Erlösers*]" (GS 1.1:157). Substitution, including Spengler's idea of historical "substitutability" (*Vertretbarkeit*), mistakes individual life for a representative form or for a mere function. This representational function is defined by the ability of the hero's image to produce exemplary and ideological effects of cohesion and bonding. But neither *individual* responsibility nor individuality itself exists in this sphere of mythic instrumentalization or in the replaceable aspect of the individual's part within a larger whole. Such conceptions abdicate individuality in favor of the representative function of an idealized heroic proxy who does what we cannot and is what we cannot be. The "we" who is substituted by the hero is let off the hook and simultaneously made into the object of a typological conformism.

The *Elective Affinities* is not tragic, and Ottilie is no hero. Greek tragedy alone was able to show that the "heroic" model was not without its redeeming aspects. In this context, Benjamin sketches a highly condensed reading of the Orphic "Urworte." His interpretation draws its evidence from Gundolf's misreading; by emphasizing hope (*Elpis*), whom Gundolf ignored, Benjamin foreshadows his essay's concluding emphasis on the "star of hope" in the *Elective Affinities*:

One of the most powerful sources of this symbolism [the "evident symbolism" of figures like Orpheus and Hercules who are "clearly differentiated" from non-heroic humans] flows from the astral myth: in the superhuman type of the redeemer, the hero stands in for humanity through his work that grants him a place among the stars. It is he for whom the Orphic "Urworte" were coined: it is his *Dämon* that is like the sun, his *Tyche* that is changing like the moon, his fate that is inescapable like the astral *Ananke*; even *Eros* does not point out beyond this star-struck configuration—only *Elpis* does. When the author [Goethe] had the idea of including *Elpis* among them in order

to bring the first four down to earth, it is no coincidence that she
alone needed no additional explanation, and it is also no coincidence
that she has no part in the schema of Gundolf's *Goethe,* which is
entirely defined by the rigid canon of the other four. (GS 1.1:158)

Benjamin's reading of Goethe's "Urworte" is risky, especially his interpretation of the contradiction between the stanzas and Goethe's commentary.
Goethe seemed to understand all five *Urworte* as a universal (non-heroic)par-
adigm of human development, but for Benjamin, this reading is only made
possible by *Elpis* (Hope). For Benjamin, the first four figures only represent
a classic mythic-heroic schema governed by an "astral" infrastructure. Like
Gundolf, Benjamin is thus also selective and arguably even reads Goethe differently than Goethe reads himself; but unlike Gundolf—and perhaps even
to a greater degree than Goethe does himself—he reads the "Urworte" as an
indissoluble unity: without *Elpis,* Benjamin argues, the universalizing intent
of Goethe's commentary would not have been possible; the lack of an *Elpis*
commentary introduces a change of register to include non-heroic life; the
ascended hero, whose fate was guided by the gods, has no need of hope. Thus
Benjamin's short reading of the "Urworte" manages to produce a rich interpretation of the poem and Goethe's commentary.

Whether or not one accepts the claim that *Elpis* was necessary to "human-
ize" the Orphic conception, her exceptionality is in fact emphasized in the
commentary's claim that she needs no commentary. In support of Benjamin's
reading, one might also observe that without *Elpis*'s closing gesture of openness, the four initial poems would have exhibited a fierce didacticism and
even pedantry, which would have appealed to the "lax literary critics" who
are mostly interested in such qualities. The best evidence of Benjamin's reading of *Elpis*'s essential role in transcending the mythic constellation of the
"Urworte" is thus indirectly given by Gundolf's attempts to exclude her from
the Orphic and "morphic" terminology that he uses to characterize Goethe's
life and work.[29]

The fact that *Elpis* plays a decisive role in Benjamin's reading of the
Elective Affinities is well known, but to some it may seem exaggerated or
arbitrary to invest so much in a single sentence of the novel: *Die Hoffnung
fuhr wie ein Stern, der vom Himmel fällt, über ihre Häupter weg* ("Hope flew,
like a star that falls from heaven, above their heads and away"). Based on the
connections to the "Urworte," however, the centrality of *Elpis* may become
more convincing, even if her placement and specific interpretation in the
wider contexts of Benjamin's essay remains challenging; and the closing passages' reliance on the *Trauerspielbuch*—in the words "mystery" (*Mysterium*),
"the dramatic" (*das Dramatische*), and "representation" (*Darstellung*)—pose
many questions. Without claiming to resolve this complexity, I would call
attention to the idea of mourning (*Trauer*), which allows Benjamin to interpret the novel as a work of mourning—Goethe's mourning—for his character

Ottilie. This authorial affect is inscribed in the novel in the sentence about the "star of hope," and the dynamic of *Trauer* outlined in the relation of hopelessness and hope corresponds to the "inversion" (*Umschwung*) characteristic of the *Trauerspiel*. Crucially different, however, is the identification of the hope-sentence with Hölderlin's idea of "caesura" (GS 1.1:199), which is connected with *das Ausdruckslose* ("the expressionless," "the inexpress," "the inexpressive") and finally with the novel's evanescent truth content. Given this difficult chain of ideas, each of which may have some ability to clarify the others, it would be possible to start at any point. The structure of Benjamin's essay, like that of Goethe's "Urworte," is not linear but cyclical, making definite conclusions impossible.

I will start with the hope-sentence and work backward to *das Ausdruckslose*. The emphasis Benjamin places on the "star of hope" is not exaggerated, because in the novel it represents an unprecedented intervention of the voice and perspective of a narrator who mostly appears to be omniscient. He otherwise only reveals himself indirectly, for example, in the montage of documentary materials such as Ottilie's diary. Benjamin's emphasis on the hope-sentence thus has a solid narratological foundation, even if he does not argue in these terms. The reflections *das Ausdrucklose* and the connections to the *Trauerspielbuch* have raised the stakes to a point where the star sentence is not a narrative problem because it pertains to representation and art in general (*Kunst schlechthin*, GS 1.1:181). Despite this broadness and the difficulties it poses, Benjamin still manages to include the arguments necessary to establish the more limited importance of the sentence: particularly his claim that the hope cannot be that of the characters (for themselves), but only that of the narrator for the characters (and particularly for Ottilie) is borne out by the sentence's simile ("hope flew *like* a star"), which indicates that the passing of hope (the fall from hope into hopelessness) occurs beyond the vision and awareness of the protagonists ("behind their heads"). There is no star in the diegesis of the scene, because it only appears in a simile representing the viewpoint of a narrator who knows the final outcome. When Benjamin speaks of the sentence as a dramatic configuration, this may refer to a fictionalized dramatic irony with respect to the action. The dramatic configuration gives itself away in the narrator's affect of *Trauer*. He feels it as the affective side of hope in the moment when hope is gone and includes a sign of it in the narration itself.

Benjamin could have presented this insight more clearly, but instead he pushes it to the breaking point in his decision to identify it with *das Ausdruckslose*. If the "caesura" or "transport" or "counter-rhythmic interruption" (GS 1.1:181) takes the form of the inscription of an affective and narratorial standpoint, then the caesura, rather than being "expressionless," to the contrary, would seem to cause the work to "express" both feeling and perspective. This is not wrong, but in Benjamin's conception what makes the work "express" is not itself "expressive"—because it is a merely technical aspect of the representation. In the essay's first part, he writes that "technique" (*Technik*) is what allows the novelist to "hide" the "mythic meaning" as an "open secret" within the material content (GS 1.1:145–46). The truth content, on the other hand, lies within the mythic content and has no existence outside of it. Though the novelist has technical command of the material content, he has no privileged access to the ultimate meaning or truth content of the work. And even criticism, which by definition specializes in truth content, is mostly a negative function: the critic cannot give positive and definite meaning to truth content but can only block those who reduce truth content to an aspect of material content. *Das Ausdrucklose* is another name for the "critical force" (*kritische Gewalt*) at work in the work and in history, "which cannot separate appearance and essence within the work, but which prevents their confusion" (GS 1.1:181).

Elpis from the "Urworte" and hope in the *Elective Affinities* conceptually represent the interruption of a stagnant and pre-ethical world of myth, whereas *das Ausdruckslose* shifts this conception toward a theory of art. "The expressionless" refers to a technique—both deliberate and accidental—of inscribing an ambiguous transcendence into a work in a way that gives rise to its truth content by destroying its systematic unity and the unequivocal coherence of its meaning. This technique of "the expressionless" is nothing other than the literary *device* as such and par excellence. It is the moment of ambiguous self-transcendence within a work, which only seems to place its meaning under the control of a narrator or author. It is not possible, Benjamin indicates, to name the expressionless, its "counter-rhythm," more precisely than as "something beyond the author that cuts his work off in mid-sentence" (*etwas, [daß] jenseits des Dichters der Dichtung ins Wort fällt*, GS 1.1:182). The constant emphasis of the idea of an interruption coming from the outside, the loss of control in and through the perfection of technical mastery, makes the finished work a *fragment*, but a fragment of the *true* world (*ein Fragment der wahren Welt*, GS 1.1:181). The work is not a lie, a fiction, or a deception, nor is "appearance" (*Schein*, GS 1.1:181), "conjuration," or illusion (*Beschwörung*, GS 1.1:180)—nor is it an immediate manifestation of beauty (*das Schöne*, GS 1.1:180). Ruined by the interruption of the expressionless, the work takes on affinity with the world in its lack of coherent closure, its openness to the historical horizons of meaning, redemption, and critical force. In narratological terms, the expressionless would be both extra-diegetic, as its connection to the narrator of the *Elective Affinities* suggests, and extra-authorial: it is a part of the formal precondition of the "work-ness" of the work, that which makes it a work in the first place (and not a hallucination or an accumulation of raw material or a sheer manifestation of beauty or harmony). The expressionless is that which cuts off the work's "excuses" (*Ausflüchte*) and freezes them (*bannen, einhalten, erstarren*) into a constellation analogous to a facial expression. The expressionless cannot make the work *speak* the truth, nor is it in any way equivalent to *the author's* truth, but it is that which causes the work to *betray* its own truth as an unspoken and unspeakable revelation.

Instead of the star in the *Elective Affinities,* Benjamin could have modeled *das Ausdruckslose* on the excurses on the demonic from *Poetry and Truth,* as a comparable moment in which ambiguity is pushed to the point of producing a loss of authorial control. A sentence from the *Trauerspielbuch* most succinctly covers all such strategies: "The tragic is to the demonic as a paradox is to ambiguity [*Das Tragische verhält sich zum Dämonischen wie das Paradoxon zur Zweideutigkeit*]" (GS 1.1:288). The paradox stands in a special relation to the demonic in that it is uniquely able to bind demonic ambiguities by giving them a specific form without permanently banishing or resolving them. The "idea that it is impossible to lift the veil [of appearance in works]" (*die Idee der Unenthüllbarkeit*) is "the idea of art criticism" (GS 1.1:195). This idea of *Unenthüllbarkeit,* the inability to separate appearance from essence, corresponds to the undecidability and unresolvability of demonic ambiguities. Despite the "critical violence" of *das Ausdrucklose,* the demonic persists, and will continue to persist, in the primal "mythic" forms that dwell in the encrusted concepts of a mystified "modernity." Thus Benjamin does not hope for a utopian solution to the "problem" of demonic ambiguities. There is nothing that can permanently banish them from the forms of life and society in which they inhere. Works of art, however, have a special status as works of paradox that *represent* a tendency *ad absurdum* in their depiction of and relation to these ambiguities. Rather than a continuation of mythic violence with different means, art's representations are discontinuous with the regime of the demonic. This moment of discontinuity is, however, as Benjamin's name for it clearly indicates, "not express," "inexpressible," but, like the seal in wax, is inscribed *on top of* or *within* the demonic continuum of history. This point is evident in one of many "unexpressed" moments in Benjamin's own essay, his description of the "evening star," Venus, in the final paragraph: "This most paradoxical and fleeting hope finally surfaces from the semblance of reconciliation, just as, at twilight, as the sun is extinguished, the evening star arises in the dusk [*im Dämmer*] and outlasts the night. Its shine, of course, is that of Venus" (GS 1.1:200). The image is Benjamin's; it cannot be equated with the "falling star" from Goethe's novel. Throughout the essay, he associates sundown and twilight (*Dämmerung,* GS 1.1:147) with the shady hybridity of "demonic ambiguity" in contrast with the sunlight (*Sonnenlicht,* GS 1.1:132) that only shines in *The Strange Neighbor-Children.* The pairing of Hope and Love (as *Eros,* not Pauline *Agape*) is thus made to stand outside of history and the philosophy of history. The "evening star" offsets and is superimposed against the "twilight" of its background. It represents an unambiguous constant that lasts through the night, a *moral* fidelity in the face of the ambiguities of fate, character, myth, and law. Twilight as such is always ambiguous: depending where it appears, it may usher in the night or prefigure a coming dawn. By contrast, Benjamin's "philosophy of history"—if one wants to call it that— occurs against the backdrop of perpetual twilight.

Chapter Six

✦

Georg Lukács and the Demonic Novel

The Demonic as a Template for the Novel

The difficulty of giving closure to a biographical narrative may have led Goethe to introduce "the demonic" in a series of interconnected excurses at the end of *Poetry and Truth*. This underlying formal difficulty as well as the substance of the excurses on the demonic are both directly relevant to the genre of the novel. The developmental-biographical paradigms of the Orphic "Urworte" may also be taken as a framework for the "novel of education" (*Bildungs-* or *Entwicklungsroman*). *Poetry and Truth*, as a biographical narrative, could be read as an application of a developmental paradigm such as that of the "Urworte." In this reading, the demonic emerges at the end of *Poetry and Truth* as a symptom of the difficulties of fitting life's events into the phases and stages of a systematic conceptual framework. The formalization of life into a system of heterogeneous factors unavoidably relies on memory to reconstruct their relations and causations. The demonic emerges from such an attempt as a by-product of the confrontation between merely subjective recollections and an intended synthesis of life into a coherent causal narrative.

In the "Urworte," the problem of the demonic originates in the unified force of an individual's personality, talents, and drives—in the innate, unique productivity of the *Dämon*, which may produce geniuses like Mozart as well as more pathological "demons" like his protagonist, Don Giovanni.[1] In either case, the demonic drive sets the driven individual at odds with society by placing him (or her)[2] above, below, or outside of it. Without constructing a canon of demonic heroes and antiheroes, the examples of which would be endless, one might postulate that especially when protagonists are depicted as exceptional—whenever characters are characters *with qualities*—the demonic is in play. The "Urworte" thus pertains to the formation of protagonists and "characters," while *Poetry and Truth*'s encounter with the limited representability of such formations exemplifies the ironic relation of narrators to their own lack of omniscience.

These two aspects of the demonic may not evidently apply to all novels or "life stories." Kafka, for example, might represent a limit at which the protagonist-narrator polarity dissolves into something more like a dream or a pure scenario, driven not by the dynamics of character and limitations in the narrator's perspective but by demonic plot elements related to other forms of uncertainty, chance, expectation, and mediation.[3] Given the vast range of possibilities within these approaches, it may be that the paradigm of the demonic can include every possible novel—but it can only do so in the way that all paradigms relate to exceptions and limit cases. It is not my intent to pursue such a paradigmatic-taxonomic project, but, broadly, one might surmise that the traditional novel, at least up to Thomas Mann, fits easily into the framework of Goethe's conceptions of the demonic.

This coherence is reflected in Lukács's 1916 *Theory of the Novel*, which represents a broadly synthetic and retrospective formalization of the nineteenth-century novel. Using the methods of the philosophy of history,[4] Lukács seeks to perceive the basic form of the genre's underlying conflicts and define the transcendental status of the novel as the latest epic form. He treats the novel as a form that has reached its end, tested all of its limits and exhausted its possibilities. In order to establish the parameters of the genre in such a way as to permit this kind of historicization, he relies implicitly and explicitly on Goethe's idea of the demonic. Lukács's citation of the most enigmatic passage of book 20 of *Poetry and Truth* gives Goethe's conception striking prominence—but the demonic never emerged as a correspondingly central conception in the reception of Lukács's theory. The reason for this is obvious: the demonic was taken primarily for a pathos formula without an evident systematic function; *The Theory of the Novel* barely indicates how the demonic fits into the theory, and insofar as it is subordinated to a philosophy of history, it can be ignored as a superfluous difficulty. Especially if the complexity of Goethe's concept is not recognized, or if Lukács is not credited with a solid grasp of it, the citation from *Poetry and Truth* looks like an afterthought.

Setting aside Lukács's direct engagements with the demonic, his familiarity with it is suggested by the similarity between Goethe's analytic parameters and those of Lukács's theory. The "Urworte" outline a universal model of character development and socialization, whereas *Poetry and Truth* presents the demonic as the inability of retrospective knowledge to give univocal meaning to a biographical-developmental narrative. These two aspects precisely reflect Lukács's focus on protagonists (on the one hand) and the ironic perspective of narrators (on the other).

This schematic reduction of the two sides of the demonic to a protagonist-narrator opposition allows the notoriously convoluted paths of Lukács's text to be circumvented. Complexity-reduction is not an end in itself, however, and this formal derivation leaves Lukács's conception of the demonic essentially unclarified. Nevertheless, new perspectives may be opened up by hypothetically imagining the demonic *without Lukács* as representing an independent framework for theorizing the novel. From this perspective, Lukács appears to have been surprisingly successful at synthesizing Goethe's conception into his overall theory. Perhaps this comes as no surprise considering his proximity to Goethe biographers like Simmel and Gundolf, but what remains striking is the synthetic understanding that allowed him to incorporate the demonic into an infrastructure that might otherwise appear Hegelian.

Lukacs's way of combining the demonic with other conceptions does not allow it to be easily differentiated analytically. Goethe himself did not produce a *theory* of the demonic to which one might directly refer, while, between Goethe and Lukács, overtly theoretical conceptions such as those of Wundt and Freud had begun to explore the demonic's systematic potential. The young Lukács also subjects Goethe's understanding of the demonic to an intense systematization and, like his older contemporaries Spengler and Gundolf, he often opposed the demonic (as a figure of modernity) to an idea of originary authenticity reminiscent of the *Dämon* of Goethe's "Urworte": "The way of the soul [*der Weg der Seele*] is: To strip everything from oneself that does not really belong to it [*was nicht ihr eigen ist*]; to form the soul to true individuality [*das Formen der Seele zur wirklichen Individualität*]."[5]

Rather than presenting a critical, analytical, or philological engagement with the paradigmatic potential of the demonic, Lukács wants to realize the *Dämon* in order to overcome the demonic. In his *Theory of the Novel*, he explicitly hopes that the determinant-system of Goethe's "Urworte" can be resolved in favor of the unity and heroic authenticity of *Dämon*, whose opponent, *Tyche*, defines the arbitrariness of social conventions and institutions. In the form of the novel, the victorious hero cannot resolve the contradiction of individual and society without violating the reality principle and committing the aesthetic transgression of idealization or romanticization. Merely fictional resolutions ring false in comparison to real contradictions, to an external reality that does not allow the *Dämon*—or "the soul" (*die Seele*)[6]—to fully actualize itself. This situation defines the relation between the modern world, its art, and its epic forms:

> But this transformation [*Wandlung*, the overcoming of the duality of nature and culture] can never be accomplished from the side of art alone [*niemals von der Kunst aus*]: the form of the great epic [for Lukács: from Homer to the novel] is bound to the factual reality [*Empirie*] of the historical moment [*des geschichtlichen Augenblicks*], and every attempt to depict utopia as if it were real [*die Utopie als seiend zu gestalten*] can only result in a destruction of forms, not in a creation of reality [*endet nur formzerstörend, aber nicht wirklichkeitschaffend*].[7]

Lukács believes that soul and forms, nature and culture, *Dämon* and *Tyche*, must be unified in reality before they can be unified in representation. The peculiarity of this construction is its toleration of idealism in life and in art that is rejected in the novel. In comparison to Goethe's idea of the demonic as historically variable but irreducibly given, Lukács's idea of "transformation" (*Wandel*) means the historical overcoming of the nature-culture opposition, leading to a reunification of the epic and the aesthetic in life.[8]

The Idea of "the Luciferian" in Lukács's *Heidelberg Aesthetics* (1916–1918)

Goethe's importance for the young Lukács is not widely recognized, despite the fact that the Lukács scholarship often finds it difficult to get away from questions of influence. Goethe should at least be added to the long list, which includes Hegel, Schlegel, Kierkegaard, and Dilthey (all of whom Lukács himself names in the 1962 preface to *The Theory of the Novel*).[9] In contrast to the short 1916 preface, in which Dostoyevsky is the "prophet of a new man [*Künder eines neuen Menschen*], the shaper of a new world [*Gestalter einer neuen Welt*], discoverer and rediscoverer of a new-old form [*Finder und Wiederfinder einer neu-alten Form*],"[10] in the 1962 preface, Lukács enumerates influences in a way that diminishes his early work.[11]

The unfinished *Heidelberger Ästhetik*, a habilitation draft, written between 1916 and 1918, focuses extensively on Goethe,[12] but unlike the more essayistic *Theory of the Novel*, the aesthetics follows the conventions of a formal academic treatise. The difference of approach between the two roughly contemporaneous works is illuminating. The aesthetics, despite being more formal, contains Schlegelian stylistic breaks[13] that show Lukács to be more interested in speculative consequences than in systematic theorizing. In *The Theory of the Novel*, on the other hand, an overtly essayistic approach is complicated by the latency of its systematics. When writing essayistically, Lukács uses implicitly systematized premises as the springboard for meta-reflections, while in the *Heidelberg Aesthetics* the essayistic lapses seem to reflect discomfort with the systematic construction. The *Heidelberg Aesthetics* often gives the impression of a seamless theorization, but the moments when Lukács "brackets" and "transcends" his systematic positions therefore feel all the more exposed. Such essayistic course-corrections produce profound shifts in the apparent argument, giving the impression that Lukács is either unable to commit to his own theorization or that he was not primarily interested in producing a descriptive aesthetic theory.[14]

Before giving an example of this, I will quickly sketch the central claims of Lukács's aesthetics: he develops an idea of "aesthetic positing" (*ästhetische Setzung*) which advocates for works of art on the basis of their immanence, singularity, self-sufficiency, and internal coherence. The autonomy of each aesthetic positing, its intrinsic claim to *be* its own "reality," causes it to exclude and negate the everyday reality from which it emerges.[15] Lukács understands this negativity of the work of art as a radicalization of Husserl's idea of bracketing.[16] The work of art, for Lukács, is constituted out of the same material as "everyday reality" (*Erlebniswirklichkeit*), and for this reason the two can only be in competition. The real world does not stand a chance, however, because in every cultural formation yet known, with the exception of the ancient Greeks, "real" reality is essentially contingent and thus inferior to the work of art: "Everyday lived experience is therefore far from being something original [*etwas Ursprüngliches*] in a systematic sense; it is impossible to think of a more artificial and contrived arrangement of objects [*das gekünstelteste Objektsgefüge*]."[17] A successful aesthetic positing, which is always possessed of its own intensive reality, provides a coherence of experience that is lacking in the real world.

In short, virtual realities are more real than reality—but this power of the work of art is highly unstable, prone to being "transcended" from one of two directions: (1) the "soul," as Lukács would say, cannot be truly at home in the work of art, because the latter has the status of a Kantian *Ding an sich*, isolated both from its creator and its recipient. The soul always remains homeless: it may temporarily and partially enter the world of the work, but it can never permanently reside there. It must always return to the incoherence of the "empirical" world. (2) The work may be transcended by philosophical-conceptual abstraction. In thinking about and justifying art, the "everyday reality" of works is constantly counter-bracketed by their "idea." The experiential immanence of the work as "aesthetic positing" leads Lukács to reject the canonical conceptions of beauty from Plato through Kant, Hegel, Schelling, and Goethe.

Such are the apparent claims of Lukács's aesthetics. I now turn to a passage (at the very end of the chapter entitled "Subject-Object-Relation") which represents the most extreme case of Lukács's tendency toward essayistic reframing:

It however also cannot be left unsaid [*kann nicht verschwiegen werden*] that the will to produce a system [*der Wille zum System*] with its necessary will to produce a harmony of values [*die Harmonie der Werte*], almost always strives from the outset to produce, through a process of synchronization [*Abstimmung*], the harmony it presupposes. This kind of systematic approach attempts to veil and diminish [*verschleiern und vermildern*] the essence of the aesthetic [*das Wesen der Ästhetik*], which strives to go beyond the level of the other values [*aus der Ebene der anderen Werte hinausstrebt*]. Here, however, an appeal will be made in the name of the simple understanding of the aesthetic sphere [*im Namen der einfachen Erkenntnis der ästhetischen Sphäre*], which leads me also to emphasize that the metaphysical "enemies" of art—such as Plato, Kierkegaard or Tolstoy—have recognized its normative essence [*ihr normatives Wesen*] as well as its metaphysical significance [*ihre metaphysische Bedeutung*] with much greater clarity than its harmonizing defenders. Thus, if someone were tempted, on the basis of the present purely value-theoretical analysis, to think that the Luciferian [*das Luciferische*] is the proper metaphysical "location" [*der metaphysische "Ort"*] of the aesthetic, I would not be able to contradict him (nor would I wish to do so). (HÄs 131–32)

At the beginning of the passage, Lukács argues that because philosophical aesthetics itself has the goal of producing systematic harmony and coherence, philosophy obscures the oppositional—negating, contrary—character of art. This will to harmoniousness contrasts with the chaos of everyday reality in the same way that art does, thereby revealing philosophy's complicity with the aesthetic. That which "cannot be left unsaid" (*nicht verschwiegen werden kann*) is philosophy's own aesthetic tendency.

Once a philosophical system is bracketed in this way, its meaning is no longer stable. Lukács calls his own system into question in an exposed self-contradiction. With false modesty, he stresses that his work is only an "immanent value-theoretical analysis," thereby calling attention to the limitations of such an analysis. This does not mean that he retracts his theory of aesthetic positing; but what counts here is not the theory's internal coherence or descriptive accuracy, but the horizons of its possible meanings. In view of such horizons, Lukács displays obvious ambivalence toward his own conception of art. He is unsure whether to side with the metaphysical "enemies" of art or with its "defenders." He concedes that the enemies would be right to conclude that the "metaphysical location" of the aesthetic is "the Luciferian,"[18] but the "somebody" (*jemand*) who plays the devil's advocate here is, however, Lukács himself. The radical defender of the autonomy of art unexpectedly changes sides and raises doubts about his defense. The traditional defenses were based on art's double tendency toward transcendence—either toward life and "reality" or toward norms of beauty, ethics, and morality—but in Lukács's conception, these rationalizations and justifications are disallowed. The oppositional character of art in the *Heidelberg Aesthetics* makes it Luciferian in its *essential* tendency to replace *the* world with a plurality of seductive, short-lived, and ultimately unlivable counter-worlds. In the terms of Maurice Blanchot: Luciferian art is a siren's song that calls away from the world.[19]

Lukács's idea of the immanence and autonomy of art is blocked by an idea of reality that prevents him from affirming his defense of art. With respect to a singular reality, art tends to produce virtual realities. The "better" a work, the more Luciferian it is. On the flip side, the philosophical-conceptual rationalization of art—toward the beautiful, the sublime, the ethical, or the political—neutralizes its Luciferian aspect, but does so in a way that makes art itself irrelevant. Thus, according to consequences Lukács does not explicitly draw: art is utterly otherworldly—but this is precisely what causes it to be of the utmost consequence for the "real world." Its "Luciferian" aspect, which its "enemies" perceived, is that if it does not lead upward—if it cannot be instrumentalized—then it must lead downward. If it is not self-transcending, then it is hostile to every system that seeks to stabilize its meaning.

Art is an unsublatable, "Luciferian" principle of opposition, and its seductions are even more seductive and uncontrollable when their normative instrumentalization is revealed as the defense mechanism of a beleaguered reality. Given this setup, it is still not easy to say what side Lukács takes. Precisely the harmoniousness of art's siren song makes it dissonant and false with respect to reality. This might mean that, instead of working on works, artists should work on reality itself. Lukács cannot go in this direction without turning his habilitation into a manifesto, and thus the degree of his sympathy with the enemies of art remains ambiguous. If he were to fully side with them, his "defense" of "aesthetic positing" would become the pretext for its condemnation. This reading cannot be ruled out, but it overlooks Lukács's obvious fascination with the unstable and destabilizing functions of art. The idea of the Luciferian suggests its author's susceptibility to it; he may have found its anarchist "negation" of a deficient reality more salutary than this reality's attempts to rationalize and harmonize art as propaganda or "aesthetic education." Without trying to resolve this point, I find it plausible to imagine that Lukács identified with art's Luciferian aspect—not because it represents a revolutionary potential, but because it represents a this-worldly beyond, a normative inversion with respect to the world and the polarities of its conceptualization (good/evil, idealism/realism, state/society, progress/decline, etc.).[20]

There is no evidence that Lukács takes his idea of the Luciferian from Goethe, but because *The Theory of the Novel* cites the demonic from book 20 of *Poetry and Truth*, it seems reasonable to read the Luciferian in connection with book 8's "pulsing" conception of man's simultaneous participation in the Luciferian and the divine. Lukács's and Goethe's versions of the Luciferian are roughly compatible in their reading of the impulse toward individualization and specification (in the form of "aesthetic positing") in terms of an opposition or distance from the divine. Goethe's opposition of the Luciferian and the divine in the figure of systole and diastole, however, differs greatly from Lukács's more schismatic understanding. Goethe allows the individual to have a double home, whereas for Lukács this doubleness is the essence of homelessness. For Lukács, perfect specification is only possible through "aesthetic positing," whereas "real life"—including the life of the artist—is defined by alien contingencies. In comparison to Goethe, the most difficult question posed by Lukács is whether the ideal of "specification" might be realizable in life—outside of the artificial closure of aesthetic positing. The choice of the word "Luciferian" itself seems to be premised on the idea that the lure of the aesthetic always breaks its utopian promise.[21] In a naive way, one might wonder if Lukács is not asking too much of art. He wants works to *be* concrete utopias in themselves *and* simultaneously to *promote* concrete utopia in the world. These imperatives are contradictory—and the second is explicitly forbidden in Lukács's theory's rejection of the political or ethical transcendence of the immediacy of aesthetic positing. As long as this transcendence is disallowed, art's production of short-lived virtual and subjective utopias will constantly divert energy from the *real* utopian project of creating a more just world. Thus Lukács suspects—against the prevailing assumptions of aesthetic theory and practice—that art is a source of a breakdown in the historical dialectic whose ultimate ends were supposed to be reason and progress.

A somewhat unexpected consequence of this is that the unified life ideal of the Greek epic[22] invoked in the opening of *The Theory of the Novel*—"Selig sind die Zeiten" ("blessed were the days," TdR 21)—cannot be taken as an ideal of *artistic* perfection. When Greek life, reflected in Greek art, is the ideal toward which modern art strives, modern art becomes Luciferian. Greece is *the* ideal for Lukács, but this ideal is profoundly misunderstood if it is taken only as a model for artistic imitation. It is Greek *life*—which produced the "art"—that must become the model for the transformation of the world. "Art" as aesthetic positing is a phenomenon of modernity that stands in contrast to Greek culture.[23] In the role of the "metaphysical enemy" of art, Lukács believes that this original unity can be re-achieved. The epic unity of subject and object, of inside and outside—"the world is wide and yet like one's own home" (*die Welt ist weit und doch wie das eigene Haus,* TdR 21)—cannot be achieved "through art" (*von der Kunst aus,* TdR 137).[24]

The turn from aesthetics to culture—and to politics—marks the point, one might say (contra Lukács), where it gets really Luciferian. A divided or alienated existence may not be the worst thing imaginable. In comparison, the possibilities of inauthenticity and self-alienation presented in Goethe's Orphic "Urworte" represent resigned realism. For Lukács, on the other hand, in keeping with his aesthetics' general basis in an idea of "spheres"—the transcendental equivalent of fields, disciplines, or genres—the historical tendency of art's autonomy and "virtuality" is increasing mutual exclusivity and pluralization. At the limit, each individual—each work—will define its own sphere, and the overwhelming proliferation of such works would cause art to fail even in its negative function of casting critical light on a deficient reality. Aesthetic positing thus ultimately posits the disparateness of aesthetic *spheres* in an equally disparate experiential reality.

Goethe and Lucifer in the *Heidelberg Aesthetics*

There is no need to introduce Goethe into Lukács's aesthetic theory, because it contains a full (and surprisingly approving) section on him (HÄs 183–92); only in the next subsection does the tone become more critical (HÄs 193).

The question Lukács pursues in Goethe, after having dismantled Hegel,[25] is whether Goethe's conception of organic-developmental form might not allow an idea of beauty—above all of artistic beauty—to be conceived, which would be simultaneously concrete, immanent, and empirical throughout all of its moments and stages. Hegel's dialectical system reports an error when it comes to explaining the concrete developmental manifestations of aesthetic objects. Hegel was, according to Lukács, unable to conceive the (Luciferian) particularity of singular aesthetic objects in their self-sufficient "spheres." In comparison with Hegel, Goethe's morphology (which Lukács never refers to by this name) is an advance, because it stands a better chance of producing an idea of the aesthetic that is at once immanent and developmental. In light of Hegel's failure to vanquish Kant, Goethe's "way of observing nature" (*Art der Naturbetrachtung*) is an intervention "in the development of speculative philosophy" (*in die Entwicklung der spekulativen Philosophie*), which Lukács characterizes as "fatefully decisive" (*schicksalhaft-entscheidend*, HÄs 183). To support this, he draws on a variety of mostly later works of Goethe, including the "Maxims and Reflections," *The Theory of Colors, Faust,* and *Wilhelm Meister's Journeyman Years.* Famous lines of Plotinus from *The Theory of Colors*—"If the eye were not like the sun / How could we behold the light?" (*Wär' nicht das Auge sonnenhaft, / Wie könnten wir das Licht erblicken?* HÄs 186)—set up an opposition between Faust and Makarie (from *Wilhelm Meister*), in which the latter represents the "utopian-real cosmic completion" (*utopisch-real kosmische Vollendung*) of Faust's human inadequacies. Makarie is "the highest realization of this form of life [*die höchste Verwirklichung dieser Lebensform*], . . . in which the solar system has become truly alive, who is the solar system and lives it immediately [*die das Sonnensystem ist und es unmittelbar lebt*]" (HÄs 187). These lines illustrate Lukács's idea of the "spherical" life and "rounded" existence that is impossible in the fragmentary reality of modernity. The young Faust, on the other hand, exemplifies the modern predicament in solipsistic limitations defined by the earth-spirit (*Erdgeist*): "you are like the spirit that you conceive, but not like me" (*du gleichst dem Geist, den du begreifst, / Nicht mir,* HÄs 187).

Lukács is more convinced by this "tragic" figure of Faust than by the possibility of a development leading to perfection (*Vollendung*) or redemption (*Erlösung*). Faust's encounter with the earth-spirit represents a struggle with the Luciferian in which "reality" triumphs, even before there is a wager that can be lost. Lukács sees *the* definitive and inescapable reality in Faust's restless striving, and on this basis he rejects the later harmonizing moments *as ideals*—or as ironic-critical abstractions. Yet Goethe's organological aesthetics is nevertheless emphatically affirmed:

> The doubly guiding role [*die doppel-leitende Stellung*] of the organic in the system is that which is ultimately determinant [*als letztlich Bestimmendes*] for both the construction and nature of the object

[*Aufbau und Wesensart des Objekts*] as well as for the constitution
and level of the subject [*Beschaffenheit und Niveau des Subjekts*].
This resolves the anthropological aporias of Platonism [*hebt die
anthropologischen Aporien des Platonismus auf*] ... [and] makes
possible a philosophically affirmative and positively valued relation
to art [*ein philosophisch bejahendes und positiv bewertendes Verhalten zur Kunst*]. (HÄs 189, 191)

In Goethe's conception, Lukács continues, "in diametric opposition to
Platonism,"

> it is no longer the mathematically well proportioned [*das mathe-
> matisch Wohl-Proportionierte*], the crystalline [*das Krystallinische*],
> which is the real carrier of the idea of beauty, but rather that which
> is enigmatically perfected in itself [*das rätselhaft in sich Vollendete*],
> that which lives and is full of spirit [*das Lebendige, Seelenerfüllte*],
> which radiates this fulfillment in its very appearance [*diese Erfülltheit
> in seiner Erscheinungsform Ausstrahllende*]. And this is why also in
> art [as well as nature], the adequate objectivation of beauty is that
> which transcends all rules [*das allen Regeln Entrückte*], that which
> has apparently grown out of itself [*das scheinbar von selbst Gewach-
> sene*]. (HÄs 192)

This ideal of both art and nature corresponds with Lukács's characterization
of modern works of art as microcosms. The experience of worlds in works
defines modern art: works are more alive than life, and life lives only through
art.

Ultimately, the Makarie ideal itself is Luciferian in its relation to modern
reality. Lukács rejects the idealization of sense perception and apperception as
a means of unifying subject and object over time on the grounds that even—
and especially—at its most ideal, aesthetic perception is governed by a form
of solipsism that is essentially equivalent to its non-idealized form (Faust's
encounter with the earth spirit). The risk of solipsism is in fact greater when
less resistance comes from the side of the "object" (when the *Erdgeist* does
not intervene and call attention to the limitations of the subject-position).
Thus the most Luciferian figure for Lukács is Makarie, and thus the most
Luciferian art, next to that of ancient Greece, is Goethe's in its ability to idealize and transfigure the solipsism of all perception and promote the confusion
of perception and reality. Lukács's interpretation of *Wilhelm Meister* in *The
Theory of the Novel* (TdR 117–28) similarly argues that, while appearing
to present a prosaic depiction, Goethe romanticizes reality in a way that
bears false witness to the achievability of the ideals represented. Lukács thus
sides more with the Tower Society of *Wilhelm Meister* than with Makarie—
but not because he supports its model of concrete management: the ideal

Makarie represents *must be realized,* not by isolated individuals and not only aesthetically, but *socially and intersubjectively.*

Read in this way, it is uncertain whether Lukács is the one who diagnoses the problem of the Luciferian—or if he is its victim. One could argue, for example, that he is unable to read the aesthetic aesthetically; he only perceives art in view of the unrealizability—*nicht von der Kunst aus*—of the ideals it merely represents. Even after distancing himself from the morphological idea of nature, the (Luciferian) harmony of which seductively leads away from reality's contradictions, he still implicitly subscribes to this ideal. He sees aesthetic positing as the main obstacle to the realization of that which *only it* can promise:

> The grandeur, however, with which it [Goethe's "cosmic" conception of the unified subject] was able to realize both [the theoretical and the aesthetic] in his creative praxis [*in der gestaltenden Praxis*] with respect to art and nature, as well as in the conduct of his own life, is very well suited [*ist sehr geeignet*] to covering over [*zu verdecken*] the insoluble problems that are hidden within it [*die darin verborgen sind*] and to awakening the appearance [*den Anschein zu erwecken*] of a well-shaped unity of life [*eine gestaltete Lebenseinheit*], as if such an apparent unity would be able to simultaneously guarantee the systematic unifiability of its actual elements. (HÄs 193)

Lukács rejects the "apparent unity" of the necessarily disparate elements of Goethe's life and art. Life and art can at best produce *the appearance* of organic unity, which hides the fact that these apparent unities are actually artificial composites. As mere appearances, aesthetic unities seek only to put a good face on a deficient reality.

The Demonic Infrastructure of *The Theory of the Novel*

Lukács was looking for something in Goethe that Goethe never claimed to provide. This is striking in the first pages of *The Theory of the Novel,* which begin with the Luciferian spell of Greek antiquity. The Plotinus quote from the *Theory of Colors* ("If the eye were not like the sun / How could we behold the light?"), which Lukács cites in the *Heidelberg Aesthetics* (HÄs 186), is paraphrased and ornamented, not to define a certain possibility of aesthetic perception, but to hypostasize the real possibility of a complete sensuous unity of inside and outside, subject and object: "the fire, which burns in the soul, is of the same essence [*Wesensart*] as the stars . . . because fire is the soul of every light and every fire clothes itself in light" (TdR 21). This unity, which Lukács attributes to the Greeks, conforms to his reading of Goethe. When Lukács contrasts "our" Kantian understanding of the stars with that of the Greeks, Makarie's internalization of the heavens provides the implicit model: "Blessed are the times . . . whose paths [*Wege*] are lit by the light of the stars" (TdR 21). The motif is again repeated and developed:

> Even if threatening and incomprehensible powers [*drohende und unverständliche Mächte*] make themselves felt from beyond the circle [*jenseits des Kreises*] that the constellations of present meaning [*die Sternenbilder des gegenwärtigen Sinnes*] draw around a cosmos that is meant to be experienced and shaped by man [*der erlebbare und zu formende Kosmos*], such forces are still never able to suppress the presence of meaning [*die Gegenwart des Sinnes*]. (TdR 25)

And finally comes the explicit contrast with Kant: "Kant's starry sky [*Sternenhimmel*] now shines only in the dark night of pure knowledge [*in der dunklen Nacht der reinen Erkenntnis*] and no longer lights . . . the lonely wanderer's paths" (TdR 28).

In the course of this sidereal exposition, the word Luciferian makes one of its two occurrences in *The Theory of the Novel*; here it is the result of the modern uprooting of art from the immediate sensuous totality of its Greek origin. In modernity, the totality can no longer be found in the "rounded" unity of life but only in "autonomous" works:

> The visionary reality [*visionäre Wirklichkeit*] of a world made to our measure [*uns angemessen*], art, has become . . . independent [*selbständig*]; . . . it is an artificial totality [*eine erschaffene Totalität*], because the natural unity of the metaphysical spheres has been permanently ripped apart [*für immer zerrissen*]. (TdR 29)

In modernity, art becomes artificial, a merely manufactured formal perfection without correspondence to a larger and equally organic reality. Modernity misunderstands the Greek "totality of being" as *mere* art and turns the ancient light-bearer into a

> seductive power [*verführerische Kraft*] that still lay dormant even in dead Greek culture [*noch im toten Griechentum lag*], the blinding Luciferian reflection [*luciferisch blendender Glanz*] of which made it possible to forget the world's unsealable fissures [*die unheilbaren Risse der Welt*], while constantly allowing new unities [*Einheiten*] to be dreamed up [*erträumen ließ*], which however always contradicted the new essence of the world [*dem neuen Wesen der Welt widersprachen*] and therefore always fell apart again [*immer wieder zerfielen*]. (TdR 29)

The anti-artistic undertone, which appears in the *Heidelberg Aesthetics* in the form of the ironic devil's advocacy, is more emphatic in *The Theory of the*

Novel. The "blinding reflection" (*blendender Glanz*)²⁶ of the Greek world, carried across the ages in art, makes modernity oblivious to the fragmentariness and artificiality of its own world. A world of constantly dreamt-up new creations—which dissolve again like dreams—is a world of superstructures that exist only in the denial of their base. Art perpetually re-creates "Greece" at the level of mere appearances.

In the *Heidelberg Aesthetics,* this interpretation of art as an endless Luciferian falling away from being—as a sentimental consolation in the absence of true being—reactivates Plato's suspicions about art. Such metaphysical doubts about the Luciferian spell of antiquity may explain Lukács's focus on the novel. The post-Homeric epic, because it has no hope of living up to Homer's perfect unification of art and life on the basis of an underlying unity of existence (TdR 46), has no choice but to reflect the fragmentariness and disunity of reality. Homer was able to produce a unified totality, not primarily because of the unifying power of his "genius," but because the world he lived in was a unified one. By contrast, all efforts to epically reflect the reality of modernity can only produce works that are fragmentary, incomplete, inconsistent, inadequate, abstractly normative-imperative, or subjectively moral-ethical in relation to a world for which there is no coherent metonymy to represent its entirety. In the terms of the *Heidelberg Aesthetics,* the novel is not an "aesthetic positing" because it does not create an autonomous "world" in opposition to the real one. According to *The Theory of the Novel,* epic form "is never the making [*das Schaffen*] of a new reality [*einer neuen Realität*], but only always a subjective mirroring [*ein subjektives Spiegeln*] of the reality that already exists [*der bereits daseienden*]" (TdR 39–40).

It is precisely aesthetic deficiency and heterogeneity that allow the novel to avoid the Luciferian. Its lack of autonomy and its dependency on empirical reality define the novel's historicity and set it apart from the other modern arts. Epic narration in modernity is always a partial reflection of historical reality, a fragment of objectivized subjectivity—or subjectivized objectivity: "it is always his subjectivity [that of the narrator] that manages to wrench one piece out of the measureless infinity of everything that happens in the world [*aus der maßlosen Unendlichkeit des Weltgeschehens ein Stück herausreißt*]" (TdR 41). The epic narrator, according to Lukács, is responsible for the selection and the meaning of what is narrated; the latter stands for the meaning of life itself. Unlike dramas, which systematically focus on an abstract problem, the novel is engaged in an existential analytic with respect to historical reality. Even if the novel's search for meaning always remains projected toward an uncertain horizon—and even if its meaning turns out to be sheer meaninglessness, as is typical of the more "artistic" genre of the novella (TdR 42)—the epic narrator is responsible for his narrative's representativeness with respect to the meaning of life in all of its material density (and not just as a "moral of the story"). The novel is unique among epic forms in that it must try to mediate its own process of selection within the totality of everything that it does not and could not possibly hope to address (TdR 43). Only at the genre's limits, in its most exemplary works,[27] are the narrator's subjective limitations made to indirectly *appear*—passively, by an act of grace (*Gnade*, TdR 44)—such that the boundaries of the novel are transformed into those of the world itself (*seine Grenze zur Grenze der Welt zu verwandlen*, TdR 44).

Limit-cases define the novel in Lukács's theory. If a novel rivals Homer's achievement in its synthesis of reality into an aesthetic whole, or if it transcends the novel in the direction of another genre, it may be at once the most aesthetically satisfying and the most Luciferian. The most ideal syntheses do not ring true, because as long as it is a novel, formal autonomy has the potential to conflict with the external reality whose meaning the epic is obliged to supply. Irony thus functions as a corrective when it reveals the novel's idealizations to be relative or counterfactual. According to Lukács's summary at the end of the fourth section of the first part, the meaning of a novel can never be totally internal and aesthetically autonomous, because this meaning ultimately refers to "a specific problematic of the world" (*eine bestimmte Problematik der Welt*, TdR 72). Lukács thus characterizes Dante's immanent depiction of transcendence as follows:

> However, only in a transcendent beyond [*nur im Jenseits*] is the meaning of this world [*der Sinn dieser Welt*] able to become concretely visible and immanent [*abstandlos sichtbar und immanent*]. In the world itself [*in dieser Welt*], the totality is one that is either unstable [*eine brüchige*] or merely yearned for [*eine ersehnte*] . . . (TdR 51)

Dante is able to harmonize the reality of this world and its meaning only by recourse to transcendence. A meaningful totality is possible only by completely separating the world from its meaning, by positing an alternate world as the meaning and fulfillment of this world. In novels, however, aesthetic harmoniousness becomes dissonant with respect to the randomness and incomprehensibility of the world.

With the help of Virgil, who gave him a guided tour, Dante was able to postulate a transcendent totality. The novel's narrator and protagonist, on the other hand, must search for it in the ruins of a world that cannot be *immanently* "harmonized" without giving lie to the novel's meaning. By defining the novel as a process in which meaning is *sought*, the lack and absence of given meanings (and thus a certain state of the world) is presupposed (TdR 51). Even when seeking reaches an end, when a given plotline reaches its fulfillment or the seeking subject finds its object, it takes the form of a temporary insight into "the meaning of life" (*der Sinn des Lebens*, TdR 70, 134) which can only occur against the backdrop of a world in which fulfillment is not the norm (TdR 53) and in which the "finding" is often a source of disillusionment. The hero's accomplished insight into the searching-process of his own development can only have the character of an exception, which precisely does not stand for the general experience of everyone, but rather displays what the world and life normally *are not*. Most do not seek, and most seekers do not find. Exceptional moments of the immanent unification of world and meaning—Makarie moments—allow the *merely* formal closure of the novel's world by way of an exception that proves the rule. Thanks to such moments of subjective illumination, the hero's experiences can be experienced vicariously, as exceptions to the norm that occur *despite* the novel's faithful reflection of the fragmentariness and meaninglessness of the world. The exemplarity of the novel's resolutions is counter-exemplary (TdR 53) and at odds with "the world as it is" (*das Leben, so wie es ist*, TdR 27) and thus also—anticipating the next step of Lukács's argument—ironic.

In the transition to the idea of irony, Lukács discreetly alludes to the *Dämon* of Goethe's "Urworte." Lukács characteristically glosses the *Dämon* idea with the word *soul* (*Seele*, TdR 56) and explains it as an experience in which the external world is able to become the extension and medium of the soul: "for the soul itself is the law" (*denn die Seele selbst ist das Gesetz*, TdR 56). The life of this soul is not that of modernity, but of Greek antiquity; it refers to a soul that does not (yet) encounter anything fundamentally opposed or foreign to it, which does not (yet) know the "searching" quality that Lukács attributes to the novel's hero:

> The human world that comes into view is one in which the soul is at home [*zu Hause*], whether as man, god or demon [*Mensch, Gott oder Dämon*]. In this world the soul finds everything it needs [*alles, was not tut*]; it has no need to create or animate something out of itself [*aus sich selbst heraus zu schaffen*], because its existence [*Existenz*] is copiously fulfilled [*überreichlich erfüllt*] in the finding, collecting and shaping [*Finden, Sammeln und Formen*] of that which is immediately given and related to it as a soul [*was ihr unmittelbar, als Seelenverwandtes, gegeben ist*]. (TdR 56)

The fact that this "soul" may ambiguously be that of "man, god or demon" indicates a prelapsarian existence more superhuman than human. Its language reconceptualizes Goethe's *Dämon*.[28] Thus, more implicitly than in the *Heidelberg Aesthetics*, Lukács here also relies on Goethe to theorize the unification of subject and object.

A comparison with Goethe makes the one-sidedness apparent with which Lukács focuses on the *Dämon* (or "soul") without regard for the balancing powers of *Tyche, Eros, Ananke,* and *Elpis*.[29] For Lukács as well as Goethe, however—at least in the modern state of the world—the idea of a completely unchecked *Dämon* is only a foil, a momentary ideal standing for everything that human life generally is not. Lukács's next paragraph thus posits an impeding if not malicious *Tyche:*

Interiority's life of its own [*das Eigenleben der Innerlichkeit*] [inte-
riority split off from a coherent connection to the outside world] is
only then possible and necessary . . . when the gods are silent [*wenn
die Götter stumm sind*] . . . , when the world of deeds [*die Welt der
Taten*] has disconnected itself from humans. The independence [*Selb-
ständigkeit*] of this form of interiority has made it hollow [*hohl*]
and incapable of receiving the true meaning of deeds within itself
[*unvermögend, den wahren Sinn der Taten in sich aufzunehmen*].
Interiority has become unable to make a symbol of itself in deeds [*an
ihnen ein Symbol zu werden*] and to dissolve them into symbols [*und
sie in Symbole aufzulösen*]: the connection between interiority and
adventure [*die Innerlichkeit und das Abenteuer*] is forever severed
[*abgetrennt*]. (TdR 57)

For Lukács, this disconnection between the authenticity of the *Dämon* and
a godless, meaningless world of contingent forms defines the modern world
and its characteristic epic genre. Older epics told of heroes who symbolically
represented communities—who did not search, but were led. This idea of
heroism presumed the unity of "interiority and adventure"; whereas *Tyche*
in antiquity was opportune and auspicious, in the modern world she is a
hindrance to the *Dämon*'s self-actualization.

Lukács reproduces of the basic schema of Goethe's *Dämon-Tyche* opposition, but he reads it very differently. Instead of viewing *Tyche* as a potentially
productive socialization, he interprets her exclusively as an agonistic opponent of *Dämon;* he resists Goethe's attempt to bridge antiquity and modernity
in the enduring validity of the "Urworte." Whereas Goethe saw in them a
timeless analytic system, for Lukács they express a unified relation of life and
world that only existed in Greek antiquity. On this point, Lukács is close to
Benjamin's reading of the "Urworte," which argues that the imagined unity
of *Tyche* and *Dämon*—of fate and character—is always a regression to the
mythic concept of the hero. Lukács sees it that way too but inverts the valuation. Where Benjamin posits the unity of life and world as a perpetual
phantasm of "myth," Lukács supposes a primordial whole, which not only
actually existed, but which remains the only possible goal of history. He thus
characterizes modernity and the modern novel in the absent connection of
Dämon and *Tyche* as "the non-compatibility of empirical life and the sensory
immanence of meaning" (*das Nicht-eingehen-Wollen der Sinnesimmanenz in
das empirische Leben,* TdR 61).

The immediate unity of life and meaning may look like a sentimental ideal,
but the current unrealizability of this ideal means that Lukács (unlike Gundolf) does not seek a contemporary epitome (such as Goethe) to show the
achievability of "heroic" existence. One might want to say that Dostoyevsky
fulfills this function, with the difference that his epics—perhaps no longer
novels—anticipate a *future* life ideal.[30] Lukács saw Dostoyevsky as a figure

pointing toward the dawn of a new epoch, but there is no unified perspective available at present through which the meaning of life can be universally mediated without lapsing into a subjectivity that would contradict the universality intended. To get around this problem, Lukács introduces irony in order to theorize the novel as a perspectival matrix, a system of foils that prevents access to final or authoritative meaning. The alternatives represented in the world of the novel are suspended by the limitations of a narrator who recognizes divisions without being able to overcome them. This limited acceptance reflects and partially stabilizes the rift at the base of the modern experience represented through the novel's hero.

Given various splits, but especially the one between individual and world—*Dämon* and *Tyche,* "soul" and "forms"—irony allows the novel's given world to be structured into two perspectives that mark the extremes of interiority and exteriority. These perspectives are typically represented by a protagonist and a narrator:

> [Irony] means . . . an internal splitting [*eine innere Spaltung*] of the normatively poetic subject [*des normativ dichterischen Subjekts*] into [1] a subjectivity as interiority, which stands in opposition to alien power complexes [*die fremde Machtkomplexen gegenübersteht*] and strives to imprint this alien world with the contents of its longings [*die Inhalte ihrer Sehnsucht*] and [2] a subjectivity that is able to see through the abstractness [*Abstraktheit*] and thus through the limitations [*Beschränktheit*] of the opposing and mutually alien subject- and object-worlds [*Subjekts- und Objektswelten*]; this perception [*Durchschauen*] indeed leaves the duality of the world untouched [*die Zweiheit der Welt bestehen läßt*], but at the same time, in the reciprocal conditionality [*die wechselseitige Bedingtheit*] of the two elements that are mutually and essentially alien to one another, it catches sight of and shapes [*erblickt und gestaltet*] a unified world [*eine einheitliche Welt*]. This unity is however purely formal [*rein formal*]. (TdR 64)

The novel is the genre of the negative—ironic and counter-exemplary—depiction of the unity of fate and character. With irony, the universal lack of unity can become the basis of a speculative unification. In order to tell the story, the narrator must be able "to recognize as necessary" (TdR 64)—and perhaps even to accept, from a standpoint of "resignation" (TdR 61)—the unfathomable split within the world. Importantly, this realization "of limits" (TdR 64) on the part of the narrator—of the limitations of any unifying perspective—is only possible on the basis of the paradoxical and partial knowledge called *irony* and not, for example, by a more stable figure, such as "renunciation" (*Entsagung*), which would seek to unify this perspective into an ethical norm and universal possibility of conflict resolution. Novelistic irony, though it

walks the fine line between ambivalent resignation and ambiguous moral-
ization, allows problematic subjects to be depicted without moralizing or
generalizing.

The split between subject and narrator also reflects a temporal split
between the time of experience and its later narration. In *Poetry and Truth,*
in the context of the demonic, Goethe ironically characterizes this idea of
irony: "That's what makes it youth and life in general: we generally first learn
to perceive the strategy after the campaign is over" (HA 10:183). Goethe
takes irony ironically where Lukács takes it seriously (in that he implies that
the problem that necessitates it is solvable). Thus the novel does not affirm
the solution—the *Notlösung*—of irony, but employs it as a "merely formal"
device to keep the real problem in focus: that the world is not a utopia but an
"ever-lost paradise" (*ein ewig verlorenes Paradies,* TdR 74).

Significantly, irony is less central in part 2 of *The Theory of the Novel,*
which focuses on the problems of protagonists. Lukács, it seems, is unable
to reintroduce irony in its proper place, the narrator-protagonist differential,
which resurfaces in part 2's discussions of memory (TdR 110–14). The context makes it clear, however, that hero and narrator are not fixed positions:
the process of aging—of achieving "mature masculinity" (*gereifte Männlichkeit,* TdR 74–75)—turns demonic heroes into ironic novelists.

The Demonic and the Luciferian in *The Theory of the Novel*

By the time Lukács names the demonic in the fifth section of part 1 of his theory, the general outlines of the topic are already so implicitly ubiquitous as to
make it almost superfluous to introduce Goethe directly. The fact that Lukács
does so can perhaps be read as a sign that he does not expect readers to make
the connection without a hint—or, on the other hand, that he thought readers *would* notice it and he wanted to address it directly. Either way, the overt
recourse to the demonic suggests that he wanted his theory to be read in this
context. The explicit invocation of the demonic thus looks like the tip of an
iceberg which, implicit in the rest of the theory, is now announced.

When Lukács names the demonic and makes it into a manifest topic, he
does not do so in a simple way. He characteristically jumps in at the level of
consequences and implications. Also, in comparison to the first four sections
of his theory's first part, the passages on the demonic appear oddly fragmentary or even vestigial. Overall, the concluding fifth section has a summary
function with respect to the sections that preceded it, and the demonic flows
directly out of preestablished contexts. The introduction of the demonic by
name thus appears to be motivated by a desire to amplify and expound. But it
is not only an emphatic reiteration. Like the Luciferian in the *Heidelberg Aesthetics,* Lukács's reflection of his thesis in Goethe's concept introduces decisive
new elements that broaden and perhaps contradict the preceding theory.

The idea of the demonic first comes into play in a Novalis citation to the effect that the belief in the identity of "fate and character" (*Schicksal und Gemüt*) is "the youthful faith of all poetry" (*der Jugendglaube aller Poesie*, TdR 74). The genre of the novel painfully breaks faith with this primal unity. Starting from this thesis, the demonic emerges as part of a reflection on the extended consequences of novelistic irony. Irony suspends "poetic" faith in the heroic unity of fate and character. Despite and because of this point's apparent redundancy, its extension in the direction of the demonic allows it to be reformatted in a language expressing the urgency of the underlying historical problem. Irony, the symptom of the present epoch, is a symptom of the narrator's inability to concede the pointlessness of the hero's aspirations and give up "the youthful faith of all poetry":

> This insight [*diese Einsicht*], his irony, turns against his hero, who perishes [*geht zugrunde*] out of poetically necessary youthfulness [*in poetisch notwendiger Jugendlichkeit*] in the realization of this faith, but the narrator's irony also turns against his own wisdom by forcing him to admit [*einsehen*] the futility of the hero's battle [*die Vergeblichkeit dieses Kampfes*] and the final victory of reality [*den endgültigen Sieg der Wirklichkeit*]. His irony comprehends [*erfaßt*] not only the deep hopelessness of the battle, but also the even deeper hopelessness of giving it up . . . By figuring [*gestalten*] reality as the victor, irony reveals [*enthüllt*] the vain inanity [*Nichtigkeit*] of this reality in the face of the vanquished hero. (TdR 74)

If the narrator did not have some residual investment in the representativeness of the protagonist, the narrative would be pointless. The narrator, whom Lukács frequently characterizes as representative of "mature masculinity" (*gereifte Männlichkeit*), knows that he should *know better* than to worry about young heroes and the *youthful* hopes of all poetry. But he cannot help wishing he were wrong in this knowledge. He narrates the hero's downfall *with irony*, thereby causing reality's triumph over "the youthful faith of all poetry" to appear ambiguous. The meaning of his defeat remains uncertain, especially with regard to its justice. The hero may end up in the wrong on the world's terms, but the world is not thereby vindicated. In Lukács's hero-centric conception, the narrator's staged reflection of "world" and "soul" leads to the insight that, regardless of the inevitability of the soul's submission to the world's ironclad necessity (*Ananke*), the latter is illegitimate as long as *Tyche* defines its essence. The protagonist may fail, but the soul cannot be made to forsake itself, its *Dämon* or nature: soul remains soul, and world remains—mere *fortuna*.

To illustrate this, Lukács recalls the mythic heroes of antiquity (*die Helden der Jugend*, TdR 75)—and of modern operas—who eternally incarnate the "naive faith of all poetry" in the unity of fate and character. Even heroes like

Ariadne, "crying on solitary isles," or like Orpheus or Dante, "who plum-
met to the very gates of hell," are always "led" (*geführt*) by a god who gives
their path "the atmosphere of security" (TdR 75). This vision of heroic youth
predictably introduces a contrast between the ancient unity of life and its
modern dissolution. Out of this familiar setup, Lukács attempts a freehand
reading of the demonic. Unlike Goethe, for whom the demonic is *always* only
a placeholder for the various possible combinations of life's basic determinants, Lukács interprets it as the modern lack of a coherent and universal
system of meaning, causation, and determination. In Goethe, all conceptions
of the demonic in all eras are relatively unsuccessful attempts to give reason
and coherence to underlying uncertainty. But for Lukács, the term declares
the bankruptcy of the modern world when it comes to providing coherent
paths that would offer even the "atmosphere" of security.

One might attribute the difference between Goethe's conception and
Lukács's either to the increasing uncertainty of the modern world, or, on the
other hand, to an increased expectation that the world *is meant to be* a safe
place. Lukács addresses this question of modernity's theological or metaphysical deficits: "The gods that have been driven out [*vertrieben*], or which
have not yet come into power, become demons" (TdR 75). Lukács's image of
modernity is that of an interim, the *long* interim that followed the dissolution
of the ancient world. Though literally ancient history, this collapse remains
utterly contemporary for Lukács. The holdover in modernity of *all* poetry's
misguided "youthful" faith in the formative power of character produces the
hero's "Luciferian defiance" (*luziferischer Trotz*, TdR 80). Heroes may have
always been defiant, at least potentially, but what makes them modern and
Luciferian is the complete deregulation of this defiance in a "godless world"
(TdR 81). The *young* hero, even in modernity, wants to be *a real* hero, a hero
for *all time*, who can live up to the standards of antiquity. No longer "led"
by divinity, he is possessed of a "demonic" psychology (TdR 79)—closed and
self-sufficient "like a work of art or a divinity" (TdR 86). This modern situation makes him even more heroic and precisely demonic because, without
divine guidance, he must stage and execute the entire performance himself.
What this hero lacks, however, in his emulation of the heroic feats of antiquity, is the narrator's knowledge, gained through hard experience, that the
heroic model is no longer current—no longer possible. The narrator knows
that modern heroes are not led by gods, but must search for them—only to be
abandoned. Antiquity's Luciferian role in the modern world causes modern
heroes to fail. The modern world is seduced into believing in unified forms
that no longer apply. The Orphic "Urworte" may have once defined a coherent system, but for us their relation has dissolved into a complete non-relation.

The demonic in Lukács's theory of the novel thus breaks into two variants:
(1) on the side of the hero, there is the "Luciferian" aspect, which stands for
the pressure that ancient ideals exert in the modern age. The Greek inheritance becomes virulent whenever it is approached with the expectation of its

modern realizability. Further complicating matters is the fact that precisely this expectation seems to be not only that of artists or heroes in novels, but of numerous political programs. (2) The second aspect is the "demonic" irony located on the side of the narrator. Demonic insight into the demonic means recognizing that there is no divine plan. This perspective knows the truth about the "Luciferian" status of inherited ideals and knows the hopelessness of all attempts to realize them in the current state of the world. The sum of these two aspects is that in modernity—and in the novel—the demonic irony of the narrator's perspective trumps and relativizes the hero's "Luciferian" defiance. The latter has only the status of a misunderstanding, a misplaced classicism. The demonic quality of the modern world is displayed in the novel as the incoherence of an existential coordinate system that would be both subjectively meaningful *and* objectively valid. The "demonic" atheism of a world without gods ultimately impacts not only the modern applicability of ancient *Urworte,* but every conceivable system of relation and coherence, whether it be fate and character, individual and society, means and ends, history and progress, law and order, lifeworld and system, and so on. In the completely ironic novel, every thinkable basis of narration would be retracted and crossed out. A "demonic" or "godless" world is one of the instability of every attributed meaning. *Attributed* meaning is the only meaning: significance can be generated relatively and subjectively—ironically—but never presupposed as immediately given or collectively or intersubjectively reliable.

The theological master-narrative that emerges from Lukács's reading of the demonic is that of the failure of Christian monotheism[31] to replace the gods that it displaced. The resulting power vacuum produced a world of fragmented powers with limited jurisdictions. A Gnostic situation dominates: "the being of the new God is borne [*getragen*] by the passing away [*Vergehen*] of the old one" (TdR 76). At the very end of the section, Lukács introduces this "Gnostic" theologeme even more dramatically as the culmination of a series of metaphysical poles that narrative irony, "itself demonic," encapsulates in the "metasubjective *Dämon*" of the hero. Irony, unable to find a world proper to itself even after it has finished tracing the path of the martyrdom of the protagonist's subjective interiority, encompasses (1) the narrator function as "the *Schadenfreude* of the creator-God at the failure of all weak insurrections [*das Scheitern aller schwachen Aufstände*] to overturn His powerful yet insignificant, botched creation [*sein mächtiges und nichtiges Machwerk*]" and (2) the protagonist function as "the inexpressibly sublime suffering of the redeemer-God at His inability to come in this world [*über sein Noch-nicht-kommen-können in dieser Welt*]" (TdR 81–82).

It is not easy to determine the precise sense and reasons for Lukács's presentation of the novel's formal polarities in terms of a Gnostic—Marcionistic—dualism of Creator vs. Redeemer. This specification or redefinition of what he understands as the "state of the world" risks ruining the in any case dubious historical specificity of his conception of modernity, which was previously interpreted as a discontinuity with respect to a different origin (that of Greek antiquity). If, on the other hand, the talk of creators and redeemers, old gods and new gods, gods and demons, is not taken literally, but only as an extended metaphor, an elaborately ornamented analogue of the "modern" situation, it would have a devastating effect on the persuasiveness of the philosophy of history upon which Lukács's thesis is premised. If *naming* of the demonic only allows for improvised "metaphorical" extensions, then the result is only a confusing exaggeration that casts doubt on the initial theoretical claims.

It is also not easy to justify Lukács's decision to quote the most famous lines on the demonic. Goethe's words neither follow directly from Lukács's thoughts about demons as dethroned gods (TdR 75), nor do they lend any direct support to his next claim that "the novel is the epic form of a world that the gods have abandoned" (TdR 77). In this context, Goethe's words seem to testify to the *experience* of life in a godless world:

> It [the demonic] was not divine [*nicht göttlich*] . . . , because it seemed to lack reason [*es schien unvernünftig*]; it was not human, because it had no understanding [*hatte keinen Verstand*]; it was not devilish, because it was beneficent [*wohltätig*]; not angelic, because it often betrayed *Schadenfreude*. It was like chance [*Zufall*], because it did not prove consequent [*beweise keine Folge*]; it resembled Providence [*Vorsehung*], because it gave indications of coherence [*deutete auf Zusammenhang*]. Everything that limits us [*alles was uns begrenzt*] appeared permeable [*schien durchdringbar*] to it; it appeared [*schien*] to arbitrarily operate [*schalten*] upon the necessary elements of our existence [*die notwendigen Elementen unseres Daseins*]; it drew time together [*zog die Zeit zusammen*] and expanded space [*dehnte den Raum aus*]. Only in the impossible did it seem content [*schien es sich zu gefallen*], while disdainfully thrusting away the possible [*das Mögliche mit Verachtung von sich zu stoßen*]. (TdR 76)

Lukács offers no direct comment or interpretation on this enigmatic passage. He also makes no special effort to introduce or mediate Goethe's words. An interpretive commentary would have bordered on superfluity in any case, insofar as the passage itself has the form of a riddle, the answer to which is given as "the demonic." It would be ludicrous to try to add or subtract from Goethe's meticulously crafted personification, and every attempt to "solve" the riddle and call the demonic by another name would only reduce it to a more familiar and non-enigmatic conception.

By foregoing interpretation, the main role of this quotation in Lukács's text is to be enigmatic—and perhaps to give credit to one of his theory's sources. The Goethe quote is a cipher or token, which Lukács uses to characterize the world of the novel and the psychological dynamic of its protagonist-narrator couplet (which is the main topic of his theory's first part). By explicitly introducing the demonic in the Goethe citation, he installs a hiatus between the name ("the demonic") and the thing it refers to (the modern state of the world that gave rise to the novel). Such a rupture is inevitably introduced whenever the demonic is called by name: as a name for the problem of the relation of fate and character, of human development and socialization, "the demonic" can only be highly improper. When any relation—including that of protagonist and narrator—is formalized as "demonic," it is an affront to the expectation of coherence implied by the analytic terms that underlie it. From a certain perspective, in other words, the idea of the demonic always sounds like an exaggeration or a distortion. Terms of relation like "individual and society," "freedom and history," "fate and character," "part and whole" implicitly presuppose the possible coherence of their objects, whereas the demonic blasphemously assumes that such categorical relations reflect only nebulous interrelations or non-relations.

The word "demonic," already in Goethe, comes with a strong presupposition of incoherence, and "a world forsaken by god" *means* the demonic instability of meaning for which the word "demonic" is only the placeholder. Lukács, however, was not necessarily ready to resign himself to the world of this word. His citation of Goethe on the demonic produces an exposed moment similar to the introduction of the Luciferian in the *Heidelberg Aesthetics*, but it does so with respect to familiar dualisms. The interjection of the demonic shows Lukács himself to be ironically focused on the potentials of Luciferian heroes. He casts himself as a demonic ironist—a narrator who sings the downfall of the Luciferian in the face of the demonic. But even when his own discourse reflects the narrator's demonic irony, it leads him back to the problems of the heroes. Though he knows the demonic, the modern, he is fixated on mythic and tragic heroism, on divinely secured and representative experiences. The Luciferian hero promises an experience and perhaps even a victory that can, the narrator hopes, just as easily happen without gods or in defiance of them. The experience of the Luciferian, of the realization of art's promise—even vicariously, artistically, and in its failure—may be the best the modern world can hope for.

The constant permutation of the ancient-modern dualism (projected, for example, onto the protagonist-narrator relation) follows a logic of "overextended transcendence"[32] that results from the condemnation of *this* world. The problem is brought to a point at the end of part 2 of *The Theory of the Novel* in words borrowed from Fichte on the "perfected sinfulness" (*vollendete Sündhaftigkeit*, TdR 137–38) of the modern and (novelistic) world. In context—with Dostoyevsky pointing to the horizon—this stereotypically "Gnostic" insight into the utterly debased state of the historical world clearly contrasts with a promise of future redemption. The assumption of a cosmic conflict between a heroic Redeemer and an incompetent Creator whose main attribute is *Schadenfreude* ironically reflects the extremes of the narrator's possible relation to the hero, but it may also be a symptom of Lukács's search for a *real* hero to restore meaning to the world. The demonic is invincible to the extent that it is defined by the limits of time and space, whereas the Luciferian, incarnated in the demonic hero "who thrives on the impossible," represents the possibility of the demonic's impossible overcoming. The Luciferian is only Luciferian as long as it falls and fails. If Lucifer succeeds, he turns out to be the Redeemer. If he succeeds, he lives up to his name—"light-bringer"—and restores meaning and unity to the world. The demonic in Goethe's conception, by contrast, does not imply an eschatological horizon or a philosophy of history; to the contrary, its philosophy of history, to the extent that one can speak of one, posits the absence of such horizons. Goethe also does not dualistically pit various aspects of the demonic against each other; his famous words on the demonic from *Poetry and Truth* proceed strictly through figures of negation ("not divine, . . . not human, . . . not devilish," etc.) and resemblance ("resembled," "appeared").

Lukács perceived that the problem of the demonic has two sides (a serious one and an ironic one), but he was not ironic enough—perhaps not old enough—to perceive that consequent irony will always trump the philosophy of history. As a reader the young Lukács took the problems of heroes seriously, whereas the aging Goethe, when he came to write about the demonic, looking back on his youth in his later years, is clearly a "narrator" in Lukács's sense. And this represents the minimal premise of a demonic philosophy of history: demonic irony, *Schadenfreude,* comes after the age of heroes.

Epilogue on Gnostic Relapses

Lukács's "Gnostic" turn in *The Theory of the Novel* anticipates postwar debates on the demonic, which crystallized around the figures of Carl Schmitt and Hans Blumenberg.[33] In the terms of this later debate, the demonic, and especially the "monster motto" (*der ungeheurere Spruch, Nemo contra deum nisi deus ipse,* "only a god can go against a god") either formats (according to Schmitt) a Gnostic-dualistic conflict that is inherent to monotheism, or else (according to Blumenberg) it is the formula of a mythic-polytheistic balance of powers in which individual self-assertion is both possible and ethically allowable but simultaneously subjected to an extensive system of limitations and checks. What Lukács shows in this context is how difficult it may be to separate these two options—given that the decision between them is never simply a question of how to read Goethe. The case of Lukács poignantly shows that even (and especially) the highest levels of reading are never free from political-theological and metaphysical assumptions.

Goethe's work, and especially his idea of the demonic, perhaps unsurprisingly, provides the ideal stage for playing out metaphysical intuitions. If Lukács shows anything, it is that the demonic can easily become the medium for the kind of self-seeking and self-finding that defines the "quests" of modern heroes. But what any given individual actually finds under the heading of the demonic is ultimately governed by the vagaries of the demonic itself. Certainly, it is easy to stand against anti-modern Gnostic "recidivists"—especially when they are characterized that way. But, then again, perhaps it is not so easy, when things get serious. The young Lukács was nothing if not serious, and in this sense his attempt to use the idea of the demonic to depict the modern world as a world system predicated on unmitigated atheism may still contain some arguments against Blumenberg's idea that the modern world, at least in its ideal state, should be conceived as a stable polytheistic "balance of powers." If Lukács were right, then Gnostic relapses, including his own, would be more than understandable. But to the extent that the "reality" of the demonic apparently lies mostly in individuals' presuppositions about it, this might be a minimal reason—assuming one is needed—to side with Blumenberg.

The demonic in Lukács's conception, like Spengler's, tends to anticipate crises, toward which it can only relate as an overreactive overcompensation in the direction of a form of transcendence that is not only utopian but hostile to the world as such. In contrast with such scenarios, Blumenberg (and Goethe) would assume that the "demonic" state of the world is not uniquely modern, but is only a residual condition, the perennial endurance of a relative lack of absoluteness. This lack, however, is one that modernity and the modern novel have often tasked themselves with overcoming, not always with foreseeable consequences.

Chapter Seven

✦

Demonic Inheritances

Heimito von Doderer's *The Demons*

> Mythic ages display the highest degree of reality [*den höchsten Grad der Wirklichkeit*]. In them, inside and outside are almost one and the same, which means that there are no events that are disturbingly disconnected or merely superficial [*es gibt ein beängstigend-beziehungsloses, bloss äusseres Geschehen überhaupt nicht*]. Everything is real. [*Alles ist wirklich.*] Gods are at work everywhere. [*Überall wirken Götter.*]
> —Heimito von Doderer, diary entry from August 17, 1936

The Demonic Novel

As in the preceding chapter, this one pursues the hypothesis that Goethe's conceptions of the demonic may reflect, wittingly and unwittingly, an infrastructure of the novel that is focused on character in the nineteenth century—and, in a somewhat different configuration, focused increasingly on event and situation in the twentieth century. At the latest since Lukács's strange overemphasis of the demonic, there must have been a general but not necessarily fully articulated awareness of it and of its possible connections to the novel. The demonic in Lukács was simultaneously overstated and implicit, but his grasp of it went far beyond that of his contemporaries (with the exception of Benjamin, who also read about it in Lukács). This situation seems to have impeded a coherent reception—in Goethe, in the novel, or otherwise.[1] Fate and character (the demonic's lowest terms, according to Gundolf) are analyzed by Lukács in a way that mostly avoids reference to the demonic, which is first called by name only in the middle of the theory in a way that can easily make it appear to be a separate topic.

In the German-speaking world around 1920, however, the appearance of Dostoyevsky's novels in German in translations by Less Kaerrick (a.k.a. E. K.

Rahsin) combined with the widely read treatments (by figures like Simmel, Gundolf, Lukács, and Spengler) of the demonic in the context of Goethe's philosophy would have certainly contributed, especially in literary circles, to a general awareness of the demonic. Such an awareness made it possible for authors to intentionally engage with and incorporate the demonic at various levels of the writing process. The difficulty, however, of using existing material as a recipe for writing the "demonic novel" would not have been unfamiliarity (since the sources themselves were extremely well known) so much as the complexity, variety, and limited compatibility of the versions of the demonic in circulation. And another more subtle difficulty is that, according to Lukács's theory, the demonic was *already* the basis of the traditional novel, which he conceived as a genre whose history was essentially finished.

Lukács's philosophy of history implicitly discourages the formulaic application of the demonic to contemporary novels. Lukács argues that the novel—from Cervantes to Tolstoy—was always defined by the *disintegration* of antiquity's unified and coherent conception reflected in Goethe's Orphic "Urworte," which present life and development as a "quintessence." In Lukács's theory, a matrix of coherence stabilized both the "heroic" world of antiquity and its exemplary literary form, the Homeric epic. The dissolution in modernity of this coherence of the individual *Dämon* and its world produces the demonic; modernity is not a secularized but a demonized Christianity, which killed its god but failed to find an adequate replacement. On the basis of this extreme polarization of ancient and modern, the novel's efforts at epic cohesion only produce provisional attempts—pseudomorphoses—with respect to an unperceived epochal rift. The novel tries to reproduce the parameters of Homeric antiquity in a world in which they have fallen apart.

To make this conception plausible, Lukács relies on an absolutely harmonious view of antiquity, which is opposed to an absolutely dissonant modernity. Goethe by contrast often assumes the underlying continuity of all ages and thus does not so drastically split the demonic along an ancient-modern fault line. Benjamin, on the other hand, like Lukács also assumes such a split but sees continuity in his idea of "the mythic," which is conceived as problematic remainder and not as a lost ideal (as Gundolf, Lukács, and Spengler imagine). For Benjamin the epochal breaks are less strict—and the valence of his cultural critique is reversed: he is not against modernity per se, only against mythic holdovers that are masked and worsened by modernity's misguided belief in its own modernity.

Lukács's theoretical architecture is troubled by the nebulousness of his emphatic claim of the non-relation of the modern world and epic categories. Cut loose, without anchor, "homeless," the lost life system of antiquity demonizes a modern world to which it cannot apply; Lukács expresses this as a disconnection of "inside" and "outside," "soul" and "forms," *Dämon* and *Tyche*. This "homelessness" of the modern soul becomes doubtful, however, especially in the second part of the theory, when Lukács tries to illustrate it in the interpretation of novels. For him, novels paradigmatically deal with the life and socialization of characters—but precisely this subject matter can easily give the impression that the split between inside and outside is not absolute. The novel is presupposed as the genre of the incompatibility of epic form and modernity, forcing Lukács to read novels' apparently success- ful mediations of the relation of individual and world as counter-exemplary (exceptional), ideological, or ironic. But the process-oriented depictions of novels themselves may give a different impression: in order to actually write a novel—to design such a process through which exemplarity or counter- examplarity is to be proved—the possibility of a coherent relation of subject and world cannot be ruled out a priori. To the contrary, precisely the counter- exemplarity of novelistic protagonists and their experiences implies that—if anywhere—the connection of inside and outside must be possible here.

Lukács's abstractly historicized conception allows him to claim that the tradition of the novel is finished and that Dostoyevsky is the sole figure who points beyond it toward a new epic genre with a more cohesive transcenden- tal base. The philosophy of history that underpins Lukács's theory would force a novelist who accepted it to comply with a norm whose time has either passed or is yet to come, and thus *The Theory of the Novel* has no obvious implications for a normative poetics of the novel. In order for the demonic to be put to work in new novels, Lukács's utopian anticipation of a new epoch would have to be at least partly set aside in favor of the assumption that the underlying conditions of modernity have not fundamentally changed—and neither have those of the novel. In fact, not much time would have needed to pass for the transformation of the novel that Lukács foresaw to become questionable. His tendency to give "history" credit for changes in literary form also would have encouraged novelists who wanted to write on the basis of his theory to supplement (and contradict) it with some kind of a practical poetics. One avenue for such an unorthodox application is the open system of the demonic—which only partly belongs to Lukács's theory. Especially if a hypothetical novelist were aware of Goethe's conceptions of the demonic, it could be reinterpreted in novelistic practice. The minimal condition for the application of Lukács's theory is thus the willingness to look into his sources as well as other contemporary theories of the demonic.

Beyond these basic requirements, the conscious redesign of the novel based on the demonic would have required an increase in the overall level of abstraction, a willingness to think about the transcendental base of epic form. This theoretical approach precludes both the unself-conscious continu- ation of inherited models and the deliberate revolutionization of them. The former approach would be conservative or merely conventionalist, whereas the latter would represent a willed transgression of the limits of the form itself. Lukács's introduction of the demonic blocks these familiar ways of dealing with inherited genres. In view of novelistic practice, the transcenden- tal presets of "the demonic" necessitate meta-levels, layers of reflection, and an overall increase in self-consciousness. A well-known example of the kind of meta-novel I have in mind—by an author who knew something about the demonic—is André Gide's *The Counterfeiters*. The title raises genre-based expectations that the novel will be about crime or at least about counterfeiters—but these expectations are only partly realized. The title refers, if anything, to the act of forgery—of fiction—through which experiences are turned into novels. Gide's title, *Les faux-monnayeurs*, refers, if it refers at all, beyond content, narrative, plot, or thematic elements to the genre of the novel—but also to the novel of the same title that Édouard is writing in the novel. Gide's novel is, however, not identical with Édouard's; it cannot be the case that *The Counterfeiters* of the diegesis literally *is* Gide's novel—at least not without producing an infinite regress and subordinating external reality to the reality of the novel and thereby reversing their hierarchy. The most that can be said is that Gide's novel is *about* Édouard's novel (of the same title) and perhaps that "counterfeiting" defines both novels' form and content.

In the counterfeit yet exemplary world of *Les faux-monnayeurs*, the secret title of the novel—of every novel—is *The Counterfeiters*. In the same way, Heimito von Doderer's *Die Dämonen* (*The Demons*) is a novel of the novel, whose title places it at the limit of novelistic meta-reflection. Setting aside for the moment Lukács's and Goethe's concepts of the demonic—both of which Doderer was familiar with—the usurpation of the title of Dostoyevsky's *Die Dämonen* alone suffices to make Doderer's novel a meta-novel in the manner of Gide. Since 1906 when *Bésy* (*The Possessed* or *Demons*) was published in German as *Die Dämonen*, the title belonged to Dostoyevsky. The similarities do not end there: the narrator, Geyrenhoff, is a clear variation of "G—ff," the narrator of Dostoyevsky's *Demons;* like G—ff, Geyrenhoff is a self-appointed chronicler of strange events that befall an extended group of friends and co-conspirators; in Doderer's novel as in Dostoyevsky's, the first-person narrator who introduces the story is mysteriously superseded (or replaced) by a semi-omniscient perspective. Such obtrusive connections make it clear that Doderer's novel is a variation on Dostoyevsky's, a reflection of it, a novel about a novel—and not a purely autonomous effort of world-creation.

At the beginning of Doderer's *Demons,* Kajetan von Schlaggenberg accuses Geyrenhoff of authoring "novelistic reports" (*romanhafte Berichte*).[2] These "reports" refer to the chronicle upon which *Die Dämonen* is based (according to the fiction of the novel itself); Doderer's *Die Dämonen* is thus subtitled "According to the Chronicle of the Section Councillor [*Sektionsrat*] Geyrenhoff." One key difference between this design and Gide's *Counterfeiters* is that the former never refers to the novel-within-the-novel by the title *Die Dämonen*. Geyrenhoff's chronicle or "journal" (*Tagebuch*) is a compendium of which Geyrenhoff is—in the beginning—the primary author; he also accepts contributions from others, over which he—initially—exercises primary editorial authority. This, combined with the systematic reference to Dostoyevsky, eliminates the need for Gide's more overtly self-referential device of giving the novel the same title as the "novel in the novel." Gide pioneered the form, but Doderer's decision to "remake" Dostoyevsky establishes a comparable self-referential continuum that highlights the importance of "demons" for the genre of the novel in much the same way as Gide emphasized "counterfeiting." The point in both cases is to introduce a theoretical meta-register that otherwise would have been absent or much less evident.

When the title of a novel becomes an intransparent self-referential device, its meaning is not (as one might expect) hollowed out and emptied, but rather, opened up to the spectrum of meanings that can find their way through the lens of the word "demons." The proper name of the title—*Die Dämonen,* with the definite article—does not evidently refer to the characters or plot events;[3] this makes the title mysterious and causes it to resonate at other levels. This is facilitated by the systematic reference to Dostoyevsky and the fact that his novel also does not exhibit a transparent relation between title and story. The net result is a highly ambiguous relation between the proper name—*Die Dämonen*—and *this novel* (by Heimito von Doderer) and its specific contents. Lacking a clear internal referent for the titular demons, the many ambiguous meanings of the word "demons" become a question and a problem. Doderer thus deeply disturbs the possibility of establishing a single referent behind his novel's title; secret, symbolic, or thematic meanings are also made problematic by the complex system of internal and external references, behind which hide a multiplicity of real or imagined demons.

Even before Doderer employed this strategy, Dostoyevsky's title arguably functioned in much the same way. Thomas Bernhard's autobiographical novel, *Die Kälte* (*The Cold*), illustrates this by referring to Dostoyevsky's *Demons* in a way that makes it unclear whether he means "Dostoyevsky's *Demons*" or "Dostoyevsky's demons." The passage in question describes a literary awakening, the moment in which the young protagonist (who will eventually become a novelist) hears the demonic call of literature. The confusion of *Demons* and "demons" is made possible by the German language's capitalization of all nouns (proper and common) and Bernhard's failure to mark Dostoyevsky's title with italics or quotation marks:

> I read The Demons by Dostoyevsky [*ich las Die Dämonen von Dostojewski*]. Never in my life had I read a book of such insatiability and radicality [*von dieser Unersättlichkeit und Radikalität*] and never such a thick book. I intoxicated myself [*ich betäubte mich*], I dissolved myself for a time in the demons [*ich löste mich in den Dämonen auf*]. After I came back, for a while I did not want to read anything else, because I was certain that I would fall into a monstrous disappointment [*eine ungeheure Enttäuschung*], into a horrifying abyss [*einen entsetzlichen Abgrund*]. For weeks I abstained from all reading. The monstrousness of the demons [*die Ungeheuerlichkeit der Dämonen*] had made me strong, had showed me a way [*Weg*], had told me that I

was on the right path [*Weg*]—the way out [*hinaus*]. I had been struck
by a wild and great literature [*eine wilde und große Dichtung*], in
order to myself emerge as the hero. It did not happen frequently in
my later life that literature [*Dichtung*] had such a monstrous effect
[*eine so ungeheure Wirkung*]. (Bernhard, *Die Kälte* 141)

The language of the passage is typically Bernhardian in its extremity. The
adjectives—insatiable (*unersättlich*), radical (*radikal*), monstrous (*ungeheuer,
Ungeheuerlichkeit*), horrible (*entsetzlich*)—all describe Dostoyevsky's novel
and simultaneously characterize the unbelievably positive and exhilarating—
"heroic"—experience of reading it. The complete lack of any reference to
plot, characters, or themes puts all of the weight on the title, which, especially
in its second and third iterations, seems to refer to "the demons" in a way
that makes it sound like Dostoyevsky's novel *is* "the demons" to which its
title refers. This implication is confirmed a few pages later:

> In the demons I had found my correspondence. [*In den Dämonen
> hatte ich die Entsprechung.*] I looked in the institute library for fur-
> ther such monsters [*nach weiteren solchen Ungeheuern*], but there
> were no more. It is superfluous to recount all of the names of those
> whose books I opened and then immediately closed again, because
> they necessarily revolted me with their pettiness and worthlessness
> [*Nichtswürdigkeit*]. The literature outside of the demons [*die Litera-
> tur außer den Dämonen*] was nothing for me, but I thought: there
> must certainly be other such demons [*es gibt mit Sicherheit andere
> solche Dämonen*]. These, however, were not to be sought in this insti-
> tute library, which was stuffed full of tastelessness and tedium, with
> Catholicism and National Socialism. But how was I to get ahold of
> other demons? [*Wie komme ich aber an weitere Dämonen heran?*]
> (Bernhard, *Die Kälte* 142–43)

Dostoyevsky's novel is *the novel*—against which all of literature is compared
and found wanting. "Demons" is the name of that which all literature deserving of the name should be, and its demonizing effect stands for that of literature
itself. No actual work, however—not even Dostoyevsky's *Demons*—could
stand up to such an idealization, which is clearly at least partly an effect of
what the reader brings to the work. In context, the word "demons" thus refers
to a conversion experience, to the discovery of a calling, mediated in and
by literature; the autobiographical narrator is placed on a path to find—or
write—the works that "demons" inspired him to search for.

At the time when Bernhard's demonic self-discovery supposedly took
place, Doderer's novel was unfinished, but at the time of the publication of
Bernhard's book, Doderer's *Die Dämonen* had become an acknowledged
if controversial milestone of postwar Austrian literature. In Bernhard's

anecdote of his Dostoyevsky epiphany, the title of Doderer's novel may also resonate, perhaps especially in the words "National Socialist" and "Catholic." Bernhard refers to his countryman Doderer obliquely at the same time as he effaces and replaces him with the Russian Dostoyevsky. Creative paternities thus move across national boundaries and generations; this problem is echoed, on the one hand, in Bernhard's notoriously negative relation to Austria and, on the other, to his grandfather Johannes Freumbichler, who inspired him to become a writer.[4]

To produce these implications, Bernhard exploits the specific ambiguity of the word "demons" and the lack of singularity of the title *Die Dämonen*. In Germany after 1956, and especially in Austria, this title existed solely as a dyad, which allowed Bernhard to return to Dostoyevsky and at the same time resist Doderer's appropriation of his title. This reading is confirmed by an interview in which Bernhard criticizes Doderer for choosing the title *Die Dämonen:* "He called one of his books 'The Demons.' Only I never found a demon in there. [*Ein Buch hat er 'Die Dämonen' genannt. Nur hab' ich nie einen Dämonen drinnen gefunden.*]"[5] Unlike Dostoyevsky's novel, which is the incarnation of its title, for Bernhard Doderer's is a misrepresentation. The key to the success of this title, however, in both Doderer and Dostoyevsky, is arguably its extreme ambiguity: a story that literally contains demons might be called many things— for example, *Faust*—but just because it contains demons or is "about" demons, that does not mean that "the demons" is the best title. As the condensation of a novel's subject matter, "The Demons" *only makes sense* if the causations, relations, and dynamics thereby named cannot be captured otherwise.

Beyond this specific literary-historical constellation, the problem with demons is their ambiguity, the lack of certainty as to their presence or absence, their good or bad intents, their precise role in events. This ambiguity corresponds to the "transcendental homelessness" that Lukács attributes to the novel. For him, a world in which there is certainty about the presence and absence of demons, about their precise intents, spheres, and cognizances, is the world of the Homeric epic. Here, regardless of what happens, the fates of heroes are subject to divine wills. Dante actually mapped infernal space, giving demons specific jurisdictions and localizations, but in the novel—in "demons" from Dostoyevsky to Bernhard—it is unclear which powers govern the course of things. Goethe's *Elective Affinities* in Benjamin's reading characterizes this situation as "mythic" ambiguity, the hopelessness of which may be resolvable in momentary flashes of divine meaning (or authorial mourning). Lukács also emphasizes such possibilities, but reads their mere subjectivity and obvious constructedness as a sign of their falseness. For him, the glimmer on the horizon is only put there for show. It is a piece of "congealed transcendence" (*geronnene Transcendenz,* TdR 38) that must be removed if a work is to live up to the title *The Demons*. In this sense, the "demonic novel" would stay strictly within what Benjamin calls the mythic—but not for the sake of glorifying this condition of atheistic incoherence and senselessness.[6]

The complete lack of "congealed transcendence" would correspond to the *Trauerspielbuch*'s idea of baroquely "overextended transcendence." In this sense, the title "the demons" congeals the "transcendent" (authorial) perspective not in the direction of hope, but of hopelessness. It takes a "hopeless state of the world," to which Lukács believes the novel indirectly attests, and directly states it, making it overtly emblematic of the world of the novel. Such a consciously demonic novel no longer presupposes a coherent world, but instead supposes its incoherence in a way that makes every narratable thread seem like an unexpected epiphany. Such a becoming conscious—and *making conscious*—of a given state of the world may indicate, in Lukács's sense, a shift of epochal significance, a change in "transcendental location" and in the constitution of the genre. In this reading, "Demons" is the new proper name of the novel's fully recognized counter-exemplarity. A "demonic" world, in which all forms of development are out of synch, is not entirely hopeless, but its hopes have become completely worldly. There is hope—such as Bernhard's retrospectively stylized hope that he will emerge as a hero—but there is no longer any hope that the world will be permanently redeemed (as Lukács seemed to expect) or that Goethe's Orphic demons will turn out to be divinities.

The deliberate introduction of the demonic into the design of the novel is thus more than the "application" of a theoretical model. For Lukács, the demonic was always the genre's latent paradigm, but, after Lukács, "demons" is the word through which, perhaps partly for contingent reasons, this paradigm begins to make itself manifest.

The Genesis of Doderer's Demons

In July 1936, Doderer writes in his diary: "Around the turn of the year 1930/31, I started writing down the novel . . . 'The Demons,' a work predisposed toward great scale [*eine sehr umfänglich veranlagte Arbeit*]" (TB 819).[7] At the end of 1930 he first read Lukács's *Theory of the Novel*. As promising as this coincidence may appear, Lukács is not the sole source of Doderer's conception. The search for origins leads to complexities,[8] but whatever sources one may want to imagine, the literary attractiveness of "demons," starting with Goethe, certainly lies in their polyvalence, ambiguity, and ability to flexibly encompass many levels and aspects of worldly existence.

Already in September 1925, Doderer uses the adjective "demonic" (*dämonisch*) with a high degree of sophistication as a part of a reflection on how the cultural foreignness of Dostoyevsky's works may have promoted their systematic misunderstanding among German-speakers. Doderer conceives a reading of Dostoyevsky like that of Bernhard's *Die Kälte,* in which the real and perceived strangeness of the novels allow for intense subjective appropriation. "Precisely the non-understanding" (*gerade das Nicht-Begreifen*) of the

Russian character leads Germans (and Austrians) to act "as if they themselves were somehow or somewhere just as 'demonic' and absolute [*so 'dämonisch' und unbedingt*]" (TB 287). The words "demonic" and "absolute" appear to be meant synonymously. The word "demonic" itself, set in quotation marks, may invoke the German title of Dostoyevsky's novel—but the unclarity of what it means is the precondition of the appropriative reading. This unclarity necessitates a further circumlocution in the word "absolute." Based on the *Dämon* stanza of Goethe's Orphic "Urworte," the rendering of the word "demonic" as "absolute" (*unbedingt*) is plausible: *Dämon* describes the starting-state of individual character, prior to all "conditions" (*Bedingungen*) that may be placed on it from the outside. Reflected back at Dostoyevsky, the unconditional defiance of the social order may make his characters seem demonic to non-Russian readers who pretend to such defiance.

This example shows that Doderer was lexically competent with the demonic well before he read Lukács and before he had the idea of giving the title *Die Dämonen* to his longest novel. Beyond Lukács and Dostoyevsky, it is impossible to determine with certainty which sources may have contributed to Doderer's conception, but in the 1920s he must have encountered the demonic in connection with Goethe. According to diary entries, he read the first part of Spengler's *Decline of the West* in 1922 (TB 93, 95); Goethe's *Poetry and Truth* and *The Conversations with Eckermann* are also mentioned in his diaries of the 1920s. A reading list from August 1924 (TB 238–41) contains, in addition to the works already mentioned, *Wilhelm Meister*, *The Italian Journey*, "Benvenuto Cellini," and Goethe's correspondence with Schiller. If "Wundt / Psychologie" (TB 240) refers to Wundt's *Völkerpsychologie* (*Social Psychology*), then this would be yet another possible source.[9]

The 1924 reading list also overlaps to a surprising degree with the canon of Lukács's *Theory of the Novel*. In addition to Goethe and Dostoyevsky, the list includes Cervantes's *Don Quixote* as well as nineteenth-century fictions like Tolstoy's *War and Peace* and *Anna Karenina*, Goncharov's *Oblomov*, Gogol's *Dead Souls*, Kleist's "Michael Kohlhaas," Flaubert's *Éducation sentimentale*, and a slightly more recent novel, Pontoppidan's *Lykke-Per* (*Lucky Peter*, translated into German in 1906 as *Hans im Glück*). However, there is no reason to assume that Doderer based his readings around Lukács. There is no evidence that Doderer read *The Theory of the Novel* in the 1920s, and a November 27, 1930, diary entry gives the impression of a first reading:

I have read the first part of the *Theory of the Novel* by Georg Lukács. Here a conceptual explanation is presented of something that I found out for myself by experience [*auf dem Wege der Erfahrung*]. Though it is written in a different language than mine, certain passages of this book (S. 31ff., S. 41)[10] thoroughly describe the point where I hope to make my mark today [*bezeichnen durchaus den Punkt, auf dem ich heute antreten will*]. (Nov. 27, 1930; TB 367)

According to this note, in 1930 Doderer's reading of Lukács helped him to crystallize his own thinking.

Lukács confirmed to Doderer that he was on the right track with respect to his plans and future artistic ambitions. The overlap of both authors' "canons" thus probably primarily reflects a shared basis for their compatible conceptions of the novel. One notable difference, however, between theorist Lukács and the novelist Doderer is the latter's greater interest in recent works. Of course, Lukács's theory predates many of Doderer's readings, but the inclusion of Rilke, Thomas Mann, Frank Wedekind, and Stefan George reflects a shift toward modernism. In diary entries from the same period, Doderer also notes enthusiastic reactions to Kafka and Rilke (TB 203, 212, 259, 273, 286).[11] Doderer's diaries in the 1920s are also punctuated with reflections on Dostoyevsky (TB 19, 164, 176, 239, 275), whose centrality is underscored in 1925: "Dostoyevsky . . . is today . . . without a doubt the most widely read author in the entire German language (I mean the red Piper volumes)" (TB 287). Only in the later 1930s, after Doderer has begun his own *Demons*, does Dostoyevsky's *Demons* emerge as an important topic in the diaries (TB 584–85, 608, 983–86, 1062). The earliest entry, from April 1933 (584–85), is of outstanding importance. Dostoyevsky's novel appears here together with many other names, words, and phrases; the list is labeled as "thematic" (for Doderer's *Demons* novel?), but its date makes it doubly significant: this diary entry was written a little more than a week after Doderer joined the Austrian Nazi Party. It thus likely—despite the appearance on the list of the term "fulfillment-recoil" (*Erfüllungs-Rückstoss*)—that these themes were noted at a time when Doderer was deeply committed to the Nazi movement.

Despite this clue, the full intent behind such a cryptic list of titles and themes will never be certain. What makes the list important, however, despite the difficulties of deciphering, is its inclusion of many of Doderer's main preoccupations of the early 1930s. Many of the list entries may relate to his nationalist (and National Socialist) convictions at the time; these are fairly easy to identify because they are expounded at length in other entries. The mention of Dostoyevsky, Lukács (TB 584), and the parenthetical inclusion of the word "Demons" (*Dämonen*) are strong indications that the "themes" of the list relate to his ongoing work on *The Demons* (which did not yet have a definite title). Close to the top of the list is Arthur Moeller van den Bruck, the German right-wing publicist and editor of the Dostoyevsky edition from Piper. Moeller took his own life in 1925; his appearance on Doderer's list in 1933 establishes a connection between the political and literary "themes."[12]

Doderer's political convictions as they relate to the work on *The Demons* are fully articulated in the "aide mémoire" to *The Demons of the East-Mark* (*Die Dämonen der Ostmark*, the novel's working title in the 1930s).[13] The aide mémoire, dated 1934, would have been written only a few months after the "thematic" list; as late as July 1936, Doderer composed a diary-letter to the publisher Gerhard Aichinger, which includes a shorter version of the aide mémoire. Aichinger was the primary editor of the *German-Austrian Daily* (*Deutschösterreichische Tages-Zeitung*), a newspaper which was—in the words of Doderer's biographer, Wolfgang Fleischer—"the organ of the Austrian NSDAP-Hitler movement" (Fleischer, *Das verleugnete Leben* 232). Fleischer emphasizes, as does Alexandra Kleinlercher's 2011 biography, that Doderer's publications with Aichinger were short literary texts without a clearly discernible political orientation. However, it seems likely that Doderer hoped that overtly political elements would help him on the way to literary success. In 1936 he moved to Dachau, perhaps in hopes of advancing his career in Germany, and to this end he wrote to ask Aichinger to support his admission to the Nazi literary bureaucracy (*Reichsschrifttumskammer*). The application was successful, but the fulfillment of this nominal requirement to publish in Germany did not bring Doderer any immediate advancement.

Despite the fact he wanted his novel to be "high literature" in the tradition of Dostoyevsky, the work he describes to Aichinger (TB 819–21) and in the "aide mémoire" is a vehicle of nationalist and anti-Semitic ideology. The plot focuses on a Jewish conspiracy, a "three-level *Theatrum Judaicum*" operative within Austrian society (TB 820). The first part of the projected novel, entitled "Stew" ("Eintopf"), follows various characters and their relationships in order to demonstrate the impossibility of Jewish integration and assimilation. The second part, called "Watershed" ("Wasserscheide"), which Doderer never completed, was supposed to depict a parting of ways, a self-imposed apartheid of incompatible elements. Without speculating extensively on why this version of *The Demons* was never completed, I will summarize key points from Alexandra Kleinlercher's biography, which substantially revises previous accounts: the origins of Doderer's sympathy for Nazism are not fully known; they may go back as far as 1927 (Fleischer, *Das verleugnete Leben* 190–91). Low self-esteem combined with Doderer's inability to support himself through his work as a writer may have led him to blame others for his lack of success. This dynamic also played a role in his first marriage to Gusti Hasterlik, a Catholic of Jewish descent. The failure of this relationship may have catalyzed Doderer's anti-Semitism; both versions of *The Demons* can be read as advancing this thesis. According to Kleinlercher, Doderer's enthusiasm for right-wing causes reached its high point in the early 1930s. His move to Germany in 1936, instead of deepening his commitments, was the beginning of his disillusionment. Kleinlercher cites Doderer's characterization of Nazism as a metaphorical "ex-lover" (*eine ehemalige Geliebte*)[14] to argue that opportunism was not his only motive. The diaries of the 1930s confirm this interpretation. Doderer may have been generally susceptible to ideology and authority claims, in which case his literary writing may have given him a means of distancing himself from them. In any event, his turn away from fascism was most likely gradual. There is no specific date when he decisively and finally rejected Nazism—but it was certainly after 1936 (the date which Doderer and others have often put forth). He never officially left the

Nazi Party, and his behavior after the Anschluss could probably be characterized as passive complicity. His 1938 conversion to Catholicism, however, went strongly against official Nazi ideology, and there is no evidence that he was ever militaristically inclined; even at his worst, he never espoused political solutions to social problems. War in particular was never in his perceived self-interest: he was conscripted into the Wehrmacht in 1940 at the age of 46, and this experience seems to have finally shattered whatever hopes he had invested in the Hitler movement. Like Lukács, Doderer was committed to the possibility of revolution and self-revolution—but he also often generalized his disillusionment with fascism into a theory of the impossibility of both individual and collective revolution. According to his 1948 "Sexuality and the Total State," revolutionary transformation—in life as in society—can never be rationally planned, managed, or implemented, but must emerge from the immanent dynamics of life and situation. These changes in Doderer's politics, to the extent that they can be reconstructed, have no immediate bearing on the interpretation of his works, whose style and themes remain surprisingly constant through his long career.

Against this background, I return to my main topic: in the 1936 letter to Aichinger, Doderer does not mention Dostoyevsky's *Demons,* despite the fact that it is central in his diaries. Perhaps Doderer wrote what he thought Aichinger wanted to hear, but the diaries from this period reflect an increasingly careful reading of Dostoyevsky that may have been leading him away from the letter-draft to Aichinger. His initial right-wing reading of Dostoyevsky's *Demons* makes sense up to a point: the novel draws on current events surrounding the figure of Sergey Nechayev and generally explores, in a tone that is at once satirical and deadly serious, the social and ideological fragmentations that result from the alliance of liberal-progressive movements and revolutionary socialism, nihilism, and anarchism—but this reading ignores aspects of craft and composition that are extraneous to the political message. Doderer's decision to copy Dostoyevsky's unusual narrative design reflects a focus on formal elements that do not lend themselves to political messaging. The events of Doderer's novel, like Dostoyevsky's, are chronicled by an unreliable narrator, "G—ff" or "Geyrenhoff"; the narrative itself is anything but linear, introducing a large number of characters in a way that makes it very difficult to perceive plotlines and character motivation. In Doderer's final version, the fundamental unclarities are arguably more coherently resolved, but ultimately there is no clear answer to the question of how the perspective of the first-person chronicler is ultimately synthesized into a coherent multi-perspectival whole.

Going back to 1933 and the thematic list, however, one finds no sign that Doderer was interested in such complexities. The list contains a quote from Dostoyevsky's *Demons,* which clearly fits with Doderer's nationalist agenda: "Whoever belongs to no people also has no God!" (*Wer aber kein Volk hat, der hat auch keinen Gott!*).[15] Moeller von den Bruck quotes this line in his preface to Dostoyevsky's *Demons* (Dostojewski, *Die Dämonen*, 1919, XXII), raising the possibility that Doderer may not have even read the novel to the end in 1933.[16] The line comes up repeatedly, always from the same character, Shatov, who often voices Slavophile sentiments. The novel shows him (like most if not all of the characters) living in a way that is at odds with his convictions; his painful awareness of his latent hypocrisy emerges in the long dialogue with Stavrogin (Dostojewski, *Die Dämonen*, 2008, 339–53), in which nationalism's self-contradictions are highlighted: nationalism, like all -isms, reflects an ideology; it presupposes the inability to immediately belong to a nation that is only *espoused* as an absent ideal to be achieved by way of a political program. According to Shatov's sentence at the end of the novel: "As a result of the impossibility of being a Russian, I became a slavophile" (Dostojewski, *Die Dämonen*, 2008, 840). This sentence, which Moeller does not cite, may even imply that every ideology is by definition abstract and compensatory in its relation to its ideals. Dostoyevsky's novel presents a further devastating critique of political ideology by depicting the ease with which political programs may be adopted, disseminated, and exchanged: Shatov inherited his Slavophile thinking, apparently almost verbatim, from Stavrogin—who himself no longer believes it (if he ever did). But neither Doderer nor Moeller is interested in the formal or anti-ideological aspects of the novel; thus the word "national sentiment" (*Nationalgefühl*), which appears on Doderer's 1933 list, almost certainly refers to nationalism in Moeller's sense.

Doderer, like Moeller, reads Shatov's sentence as a piece of "congealed transcendence"—as the direct expression of the author's opinion or perspective; according to Lukács, such unconditional expressions of authorial opinions violate a fundamental principle of the form of the novel.[17] A few years later, Doderer returns to the topic of nationalism in Dostoyevsky (TB 985); this diary entry is now clearly based on more than Moeller's introduction, and Doderer clearly has difficulty reading the novel as a simple advocacy of nationalism. But he still closes with Shatov's sentence: "Whoever belongs to no people also has no God!" The definitional unity of "people" and "god" is clearly modeled on the one God of *the Jewish people* and *the nation of Israel*—which might lead one to wonder what Shatov's sentence means to a Christian. To the extent that he assumes a plurality of peoples (and a plurality of gods), his version of nationalism is not (Christian) universalism but (idolatrous) polytheism. This background may give a limited insight into why Doderer, born an Austrian Protestant under the Habsburg monarchy, may have looked to Jewish, Russian, and German ideals of nation for an identity that he felt he lacked; his conversion to Catholicism also fits this narrative.

The details of the transformation of the 1930s version of *The Demons* into a different (but still similar) novel have been documented in detail, and the manuscript of the long fragment of the first version, though unpublished, is available to read.[18] The story of this transformation is not my primary concern. I would observe, however, that the "demons" paradigm itself permits vast ideological swings: the title itself posits the ambiguous presence of seemingly malevolent or at least unexplained forces, but the novel by this title need not actually identify or reveal the ultimate sources of demonic influences. It also need not explicitly "demonize" specific groups or individuals. The anti-Semitic version, by definition, would have pursued such a demonization, whereas the tendency of the later revisions is, if anything, to demonize the proto-fascist elements.[19] This demonization is, however, left rather implicit, no doubt so as to avoid "congealed transcendence," and perhaps also because the demonic, rigorously understood, is antithetical to demonization. If "the demons" are finally identified and a single chain of causation is established, then there are no demons anymore. Supposedly demonic forces are thereby localized and demystified. Villains and the dynamics of vilification are thus central to the creation of demonic effects, but the more obvious this becomes, the more the demonic—which inheres in the uncertainty and unknowability of historical and narrative causation—will be eliminated.[20]

"The Pure Types"

Considering Doderer's prolificness as a diarist and in general, and given the obvious importance of the demonic throughout his work, he wrote surprisingly few extended reflections on the topic and none definitively tying him to a single conception. Nowhere will Doderer write or say, even in his diaries, that his idea of the demonic comes from Goethe, Spengler, Lukács, or anyone else.[21] Nevertheless, I have an interest in pinning him down, and thus I turn to relatively far-flung clues that show his familiarity with the demonic in the senses that began to proliferate during his lifetime.

One such clue, perhaps the most important one, can be found in the April 1933 "thematic" list (introduced in the previous section). Following the name "Moeller van den Bruck," Doderer notes—in quotation marks—the decisive words of the *Dämon* stanza of Goethe's "Urworte": "imprinted form" (*geprägte Form*). This minimal citation is set next to the words "the pure types" (*die reinen Typen*), which are followed by the name, in parentheses, of Doderer's main literary mentor, the painter-novelist and Klimt protégé Albert Paris Gütersloh. The Goethe citation, though fleeting—and distressing insofar as his morphological conception here appears in the service of a nationalist and anti-Semitic agenda—is a good indication that Goethe's idea of the *Dämon* may have been a part of the earliest phase of Doderer's *Demons*.

It is not so easy to say what the "pure types" may be. In Gütersloh's work that was most important for Doderer at the time, the *Bekenntnisse eines modernen Malers* (*The Confessions of a Modern Painter*)—also known as *Die grosse und kleine Geschichte* (*Big History and Little History*)—the idea of "types" appears frequently. Gütersloh's usage is close to what Carl Schmitt in *Roman Catholicism and Political Form* calls "representative" types, which, according to a "Catholic" concept of representation (as opposed to the predominant modern "Protestant" economic reason), are the basis of society and of social roles. This role-based representational understanding of identity does not provide a solid basis for reading the idea of "pure types" in conjunction with the idea of "imprinted form" (*geprägte Form*), which invokes a more internalized individual-developmental model. More productive, however, is Doderer's 1929 essay, *Der Fall Gütersloh* (*The Gütersloh Case*), in which human developmental possibilities are theorized in an opposition between two "pure types." Thus, in light of the citation of Goethe's *geprägte Form* in the 1933 thematic list, the "Urworte" appear to have served as the model for the 1929 essay's attempt to explain the origins of a genius like Gütersloh in a world or society that typically does not foster artistic genius.

This presentation on genius from 1929—the year before Doderer read Lukács—is of particular interest because there is no way to ascertain how much Doderer knew about Goethe's various conceptions of the demonic. Even a partial re-theorization of the "Urworte" in 1929 suggests, however, that by April 1933 at the latest he had consciously made the connection between *geprägte Form* and the demonic. In the 1933 list, "imprinted form" and "pure types" are juxtaposed (in the context of themes related to *The Demons*) in a way that suggests a developmental, typological, and morphological understanding of *geprägte Form*. Doderer's reading of Spengler in the early 1920s is a possible source for his knowledge of the "Urworte" and related contexts. This means that when Doderer read Lukács in 1930, the demonic would have been an aspect of Lukács's argument that was already quite familiar to Doderer. Thus it is unlikely, in my view, that in 1929, without any prior knowledge of the demonic, he spontaneously generated his theory of "pure types" and only later drew the connection to Goethe's *Dämon*.

The first section of the 1929 essay is titled: "Two Ways into Life" ("Zwei Wege in's Leben"); the first sentence reads: "A child is born and a new world is thereby made possible."[22] Unlike Goethe's *Dämon*, for Doderer the moment of birth itself is not symbolic of the emergence of a new, unique, and discrete identity—a "world" defined by "strict limits" (*die strengen Grenzen* of the "Urworte"). Instead, Doderer's newborn *looks at* a "new world," which appears at first to be "peculiarly and uniquely deformed," which is "too close" and produces a "correspondingly distorted perspective" (WdD 40–41). Rather than defining the individual as an autonomous entelechy with pre-given limits, Doderer's newborn *sets its own limits* together with those of the external world, in order to produce a "self-made apparentness" (*selbstgeschaffene Anschaulichkeit*). The newborn *is not itself* a new world (and is not pre-programmed with any kind of anamnesis), but instead *creates* a new world in its perceptual misunderstandings of the world it is born into. The main illustration of this is language acquisition: the infant's "own tangled and very dense impressions [*Vorstellungen*]," which it "attaches to whatever words it may have snapped up [*irgend einem aufgeschnappten Worte unter-schiebt*]," define a moment of subjective world creation—which is inevitably destroyed when the infant learns the "fixed meaning [of words], which the adults have all agreed upon" (WdD 41). In this account, the coercive effects of "world" begin very early—with the word. There is no individual before or outside of this world, because the encounter with the "adult world" is by definition the victory of existing conventions over the infant's creation.

The second paragraph introduces the further possibility that the infant might be allowed to work unimpeded on the project of its "world creation" (*Weltschöpfung*). The self-made world of infancy is hypothetically extended and allowed to gain ground against the "real world" ("the chaotic ocean which washes up against the known world [of the infant]"). The only way this can happen, Doderer contends, is if the infant resists the temptation and pressure to use words and names to assimilate an untransparent outer world. If the infant were able to *create* its relation to the world without the "short-cut" of language, then it would be able to remain for its whole life in this "ideal condition" of a self-made world "whose limits [*Grenzen*] precisely correspond with those of its own abilities" (WdD 41). Reflected against the norms of the real world, however, Doderer concedes, most children's realiza-tion of this ideal would produce "the worldview of an idiot" (*das Weltbild eines Idioten*). But such an idiosyncratic and idiotic world would nevertheless be a more pleasant one in which to live, because it would never have to sacri-fice its own primary creative role to the creations of others. It would never be disrupted, in Doderer's words, by "relations with an outside" (*Beziehungen nach außen*)—with the contested realities that define the adult world (WdD 41). The unity of interiority and exteriority, of individual and world—the "home" which Lukács and Spengler locate in the infancy of world history—lies in the actual infancy of all individuals; it is a home that they are always already in the process of losing.

Doderer remarks that the infant's "autochthonous construction of its own horizons" (*der autochthone Ausbau ihres Gesichtskreises*) is the last thing that systems of socialization (Goethe's *Tyche*) encourage. From the perspec-tive of education, it would be inefficient to let everyone find their own way. Even assuming it were possible to allow each their own development, this would be infinitely more time-consuming than a standardized training pro-cess, which distributes a "fixed guideline for orientation" (*ein fertiges und orientierendes Schema*). In addition to this problem of efficiency, Doderer admits that institutionalized autodidacticism would "probably never" suc-ceed in allowing each individual to independently create a valid and viable world (*ein giltiges, lebensgerechts Bild*). In order to avoid producing idiots—which nobody wants, Doderer ironically underscores—"the little god" (*der kleine Gott*) is mercilessly subjected, "long before school," to the "tried and true forms of language, opinion and every other field," thereby "altering and irritating the process of his independent creation (the dubious life-value of which is known to the adults)" (WdD 41).

Rather than a complete split between interiority and exteriority (which Lukács takes as definitive of the modern condition), Doderer supposes that the entire point of socialization is—"breach by breach" (*Bresche auf Bresche*, WdD 41)—to overcome this split. The most intense and effective way of appropriating and affirming the fixed forms of society is by way of "talents," which are the vehicles through which the child (the object of socialization) proves its "specific capacity in the correct and skillful combination" of given forms (WdD 42). The child's first words testify that "it has accepted its parents" and "has given up its ambitions of world creation" (WdD 42). However, the disciplinary force of reality may still produce some reticence, and the drive toward an otherworldly self- and world-creation—a twist on Goethe's *Dämon* that "can never be cast out"—may slumber "beneath the crust" of fixed forms. This situation continues, as in Goethe's "Urworte," until *Eros*—"awakening sexuality"—intervenes and "produces (as they now freely admit) a really authentic connection to the external world [*eine wirklich echte Beziehung zur Außenwelt*]" (WdD 42). As was the case with the process of socialization, however, ironic notes ("as they now freely admit") indicate that even sexuality, like the forms and conventions of socialization, may not define a completely authentic connection to reality that can fully displace the self-made forms of childhood. Especially sexuality may seem uncanny: "This connection, which seemed to completely originate from the most internal and intimate sources, is experienced in many moments, strangely enough, as something foreign approaching from without" (WdD 42).[23] The "dull impact" (*der stumpfe Stoß*) of sexuality nevertheless gives momentum and eliminates "any last remnants of the unfinished" (*alle noch vorhandenen Reste des Unfertigen*) (WdD 42).

Having sketched the norm of development, Doderer turns to his primary interest, the exceptions. The typological division into two "pure types" takes a predictable form: "In very few cases," the normative forces of socialization are not able to "entirely destroy" the loyalty to the forms of pre-childhood (*das Kindergelöbnis*).[24] In adulthood, the forms and forces of normalization may continue to produce a space "beneath the crust," in which the child "continues its secret efforts" while the adult "proceeds through a life" whose reality is not fully admitted. The grown child feels "strangely separated" from reality "as if by an empty space" (*wie durch einen stets noch vorhandenen leeren Raum getrennt*, WdD 42). Such a distance from the norms and forms of life, Doderer emphasizes, does not produce "productive members of society"; this "type"—initially defined negatively by its discomfort with given forms—is not "sympathetic" with the others who promptly and unquestioningly conformed. Doderer's construction, in contrast with that of the young Lukács (who believed in a complete split between interiority and exteriority, between "soul" and "forms" as definitive of modernity), admits the normality of norms and characterizes the strong split between inside and outside as an exception with respect to a universal developmental potential. There is no way to decide between these two theories—but they have very different implications with respect to the givenness of norms: Lukács's model denies given forms legitimacy to the degree that no souls can find a genuine home in them, whereas Doderer—closer to Spengler—accepts their legitimacy based on the assumption that there will always be some kind of alienated and alienating regime of forms, languages, and conventions. The world's forms are legitimate to the extent that the production of forms is inevitable. Doderer thus focuses on the question of what individuals can possibly do with or against an unpleasant superstructure of externally imposed forms.

The difference between the form-acquirers and those who tend to be idiotic is the basis of the theory of the two "pure types" or "two physiognomic peoples" (*zwei physiognomische Völker*) that inhabit our "civilized life" (*zivilisiertes Leben*, WdD 42). Doderer's reliance on the idea of physiognomic tact—*physiognomischer Takt*, a conception from Spengler—suggests that the developmental difference between the two types is immediately evident on the surface, even if its causes go unrecognized. The two types are: (1) the creative type who is in touch with his or her "inner child" and (2) the outwardly successful type who is completely in touch with current forms. Doderer concedes that there is a whole spectrum of intermediary possibilities, but for the purposes of his theory he focuses on the two "pure types." The second type (the one with great facility in acquiring forms) is not a rare specimen, whereas the pure form of the "creative type" is almost impossible to discover: "The one population is large, the other is diminishingly small" (*Das eine Volk ist groß, das andere verschwindend klein*, WdD 42). Intermediary forms and numerical differences notwithstanding, the two pure types represent a "fundamental difference" (*ein gründlicher Unterschied*) which, unlike Goethe's *Dämon*, does not play out at the level of character, but is foundational for a difference of spiritual or intellectual type (*geistiger Typus*, WdD 42).[25]

Doderer addresses the lack of any pure examples of the second pure type. One might imagine, not wrongly given the time and his political leanings, that the "spiritual type" will turn out to be a spiritual elite—but this intent is impeded by the near impossibility of discovering or producing this type in its purity. To the extent that the theory of pure types is only meant to introduce the artistic physiognomy of Albert Paris Gütersloh as the epitome of a new kind of genius, the theorization of the "pure types" can be taken with a grain of salt. But my claim is that this material remained of great importance for Doderer, especially in his *Demons* project. The pure types provided building blocks not only for the unfinished manuscript of the 1930s, but also for the published version. Based on the plans of the version from the 1930s, recorded in the "aide mémoire," it appears that the anti-Semitic "watershed" was to be subordinated to a final apotheosis of "spiritual purification" centered around the figure of "Kajetan's teacher" (Kyrill Scolander in the published version).

"Scolander" was a pseudonym, not only in the novel but also in Doderer's diaries, for Albert Paris Gütersloh. Kajetan, on the other hand, is a writer and Doderer proxy who contributes to Geyrenhoff's novelistic reports; Kajetan is identified at the beginning of both versions of the novel as the author of a book about his teacher, the writer-painter Scolander.[26] The last paragraph of the aide mémoire projects an ending in which Kajetan's teacher, "only occasionally named in the novel and indeed only in connection with one of Kajetan's books on his teacher's biography," "constitutes, so to speak, the symbolic center for the new circle, which has now been purified" (*bildet sozusagen den sinnbildlichen Mittelpunkt für den jetzt neuen, gereinigten Kreis*);[27] the new direction of the circle, its "spiritual position" (*spirituelle Stellungsnahme*), is "most strongly embodied by precisely this one man" (*sich eben in diesem einen Mann am stärksten verkörpert*). At the very end of the novel, Kajetan will give a speech on "the new empire" (*das neue Reich*).

Given the almost thirty-year genesis of *The Demons*, it could hardly be expected that Doderer would precisely follow the initial plan. The attempted ideological revision is another story, but, all things considered, what is most surprising is that he finished it at all—and that he, in many large and small ways, mostly retained the original conception. The final chapter of the published version is still called "Schlaggenberg's Return" ("Schlaggenbergs Wiederkehr"), just as it is called in the last paragraph of the aide mémoire, but rather than a "watershed," in the end of the published version the characters go their own ways at the end of the 1920s, with the future history of the twentieth century looming. Rather than a new coherence of the circle around its master, Scolander (a.k.a. Gütersloh), the published ending centers around various inheritance stories, marriages, and the burning of the Justizpalast in Vienna on July 15, 1927. Doderer had always intended to incorporate the latter event, but in the published novel this event is without unifying function with respect to the circle of friends and co-conspirators; the marriages that tie up the various plotlines are also represented as entropic with respect to the unity of the circle. Rather than discovering a new spiritual center, the group splinters.

Focusing on the implementation of the theory of "pure types" between the two versions of *The Demons* circumvents the question of Doderer's personal convictions. At a pragmatic level, in the 1930s the nationalist and anti-Semitic narrative of the aide mémoire would have become increasingly irrelevant.[28] Even under the pretext of "backward-looking prophecy" (DD 11, 301), utopian social transformation through racist self-segregation and the crystallization of "pure spiritual types" would have been superfluous after the Nuremberg laws. Established National Socialism had little to offer to Doderer's antisocial "creative types." The anti-Semitic and pan-Germanic nationalist agenda of the aide mémoire thus lost its object. Regarding Gütersloh, it is a question of the degree of disillusionment that Doderer may have experienced: by the 1950s it would have been pointless—recalling Egon

Schiele's 1918 portrait of Doderer's master—to make *The Demons* a pedestal for a self-styled genius of an earlier era. What does endure in the 1950s, however, is the 1929 theory's assertion of the difficulty or even impossibility of realizing the second pure type. This unrealizability sets limits on the overtly idealized (counter-exemplary) models of self-realization presented by the figures of Leonhard Kakabsa and "Kaps" (who are new to the published version of the novel).[29] Both are also eccentric to the circle, which fails to define the difference between the novel's "central" and "peripheral" characters.

The introduction of new exemplary characters extrinsic to the circle of *die Unsrigen* ("our group") is significant; it is also possible to identify many of them as cases of "latent genius" (*Genie in Latenz*).[30] In Kaps and Kakabsa, the creative type's fundamentally autodidactic relation to world and forms comes closest to being realized. But this realization does not occur in figures of great societal, historical, or political significance, but, to the contrary, in characters who measure success in their own terms. Among even more minor characters, the figurations of "genius in latency" become shadowy and nocturnal: undeveloped autodidacts are demonic and hybrid existences, grotesques who populate and cultivate private worlds at the margins of society. Regarding such figures, Doderer's 1929 description of "creative types" applies: "The smallest minority appears in relatively coherent shapes [*in einigermaßen ausgeprägten Gestalten*], but mostly only in every conceivable more or less poorly worked out—blurry or distorted—preliminary stage [*in allen möglichen mehr oder weniger übel geratenen, verschwommenen oder verschrobenen Vorstufen*]" (WdD 42). What goes for geniuses in latency who are unable to achieve a coherent shape also obtains for many of "our group"—who may not be geniuses, but who are uncomfortable with their current state of latency. They are not demonic in the sense that they have strong characters, but because they are suspended at a purgatorial phase in a perhaps impossible development.

No figure in *The Demons* represents this more than "Quapp," Charlotte von Schlaggenberg, Kajetan's sister, who stands at the center of the novel's multiple inheritance narratives. Her nickname (*Kaulquappe* = "tadpole") designates her as an unfinished nature, and her life is lived, in the words of Doderer's Gütersloh essay

> as if in two parts, . . . like a compound word that produces a contradiction or like a name that is composed of a natively familiar surname and a strangely foreign first name [*aus einem heimatlich vertrauten Zunamen und einem seltsam fremdländischen Vornamen besteht*] and thus cannot be pronounced without breaking apart in the middle [*beim Aussprechen in der Mitte entzweibricht*]. (WdD 44)

I will let the xenophobic potentials of this analogy pass without comment. The main reason to cite them is that "Quapp," like her author "Heimito," fits the bill. None of her names are proper: known as "Quapp" and also "Lo," her last name is not that of either of her biological parents ("Ruthmayr" and "Charagiel"); her given name, "Charlotte," is the diminutive of the French "Charles," which sets it off against the bombastically Germanic surname "von Schlaggenberg."[31] Charlotte was a bastard child, who, adopted as a baby by the Schlaggenbergs, turns out to be the recipient of multiple inheritances. A farce like this can hardly be presented without irony, and the narrator, Geyrenhoff, is aggressively critical of the effects of these inheritances on her development. But at least superficially, Quapp's story appears to have a happy ending: her multiple *monetary* inheritances seem to resolve the contradictions of her biological inheritance (the disharmony of the characters of parents she never knew) *and* within her "spiritual" development; previously a struggling violinist, Quapp's newfound wealth and marriage lead her to abandon her creative efforts, which retrospectively look like they were always a false path.[32]

The novel's depictions of Quapp leave no doubt that reconquests of the inner realm of childhood are painful and do not always work out. Quapp's brother, Kajetan, claims that she, like her mother, "knew how to inherit" (*Sie hat zu erben verstanden,* DD 1077, 1141) and that this ability will allow her to resolve the dissonances of her various inheritances. Beyond the irony of the phrase "knowing how to inherit" (which suggests that one could be skilled in passively receiving things that originally belonged to others),[33] the narrator, Geyrenhoff, never accepts Kajetan's interpretation of Quapp's "second biography" (*zweite Biographie,* DD 1077). Geyrenhoff points out that he also knows how to inherit,[34] and in the novel's final pages he violently expresses his unhappiness with the transformations brought about by the monetary realization of the other half of Quapp's biography. His final reflections (DD 1344–45) are provoked by his anger that Quapp, after her inheritance, never asked him about her former boyfriend, Imre Gyurkicz, whose death Geyrenhoff witnessed on July 15, 1927. Gyurkicz can hardly be counted as a character who comes off well in *The Demons,* but Geyrenhoff suddenly and unexpectedly comes to view him differently after witnessing Imre's death: "truly he [Imre] became my friend at the very last moment!" (DD 1344). This aside in the novel's final scene repeats an earlier line, which Geyrenhoff uttered to the Hofrat Gürtzner-Gontard at the time of Imre's death: "'he was a friend of mine' (now I could really say it!)" (DD 1249).

The reason for this change of heart, apparently, is that Imre, whom Geyrenhoff and others clearly perceive as a superficial and outwardly oriented "successful type" with excessive facility in acquiring finished forms, was ultimately able to resolve the contradiction between inside and outside. Imre, "unlike Quapp," Geyrenhoff writes, "was finally able to resolve" his version "of her 'trema'-cramp, to annihilate his darkest, most deeply internal, abject ignominy [*Schmach*]" (DD 1249). The strange word "trema" is (among other things)[35] a diacritical mark (¨) that looks like the German umlaut but indicates (unlike the umlaut, which produces diphthongs) that two adjacent vowels are to be pronounced separately (as in the word "naïve"). This meaning of *trema* is, however, not the primary one in *The Demons:* Geyrenhoff clearly uses the word to refer to a problem that affects Quapp's vibrato; she suffers from a *trema*, which causes her fingers to tremble in a way that negatively affects her tone production (DD 943–44). The diacritical mark is, however, perhaps also relevant as yet another figure of Quapp's split identity. In any case, Quapp's spastic performance (DD 1007) is interpreted by the narrator (who is not Geyrenhoff in this case) as the symptoms of a wound—a trauma:

> Her experience of the *trema* was the most deeply seated, the darkest in Quapp's life up to that point, a dark scar in the core of her person and simultaneously a demon [*ein Dämon zugleich*] that came to her as if entirely from the outside as soon as she was supposed to show her art. (DD 944)

Quapp's daemon, the core of her person and identity, is "simultaneously" a demon (*Dämon*), which torments her "as if from the outside" as soon as she tries to express what is inside.[36] No longer a problem of character (as in Goethe), here, as in the theory of pure types, the daemon-demon represents the contested point between a *new* self-creation and the inability or unwillingness to master or comply with inherited forms. A few pages later, the idea of the *trema* is used as a metaphor for a more general problem: Imre, despite his superficiality and because of the impending failure of his relationship with Quapp, is suddenly able to look beneath his own surface to discover "the wound, the dark scar at the core of his existence, his '*trema*,' one might say" (DD 949). A difference with Doderer's 1929 conception can be noted here: even the outwardly oriented types, who are excessively interested in the mimetic acquisition of forms (without internally *re-creating* these forms), may still suffer due to the forms' inability to fill the void left behind by the unrealized world of childhood.

The metaphor of the *trema* culminates in the scene of Imre's death. Why does Geyrenhoff think that Imre, in his death, was able to resolve his *trema* in a way that Quapp was never able to? The answer to this question revolves around the contrast between the two polar types, both split by an unresolved primal trauma: Quapp tries (but fails) to re-create the prelinguistic world of childhood through art, but she can never "find herself" or "express herself" authentically there.[37] Imre, on the other hand, seeks to find himself in the representational forms of the outside world; this motivates his eclectic acquisition of trophies and "emblems" (DD 949), which fail to meaningfully reflect a coherent interiority. According to Geyrenhoff, Imre manages to resolve his *trema* where Quapp fails, because his arbitrary assumption of poses and postures leads him to his destiny in the end—to his death—which is something different from an arbitrary symbol to fill an internal void; it is something the world gives back to him that allows him to realize an identity that was previously only put on. His death is thus functionally equivalent to Quapp's "inheritance," except that, in her case, it is not clear that solving the *trema* with money actually solves the problem. Money, in Geyrenhoff's reading, may be simply an anesthetic that dulls the pain of the *trema*. This is the sense of his internalized rage during their final farewell at the train station: "Of course, I also—understood how to inherit. But at least I did not have the memory of a hen and—no! because of this amnesia! [*nein! daher!*]—a heart of stone" (DD 1344). For Geyrenhoff, the result of Quapp's lack of memory is an inability to mourn. She not only apparently fails to mourn Imre's death but also forgets the loss of the *trema*, her *Dämon* that connected her to her pre-adult world. Thus, according to Geyrenhoff (in opposition to Kajetan), Quapp does not understand how to inherit, because she does not value her own memories.

Split or bastard natures who spend their lives waiting to inherit—who knows how prevalent they are?—represent the developmental norm of the life stories of *The Demons*. They in no way reflect the process of "purification" that Doderer envisioned in the 1930s. In Lukács's terms: modern heroes will never be purified of their "halfness," which is precisely what makes them exemplary in comparison to idealized counter-examples. The sum of the novel's inheritance stories shows the contingency of development in modernity and in general. Chance (*Tyche*), for example, plays a role in the opportunities and external factors (including money) that govern the fates of "talents" and the specific forms of their eventual realization or non-realization. If Quapp and Imre are taken as cases of the "pure types" that Doderer had in mind in 1929, they reflect—Leonhard's success story notwithstanding—a rupture that runs through every individual, which is precisely *not* healable by the bourgeois happy ending. At best, external pressures fall away and the figure in question becomes narratively uninteresting once the battle with the demon is given up; at worst (in the case that Quapp's real talent is being rich, as Kajetan suspects), the result would be a kind of "demonic" automatism, a purely natural development, a fatefully pre-programmed biological proclivity that does not allow the individual to play a role in the outcome of her talents.

The final version of *The Demons* emphasizes the uncontrollability of the forces that may activate—but more often block—the free use of inborn gifts. These forces may be felt internally (like Quapp's "demon"), but they are shown to originate outside of and ultimately to transcend the internal dynamics of the discrete individual. The Gütersloh essay, on the other hand, suggests a kind of natural selection through which the "starting speed" (*Anfangsgeschwindigkeit*) of the childhood "act of creation and ordering [*Schöpfungs- und Ordnungsakt*]" affects the ability to resume this creation as an adult (WdD 43). Complicating things further, Doderer's early theory of the "pure types" supposes the contingency of talents themselves, which are not simply the "gifts" they are often mistaken for (in the eyes of the adult world) but highly specific *bridges* or *access points* to the given world and its arbitrary forms. The moment of "talent" is thus demonically charged already in 1929, not as an avenue of pure self-expression (of the daemon), but as a highly conflicted space that lies somewhere between autonomous self-creation and the automatic appropriation of inherited forms.

In 1929 Doderer was under no illusions about the fact that artists may belong to either "type." The artist, he explicitly indicates, "can belong to either of the aforementioned physiognomic populations [*Völker*]" (WdD 46). The more raw talent a developing artist possesses, the stronger will be the connection to *already existing* forms—and the weaker and more beleaguered will be "the realm of childhood" (WdD 45). Artistic talents are "specific abilities" (*spezifische Fähigkeiten*) that "are not at home in the innermost cell of the individual [*in der innersten Wesenszelle des Menschen*]" but are instead "encountered there" as "something that is to a certain degree foreign [*gewissermaßen als ein Fremdes*]" (WdD 45). The further problem, as it emerges in the next paragraph, is that "specific abilities," even when the individual is able to make "free use" (*freien Gebrauch*) of them, inevitably become destinies (*Schicksale*)—careers—which shape the external form of life and eventually bring it into line with the given forms of the adult world (WdD 46). The true artistic project (and for Doderer in 1929 also the true *political* project) is the resumption of the unfinished work of childhood. True artists must not only accept and make "free use" of their talents in order to become successful. Instead, the reconquest of the *Kinderreich* forces the individual to "become the destiny of his own talents" (and not only the other way around) (WdD 46) and to engage in a "war against the talents" (*Krieg gegen die Talente,* WdD 49). Gütersloh represented this artistic model in 1929—but the problem at issue is independent of this model. Evidence of this can be seen in Doderer's continued engagement with the "pure types" in the final version of *The Demons,* after Scolander has become a truly vestigial figure. In 1929 Doderer used Gütersloh's double talent (his gifts both as a writer and a painter) to exemplify a "type" who does not accept the self-evidence of a single defining ability. In this model, art draws on the *Kinderreich* and gives its unborn forms expression in the medium of a pre-given and essentially external talent. Art "creates everything anew, which was encountered in the already extant creations of others" (*alles das neu schaffend, was von Anderen bereits vorgefunden wurde,* WdD 47).

This "re-creation of what is already given" results in the creation of something entirely new. This conception is evident in the role of writing in *The Demons.* Regardless of its object, writing is intensely determined by preexisting forms of language and always reflects inherited forms of givenness. A limit case of this is Kaps's dream diary, which transcribes an especially internal form of antecedence. The writer is especially dependent not only on others, but on everything—including and especially language—other, external, or foreign to the self. This relation of dependency is primarily developed in the narrator figure of Geyrenhoff, who intends to "chronicle" the doings of "our group" in a diary, but in the process discovers that "writing simultaneously with the events" implies the "total transcription" (*eine Totalität des Aufschreibens*) of reality (DD 61). He is constantly forced to retrospectively account for the gaps in his past and present knowledge of unfolding events. The passage of time compounds the impossibility of a "total writing" of reality, constantly transforming it into an exponentially greater *total rewriting* of reality. The effort necessary to keep up with even a very small excerpt of the past (much less to keep up with the present) totally exceeds the processing ability of writing.[38] Rather than a mimetic or "realistic" relation, which is completely out of language's grasp, the genesis of a novel as it is represented in *The Demons* only takes its start in an attempt to "re-create" or duplicate what is already there. In the moment when the writer sees that the re-creation is creating something new—out of the depths of his or her "second biography"—the pretense of an objective chronicling is abandoned. The work of writing continues, if it continues, as a novel.[39] The novel is thus the most exceptional form of what *The Demons* calls "second reality" (*zweite Wirklichkeit*); the successful novel is, as Lukács knew, the reconstruction of a "given" reality—but if it is based on an alternate pre-reality that the writer inherits from childhood, then it is far more real and more primary than the so-called reality of the adult world.

Such an approach protects the novel from its own tendencies to become tendentious by reducing its polemical and critical aspect—which for Lukács defines the genre up to Dostoyevsky. In a passage of *The Theory of the Novel* on "congealed transcendence," which Doderer often references in his diary, Lukács states that "the implication of an 'ought' destroys the sense of life" (*das Sollen tötet das Leben*) and that "an epic hero built out of an imperative 'ought' [*ein aus sollendem Sein erbauter Held der Epopöe*] will always only be a shadow of the living individual in the historical world" (TdR 39). At the very end of Lukács's theory, Dostoyevsky stands for the possibility of a *sheer* representation of the world. Unlike Tolstoy, whose works remain "polemical," Dostoyevsky's novels display sovereign indifference—"neither affirming nor denying" (*weder bejahend noch verneinend*)—to history and the representational imperatives of the traditional novel (TdR 137). The overcoming of the novel's critical-polemical character and correlated tendency to idealize is itself an ideal which Doderer, following Lukács, strove to realize. On March 30, 1935, he wrote in his diary:

> Criticism [*Kritik*] of "existing conditions," whatever its object may be, contains a will to improve the matters under consideration, which means the will toward some kind of an "ought" ["*Sollen*," quotation marks by author]. The writer, however, always has to do with the world in me as it *is* and never with a world as it *should be*. (TB 671)[40]

The plan of the first version of *The Demons* is as a massive deviation from this ideal. It is also debatable whether the anti-ideological ideology of the final version resolves the problem. But formally—given the possibility of lapses—the solution, which Doderer borrows from Dostoyevsky's *Demons*, is to splinter the narrating voice into separate instances that are not omniscient and to overtly reflect on their relative cluelessness and differences of perspective. Instead of denying the narrator's perspective and opinion, in this "objective" style the narrative voice reflects a lack of omniscience. The obvious fallibility of the narrator obstructs the production of "congealed transcendence" by leaving the reader free with respect to the narrator's reports and dubious attempts to interpret them. In this sense—in contrast with Benjamin's essay on Goethe's *Elective Affinities*—the "demonic" novel in the tradition of Dostoyevsky is supposed to lack a moment of decisive perspectivization that would point toward an outside or a beyond.[41] In the model of *The Demons*, the novel itself is simultaneously the inside and the beyond. Thus the demonic novel is—or is meant to be—bottomless and uninterpretable in its lack of closure and limitless interpretability. In the end it may not be important (or decidable) whether this ideal reflects a new kind of novel (as Lukács and Doderer hoped), or whether it reflects the old problem of demonic ambiguity (which for Benjamin was always constitutive of the forms of literature and life in the inseparability of truth content and material content). What is certain though is that the universal title for such an ideal or "total" novel is *The Demons*.

On Irony and the Demonic Character

In comparison with the predicament of "creative types," who are plagued by the demons of their failed and partial self-realizations, the "demonic characters" of *The Demons* are fewer and simpler. In an inversion of the "pure types" hypothesis of Doderer's *Der Fall Gütersloh* (*The Gütersloh Case*), *The Demons* follows a presupposition that there are no pure types—or that they are diminishingly few. Unlike the 1930s version of the novel, which was supposed to culminate in a "purification" of the struggling creative types around the figure of Kyrill Scolander (a.k.a. Gütersloh), the published version focuses on the normal situation of creative and non-creative types without explicitly differentiating the two; this can be seen in the Quapp-Imre pairing, as well as in figures like Williams, Drobila, Mary K., and Kakabsa—to say nothing of the younger generations. In the context of *The Demons*, therefore, demonic characters—strong characters or pure types—are in the minority, as are characters (to use Lukács's terminology) who are "narrower" (*schmäler*) "than the external world that is given to them as the stage and substrate of their deeds" (TdR 83). Lukács describes these figures, who are possessed of a "demonic character," as the protagonists of an "abstract idealism." Doderer, however, hyper-aware of the pitfalls of idealism and ideology, explicitly configures these "idealist" types as victims of delusional "second realities" (*zweite Wirklichkeiten*), which refer, for example, to the fanaticism, pedantry, and sexual obsessions exemplified by Kajetan and Herzka.

The key metaphorical depiction of the idea of second reality appears in the fictional 1517 manuscript of Ruodlieb von der Vläntsch, which details the exploits of Herzka's ancestor, Achaz von Neudegg. The sentence in question speaks of a split, of an internal demonization, which makes these characters—who are numerous—distinctly different from those who may be *possessed by* a demonic character: "Undt mir ist, als wuerdt ich aus zweien halbeten mannern wyder ain gantzer; und war von den halbeten der ain von holtz" (And it was to me as if out of two half men I became whole again; and of the two halves, one was made of wood, DD 805).[42] When René discusses this sentence with Williams, he connects it to the idea of "second reality." Williams says: "Back then they called it a demon"; Stangeler replies: "And rightly so" (DD 1023). René goes farther than the theory of the pure types, arguing that not only "abstract idealisms" and creative pursuits (especially writing) but also everyday "opinions" (*Meinungen*) and "worldviews" (*Welt-anschauungen*) are essentially irrational (DD 1023).[43] For this reason it may have been better and more accurate to view every more or less crazy violation of the given orthodoxy of the "adult world" as a form of demonic possession. Such "demonic" impulses are without rational basis to the extent that they are futile attempts to restore a counter-world of childhood. The theory of "second reality" thus supposes a different split between "inside and outside" than that of Lukács: it is a *temporal* split *within the inside,* which produces wildly divergent "worlds" from each individual to the next. This split is not exclusively a problem of modernity, and revolutions in the "adult world" or "social contract"—though some may be better than others—can never (as Lukács imagined) completely resolve the split within individuals, to the extent that the latter are conceived as an infinity of unrealized (and unrealiz-able) worlds.[44]

As in the case of Quapp, the various splits of second realities are produc-tive of demons—or are the product of them. Such demons are spirits that emerge from the depths of individual biography and collective history. Rather than allowing even a partial realization of the dream of childhood, they tor-ment their victims with the experience of unrealizability. This corresponds to one of Goethe's definitions of the demonic, its "thriving on impossibil-ity": *nur im Unmöglichen schien es sich zu gefallen* (HA 10:175). If this is the norm of demonic possession in Doderer's novel, then the truly demonic characters appear to be exceptions or experiments, attempts to imagine what an undivided character or unobstructed self-realization might look like in reality. One such case is Quapp's mother, "the Baroness Claire Neudegg, later the Countess Charagiel" (DD 54). Geyrenhoff remembers encountering her when he was only sixteen, a very brief interaction that impressed upon him the "limitless stupid gall" (*grenzenlos dumme Frechheit*)[45] and "completely inimitable overbearance" (*ganz unnachahmliche Anmaßung*) of her behavior and facial expression (*Gesichtsausdruck,* DD 114). The word "arrogance" (*Arroganz,* DD 114) connects Charagiel to the novel's central villain, Leveille, whose character, like Charagiel's, is primarily developed through the impressions it makes on others.

Recalling encounters with Charagiel and Leveille, Geyrenhoff asks himself the same question as when he first met the Countess Charagiel. It is a question of inheritance: "Where do these people get it from?" or, even more literally: "Where do these people *take* it from?" (*Woher nehmen diese Leute das nur?* DD 114).[46] Almost everyone may have themselves asked this question at some point after encountering an arrogant or overbearing person. The question is not answered until much later in the novel. The importance of this answer is indicated by its verbatim repetition in two different contexts (separated by many pages). In the first appearance, narrated by Geyrenhoff, the Prince Alfons Croix speculates about the character of Charagiel. Croix is himself arguably another kind of demonic character; he is indirectly marked as a Goethe surrogate by Geyrenhoff's characterization of Croix's sidekick, Mucki Langingen, as a "miniature Eckermann" (DD 846).[47] Unlike most of the novel's characters, Croix is a power center without a psychology and apparently without an internal split. But instead of being animated by the demonic "gall" of villains such as Charagiel and Leveille, Croix is a wise and benevolent figure who helps Geyrenhoff in a moment of crisis.

Croix's comments about Charagiel are part of a longer conversation, but—in case the reader missed them the first time—they are cited about two hundred pages later by a different narrator who apparently had access to the manuscript of Geyrenhoff's account of the conversation with Croix. The later narrator, whose viewpoints may make it possible to identify him as Kajetan, ignores the original topic (Charagiel), cites only the first half of Croix's discourse, and reads it as a commentary on the bad company that frequents the Café Alhambra.[48] This narration not only recontextualizes Croix's speech, it dismisses the context and understanding established by Geyrenhoff, thereby greatly expanding its potential applicability to include the borderline and criminal existences of a nocturnal Vienna. This citation thus generalizes Croix's concept in a way that implicitly characterizes the malevolent killer Meisgeier. Either way, however, it attempts to answer Geyrenhoff's question: *Where do they take it from?*

> "Selbst die unmöglichsten Personen mit ihren sicher indiskutablen Verhaltensweisen sind immerhin Konkretion geworden, haben, von sich selbst aus betrachtend, immer recht—sobald sie daran zweifeln, sind sie eben keine unmöglichen Personen mehr—und man muß mit Aufmerksamkeit jene anschauen, welche so undankbare Rollen spielen: denn diese Rollen sind unentbehrlich." (DD 846, 1040)

[Even the most impossible people (with their behaviors that are undoubtedly completely out of the question) have nevertheless become concretions and are always in the right from their own perspective—as soon as they doubt it, they cease to be impossible people—and we should be especially attentive to those who play such thankless roles: because these roles are indispensable.]

The desire to pose an "answer" to a central question in the form of a questionable reflection—not as "congealed transcendence"—may explain why these words were included twice in the novel.

Based on the more generalized perspective of the second citation of Croix's words, which applies them to all "villains" and demonic characters, it is possible to make a few observations: the language of "roles" emphasizes the artificiality of demonic characters; villains do not necessarily see themselves—"from their own perspective"—as villains; the very idea of a villain is first and foremost a literary type, a personified version of evil and things that go wrong in the world. The identification of such evils with specific individuals or groups may give some comfort to the reader or viewer of works of fiction. Perhaps life even imitates art to the degree that it is possible to actively assume such roles. But being someone else's idea of an incarnation of the demonic can never be a rewarding self-actualization, and the introduction of a logic of roles makes it impossible to see individuals or groups as the origin or cause of a given story. The role always preceded the actor, and for this reason, Kaps's imagination of a kraken lurking in the sewers of Vienna is a far more adequate metaphor for the unknown origins of trouble than is the petty criminal Meisgeier, who in the end fails to personify the kraken. The two figures are identified with each other only for the sake of their difference: Meisgeier, who dies on July 15, 1937, is a comic-book killer—an obvious literary device—whereas the "metaphor" of the kraken is an image of everything that unknowably surfaces from the depths. The latter is much more real than any individual "demonic character."

Croix's speech seems to say that even "villains," who are only *perceived* as demonic characters, are ultimately playing a "thankless" yet "indispensable" role. The thanklessness of such roles is obvious, but their indispensability is less so. Croix offers no analysis of why a society cannot function without such figures or how they may have been scapegoated for the benefit of the rest. He implies, however, that apparent "demonic characters" may be the concrete results of either psychological coping mechanisms or of morally neutral aspects of character. The novel's depictions lend little support to this hypothesis, because the sources of such compensations are left in the dark, leaving the reader to ask Geyrenhoff's question: "Where do they get it from?" Because the reasons for apparent malevolence or villainy cannot be known at second- or third-hand (perhaps not even at first), the motivations of "demonic" figures are off-limits for the novel's non-omniscient narrators.

Thus, though Croix's speech invites the consideration of various possibilities, neither it nor the novel can give a definitive answer. Even the implication, however, of the artificiality and externality of demonic characters reintroduces the possibility of a split psychology based on the difference between the *apparent* unquestioning arrogance of demonic characters and the possibility that this unquestioned lack of self-doubt is only a given or chosen role.

As long as there is a split—which everyone has to a degree, according to *Der Fall Gütersloh*—it will be uncertain if a given character *is* demonic or if he or she only *seems* demonic. *The Demons* thus resists the idea that there are any actual "demons" and avoids a narrative politics of "demonization." Literal demons are subordinated to the nebulous causal and interpretive matrix of the demonic. In 1952, in an entry in his *Repertorium existentiale*, Doderer wrote under the heading "CHARAKTER—DÄMONOLOGIE" (*Character—Demonology*): "Every person who realizes only his or her own character is demonic" (*Jeder Mensch, der nur seinen Charakter realisiert, ist dämonisch*).[49] The idea of the pure realization of one's own character seems to have been a prevalent fantasy in the wake of Goethe, promoted both by his life and by his idea of an unchecked demon of individual identity (as *geprägte Form, die lebend sich entwickelt*). The degree to which Doderer invested in such fantasies (or tried to invest them in Gütersloh) is not of primary importance—but, already in 1929, his *Der Fall Gütersloh* presented such a powerful conception of *Tyche* (as "world," "education," and "socialization") that he concluded that the only way for the individual to actualize its demon is to resurrect it in the middle of life. In the published version of *The Demons*, he remains unable to make a compelling case for the realizability of demonic characters.

Instead, the typical self-relation of *The Demons* is described in a 1963 *Repertorium* entry on irony: "Irony is our relation or comportment with respect to the figural remnants within us, to the figures that we were unable to become" (*Ironie ist unser Verhalten [im Doppelsinne des Wortes] dem Rest von Figur in uns gegenüber, die wir nicht haben werden können*, R 126). Irony names the relation to a past self or other self, an alter ego, whom "we" *never were* or *were never able to become*. "We" are always already plural, populated by the remnants of "figures" and characters that might have been. Irony in this sense is the true sphere of the demonic. It "thrives on impossibility" and is the inheritor of that which was unrealized and remains unrealizable. And yet, by retrospectively inhabiting such past possibilities, it is especially the writer—the prose narrator and novelist—whose task it is to realize the unrealized in fictional characters. This corresponds with Lukács's conception of irony as a split between an (older) narrator and a (younger) protagonist, but it fits even better with Goethe's words from *Poetry and Truth*: "We usually learn to perceive the strategy only after the campaign is over" (*wir [lernen] die Strategie gewöhnlich erst einsehen, wenn der Feldzug vorbei ist*, HA 10:183). Geyrenhoff says something similar in the "Overture" to *The Demons,* when he is confronted with the narrative challenge not to depict himself as "less stupid and unknowing than [he] actually was, as we certainly all are with respect to a life that is playing out right in front of us, the further extension and vanishing-point of which was impossible for us to know" (DD 11).

Geyrenhoff was hardly a young man at the time when he played the role of protagonist in his own "novelistic sketches." The novel also cannot have a definitive ending, because its ending and meaning depend on the perspective and the elapsed time from which one looks at it. Though Geyrenhoff claims to "know it all" as he writes the overture, his reflection on his previous state of knowledge indicates that the meaning of events—their eventual transformation into a novel—may always exceed him. For this reason, the demonic novel does not end on its last page—nor in "congealed transcendence," nor in Benjamin's idea of *das Ausdruckslose* (which might be considered a special case of congealed transcendence)—but rather finds its limit, in the sense of the theory of pure types, at the limits of the world.

Conclusion

✦

Transformations of the Demonic

In the introduction, I claimed that the "the demonic is not one (thing)" and that it is a "something." Lest this be taken as an indication that it is nothing at all and that I, following Goethe, have allowed it to expand into all-encompassing vagueness, this conclusion will attempt to answer the questions: What is the demonic? What revealed itself in its reception? And, to the extent that it may be taken as a renaming of other already known or more clearly defined conceptions, what are the effects of this renaming? There are no simple answers, but I will attempt to delineate a series of possibilities:

1. *Failed Secularization.* The demonic is the perceived or self-perceived situation of modernity as the result of a secularization that killed its gods without being able to fill the power vacuum thereby produced. This is Lukács's understanding, which can be put in familiar Nietzschean terms: God was killed, we killed him—but gods remained. The demonic in this sense is not a new polytheism and pluralism, because the "gods" in question are only demons possessed of a limited ability to establish general conditions of meaning, validity, coherence, stability, and authority. Lukács's conception acutely articulates this, but the problem is ubiquitous in the early twentieth century.

2. *The Lowest-Terms of Existential Analysis.* Goethe's "Urworte Orphisch" conceives the demonic as a universal coordinate system of human life and development. Goethe's complex conceptual model would be comparable to the system vs. environment or system vs. lifeworld models of the twentieth-century social sciences, but it was more often understood in a reduced way as a relation of fate vs. character, nature vs. nurture, and so on. The metaphorical registers of Goethe's five stanzas allow wide application to varied structures and systems. Though the *Dämon* vs. *Tyche* opposition primarily reflects birth vs. socialization, *Eros, Ananke,* and *Elpis* emphasize more "adult" factors such as love and sexuality, procreation and profession, resignation, disillusionment, and hope. Conceptions like the "Urworte," including the social sciences' attempts to define the conditions of human development, strive for maximum generalizability. Such conceptions thus often have a metahistorical or ahistorical consistency; this is very much the case for Goethe's "Urworte," but specific historicizations can also be derived from it.[1]

3. *Demonic History*. In Goethe's autobiography, the apparently fixed terms of the "Urworte" dissolve into infinite paths that are impossible to foresee and to unambiguously trace after the fact. The attempt to narrate any specific development, any story or history, in its lowest terms begins to confuse the unique function and discrete identifiability of supposedly separate causal factors. Given the complexity of reducing an individual life or collective history to basic determinants, events and causations become entangled, even and especially if they are approached at a high level of abstraction. The categories of the "Urworte" give the impression of an ordered and possibly objective development, but from the perspective of the one who lives through this development, the process appears mysterious. In life, it is impossible to say what came from nature, what from nurture, and what from fortune. Goethe's autobiography attempts an extended narrative sorting of such factors, but his introduction of the demonic at the end declares the impossibility of a final reckoning. Looking back, chance arguably plays the main role, but precisely for this reason the individual's role in making and taking chances is also a primary factor. This model's extreme degree of uncertainty places it in opposition to the philosophy of history (*Geschichtsphilosophie*), but this does not mean that it is ahistorical or anti-historical, only that it bears a greater affinity to positivist historiography than to meta-history. The master narratives of meta-history, philosophy, metaphysics, and religion are discourses of the repression of the demonic; in comparison to such discourses, the demonic either represents meta-meta-history—as the return of the repressed—or it represents the consequent rejection of all metahistorical and metaphysical truth claims.

4. *Demonic Ambiguity*. The suspicion that there may have been higher forces in play easily combines with the ironic awareness that mysterious "fates" can usually be explained rationally. Reason need not explain everything; it must only posit that everything is, in theory, explicable. This produces a latent differential between natural and supernatural causation, which leads the demonic to be identified with ambiguity. Especially Freud's theory of the uncanny and his idea of ambivalence in *Totem and Taboo* suppose a modernity that continually questions whether "primitive" or "modern" ways of explaining the world are applicable in given cases. Freud's near-contemporaries, Spengler and Benjamin, also produced conceptions of demonic ambiguity, but whereas Freud's theory of ambivalence supposed modernity's recidivism to primitive interpretations, Spengler associated the demonic with pre-ambivalent subjectivity. By affirming the demonic as a desirable form of atavism, modernity is in the paradoxical position of only being able to perceive this atavism through the lens of its own characteristic rationality. Benjamin's conception of demonic ambiguity goes one step further by arguing that the demonic is essentially a phenomenon of ambiguity and that ambiguities are essentially demonic. For Benjamin, modernity is not only subjectively but also objectively demonized by systems of institutionalized ambiguity, which are simultaneously more pervasive and more occulted

than those of previous eras. The ambiguities in question include the ambiguity of law-making and law-maintaining violence, law and justice, law and fate, fate and character, guilt and fate. The belief in the rationality of modern systems—which is, according to Weber, the very source of their legitimacy—systematically represses the fact that these systems remain tied to ambiguous aspects of older systems, leading to a false legitimation and profound misapprehension with respect to the general state of things. The increasingly demonic quality of the modern world is the result of its wildly self-deluded belief in itself as a rational era of disenchantment (*Entzauberung*).

5. *Morphological Demonology.* Goethean and Spenglerian morphology envision a general comparative study of the development of all forms in order to take the pulse of the cosmos itself. In Goethe's morphological writings, the demonic oscillation of *Dämon* (as form) and *Tyche* (as formlessness and entropy) are the systole and diastole, the mysterious and unidentifiable energy that flows within and animates creation. The demonic in this sense is Being or Nature, conceived as a force. This nature is not evidently benevolent, because it only applies to the natural world (and perhaps to art), whereas human lives, histories, and societies are mostly excluded or ambiguous in their relation to its cosmic ebb and flow. That which animates the cosmos is "demonic"—threatening and mysterious—in its relation to "oasis earth."[2] In Goethe's scientific writings, the morphologically ordered universe offers, at best, a precarious opportunity for human dwelling, self-development, and (as Blumenberg would say), "self-assertion" (*Selbstbehauptung*); Spengler's morphology goes further, seeing the demonic threat of "nature" as a predictable pattern, a law of the rise and fall of human cultures.

6. *Demonic Character.* To the extent that the unique identity of the individual is taken to be the decisive element in an existential lowest terms, the demonic is not a *set* of parameters of human development but rather defines the limits with respect to which *exceptions and transgressions* may be performed. In the paragraph of *Poetry and Truth* on demonic character, Goethe interprets the demonic in terms of the outer limits of existence by focusing on individuals who represent a unique challenge, not only within their own historical moment but "to the universe itself" (*das Universum selbst,* HA 10:177). The universe always triumphs over the individual in the end, but the paragraph closes with the "the monster motto" (*der ungeheure Spruch*): *Nemo contra deum nisi deus ipse* (None but a god can go against a god, HA 10:177). This formulation, perhaps due to its clarificatory or illustrative value with respect to Goethe's enigmatic definitions of the demonic, allowed "demonic character" to become a dominant understanding of the demonic more generally.[3] In book 20 of *Poetry and Truth,* however, demonic characters are presented as reactive and representational in their relation to the demonic itself. Such characters, like demons, inhabit an imaginary world into which Goethe fled in order to escape from the demonic. The self-portrait of book 20 shows a protagonist tormented by a pathological inability to decide,

who invents a perfectly unself-conscious and charismatic character named Egmont. Neither Egmont, however, nor his rival Alba define the demonic— nor does Napoleon, who famously represented Goethe's real-world ideal of demonic character. In the context of the monster motto, demonic character reflects the untransparent origins of rivalry, enmity, and titanic striving. The idea of demonic character questions the limits of what a charismatic or single-minded person can do or be despite the constant opposition of chance and history. At the limit, demonic characters may exhibit signs of demonic possession or madness, but, at the more conventional level, they reflect the fascination exerted by heroes, villains, and martyrs.

7. *Demonic Irony.* Heimito von Doderer's novel *The Demons,* which is demonstrably rooted in Goethe, Dostoyevsky, Spengler, and Lukács, focuses on forms and manifestations of the demonic while deemphasizing and problematizing demonic character. His novel shows the limits placed on the development of "demonic" geniuses or heroes (in Lukács's sense) by contrasting such figures against the obstacles to their self-realization in a supposedly "modern" world in which human lives are systematically ordered and institutionally administered. Such systems produce a multiplicity of internal and external checks upon the self-realization of character and talents. In *The Demons,* the human norm is a developmental limbo, whereas heroes, villains, and geniuses—if they exist at all—are indistinguishable from the idealizations of conventional literary types.[4] What emerges is both frustration and relief with respect to the modern requirement of living an unexampled life without precedent or role model. The antidote to demonization thus remains Lukács's novelistic irony, which reveals demonic characters as false idealizations. Irony is also demonic in a different sense: it is only possible in the interim of a "failed secularization," in which things are not what they seem to be; in which the old gods have been replaced by demons; in which a single unquestionable overarching source of value, meaning, and authority has been fragmented into semi-autonomous spheres and perspectives; in which even God Himself—Lukács's "*Schadenfreude* of the creator"—can only be conceived as ironic.

8. *Demonic Political Theology.* The demonic can also be understood as a limit case of theological rhetoric. The transformations listed above allow it to be characterized as a borderline form of what is often called political theology. The demonic is, however, not a typical case of the use of theological imagery to mask political ends (as Blumenberg's *The Legitimacy of the Modern Age* argues against Carl Schmitt). In the context of such considerations, the choice of the term "the demonic" can only be understood as theological rhetoric plus irony, with the irony residing in the fact that what is called "the demonic" refers precisely to an a-theological or atheistic situation. The demonic posits an absence of reliable providential principles (i.e., gods), which does not result in utter chaos or a completely a-teleological void but which produces a world of limited teleologies in which the coherence that

remains is ironically *called* "demonic." The point of the theological metaphor of the demonic, therefore, is that in the absence of gods, there also can be no *real* demons. But whatever is running amok in the world, for better or for worse, is the result of "demons."

This irony behind the idea of the demonic prevents it from being a classic case of political theology defined as the secularization of a previously religious or theological substance that has been legitimately or illegitimately transposed into a modern political and societal form. The demonic is, however, from a variety of political perspectives, regularly invoked to contest the desirability or realizability of proclaimed secularizations—but it is not a "secular" circumlocution of a previously religious concept of the type: "x is the secularized y." Even if one were to hypothesize that the demonic represents a modern version of the ancient idea of fate, this would not be coherent because the idea of fate itself may exist in various modern versions that may or may not correspond to prior "religious" conceptions. Benjamin argues that the correlated ideas of fate and the mythic continued to exist in modernity, which also makes it difficult to see why the demonic should be fate's "secularization." The connection of the demonic to fate only makes sense in the context of an unstable characterization of the transformation of an idealized past moment within a supposedly modern world. The word "demonic" may (negatively) characterize fate, but it implies a belief neither in "demons" nor in "secularization." To the contrary, this idea of "demonic" fate excludes the belief in demons to the extent that it is overtly metaphorical; and it is ironic in Lukács's sense to the extent that it knowingly attributes *something like* demonic influence to a world in which no actual demons are expected to appear.

In a short text by Blumenberg called "Political Theology III" (recently published in his correspondence with Schmitt), he suggests that the dubious and confusing idea of political theology may refer to and express the constantly renewable striving for new absolutes and absolutisms.[5] This definition implies that the non-absolute—the demonic—is characteristic of the secular status quo. Such a demonic state can ambiguously serve both as the pretext for its own overcoming—in the coming of new "gods"—and as the vehicle for coming to terms with the perennial absence of absolutes. The demonic in this sense is both the primary affect of a secular world and the motor of a return to religion.

9. Demonic Remainders in the History of Reason and Rationalization. The following sentences from the scene of Mignon's death at the end of Goethe's *Wilhelm Meister's Apprenticeship* were written well before Goethe had developed his "official" concept of the demonic, but they easily fit into this context:

> Er dachte mit großer Schnelle eine Reihe von Schicksalen durch, oder vielmehr er dachte nicht, er ließ das auf seine Seele wirken, was er nicht entfernen konnte. Es gibt Augenblicke des Lebens, in welchen

die Begebenheiten gleich geflügelten Weberschiffchen vor uns sich hin und wider bewegen und unaufhaltsam ein Gewebe vollenden, das wir mehr oder weniger selbst gesponnen und angelegt haben. (HA 7:544)

With great speed he thought through a series of fates, or rather, he did not think, he merely allowed something to work [*wirken*] upon his soul, which he could not remove from it. There are moments in life, in which the events [*Begebenheiten*] are like the weaver's flying shuttles that move to and fro in front of us and ceaselessly complete a textile that we have more or less spun and set into motion ourselves.

Mignon cannot be revived, and Wilhelm's experience of disorientation and shock is expressed as an idea of the demonic that is not identical to fate but reacts to a fate-like situation. The demonic here is the course of events itself, reflected in the mind of the subject-object of these events; it is the subjective calculation and retrospective permutation of possible *fates* in view of the ambiguity of (1) the degree to which the individual is productive of and responsible for the events in which he or she plays a role and (2) the degree to which other forces and instances may have set the stage and written the script. In the face of events that seem to move by themselves as a *perpetuum mobile* external to the subject, he or she is able to imagine unfolding events as a by-product of his or her intended actions and unconscious intents. This version of the demonic inheres in the individual's contradictory sense of responsibility for events and the simultaneous inability to control their course. Such a relation to events formulates itself retrospectively as guilt: the pull of the demonic is experienced most intensely at a point when it is too late to substantially alter the outcome. As in Wundt's and Freud's conceptions of primitive man's relation to demons, the demonic is essentially a "post-" construction, a relation after the fact to a completed transgression. The demonic is the justified or unjustified, unjustifiable sense of complicity with a finished course of events. Fate in this model is not a single fate, but a serial conception whose mechanics can only be determined partially and belatedly.

Regardless of whether the term "crisis" is used to describe any aspect of demonic events or the reaction to them, the relation to such events is that of a process of rationalization, not in the sense of Max Weber, but as a pragmatic attempt to make sense of a fait accompli. The explicability or inexplicability of the chain in question, its questionable unity and the degree to which it appears to be generated by or to impinge upon the freedom of the subject, makes a difference for the convincing applicability of the adjective "demonic" in any given instance. The demonic thrives on the unknowability of origins and causes; it subsists at the limits of explicability and theorizability. In Benjamin's terms: the demonic occurs within the zone of divine violence, in which an old order has not yet consolidated itself in a new one and the rationality and ends of ongoing events remain undecided.

The existence of such a zone of demonic ambiguity implies nothing about the chains of events that gave rise to it. A sequence of events may be rational or irrational, expected or unexpected, predictable or unpredictable, accidental or necessary, depending on the mode of its analysis and the perspective from which it is viewed. The demonic, on the other hand, depends on a specific perspective: even for so-called primitive man, it is an uncanny encounter with the limits of rationalization based on the presupposition that events can be brought into line with reason (in the sense of ends) and with reasons (in the sense of causes). If this were not the case, there would be no internal calculus, no sense of an unbalanced equation, no demonic anomaly—only business as usual. As a category of event, the demonic manifests itself between "systems" and their "environments"—but its perception is connected to the "lifeworld" of individual subjects. The demonic is, however, primarily an aspect of neither instrumental nor of communicative reason—but the communication of the demonic, the attempt to come to terms with it, implies specific modes of communication. For Goethe, *Urworte* are the medium of intersubjective communication (*Verständigung*) about the demonic. The demonic is also not a question of the rationality or irrationality or the good or evil intents of given subjects: it manifests itself in the subjective inability to perform a successful rationalization, but this inability itself—virtually by definition—may not be rationalizable. Having or expecting a reason for everything may itself be a form of irrationality, whereas the demonic reflects a rational deferral in the application of reasons.

This is not only a conservative finding with respect to the ongoing potentials of traditions called "theory" and their commitments to reason and rationality. My work shows how the demonic shaped a largely unrecognized or misrecognized prehistory of twentieth-century theory (especially of the Frankfurt School). The demonic refers to a structure of historical motivation that puts pressure on the differences between instrumental, theoretical, and communicative reason—and therefore also lends itself to literary formulation. The demonic may consist and persist in the recognition and misrecognition of crises, but it says nothing about the proper response to them or which (if any) genres of writing or action are appropriate or adequate. Thus, in the light of the demonic, one might be tempted to see theory as an increasingly outmoded form of discourse—but for anyone invested in theoretical problems, this suggestion itself poses pressing theoretical questions. What if previous understandings of the rationality of "lifeworlds" and "systems" no longer hold? What happens when theoretical distinctions based on an increasingly tenuous recourse to a specific "state of reality" (*Weltzustand* in Lukács's sense) can no longer be made coherent in terms of an underlying philosophy of history? What if the demonic is, as usual, in the process of shifting its paradigms?

German Text and English Translation of Goethe's "Urworte Orphisch" (with Commentary)

"Urworte Orphisch" ("Orphic Primal Words")

Nachstehende fünf Stanzen sind schon im zweyten Heft der Morphologie abgedruckt, allein sie verdienen wohl einem größeren Publicum bekannt zu werden; auch haben Freunde gewünscht daß zum Verständniß derselben einiges geschähe, damit dasjenige was sich hier fast nur ahnen läßt auch einem klaren Sinne gemäß und einer reinen Erkenntniß übergeben sey.

[The following five stanzas are already printed in the second issue of the morphology, but they certainly still deserve to become known to a larger public. Certain friends have also expressed the desire that something might occur for the sake of their comprehension, in order that what is at present almost exclusively the object of an uncertain premonition be rendered in accordance with a clearer meaning and a purer understanding.]

Was nun von älteren und neueren orphischen Lehren überliefert worden, hat man hier zusammenzudrängen, poetisch, compendios, lakonisch vorzutragen gesucht. Diese wenigen Strophen enthalten viel Bedeutendes in einer Folge, die, wenn man sie erst kennt, dem Geiste die wichigsten Betrachtungen erleichtert.

[In the following I have tried to compress whatever has been passed down of older and newer Orphic teachings, to present them in a way that is at once poetic, compendious and laconic. These few strophes contain much of great significance in a sequence, which, once one has come to know it, make the most important observations easy for the mind.]

Δαιμων, Dämon

Wie an dem Tag der Dich der Welt verliehen
Die Sonne stand zum Gruße der Planeten,
Bist alsobald und fort und fort gediehen,
Nach dem Gesetz wonach Du angetreten.
So mußt Du sein, Dir kannst Du nicht entfliehen,
So sagten schon Sybillen, so Propheten,
Und keine Zeit und keine Macht zerstückelt
Geprägte Form die lebend sich entwickelt.

[Δαιμων, *Demon*

As on the day you were granted to the world,
The sun stood to greet the planets,
You likewise began to thrive, forth and forth,
Following the law that governed your accession.
You must be so, you cannot flee yourself,
Thus sibyls long ago pronounced, thus prophets,
And neither time nor any power can dismember
Characteristic form, living, self-developing.]

*Der Bezug der Ueberschrift auf die Strophe selbst bedarf einer Erläuter-
ung. Der Dämon bedeutet hier die nothwendige, bey der Geburt unmittelbar
ausgesprochene, begränzte Individualität der Person, das Charakteristische
wodurch sich der Einzelne von jedem andern, bey noch so großer Aehn-
lichkeit unterscheidet. Diese Bestimmung schrieb man dem einwirkenden
Gestirn zu und es ließen sich die unendlich mannigfaltigen Bewegungen
und Beziehungen der Himmelskörper, unter sich selbst und zu der Erde,
gar schicklich mit den mannigfaltigen Abwechselungen der Geburten in
Bezug stellen. Hiervon sollte nun auch das künftige Schicksal des Menschen
ausgehen, und man möchte, jenes erste zugebend, gar wohl gestehen daß
angeborne Kraft und Eigenheit mehr als alles Uebrige des Menschen Schicksal
bestimme.*

[The title's relation to the strophe itself is in need of a clarification. Here
the *Dämon* refers to the necessary and delimited individuality of the person that is pronounced at birth in an unmediated fashion; the *Dämon* refers
to that which is characteristic, that by which each individual differs from
every other, no matter how great the similarities may be. This determination used to be attributed to the influence of the constellations, and it was
possible, quite ingeniously, to produce a relation quite conveniently between
the infinitely manifold motions and relations of the heavenly bodies, among
themselves and with respect to the earth, and the manifold permutations of
human births. Through this connection, the future destiny of the individual
was supposed to proceed, and, assuming the initial premise is accepted, one
can quite easily concede that innate force and individuality determine human
fate much more than anything else.]

*Deshalb spricht die Strophe die Unveränderlichkeit des Individuums mit
wiederholter Beteuerung aus. Das noch so entschieden Einzelne kann, als ein
Endliches, gar wohl zerstört, aber, so lange sein Kern zusammenhält, nicht
zersplittert, noch zerstückelt werden, sogar durch Generationen hindurch.*

[Thus the strophe pronounces the invariability of the individual with
repeated assurance. That which is most decisively individual, insofar as it is
finite, can certainly be destroyed, but, as long as its core remains intact, it can
never become fragmented or torn apart, even across generations.]

Dieses feste, zähe, dieses nur aus sich selbst zu entwicklende Wesen kommt freylich in mancherley Beziehungen, wodurch sein erster und ursprünglicher Charakter in seinen Wirkungen gehemmt, in seinen Neigungen gehindert wird, und was hier nun eintritt, nennt unsere Philosophie:

[Of course even this entity—fixed and tough, an essence to be developed only out of itself—enters into many relations that may impede the effects of its first and original character, or hinder it in its affections. That which appears in this moment of resistance, according to our philosophy, is called:]

Τυχη, *das Zufällige*

Die strenge Gränze doch umgeht gefällig
Ein Wandelndes, das mit und um uns wandelt;
Nicht einsam bleibst Du, bildest Dich gesellig,
Und handelt wohl so wie ein anderer handelt.
Im Leben ists bald hin-, bald wiederfällig,
Es ist ein Tand und wird so durchgetandelt.
Schon hat sich still der Jahre Kreis geründet,
Die Lampe harrt der Flamme die entzündet.

[Τυχη, *the Accidental*

Yet this strict limit is gently circumscribed
By a fluctuation that flows around and with us;
You are not alone, but shape yourself socially,
And must certainly act just as another acts.
In life things are often due, overdue, redone,
It is a trinket, passed in makeshift thrift.
The circle of the years is already silently closed,
The lamp awaits the flame that will ignite it.]

Zufällig ist es jedoch nicht daß einer aus dieser oder jener Nation, Stamm oder Familie sein Herkommen ableite: denn die auf der Erde verbreiteten Nationen sind, so wie ihre mannigfaltigen Verzweigungen, als Individuen anzusehen und die Tyche kann nur bey Vermischung und Durchkreuzung eingreifen. Wir sehen das wichtige Beyspiel von hartnäckiger Persönlichkeit solcher Stämme an der Judenschaft; europäische Nationen in anderer Welt-theile versetzt legen ihren Charakter nicht ab, und nach mehreren hundert Jahren wird in Nordamerika der Engländer, der Franzose, der Deutsche gar wohl zu erkennen seyn; zugleich aber auch werden sich bey Durchkreuz-ungen die Wirkungen der Tyche bemerklich machen, wie der Mestize an einer kläreren Hautfarbe zu erkennen ist. Bey der Erziehung, wenn sie nicht öffentlich und national ist, behauptet Tyche ihre wandelbaren Rechte. Säu-gamme und Wärterinn, Vater oder Vormund, Lehrer oder Aufseher, so wie

alle die ersten Umgebungen, an Gespielen, ländlicher oder städtischer Local-
ität, alles bedingt die Eigenthümlichkeit, durch frühere Entwicklung, durch
Zurückdrängen oder Beschleunigen; der Dämon freylich hält sich durch alles
durch, und dieses ist denn die eigenliche Natur, der alte Adam und wie man
es nennen mag, der, so oft auch ausgetrieben, immer wieder unbezwinglicher
zurückkehrt.

[It is however not accidental that one derives one's descent from this or
that nation, tribe or family: because the nations that are spread across the
earth are, just like their manifold branching, to be seen as individuals, and
Tyche can only intercede by way of mixing and crossing. We see the most
important example of the stubborn personality of such tribes in the Jewry.
European nations, transported to other parts of the world, also would not
cast off their character, and after several hundred years in North America,
the Englishman, the Frenchman, the German, will still be recognizable. At the
same time however, the effects of Tyche will make themselves known in the
case of crossings, just as the mestizo can be recognized by lighter colored skin.
In child-rearing and education, as long as they are not public and national,
Tyche also asserts her mutable rights. Wet nurse and babysitter, father or
guardian, teacher or supervisor, just like all of the earliest environments,
playmates, rural or urban locality, all of this conditions the individual peculiarity, whether through an earlier development, or by forcefully suppressing
or accelerating. The *Dämon*, of course, perseveres through all of it, and this
is then the proper nature, the "old Adam" and whatever else one may wish to
call it, who, so often he may be driven out, always returns again even more
irresistibly.]

In diesem Sinne einer nothwendig aufgestellten Individualität hat man
einem jeden Menschen seinen Dämon zugeschrieben, der ihm gelegentlich
ins Ohr raunt was denn eigentlich zu thun sey, und so wählte Sokrates den
Giftbecher, weil ihm ziemte zu sterben.

[In this sense of a necessarily erected individuality, every person was
ascribed with his own *Dämon*, who occasionally mumbles into his ear to tell
him the proper course of action, and thus Socrates chose to take the poison,
because it was fitting that he should die.]

Allein Tyche läßt nicht nach und wirkt besonders auf die Jugend immer-
fort, die sich, mit ihren Neigungen, Spielen, Geselligkeiten und flüchtigem
Wesen bald da bald dorthin wirft und nirgends Halt noch Befriedigung findet.
Da entsteht denn mit dem wachsenden Tage eine ernstere Unruhe, eine
gründlichere Sehnsucht; die Ankunft eines neuen Göttlichen wird erwartet.

[But *Tyche* does not relent and continues to exert its influence, especially
upon the young, who, with their inclinations, games, camaraderies, and fickle
nature, often cast themselves in this direction and that, and are nowhere
able to find rest or satisfaction. Thus emerges with the dawning day a more
earnest discontent, a more fundamental longing; the arrival of a new divinity
is awaited.]

Ἔρως, *Liebe*

Die bleibt nicht aus!—Er stürzt vom Himmel nieder,
Wohin er sich aus alter Oede schwang,
Er schwebt heran auf luftigem Gefieder
Um Stirn und Brust den Frühlingstag entlang,
Scheint jetzt zu fliehn, vom Fliehen kehrt er wieder,
Da wird ein Wohl im Weh, so süß und bang.
Gar manches Herz verschwebt im Allgemeinen,
Doch widmet sich das Edelste dem Einen.

[Ἔρως, *Love*

And there she is!—He hurtles down from the heaven,
Where he had lifted himself out of ancient chaos,
He soars and surges forward on airy wings
Surrounding brow and breast across the vernal day,
Seems now to flee, but in flight he turns about,
Creating pleasure in the pain, so happy and forlorn.
Many a heart drifts away in generality,
But the noblest devotes itself to the One.]

Hierunter ist alles begriffen was man, von der leisesten Neigung bis zur
leidenschaftlichsten Raserey, nur denken möchte; hier verbinden sich der indi-
viduelle Dämon und die verführende Tyche mit einander; der Mensch scheint
nur sich zu gehorchen, sein eigenes Wollen walten zu lassen, seinem Triebe zu
fröhnen, und doch sind es Zufälligkeiten die sich unterschieben, Fremdartiges
was ihn von seinem Wege ablenkt; er glaubt zu erhaschen und wird gefangen,
er glaubt gewonnen zu haben und ist schon verloren. Auch hier treibt Tyche
wieder ihr Spiel, sie lockt den Verirrten zu neuen Labyrinthen, hier ist keine
Gränze des Irrens: denn der Weg ist ein Irrthum. Nun kommen wir in Gefahr
uns in der Betrachtung zu verlieren, daß das was auf das Besonderste ange-
legt schien ins Allgemeine verschwebt und zerfließt. Daher will das rasche
Eintreten der zwey letzten Zeilen uns einen entscheidenden Wink geben, wie
man allein diesem Irrsal entkommen und davor lebenslängliche Sicherheit
gewinnen möge.

[Included here is everything imaginable, from the most quiet affection to
the most impassioned raving. Here the individual *Dämon* and the seducing
Tyche join together; the human seems to belong only to himself, to allow
his own desire to reign, to indulge his own instinct, and yet these are mere
contingencies that introduce themselves at this moment, alien natures, which
distract him from his own path. He means to capture and is himself taken
prisoner; he thinks he has won and is already lost. Even here Tyche plays its
game, it entices the disoriented individual to new labyrinths. Here there is no

limit to his erring: because the way itself is error. Now we are in danger of losing ourselves in the observation that that which seemed to be predisposed to the most particular and specific now floats away and dissolves into the realm of generality. For this reason, the sudden interjection of the final two lines gives us a decisive signal, as to the sole means by which one may escape this perdition and gain lifelong security from it.]

Denn nun zeigt sich erst wessen der Dämon fähig sey; er, der selbstständige, der mit unbedingtem Wollen in die Welt griff und nur mit Verdruß empfand wenn Tyche, da oder dort, in den Weg trat, er fühlt nun daß er nicht allein durch Natur bestimmt und gestempelt sey: jetzt wird er in seinem Innern gewahr daß er sich selbst bestimmen könne, daß er den durchs Geschick ihm zugeführten Gegenstand nicht nur gewaltsam ergreifen, sondern auch sich aneignen und, was noch mehr ist, ein zweytes Wesen, eben wie sich selbst, mit ewiger unzerstörlicher Neigung umfassen könne.

[Because only now does the *Dämon* show what it is capable of; he, the independent, selfish one, who has intervened in the world with unconditional desire, and only felt frustration when Tyche got in his way, here and there— now he feels that he is determined and stamped not only by nature. Now he perceives within himself that he can determine himself, that he may not only forcefully acquire the object that fate has brought to him, but also may assimilate it and, more importantly, can embrace a second being like himself with eternal, indestructible affection.]

Kaum war dieser Schritt gethan, so ist durch freyen Entschluß die Freyheit aufgegeben; zwey Seelen sollen sich in einen Leib, zwey Leiber in eine Seele schicken und indem eine solche Uebereinkunft sich einleitet, so tritt, zu wechselseitiger liebevoller Nöthigung, noch eine Dritte hinzu; Eltern und Kinder müssen sich abermals zu einem Ganzen bilden, groß ist die gemeinsame Zufriedenheit, aber größer das Bedürfniß. Der aus so viel Gliedern bestehende Körper krankt, gemäß dem irdischen Geschick, an irgend einem Theile, und, anstatt daß er sich im Ganzen freuen sollte, leidet er am Einzelnen und dem ohngeachtet wird ein solches Verhältniß so wünschenswerth als nothwendig gefunden. Der Vortheil zieht einen jeden an und man läßt sich gefallen die Nachtheile zu übernehmen. Familie reiht sich an Familie, Stamm an Stamm, eine Völkerschaft hat sich zusammengefunden und wird gewahr daß auch dem Ganzen fromme was der Einzelne beschloß, sie macht den Beschluß unwiederruflich durchs Gesetz; alles was liebevolle Neigung freywillig gewährte wird nun Pflicht, welche tausend Pflichten entwickelt, und damit alles ja für Zeit und Ewigkeit abschlossen sey, läßt weder Staat, noch Kirche, noch Herkommen es an Zeremonien fehlen. Alle Theile sehen sich durch die bündigen Contracte, durch die möglichsten Oeffentlichkeiten vor, daß ja das Ganze in keinem kleinsten Theil durch Wankelmuth und Willkhür gefährdet werde.

[This step is hardly taken, and freedom is given up through free decision; two souls must adapt to one body, two bodies to one soul, and in the introduction of this agreement, thus they are joined, in reciprocal loving duress, by a third; parents and children must likewise shape themselves into a whole, and great is the satisfaction, but even greater is the sense of lack. This body, comprised of so many members, takes ill, according to the way of the world, in one or the other of its parts, and rather than taking pleasure in itself as a whole, it suffers in its members, but such a relation is nevertheless deemed to be as desirable as it is necessary. The advantages are attractive to all, and each one concedes to go along when it comes to the disadvantages. Family follows family, tribe follows tribe; a people has discovered itself and perceives that the individual's decision is also proper for the whole, and it makes this verdict irrevocable in law. Everything that loving affection gave voluntarily now becomes duty, which develops into thousands of duties. And so that everything is resolved for all of time and eternity, neither state nor church nor tradition will permit any lack of ceremonies. All members provide for themselves through the most binding contracts and a maximum of publicness, so that precisely the whole may not be endangered even in its smallest parts by fickleness and willfulness.]

Αναγκη, *Nöthigung*

> *Da ist's denn wieder wie die Sterne wollten:*
> *Bedingung und Gesetz und aller Wille*
> *Ist nur ein Wollen, weil wir eben sollten,*
> *Und vor dem Willen schweigt die Willkühr stille;*
> *Das Liebste wird vom Herzen weggescholten,*
> *Dem harten Muß bequemt sich Will und Grille.*
> *So sind wir scheinfrey denn, nach manchen Jahren,*
> *Nur enger dran als wir am Anfang waren.*

[Αναγκη, Necessity

Now all follows once again the stars' will:
The terms and laws and the wills of all
Are but a single will, just because we have to,
And before the will all choice is silenced;
The most beloved is exiled from the heart,
Desire and fancy submit to hard compulsion.
Thus apparently then, after many years, we are
Only more tightly bound than in the beginning.]

Keiner Anmerkungen bedarf wohl diese Strophe weiter; niemand ist dem nicht Erfahrung genugsame Noten zu einem solchen Text darreichte, niemand der sich nicht peinlich gezwängt fühlte wenn er nur erinnerungsweise sich solche Zustände hervorruft, gar mancher der verzweifeln möchte wenn

ihn die Gegenwart also gefangen hält. Wie froh eilen wir daher zu den letzten
Zeilen, zu denen jedes seine Gemüth sich gern den Commentar sittlich und
religios zu bilden übernehmen wird.

[This strophe is in need of no further commentary; there is no one whose
experience has not provided him with adequate notes to such a text, no
one, who has not felt himself painfully compelled, when he even so much
as recalls such situations in his memory, and there are even quite a few who
would want to despair, when the present moment holds him captive in this
way. How happily we then must rush to the final lines, where every gentle
spirit will gladly take over the task of creating their own ethical and religious
commentary.]

Ελπισ, *Hoffnung*

Doch solcher Grenze, solcher ehrnen Mauer
Höchst widerwärtge Pforte wird entriegelt,
Sie stehe nur mit alter Felsendauer!
Ein Wesen regt sich leicht und ungezügelt,
Aus Wolkendecke, Nebel, Regenschauer
Erhebt sie uns, mit ihr, durch sie beflügelt,
Ihr kennt sie wohl, sie schwärmt nach allen Zonen;
Ein Flügelschlag! und hinter uns Aeonen.

[Ελπισ, *Hope*

But such a limit, such a steely wall,
Its most revolting portal is unlatched,
Though it may stand with a mountain's age!
A being arises lightly, without reigns,
Out of the clouds' cover, fog and rainfall,
It lifts us up, with her, by her wings,
You know her well, she swarms toward every zone;
A wing flap! and behind us lie the eons.]

NOTES

Introduction

1. Goethe translations are in all cases my own. Unless otherwise noted, citations refer to the widely available Hamburg edition: J. W. von Goethe, *Werke: Hamburger Ausgabe* (14 vols.), edited by Erich Trunz (Munich: Deutscher Taschenbuch Verlag, 1998) (abbreviated HA followed by volume and page number). When other editions contain important differences, they are also referenced: J. W. von Goethe, *Sämtliche Werke: Briefe, Tagebücher, Gespräche* (39 vols.) (Frankfurt am Main: Deutscher Klassiker Verlag, 1999) (abbreviated FA); Goethe, *Sämtliche Werke*, edited by Karl Richter et al. (Munich: Carl Hanser Verlag, 1985–98) (abbreviated MA).

2. Hans Blumenberg, *Arbeit am Mythos* (abbreviated AaM), 437; unless otherwise noted, all translations are my own.

3. On "onomasiology," see Assmann, "Translating Gods: Religion as a Factor of Cultural (Un)Translatability." Where semasiology "starts from the word and asks for the referent," onomasiology "starts from the referent and asks for the word" (139).

4. See Brodsky, *In the Place of Language*, on the architecture of the referent in Goethe: "the form of the referent . . . [is] demarcation rather than signification . . . as neither given in nature nor by thought . . . but made . . . through . . . the forming of a place to which perception returns, on which imagination lingers" (xv).

5. Mephistopheles himself is not a conventional personification of evil. He famously claims to be "a part of the power that always wishes for ill and always makes good" (*Faust,* vv. 1335–36; HA 3:47). See Schmidt-Dengler, "Teuflisches bei Goethe," which argues that after Klopstock's *Messias* the German *Spätaufklärung* became unable to identify the devil. The increasing fuzziness of religious-metaphysical competencies allowed the devil to cede his position to the demonic. But this is not the end of demons. To the contrary, lacking a single personification of evil (Satan), *evils* become decentralized, depersonified, inexplicable. See also Muschg, "Goethes Glaube an das Dämonische" (336); and Anderegg, *Transformationen: Über Himmlisches und Teuflisches in Goethes Faust* (100, 170). Contrary to Goethe's remarks to Eckermann, Anderegg establishes affinities between Mephisto and the demonic.

6. Muschg, "Goethes Glaube an das Dämonische," says almost the same thing, with a broader and more drastic emphasis: "The concept of the demonic thus replaces the concept of God" (337, my translation).

7. The conception in question is that of Heraclitus's fragment 119—*ethos anthropos daimon*—which is often understood to mean that a man's character is his fate. See, for example, the discussion in Heidegger's "Letter on 'Humanism,' "

which argues that the fragment *does not* mean "Man's *Dämon* is his individuality [*Seine Eigenart ist dem Menschen sein Dämon*]" (*Wegmarken*, 354)—but rather: "Der (geheuere) Aufenthalt ist dem Menschen das Offene für die Anwesung des Gottes (des Un-geheueren)" (356). The Heraclitus connections are also developed—at a degree of separation from Goethe—in Krell, *Daimon Life;* and Hadot, *The Veil of Isis.*

8. Unlike Nicholls, I see Goethe's concept as decidedly post-classicist. See Szondi's idea of "overcoming classicism," developed in "Die Überwindung des Klassizismus" and *Poetik und Geschichtsphilosophie* 1 and 2.

9. Matala de Mazza's "Dämonologie: Anmerkungen zu Hans Blumenberg" outlines Blumenberg's relation to Goethe. Her interpretation differs somewhat from mine, perhaps because for me the demonic represents a specific mode of self-reflection in Goethe, to which Blumenberg has a particular affinity. If, as Matala de Mazza puts it, "Goethes Daseinskonzept der philosophischen Haltung Blumenbergs widerstreb[t]" (169), then the aspect of Goethe's thought that Blumenberg resists is the titanic self-fashioning of the young Goethe. Thus Blumenberg (sympathetically) sees the demonic as a late attempt to come to terms with an earlier (failed) *Daseinskonzept.* My own reading of Blumenberg is elaborated in "Working Over Philosophy: Hans Blumenberg's Reformulations of the Absolute." Wellbery in *The Specular Moment* expresses the shortcomings and the strength of Blumenberg's work in his characterization of it as "speculative fiction" (445).

10. Hofmann's 2001 *Goethes Theologie* provides a further contrast. Hofmann weaves the history of theological perspectives on Goethe together with the theological possibilities presented by Goethe's works. Hofmann represents the discipline of theology, and raises the important question of the degree to which Goethe can be adequately treated within traditional disciplinary boundaries.

11. The demonic in this understanding (addressed in chapter 3) is the sublime object of myth, religion, and metaphysics. The following sentence expresses the relation of the demonic and the mythic in Blumenberg: "Was er [Goethe] an Napoleon dämonisch nennen wird ... gehört der Kategorie des Mythischen an" (AaM 559). Goethe translates the mythic as the demonic—and Blumenberg translates it back.

12. For a detailed analysis of this figure of the "flight behind an image," see Kreienbrock's forthcoming "Bilderfluchten: Zur Goetherezeption bei Hans Christoph Buch, Hans Blumenberg und Georg Simmel."

13. In another passage, Blumenberg cites Goethe's words to Eckermann from March 2, 1831, which state that the demonic manifests itself in events (*Begebenheiten*) that cannot be resolved by understanding or reason (*Verstand und Vernunft*). Blumenberg comments that this is "not an attempt at defining the demonic but a description of the resistance that characterizes it" (AaM 518–19).

14. This is something different than Paul de Man's *Resistance to Theory.* Rather than subjects' resistance to theoretical discourses, Blumenberg means the resistance produced by *objects that cannot be fully theorized.*

15. Hofmann, based on Blumenberg, reads the demonic as a figure of discontinuity in nature and history (*Goethes Theologie,* 355–74). Hofmann's theological approach unsurprisingly emphasizes the *demonic* (not the *daemonic*), but he

underscores "the vast compass of this word, which serves . . . as an *Ersatz*-concept for the indeterminate divine beyond all preexisting models of theological interpretation" (362, my translation).

16. I realize that this aspect may be a problem for some readers, but I would respond that especially when it comes to Goethe, there is a need of scholarly work that does not latently or overtly grapple with problems of mimetic rivalry and ressentiment.

17. My approach generally accords with Mandelkow's lengthy study, *Goethe in Deutschland*. Reception history "does not seek an empathic relation to past historical standpoints but to critically reflect these standpoints in the light of contemporary research-interests [*gegenwärtiger Erkenntnisinteressen*]" (1:13, my translation).

18. Conversations with colleagues in Bonn during my sabbatical year made me concretely aware of this: Lars Friedrich traced the demonic to Hugo von Hofmannsthal, Stephan Kraft to Gottfried Benn. A less personal example of such connectivity is Jochen Schmidt, whose commentaries on Hölderlin's "Der Rhein" invoke the *Dämon* stanza of Goethe's "Urworte Orphisch" (Schmidt, *Die Geschichte des Genie-Gedankens* 1:405–6; Hölderlin, *Sämtliche Werke und Briefe*, 862). The lines in Hölderlin read: "Ein Räthsel ist Reinentsprungenes. . . . Denn / Wie du anfiengst, wirst du bleiben, / So viel auch wirket die Noth, / Und die Zucht, das meiste nemlich / Vermag die Geburt, / Und der Lichtstral, der / Dem Neugeborenen begegnet." Given that Goethe's poem was written more than a decade later and without any awareness of Hölderlin's, the connection might be read as a sign of the infectiousness of the underlying idea (e.g., genius). The infection is thus traceable—but not isolable as long as it is traced under the heading of "the demonic." The term's indefiniteness allows for a kind of unregulated traffic, which does not mean that nothing is moving. To the contrary, it is a black market of underground transactions.

19. In a broader sense, the critical awareness of the demonic represents a *critique* of forms of social-characterological-political analysis that have been endemic to countless spheres of thought and action. The demonic in this sense is a limit-concept, a conception of the limits of the world—constantly changing due to globalization and technology—as well as of the limits of history and the human. The specificity of the word "demonic" characterizes the attempt to transcend or transgress such limits. "The demonic" names a field of possible transvaluations that are often simply referred to as "modern." Calling modernity demonic is not automatically conservative or anti-modern, to the extent that it refers to the incessant dynamics of unforeseeability and unintended consequences: beyond the *ne plus ultra*, skillful navigation is all there is.

20. Together with Gide, I would mention Carlyle's *Sartor Resartus*, a complex case meriting a separate treatment. The novel's fictional translator-biographer renders the German word *Dämon* in English as "guiding genius" (109). This seems to support the reading of *Dämon* as daemon, except that this daemon belongs to a protagonist named Diogenes Teufelsdröckh ("devil's shit" in Carlyle's own translation, xiii). The "genius" is further specified as Eros, which, as Teufelsdröckh writes, "may be either true or false, either seraphic or demoniac, Inspiration or Insanity" (110), thereby implicating it in the ambiguity of the demonic. Teufelsdröckh's beloved Blumine is, in the same chapter, interpreted

as a Lucifer figure—emphasizing the *lumine* in Blumine. She is a "Light-bringer" (111) and "Morning star" (113), who leaves Teufelsdröckh "falling, falling, towards the Abyss" (113). Additional traces of Goethe's demonic are evident in Carlyle's novel, in a persistent metaphorics of spectrality: 117 ("the Future is wholly a Stygian Darkness, spectre-bearing"), 130, 143 ("the Universe is not dead and demoniacal, a charnel-house with spectres"), 151, 167 ("poor devil! Spectres are appointed to haunt him"), 196 ("Witchcraft, and all manner of Spectre-work, and Demonology, we have now named Madness"), 198 ("but a pale spectral illusion"), 201 ("the veriest Spectre-Hunt"), 223 ("an authentic Spectre"); see also the discussions of "Demon-Worship" in the chapter "The Dandiacal Body" (207–18).

21. See especially Blumenberg's *Work on Myth* (AaM 567–604).

22. Friedrich Nietzsche, *The Birth of Tragedy,* 69 and 99.

23. Next to Tillich, I would also mention Wundt's chapters on demons in his *Völkerpsychologie* (1906 and 1910), which represent an attempt to systematize the phenomena qualifiable as "demonic."

24. Otto, *Das Heilige: Über das Irrationale in der Idee des Göttlichen und sein Verhältnis zum Rationalen,* esp. 179–82. Otto relies on Goethe's definition of the demonic as that which evades both "reason and understanding" (*Verstand und Vernunft,* 179) and clearly considers it a predecessor of his idea of the numinous (*das Numinose,* 180). The change of name reflects a clear shift in emphasis: Otto connects Goethe with "heathen" irreligiosity (182). Between Otto and Tillich, Volz's 1924 *Das Dämonische in Jahwe* also develops a theological discourse on the demonic. Volz, whose essay appeared in the same series as Tillich's (Mohr-Siebeck in Tübingen), refers to both Otto and Goethe (41). See also Nicholls (*Goethe's Concept of the Daemonic,* 229–34) on Blumenberg's reference to Otto's *das Numinose* (AaM 559); both Nicholls and Blumenberg find that the substitution of "the numinous" for "the demonic" reflects a deliberate misunderstanding.

25. Muschg's 1958 "Goethes Glaube an das Dämonische" posits Goethe's "belief" in all kinds of demons. Muschg's postwar anti-Gundolf position holds the line against classicization, harmonization, and idolization. The focus on Goethe's biography, personality, and beliefs falls within a counter-tradition that tends to view the demonic as an aspect of Goethe's supposed superstitiousness.

26. Agamben's "Benjamin and the Demonic" discusses ancient traditions of daemonology (or demonology); Goethe comes up occasionally, but ancient sources are the main focus. Agamben speaks of an idealized "alter ego" that began to be conceived in the "fusion of the ancient pagan and Neoplatonic motif of the *idios daimon* of every man with the Jewish motif of the celestial image, *demuth* or *zelem,* in whose image each man is created" (145–46).

27. Scholarship on ancient demonology traces comparable semantic and orthographic borderlines: Rosen-Zvi's *Demonic Desires,* a study of the rabbinic *yetzer* and "other demonic and semi-demonic entities" (9), deals with "demons" as the sources of evil. Padel, however, cited by Rosen-Zvi (7), writes of "daemons" in the context of fifth-century Greek antiquity. The conceptions developed by Padel are in turn compatible with post-Goethean ideas of the demonic: "Something 'comes in' from the outside . . . . Something already in the mind comes out" (Padel, *In and Out of the Mind,* 134). Daemons "had to be lived with, just as

we have to live with radioactivity, carcinogens in our food, and a thinning ozone layer" (138).

28. I use the "primal words" without capitalization when referring to the five words alone (and not to the poem); even more frequently, however, I will use the German *Urworte* or "Urworte" (to refer to the poem). Also, in the three publications of the poem during Goethe's lifetime, it was punctuated differently: "Urworte. Orphisch." (1820), "Urworte Orphisch." (1820), and "Urworte. Orphisch." (1828). I concentrate on the second 1820 publication, so I have followed its punctuation; the full German text, including Goethe's commentary, and my own English translation are reproduced as an appendix.

29. Schmidt questions whether the "Urworte"—as a work—should be referred to in the singular or plural. He argues for reading them as *a poem* rather than as *poems* or a cycle of poems. Schmidt's argument is based on the interdependence of the stanzas (*Goethes Altersgedicht*, 28)—but the top title, "Urworte," is plural, and Goethe himself does not refer to this work as "a poem" but rather as "a series" of *Urworte* and as "stanzas" (Buck, *Goethes "Urworte. Orphisch*," abbreviated UO, 72). To preserve the plurality and the integrity of this series, I refer to the "Urworte" and their corresponding "stanzas" in the plural. In contrast to Schmidt, see Sewell, *The Orphic Voice* (269–75): "Each of the *Urworte* . . . is a poem" (274).

30. See Swales, "Johann Wolfgang von Goethe, 'Urworte. Orphisch'" (63). But Swales is hardly alone. Nicholls, though he largely avoids the question, indirectly follows Swales and many others in focusing on the *Dämon-Tyche* pair. The conflation of *Dämon* and *das Dämonische* is the norm—against Benjamin's critique of Gundolf and despite Goethe's indication (UO 72) that *all five stanzas* comprise a concept of the demonic.

31. The long-standing tradition of invoking unattributed snippets of the *Dämon* stanza as a part of panegyrics—nominally attributed to Goethe—on the power of fate and the lives of great men continues even in relatively recent publications. See, for example, Seibt's *Goethe und Napoleon*, 244–45.

32. Another side example is Hans Pfitzner's musical setting of the "Urworte" for vocal quartet, chorus, and orchestra, which was left incomplete after his death in 1949 (Schrott, *Die Persönlichkeit Hans Pfitzners*, 137–39). Pfitzner is a good reader of Goethe's stanzas insofar as he understands them as a cycle, and his use of solo voices with chorus balances individualizing and collectivizing moments. But it is striking that one of the last works of such a notoriously conservative composer should be an "Urworte" setting.

33. To give a sense of how established the language of the demonic had become only a few decades later, I quote from Adorno and Horkheimer's *Dialektik der Aufklärung*, a sentence that may echo Spengler or Benjamin—in addition to Otto or Freud: "Das von den Dämonen und ihren begrifflichen Abkömmlingen gründlich gereinigte Dasein nimmt in seiner blanken Natürlichkeit den numinosen Charakter an, den die Vorwelt den Dämonen zuschob" (Adorno, *Gesammelte Schriften*, 3:45).

34. The "demonic novel" is meant as a condensation of the connections between the demonic and the novel and not as a specific subgenre. Nor is it a "modern epic" in Franco Moretti's sense. But, taking a cue from Moretti, the demonic novel may fit his characterization of Russian literature, in which "epic

and novel are intertwined with an intensity unknown to other European literature" (*Modern Epic,* 50). Extending Moretti's theses, Doderer's *Demons* may
reflect Austria's exceptional relation (comparable to nineteenth-century Russia)
to the European historical norms of progress and enlightenment. For the same
reason, another important case would be Melville's *Moby-Dick:* the importance
of Goethe's idea of the demonic for the conception of the figure of Ahab is argued
in Robert Milder's "*Nemo Contra Deum . . .* : Melville and Goethe's 'Demonic.' "
This essay contains striking formulations, the importance of which is amplified
by the fact that Milder is not a Goethe scholar by trade: "the demonic occupied
an anomalous position in both a theistic and an atheistic scheme of the universe"
(225); "Goethe's solution was as appalling as the problem it addressed, for it
seemed to abandon the world to the rule of the demonic while positing a God
who, if He existed at all, was so removed from human affairs and so morally and
spiritually indeterminate that belief in Him was not far from practical atheism"
(227). Milder notes that the demonic is a subjective projection, but does not go
so far as to call it a superstition: "It gathers under one denomination and causal
scheme various undeniable elements of human experience, but whether it exists
as anything more than a projection is a moot point" (231–32); for Melville "it
may have been the very ambiguousness of the demonic which proved most lib-
erating" (232).

Chapter One

1. Compare UO 21–30; see also Staiger (*Goethe,* 3:96–99); Swales ("Johann
Wolfgang von Goethe 'Urworte. Orphisch,' " 59); Nicholls (*Goethe's Concept of
the Daemonic,* 230–40); and Schmidt (*Goethes Altersgedicht Urworte. Orphisch,*
8–11). Buck reproduces the three first publications of Goethe's text, while Schmidt
includes the facsimile of a manuscript in the hand of Goethe's copyist (41–43).
Buck also includes excerpts of diary entries' correspondences pertaining to the
"Urworte" (UO 67–76) as well as the writings of Hermann, Creuzer, and Zoëga
(UO 76–86). To my knowledge, no one (including Buck) has systematically investigated these sources in the context of the "Urworte." The reason for this neglect
may be the complexity and—for Germanists—relative obscurity of the material.
If I were to speculate on Goethe's motives with respect to debates on the origins
of antiquity, I would say that he wanted to maintain the unity and polar opposition of the Greek "classical" vs. the Israelite world (structured by polytheism vs.
monotheism). Goethe disagrees with historical methods that mix traditions "by
transsubstantiating everything with everything else" (UO 74). The "Urworte"
seek to speculatively imagine a transcendental origin of antiquity—which may
also run the risk of "confusing everything"—but I believe that Goethe's intent
was to produce a synthetic ideal of pre-antiquity from which everything else,
including monotheism and polytheism, could be derived. This attempt pertains
not only to the discourses up to Goethe's time, which are complex enough, but
to similarly motivated later works, such as Bachofen's *Mutterrecht* and Freud's
Moses and Monotheism.

2. In a letter to Sulpiz Boisserée from July 16, 1818, Goethe expresses the
desire to "bring diffuse antiquity back to its quintessence" (UO 72).

3. Jochen Schmidt (*Goethes Altergedicht Urworte. Orphisch*) underscores the
paradigmatic status of the primal words as general categories that encompass

all human life (10). However, the context of Goethe's scientific writings suggests extensions beyond the primary anthropological valence.

4. See Willer, "Urworte: Zum Konzept und Verfahren der Etymologie"; Willer describes the German "Ur-" prefix as "an inherited transfer that creates both distance and continuity" (36, my translation); he also develops early nineteenth-century contexts—etymology and comparative mythology—into which Goethe's "Urworte" intervened.

5. Blumenberg also emphasizes (AaM 165–91) that the time prior to the foundational texts of antiquity is much more vast than the times for which we have written records. What we perceive as a foundation and an origin can only have been the culmination of a lengthy process.

6. Compare Swales ("Johann Wolfgang von Goethe, 'Urworte. Orphisch,'" 62–63); Schmidt (*Goethes Altersgedicht Urworte. Orphisch,* 16 and 32); Gundolf's reading is addressed in chapter 3. Buck reads the relation as dialectical. It is, however, not a Hegelian dialectic. Rather than an immanent movement of opposition and reversal, the "Urworte" consistently reflect the intervention of an *external* force: the unity and uniqueness of *Dämon* must conform to a more general *Tyche;* this opposition is catalyzed by the appearance of *Eros,* who unexpectedly promotes social integration (*Ananke*). The *Eros-Ananke* transition is arguably the most dialectical, except that its immanent movement, like that of the *Dämon-Tyche* opposition, merely produces standstill. *Eros* and *Elpis* are winged beings who intervene from the outside and transcend a static opposition.

7. Buck reads the "Du" as the reflex of a lyric "Ich" (UO 33), but for me the "Urworte" are not essentially lyrical: the universality of the "you" apostrophizes each individual reader.

8. Georg Simmel's 1913 *Goethe* declares that an "abyss" separates "the artistic boundedness and self-sufficiency of form" from "the infinity of becoming"; *geprägte Form* covers over a "problem" and a "question" of "how form can *live* and that which has been *imprinted* can *develop*" (81, my translation). Compare Simonis, *Gestalttheorie von Goethe bis Benjamin,* 69; and Krois, "Cassirer als Goethe-Interpret," 304–6.

9. In Blumenberg's attempt to define form as the source of "meaningfulness" (*Bedeutsamkeit*), he relates symmetry to circularity and recursiveness (*Kreisschlüssigkeit*) with reference to both visual-symbolic and temporal-narrative dimensions. In this context, he cites the line on *geprägte Form* (AaM 78). Development is thus conceived as an "imprinted form" of temporal *Kreisschlüssigkeit.*

10. Compare Nicholls, *Goethe's Concept of the Daemonic,* 66–67; Swales, "Johann Wolfgang von Goethe, 'Urworte. Orphisch,'" 63.

11. The *Dämon-Tyche* relation in Zoëga and Goethe substantially prefigures Bachofen's 1861 opposition of matriarchy and patriarchy: "The paternal principle of limitation [*Beschränkung*] corresponds to the maternal principle of universality [*Allgemeinheit*]" (*Das Mutterrecht,* 13, my translation). See also Assmann's discussion of Isis in *Moses der Ägypter* (76–78).

12. Compare Nicholls (*Goethe's Concept of the Daemonic,* 242–43); Swales ("Johann Wolfgang von Goethe, 'Urworte. Orphisch,'" 70). Swales goes further than I would in attacking Goethe, while Nicholls goes further than I would in defending Goethe from Swales.

13. See book 4 of *Poetry and Truth,* which retells the story of the Tower of Babel; this collapse is offset by the "luck" (*Glück*) of a "patriarch" (*Stammvater*) who was able to "imprint his offspring with a decisive character" (*seinen Nach-kommen einen entschiedenen Charakter aufzuprägen*), thereby giving rise to a nation with longevity (HA 9:130). This political theology reduces ancient history to natural selection.

14. I agree with Swales's emphasis on gender in the "Urworte," but her analyses are often not detailed enough to draw precise conclusions. For example, I question whether *Dämon* is "fundamentally male" ("Johann Wolfgang von Goethe, 'Urworte. Orphisch,'" 69) or whether, defined as "individuality," it might not apply to all genders.

15. Compare Schmidt, *Goethes Altersgedicht Urworte. Orphisch,* 14–15.

16. See Bersier, "Sinnliche Übermacht—übersinnliche Gegenmacht," which observes a hospitable and a demonic *Eros* in Goethe. Partly for biographical reasons, she argues for an increase in the latter in Goethe's later literary works.

17. Naumann's "Talking Symbols: Ernst Cassirer's Repetition of Goethe" leaves no doubt that for Goethe (as well as for Cassirer) *Eros* is fundamentally a form of "self-reflection" (371) with profound epistemic consequences.

18. See Freud, *Das Unbehagen in der Kultur:* "Eros and Ananke are the parents of human culture" (66, my translation).

19. Pierre Hadot, *N'oublie pas de vivre* also emphasizes that "le poésie ne représente pas un genre littéraire, pratiqué par un écrivain, mais une attitude, un exercice spirituel" (232). I became aware of Hadot's chapter on Goethe's "Urworte" only after I had completed my own. In order to highlight the overlaps and discrepancies between the two independent readings, I decided not to revise my text in light of Hadot's.

20. Compare Schmidt, *Goethes Altersgedicht Urworte. Orphisch,* 26; I am perplexed by Schmidt's assertion that *Elpis,* though dominated by "freedom and expanse," is "ambivalent." The mirage character of hope is well known, and in the end the interpretation depends on the degree of hopefulness of the individual reader, but even if *Elpis* implicitly lowers expectations (through the relation with *Ananke*), she remains a figure of clear-sightedness, above "clouds, fog and rain."

Chapter Two

1. The Frankfurt edition suggests that it was written around 1798 (FA 1017) and gives it the title "Betrachtung zur Morphologie" (FA 1023).

2. For a detailed account of this synthetic method in relation to the philosophy of the period, see Förster, *Die 25 Jahre der Philosophie:* "Characteristic . . . of *scientia intuitiva* is that, unlike Hegel's science, it does not start from the supreme idea but instead seeks . . . to ascend to it through knowledge" (364, my translation).

3. Goethe's morphology is not included in the epistemic shift of Michel Foucault's *The Order of Things,* but it could probably be understood within this narrative. However, morphology's reliance on analogy and similarity may also fit in Foucault's idea of the pre-classical *episteme.* And Foucault's attempt to solve the problem of diachronic form or "structure" may be an example of morphological method. Compare Simonis, *Gestalttheorie von Goethe bis Benjamin* (67); and Pörksen, "Alles ist Blatt" (127). The emphasis of analogy over causation may

mystify or "literarize" science; see Pörksen, who argues that Goethe's method was contrary to the sciences' trend toward increasing abstraction ("Alles ist Blatt," 129).

4. Pörksen, "Alles ist Blatt," begins with a facsimile of this famous fragment. I follow the wording and orthography of the facsimile.

5. Compare Pörksen ("Alles ist Blatt," 110).

6. Förster's "Goethe and the 'Auge des Geistes' " reconstructs the philosophical underpinnings of Goethe's generative-developmental morphology. He never mentions *geprägte Form die lebend sich entwickelt,* but he does paraphrase it in the context of Goethe's "leaf": "To really comprehend [the living plant] . . . I must know the law underlying its development, its *typus* or archetype, so that I can generate imaginatively a new plant from it" (95, emphasis mine).

7. See Simonis, *Gestalttheorie von Goethe bis Benjamin* (34–39). See also Eva Geulen's recent "Urpflanze (und Goethes *Hefte zur Morphologie*)," which does not focus on "discrepancies" (Simonis 34, my translation), but argues that the *Urpflanze*-idea has been systematically overinvested: "*Urpflanze* is the name, the cipher, of the need . . . to suspend contradictions between abstract idea and concrete intuition" (Geulen, "Urpflanze," 155).

8. A morphological text called "Bildungstrieb," published in 1820 but probably written 1817, argues that the "unity and freedom" of organic beings "cannot be conceived without the concept of metamorphosis" (HA 13:33–34).

9. The morphological essay "Fossiler Stier" (published 1822) shows that Goethe himself was not immune to this way of thinking. Citing Dr. Körte, Goethe compares the skull of a fossil steer with a modern domesticated one. On the basis of formal-aesthetic criteria, the latter is clearly favored (HA 13:198). The fusion of nature and culture favors *Bildung,* progress, and development. Goethe especially focuses on the horns, which are a weapon in nature, but useless and ornamental in the domesticated animal (HA 13:202–3).

10. In "Einwirkung der neueren Philosophie" (published 1820), Goethe reflects on Kant's first critique. Here he not only conceives analysis and synthesis as natural forms, but assimilates them to the alternating rhythms of human understanding (HA 13:27).

11. For Pörksen, morphology implies *Sprachskepsis* ("skepticism of language") ("Alles ist Blatt," 112).

12. In a longer text, "Die Metamorphose der Pflanzen," first written and published after Goethe's return from Italy, then revised and republished in *Zur Morphologie* in 1817 and again in 1832, further terminological layers may be uncovered. For example, "Verwandschaft" is correlated to metamorphosis (§53, §69, §71, §80, HA 13:80–88). The "rhythmic" model of systole and diastole is echoed in §50 (and repeatedly thereafter) in the idea of "expansion and contraction" (HA 13:79).

13. In the Pandora chapter of *Goethe,* Gundolf writes: "Symbol is to the individual what myth is to the collective: organic expression, involuntary self-externalization, the becoming image of inner life. Allegory is the conscious attempt to find the significant image for such a life (individual or collective)" (583, my translation).

14. My idea of *analogia entis* owes more to Heimito von Doderer than to Saint Thomas—but Doderer's idea of it may have also owed something to morphology.

15. A further analogue of the Lucifer function is Goethe's sonnet "Mächtiges Überraschen," which conceives the genesis of a new world in the collision of "demonic" unities. See Campe, "Goethes *Mächtiges Überraschen*," especially his reading of the reflected "flickering" (*Blinken*) of the stars (90).

16. The negation and transcendence of the (narcissistic) self-ness of the self may be a "Plotinian" moment. See Davidson's introduction to Pierre Hadot, *Plotinus, or The Simplicity of Vision* (10–13). Goethe's figure of pulsation, however, suggests a continuous and immanent—less mystical—version of this process.

17. In an alternate version of the end of book 8, Goethe does not allow his own ideas to flow as smoothly into general words of wisdom, but criticizes the "embarrassing efforts" (*peinliche Bemühungen*) of his youth (MA 16:986). One line, however, offers support for the connection of book 8 to the demonic in book 20: "Ich enthalte mich hier aller Bemerkungen darüber um so mehr, da ich späterhin werde bekennen müssen, wie ich durch mancherlei andere ähnliche Vorstellungen hindurch gegangen" (MA 16:986). Both the passage from book 8 and the passage on the demonic from book 20 were first drafted at the beginning of the 1810s: book 8 between winter 1811 and summer 1812 (HA 9:736), and the demonic in the spring of 1813 (HA 10:644).

18. Compare Breidbach, *Goethes Metamorphosenlehre*, 310.

Chapter Three

1. For a relatively recent assessment, see Mandelkow, *Goethe in Deutschland* 1 (267–80). Mandelkow links Gundolf, Chamberlain, and Simmel by way of their shared hostility toward modernity (and the corresponding desire for cultural renewal). Despite Gundolf's shortcomings (276–78), Mandelkow notes his vast influence (276) as well as certain strengths in comparison to the scholarship of the time (278).

2. Gundolf's spelling differs from the English transliteration, *Ananke*.

3. The connection to the grey sisters from the end of *Faust* is highly interesting, however, in that they—together with their brother, Death—are also five in number.

4. The unity of the "Urworte" could be demonstrated by the fact that the other allegorical figurations that Gundolf names could be read as subordinate moments of the "Urworte." Death's absence is undoubtedly significant, but the numerous figures of its transcendence may reveal it to be derived rather than "primal." Gundolf's invocation of karma in the same breath as entelechy gives a sense of just how open the demonic is to projections from various sources. *Poetry and Truth*'s vague reference to sources—"after the example of the ancients and others who thought of something similar" (HA 10:175–76)—gives license to free association.

5. Staiger's *Goethe* equates the Orphic "Urworte" with "the complete depiction of Goethe that lies before the reader [in Staiger's biography]. For everything which the poet and scholar ever thought about man is truly compressed here with maximum power into only a few lines" (3:99, my translation). This is still rather close to Gundolf. The "Urworte," as I read them, neither represent the last word on the demonic nor are they a direct self-representation of Goethe's "thought."

6. Compare Schmitz, "Das Ganz-Andere: Goethe und das Ungeheure" (428). Schmitz also understands the sentence with the exclamation point as a list of *Urworte*, but he does not cite the line about Orphic "Urworte." Schmitz treats the

demonic more systematically than and in less space than any other commentator; in the end he sees it as an *Ahnung* (435) of ideas that others were able to more clearly formalize. For me, on the other hand, Goethe's strength lies precisely in his awareness of the limitations of concepts that act as if their objects were more knowable than they actually are.

7. See Blumenberg, "Nach dem Absolutismus der Wirklichkeit" (AaM, chapter 1), as well as my essay, "Working Over Philosophy."

8. Gundolf's analysis of the "Urworte" is brief, but the language of the *Dämon* stanza clearly informs his overall approach; "geprägte Form, die lebend sich entwickelt" is a leitmotif in his introduction (*Goethe*, 1 and 5). On Gundolf and the George circle's "tendency to read morphology ideologically," see Annette Simonis (*Gestalttheorie von Goethe bis Benjamin*, 18, my translation).

9. In the first years of the twentieth century, as Geulen shows in "Nachlese: Simmels Goethebuch und Benjamins Wahlverwandtschaftenaufsatz," Simmel proposed a morphological reading of Goethe's life, the major assumptions of which are shared not only by Gundolf and Spengler. Morpho-biography arguably continued to dominate even in those, like Benjamin and Blumenberg, who disputed key elements of it.

10. For all of the sobriety and decided populism of Staiger's introduction to the first volume of his 1952 *Goethe*, it still has much in common with Gundolf. Staiger sees a quasi-morphological progression in Goethe's life (9), emphasizes the incompatibility of literature with scientific analysis (11), and monumentalizes and heroizes Goethe to establish contemporary relevance: "Wie bestehen wir heute vor ihm?" (1:11).

11. Goethe sees the significance of life in its productivity, which posterity perceives retrospectively (Eckermann, *Gespräche mit Goethe*, 650–60). Shakespeare (658) shows how all particulars of a work (*Hamlet*) may be subordinated to an overarching power that guarantees the coherence of the whole.

12. Cassirer is one of the few who situate the demonic through a retelling of the end of *Poetry and Truth*. His lecture at Yale, "Bemerkungen zum Faustfragment und zur Faustdichtung" (esp. 58–59), is not primarily about the demonic. Krois, "Urworte: Cassirer als Goethe-Interpret," notes the intensity of Cassirer's "Urworte" reception.

13. Goethe's method of neutralizing the power of the world in the interest of his own *Selbstbehauptung* is a main topic of Blumenberg's *Arbeit am Mythos* (esp. AaM 482).

14. Goethe's famous "The Sorcerer's Apprentice" may be read as an illustration of this.

15. Ironically, in *Poetry and Truth* and the *Italian Journey*, being at home implies a predominance of foreign influences, whereas travel frees one from both self- and other-determination. Travel, conceived radically, leaves the compulsions of self and identity behind. The idea of *Wiedergeburt* ("renaissance") in the *Italian Journey* does not have a precise analogue in the "Urworte."

16. In the *Gespräche mit Eckermann* (March 11, 1828), the word "aperçu" is repeatedly connected to the demonic (653, 657, 658). "Aperçu" may be another word for *Urwort*, and "der Gedanke" is another potential synonym. See Hofmann, *Goethes Theologie* (285–329), in connection to *Urworte* and Jung-Stilling (296–98).

17. This is also an implication of Dostoyevsky's *Demons*. Pyotr Stepanovich suffers when his expectations are dashed; Nikolai Stavrogin attempts to presuppose nothing at all so that nothing can challenge his system. Neither is a success. Even "insane" individuals make decisions based on "character" or some other disposition: Kirillov's attempt at self-unification—to become God through suicide—fails to convince the other characters (and perhaps the reader) this is his real motive.

18. Book 16 of *Poetry and Truth* discusses the demonic in relation to animals; "natural phenomena that show [*deutet auf*] understanding, reason or even will [*Verstand, Vernunft, ja auch nur auf Willkür*] astonish and even horrify us" (HA 10:79; also 10:177). Humans understand "nature" as *Ananke* ("the realm of necessity"); this produces "horror" (*Entsetzen*) when animals appear to exhibit a rational will. The demonic emerges out of categorical confusion, but this cannot necessarily be solved by more rigorous distinctions, because categorical presuppositions (animals = nature = necessity) are what produce the problem in the first place.

Chapter Four

1. Doderer's early diaries, the *Tägebucher 1920–1939*, will be abbreviated TB; all Doderer translations are my own.

2. See the recent study by Kleinlercher, *Zwischen Wahrheit und Dichtung: Antisemitismus und Nationalsozialismus bei Heimito von Doderer*.

3. Osmancevic, *Oswald Spengler und das Ende der Geschichte*, sees a new relevance of theories of decline in an era marked by the limitations of optimistic theories of "the end of history."

4. In Doderer's *Repertorium* (abbreviated R), a self-made dictionary of important ideas, in an entry dated 1963, entitled "Improvement [*Besserung*]," he writes: "One may feel bad about a vice that has abandoned one or a mistake that one is no longer capable of. One used to fight against it, and therein lay the tension. Now there's nothing there. Emptiness, *Erfüllungs-Rückstoß*. A door is closed" (R 37).

5. This micro-narrative can be found in Doderer's "Sieben Variationen über ein Thema von Johann Peter Hebel" (1926), "Die Bresche" (1924), and in his Siberian writings.

6. Quotations from Spengler's *Decline of the West* are marked with the abbreviation UdA; translations are my own.

7. Janensch's *Goethe und Nietzsche bei Spengler* sees Spengler's cyclical conception as a reversion to understandings of pre-Christian antiquity, whereas teleology reflects the modern, Christian, eschatological, and linear ideas of history. Spengler and Nietzsche use cyclical history to oppose the modern conception. This may be true as far as it goes, but the problem becomes abstract if other contemporary theories (for example, Max Weber) are not a part of the implicit context.

8. See Wetters, *The Opinion System*, 50–56.

9. A Spenglerian patterning may be visible in the structuralist anthropology of Claude Lévi-Strauss; see Kuhnle, "Ekelhafte Stadtansichten," focusing on the idea of "entropy" (153–54). Spengler and Lévi-Strauss have similar styles of cultural symbolic analysis; *Tristes Tropiques*'s emblematic sunset may also be read

as a symbol of decline (*Untergang*). Goethe and Spengler—and morphology—thus inform the background metaphorics of intellectual filiations extending from structuralism to cultural studies and beyond. More evidence of this can be found in Liu's 1996 dissertation, "The Question Concerning Morphology: Language, Vision, History, 1918–1939," which traces Goethe's morphology through Spengler, Propp, Mauss, Levi-Strauss, and others. Liu claims: "As the first application of morphology to culture, and thus to some degree the inspiration of the various morphologies that succeeded it, Spengler's text remains an incidental origin in the genealogy of formalist, structuralist, and poststructuralist thought" (16, footnote). (I thank Arnd Wedemeyer for calling my attention to Liu's work.)

10. Spengler is not entirely vanquished: his ideas are still present in right-leaning political discourses. In the academic context, Adorno's "Spengler nach dem Untergang" offers both critique and postwar recontextualization. When it comes to satirizing Spengler's theoretical weaknesses, Robert Musil's contribution is the last word: "Es gibt zitronengelbe Falter, es gibt zitronengelbe Chinesen; in gewissem Sinn kann man also sagen: Falter ist der mitteleuropäische geflügelte Zwergchinese. Falter wie Chinese sind bekannt als Sinnbilder der Wollust. Zum erstenmal wird hier der Gedanke gefaßt an die noch nie beachtete Übereinstimmung des großen Alters der Lepidopterenfauna und der chinesische Kultur. Daß der Falter Flügel hat und der Chinese keine, ist nur ein Oberflächenphänomen" (cited from Felken, "Nachwort" to Spengler's UdA, 1261).

11. Adorno, "Spengler nach dem Untergang," 47.

12. Despite similarities, Herder's historicism is not identical with Spengler's comparative morphology, above all because the former does not assume the substitutability of individuals within a morphologically stabilized universal history. Spengler operates with a fixed universal historical frame, whereas Herder emphasizes strict singularity. See Cassirer, *Philosophie der Aufklärung*, 309.

13. See Löwith, *Meaning in History*, 11–12.

14. A passage of part 2 of *Decline of the West* expresses this idea with tragic-heroic pathos: "The last race [*Rasse*] to keep its form, the last living tradition, the last leader [*Führer*] go through the goal victorious" (UdA 1101; see also UdA 686).

15. See Strong, "Oswald Spengler: Ontologie, Kritik und Enttäuschung"; Strong connects Spengler with later critical thought, especially Foucault's *episteme* (185–86). The insight into past epistemic moments for the sake of identifying and critiquing our own is close to Spengler's idea of archaeology: "Archaeology itself is the expression of the feeling that history repeats itself" (UdA 4–5).

16. Spengler fits into all three of the "three conservatisms" presented at the end of Habermas's "Modernity: An Unfinished Project" (53–54). This may be a problem in Habermas's typology or a sign that Spengler, due to his theory's internal contradictions, is archetypal for twentieth-century conservatism.

17. Spengler is a declared anti-classicist and anti-romantic. Renaissance, both as a name for an artistic period and as an idea, is also an object of scorn. In all of these cases, his objection is that imitation—as well as canonizing and classicizing gestures—is always inauthentic and belated in comparison to the original organicity of "culture." The eighteenth-century morphological idea of *Bildungstrieb*, though it does not appear in Spengler, is also worth mentioning here. Degner's *Bilder im Wechsel der Töne* addresses *Bildungstrieb* (171–79) in Hölderlin,

thereby producing an intensely anti-morphological conception. His poetics of *Bildungstrieb* skew perceived morphological continuity toward an aesthetics and literary practice opposed to single-outcome systems. What Degner terms a "Revision des Blicks" is the "recursive construction" (176) of alternate unrealized *Bildungstriebe*. Where the sentimental gaze remains fixated on a supposedly perfect past, Hölderlin pursues a strategy of deliberate pseudomorphosis.

18. Many readers implicitly pass judgment on Spengler and his moral character. These readings miss the "dramatic irony" and become victims of it. Spengler brought a tradition of negative portrayals down on himself, but vilification is counterproductive. For example, Jochen Schmidt, *Die Geschichte des Genie-Gedankens* (2:202–5), seems uncertain if Spengler is a cause or an effect of the historical dynamics he implicates himself in. Schmidt, citing the same passages as Hermann Heller's 1930 essay, repeats Heller's verdict. Schmidt thus appears antiquated in comparison with much earlier work such as Adorno's "Spengler nach dem Untergang" (1938, English 1941, 1950, *Prismen* 1955) or Lübbe's 1980 "Historisch-politische Exaltationen: Spengler wiedergelesen."

19. Compare Mandelkow, 240–261; on Spengler in particular, 259.

20. Spengler claims that cross-cultural borrowing occurs under the aegis of the epistemic prejudices of the target culture. Spengler views such appropriations negatively, as an impediment to the self-developing entelechy of discrete cultural monads; great cultures emerge in spite of pseudomorphosis (UdA 784).

21. Spengler at one point defines *Urworte* as axioms, deductive a prioris, which "give shape to experience rather than emerging from it" (UdA 483).

22. Another example of Spengler's confusion of author and protagonist is a famous line from *Tasso,* which Spengler puts in Goethe's mouth: ". . . Goethe gab es ein Gott, zu sagen, wie er leide" (UdA 382).

23. Spengler does not like the language of "problems," which seems too activist and trivially academic to him: "As long as we have hope, we tend to call the arcanum a 'problem'" (UdA 571).

24. The importance of Goethe's "Urworte" for Spengler (and the contrast between Benjamin's dialectical image and Spengler's analogical "simultaneity" of epochs) have been noted in Ophälders's "Dialektik eines Bildes des Abendlandes."

25. Compare Adorno, "Spengler nach dem Untergang," 65.

26. According to Spengler, in modernity only law is retrograde, an un-Faustian holdover from earlier times (UdA 617–55).

27. In part 2 of *Decline,* Spengler says that the privileged recipient of "inner certainty" is "the true statesman" who is "history incarnate" (*die Geschichte in Person*) (UdA 1113); "there are moments [*Augenblicke*] in which an individual knows himself to be identical with fate and the center of the world [*die Weltmitte*] and experiences his personality almost as a cloak [*Hülle*] in which the history of the future is preparing to dress itself" (UdA 1115).

28. Twentieth-century classics on reason and causation in history might include works of Weber, Lukács, Schmitt, Heidegger, Benjamin, Adorno, and Adorno-Horkheimer and, after the war, Koselleck (*Critique and Crisis*), Blumenberg (*Legitimacy of the Modern Age*), and Habermas (*Theory of Communicative Action*).

29. Liu, "The Question Concerning Morphology," is persuasive on this point, but he is perhaps too willing to overlook Spengler's official thesis in order to

postulate post-poststructuralist undercurrents. Liu follows Badiou in questioning philosophy's relation to the representation of infinity (116–21). The increasing general awareness of the idea of infinity, Liu argues, ushers in an era that Spengler's *Decline* anticipated and helped to precipitate. Liu daringly goes against the endemic rejections of Spengler, but for me the messianic-epochal implications he develops remain too meta-historical. Liu's findings could be productively contrasted with theories that insist on the idea of redemption vs. theories that suppose a political theological "covering" of sacred concepts with secular ones.

30. A parallel passage from part 2 shifts the emphasis away from the primal unity and toward a primal entanglement of exception and rule: "An animal is afraid of individual dangers, but early man trembled before the entire world. Everything within him remained dark and unresolved. The quotidian and the demonic are completely and lawlessly entangled [*unentwirrbar und regellos verstrickt*]" (UdA 894).

31. The "warp and weft" metaphor of the demonic is rewritten in Doderer's "Sexualität und der totale Staat" in the relation of burning logs to the grid of a grating, which allows ash to fall through (*Wiederkehr der Drachen*, 286). The unburned logs represent primitive unity, whereas the ash is the alienation of modern thought after it has passed through a rational-conceptual grid.

32. See Schmitz, "Das Ganz-Andere: Goethe und das Ungeheuere," which expands upon the idea of *sittliche Weltordnung* (427).

33. Faust imagines something like this at the end of his life (HA 3:344; vv. 11433–44) before Care (*die Sorge*) catches up to him; Blumenberg's *Work on Myth* conceives the unity of primitive man as "the absolutism of reality," which refers to a situation of pure terror and the absolute state of exception; the post-absolutist state of reality is a "work on myth" characterized by balanced (i.e., not unified) powers.

34. Compare Stern, *The Politics of Cultural Despair*: "In modern Germany there were a great many Spenglers before the master-metahistorian had his day" (188).

Chapter Five

1. An exception is Axer's forthcoming "Alldeutig, zweideutig, undeutig," which focuses on Benjamin's essay on Karl Kraus. Among older work, Agamben's "Benjamin and the Demonic" stands out, but it often overlooks the connection to Goethe or takes it as self-evident. Agamben's emphasis of messianic motifs over "demonic ambiguity," however, and his implicit equation of the demonic and the Luciferian, for example, reflect unresolved misunderstandings and conceptual difficulties.

2. Citations of Benjamin refer to the Suhrkamp edition (abbreviated GS); translations are my own. Simonis's *Gestalttheorie von Goethe bis Benjamin* includes an extended narration (323–27) of Benjamin's engagement with Goethe. Lindner, "Goethes Wahlverwandtschaften," makes an even stronger case, mentioning Benjamin's 1931 plan, which he was never able to realize, to write a lengthy book on Goethe (480).

3. See Fehér, "Lukács und Benjamin: Affinitäten und Divergenzen."

4. A letter to Max Horkheimer from 1940 (*Gesammelte Briefe*, 6:413–14) suggests a late rereading, focused on the later sections of Spengler's book. Benjamin sees *The Decline of the West* as symptomatic for the development of Hitlerian

ideology. Benjamin's criticism of the left's confused response to part 1 and relative silence about part 2 may perhaps be readable as indirect self-criticism. Whether he knew Spengler's work or not, Benjamin never refers to it by name in his published work. But Benjamin's polemics against others—especially Gundolf—leave little doubt about his position toward Spengler.

5. The remark—"Was soll ich von ihm halten? Ein trivialer Sauhund"—is recorded by Werner Kraft ("Über Benjamin," 66). The wide circulation of this anecdote has exaggerated its importance: Benjamin's negative attitude toward Spengler is unsurprising, but the 1933 comment in itself adds nothing. The full anecdote, however, is more interesting: Kraft asked Benjamin what he thought of Spengler's *politics* in the 1930s (his opposition to Hitler), but the response reflects a general indictment of Spengler's *philosophy*. Kraft implies that, despite the harsh reaction, Benjamin may have once shared his contemporaries' interest in Spengler. Kraft sees both Spengler and Benjamin as figures who are more interesting than their fate: "Gewiß war Spengler ein Verhängnis, und doch zeigt ein Photo in dem Almanach des Verlages Beck 'Das Aquadukt' [*sic*] (1963) das ergreifende Bild eines *jungendlichen* Philosophen, das auch Benjamin ergriffen hätte" (66). The volume in question, *Der Aquädukt* (1963), includes features on Egon Friedell, Franz Blei, Hilde Spiel, and Heimito von Doderer. Kraft's odd claim that Benjamin would have been fascinated by the 1910 photo of Spengler may be rooted in Kraft's desire to see a resemblance between the young Spengler and the young Benjamin.

6. See Wundt's chapter, "Dämonenglaube und Dämonenkulte," from his 1905 *Völkerpsychologie: Mythus und Religion* (457–576). Wundt's approach to the demonic in 1905 reflects a degree of similarity with Goethe's "Urworte" and *Poetry and Truth*—as well as with Gundolf's *Goethe*. Wundt's demons also exhibit "demonic ambiguity": a demon may be an evil spirit or a "guardian demon" (*Schutzdämon*), a "duplication of the personality" (*Verdoppelung der Persönlichkeit*) or a "demonic embodiment of the human fate" (*dämonische Verkörperung des menschlichen Schicksals*) (457).

7. By the time of the publication of part 2 of *Decline* in 1923, Spengler had integrated Freud's theory into his claims (UdA 693–96).

8. Scholem's remarks pertain to the two versions of Benjamin's essay ("Die Lehre vom Ähnlichen" and "Über das mimetische Vermögen"). In further sketches on this topic, dated from the mid-1930s, Benjamin wrote: "A further canon of similarity is the totem. The Jewish ban on image-making is probably connected to totemism" (GS 2.3:957).

9. Compare Sagnol, "Recht und Gerechtigkeit bei Walter Benjamin": "In opposition to the claims of the whole tradition of the philosophy of law [*Rechtsphilosophie*], law [*das Recht*] [in Benjamin] does not represent an accomplishment of man, his emancipation from mythic forces [*Gewalten*] that formerly ruled humanity but is instead their ominous remainder [*verhängnisvoller Überrest*]" (60, my translation).

10. Cf. Martínez, *Doppelte Welten,* 38; and Sagnol, "Recht und Gerechtigkeit bei Walter Benjamin," 63.

11. Thanks to Google, it is easy to discover that the line comes from chapter 7 of France's 1894 *Le Lys rouge.* The same line from France is cited somewhat more fully in part 2 of *The Decline of the West:* "Jedes Recht ist von einem einzelnen

Stande im Namen der Allgemeinheit geschaffen worden. Anatole France hat ein-
mal gesagt, 'daß unser Recht in majestätischer Gleichheit dem Reichen wie dem
Armen verbiete, Brot zu stehlen und an den Straßenecken zu betteln' " (UdA 630).
The reference functions similarly in both authors' critiques of the modern institution of law.

12. For both Benjamin and Blumenberg, myth is a polemic against a preceding
age, but for the latter it expresses a *distance* from and a polytheistic *fragmentation* of a previous "absolutist" era in which humans were utterly at the mercy
of unnamed horrors. Though not necessarily reflective of *progress*, myth at least
represents a *process* of rationalization (in both senses) in which the mere appearance of controllability is decisive. For Benjamin, the blindness that comes with
myth's progressive sublimations magnifies the final costs. Blumenberg acknowledges that modernity may only raise the stakes without ever fully breaking from
myth, but his idea of "work" pragmatically focuses on myth's ongoing ability
to mitigate the hostility of existence. Both Benjamin and Blumenberg oppose
Christianity's hybridization of myth and monotheism. Blumenberg calls it an
"absolutism of transcendence" (AaM 158) that contradicts myth's efforts to
lower the stakes (by telling stories of how a tenuous livability came about).

13. The intense interest of recent science fiction with this problem reflects the
way that it plays out under the conditions of modern technology. Especially the
idea of "apophenia" developed in William Gibson's *Pattern Recognition* explores
the question of whether there is really a "conspiracy" (a demonic force behind
unfolding events) or whether the chances that coincidences and patterns will be
perceived and realized are only increasing through more extensive technological
networking.

14. The English title of this work, *Origins of the German Mourning Play*, is
cumbersome; thus I will follow the common convention of referring to it simply
as the *Trauerspielbuch*.

15. See Blumenberg, *Theorie der Unbegrifflichkeit*; and my own "Working
Over Philosophy."

16. Doderer's "Sexualität und der totale Staat," though perhaps not perfectly
consistent on this point, is overall a clear case of the confusion of analogy and
affinity. Doderer's understanding of "analogy" may be that of Aquinas's *analogia
entis* inflected by Spenglerian morphology; compare Kleinlercher's conversation
with Wolfgang Fleischer (Kleinlercher, *Zwischen Wahrheit und Dichtung*, 355).

17. Hamacher's "Afformativ, Streik" describes the afformative as an "event of
formation that does not give rise to any form" (*Ereignis der Formierung, das in
keiner Form aufgeht*, 364). This contrasts with speech act theory's idea of the
"performative," which is apparently conclusive, executive, and formulaic.

18. Haverkamp's *Figura Cryptica* also emphasizes the Goethean *figura mor-
phologica* encrypted in the dialectical image (52–53).

19. Simonis's *Gestalttheorie von Goethe bis Benjamin* characterizes Benjamin's
version of morphology in terms of fragmentariness and dynamic openness with
respect to the form-ideals of classicism, thereby deemphasizing the anti-classicist
side of Goethe's own conception of metamorphosis. A stereotyped classicism
thus tends to overstate and mischaracterize the differences between Goethe and
Benjamin: "*Benjamin glaubt* in Goethe somit einen exemplarischen Vertreter der
Moderne zu erkennen" (330, emphasis mine).

20. Benjamin's Goethean anti-Platonism is echoed in Blumenberg's criticism of Rothacker's appropriation of the idea of *geprägte Formen* in his *Philosophische Anthropologie*. Rothacker sees a historical conservation of forms in institutions, but Blumenberg argues that apparent continuity only covers troubling discontinuities: "Zeit schleift die Prägnanzen [the significances of inherited forms] nicht ab, sie holt aus ihnen heraus, ohne daß man hinzufügen dürfte: 'was drin ist' " (AaM 79).

21. Simonis sees the Goethe essay as a work of "extraordinary significance . . . within Benjamin's oeuvre" (*Gestalttheorie von Goethe bis Benjamin*, 330). Lindner ("Goethes Wahlverwandtschaften") observes the essay's meticulous organization (from which Benjamin eliminated all subsections and subtitles); according to Lindner, it represents "a maximum" in Benjamin's theoretical stylistics (*ein Maximum seiner schriftstellerischen Darstellungskunst*, 473).

22. There is, as far as I can see, no compelling reason to strictly periodize Benjamin's work. The 1931 essay on Karl Kraus, for example, is arguably comparable to the Goethe essay in its complexity and returns to some of the same topics (including the demonic). Axer's "Alldeutig, zweideutig, undeutig" shows how the later essay reconfigures concerns that had occupied Benjamin since the 1910s.

23. The first paragraph concludes with an excursus on fate and character in relation to sign systems. I bracket it, however, because Benjamin introduces this topic primarily in order to exclude it. He concludes that "signifying relations can never be conceived causally." This rules out all semiotics of physical signs as the effects of character or as predictors of fate. The semiotic question is "an equally closed and difficult relation," but it is a "different problem." The topic of the essay is thus not *the signification of fate and character* but *the relation of fate and character itself* (GS 2.1:172).

24. According to the economical formula of the *Trauerspielbuch:* "The tragic is to the demonic as the paradox is to ambiguity" (*Das Tragische verhält sich zum Dämonischen wie das Paradoxon zur Zweideutigkeit*, GS 1.1:288).

25. According to an early fragment: "Heidentum entsteht wenn die Sphäre des geniushaft Menschlichen, der Urphänomene der Kunst, Musisches und *mechané* die symbolisch für das Dasein der Heiligkeit sind zur Sphäre der Geistigkeit selbst erhoben werden, zur dämonischen Gemeinschaft. / Das Heidentum steht in der Sphäre des Dämonischen und des Geniushaften" (GS 6:90). In striking contrast to assumptions of art's loss of its communal function in modernity, Benjamin seems to suggest that the communal and cultural potentials of art are the result of false idolization and heathen religiosity.

26. The confusion of Benjamin's reading with the one he attacks persists even in recent interpretations. In Martínez's *Doppelte Welten*, Benjamin is made into "the most decisive example" of the mythic reading, which "posits a radical difference between our modern world and the one represented in *The Elective Affinities*" (37–38). For Benjamin, the ambiguities of Goethe's novel are precisely those of "our modern world." See Liska's "Die Mortifikation der Kritik" for a comprehensive though certainly not exhaustive inventory of misreadings and deliberate distortions of Benjamin's essay.

27. Leacock's reading of Benjamin's essay emphasizes the importance of the idea of decision. I also think of Dostoyevsky's Stavrogin, who, according to the narrator, up to and including his last act, goes to great length to wordlessly show that he acts *consciously.*

28. Peculiarly, perhaps tellingly, Lindner's short list of the sources upon which Benjamin based his polemic against Gundolf does not include the "Urworte" ("Goethes Wahlverwandtschaften," 479–80).

29. Like Gundolf, Spengler tends to systematically exclude *Elpis;* see UdA 571.

Chapter Six

1. See Kierkegaard's *Either/Or* (I): "Don Juan . . . is the expression for the demonic qualified as sensuous; Faust is the expression for the demonic qualified as the spiritual that the Christian spirit excludes" (90). In Goethe's conversation with Eckermann on June 20, 1831, Mozart is cited as an example of demonic inspiration in opposition to the idea of *Komposition:* "How can one say that Mozart supposedly *composed* his Don Juan!" (Eckermann, *Gespräche mit Goethe,* 736). Goethe's position here is evidently informed by his thinking on the conflict between Cuvier and Saint-Hilaire (HA 13:245–46; FA 838).

2. The characteristic male gendering of the demonic character is deeply rooted in the connection of (male) geniuses and figures like Don Giovanni representing productive and destructive male sexuality. Perhaps the demonic might be viewed as a parallel discourse to the more negatively connoted conception of hysteria. The young Lukács's connection of the demonic with male heroes and narrators is apparently in line with this—but in other contexts Friedrich Hebbel's *Judith* epitomized his idea of heroism.

3. The narratorless demonic novel remains absolutely current. Suarez's 2006 action thriller, *Daemon,* and its sequel *Freedom*™, for example, grapple with the demonic in view of technology's possibilities of fundamentally altering the systems by which individual destinies are produced. A computer program (a "daemon" or "bot") is able to master chance and control the plot; old hierarchies of money and power are mediatized and repurposed into a rational meritocracy of individual self-realization; in *Freedom*™, the computer-daemon turns out to be a classical daemon capable of superseding positive law: "The entire concept of a daemon stems from the guardian spirits of Greek mythology—spirits who watched over mankind to keep them out of trouble" (82). (I thank Prof. Bettina Schlüter for making me aware of Suarez's novels.)

4. Szondi has remarked that Lukács's theory is "not thinkable" without Hegel's philosophy of art (*Poetik und Geschichstsphilosophie,* 1:309).

5. *Esztétikai kultura (Aesthetic Culture),* Budapest 1913; cited from Márkus, "Die Seele und das Leben. Der junge Lukács und das Problem der 'Kultur,' " 110.

6. Resembling the subject-object opposition, the title of Lukács's 1911 *Die Seele und die Formen (The Soul and the Forms)* also reconfigures Goethe's *Dämon-Tyche.* The aesthetic strives toward "the mystical moment of union of inside and outside, soul and form" (*Die Seele und die Formen,* 17, my translation). This conception is compatible with Wundt's *Völkerpsychologie,* which defines a *Dämon* as "a higher-order soul," residing somewhere between individual psyche and collectively recognized divinity: "the meaning of the concept of the *Dämon* experiences two important shifts. The one leads . . . toward the idea of the soul; the other expands it limitlessly by extending it to include everything beyond the reach of human power. On the one hand the *Dämon* returns itself to the shape of the individual soul, on the other hand it raises itself to become a god" (458–59, my translation).

7. Lukács, *Theorie des Romans*, 137 (my translation); abbreviated TdR.

8. Broch writes in *Der Tod des Vergil* of an "overcoming of the demonic [*Überwindung des Dämonischen*]" (73). Whereas Lukács's theory envisions a possibility of this-worldly transcendence, in Broch's novel death is the horizon of its overcoming.

9. See Löwy, "Der junge Lukács und Dostojewski," emphasizing the breadth of Lukács's readings in the 1910s. This can also be seen in Lukács's *Dostojewski Notizen und Entwürfe*. Hoeschen's *Das "Dostojewsky"-Projekt* focuses on neo-Kantian aspects of Lukács's thought and argues against overemphasizing Hegel; Simmel and *Lebensphilosophie* are also downplayed.

10. Cited from Nyíri's preface to Lukács's *Dostojewski Notizen und Entwürfe* (12).

11. See TdR 5–17; Spengler is also named in the 1962 introduction (10). The philosophy of history of Lukács's 1916 theory in some ways resembles Spengler's deterministic *Decline:* Lukács speaks confidently of "the present state of spirit" (*der gegenwärtige Stand des Geistes,* TdR 126), "the basis within the philosophy of history" (*geschichtsphilosophische Grundlage,* TdR 122), "the intuitive visionary of the philosophical-historical moment that will not return" (*der intuitive Visionär des nicht wiederkehrenden geschichtsphilosophischen Moments,* TdR 116); such formulations show that Lukács, like Spengler, believed in the "demonic" connection between artistic genius and the historical moment. This belief (or superstition) has since been the object of literary satires, such as Borges's "Pierre Menard, autor del Quijote." More recently and directly focusing on Lukács, Menasse's *Selige Zeiten, brüchige Welt* tells of Leo Singer, who wants to rewrite Hegel's philosophy of history backward in order to update it for the post-1968 world. In the process, Leo unwittingly follows in the footsteps of the young Lukács.

12. Lukács's Heidelberg connections would have made him aware of Gundolf's Goethe interpretation well before 1916. See Lukács, *Briefwechsel 1902–1917,* 325, 393; also Fehér's "Das Bündnis von Georg Lukács und Béla Balázs bis zur ungarischen Revolution 1918": "It is well known what a central importance Goethe's unique theory of the symbol had for Lukács's entire aesthetic development" (164, my translation).

13. According to Szondi, Schlegel "[will] neben den Gegenständen immer auch die eigene Position erkennen" (*Poetik und Geschichtsphilosophie* 2:113).

14. On the turbulence of Lukács's intellectual development, see Márkus's "Die Seele und das Leben"; on the early aesthetic theories in particular, see Márkus's "Lukács' erste Ästhetik: Zur Entwicklungsgeschichte der Philosophie des jungen Lukács." Márkus writes of "kaleidoscopic changes . . . combined with emphatic consistency of the basic problems and intents" (104, my translation).

15. Despite the fact that Adorno probably never read the *Heidelberg Aesthetics,* an affinity may be noted. See Hohendahl's "Art Work in Modernity," which finds that "Adorno's theoretical endeavors can only be understood against the background of Lukács's early work" (34).

16. Here Lukács's aesthetics may seem to intersect with Blumenberg. Unlike Lukács, Blumenberg is comfortable with bracketing's "negative" side effect of producing a plurality of semi-autonomous worlds.

17. Lukács, *Heidelberger Ästhetik,* 28 (my translation); abbreviated HÄs.

18. "Das Luciferische" only appears once in the *Heidelberg Aesthetics*, but it also appears in the *Theory of the Novel* and the Dostoyevsky notes. Márkus summarizes the conception: "The young Lukács interprets . . . art's utopian function of creating a reality that would be adequate to man . . . as precisely its 'Luciferism': The work brings about harmony and fulfillment prior to (and without) the real redemption of man" (*Die Seele und das Leben*, 101, my translation). Márkus also writes: "According to [Lukács's idea of "Luziferismus"], the perfected world of the work of art . . . can only represent . . . 'an anticipation of perfection, harmony prior to and without redemption' [*ein 'Vorschuß auf Vollkommenheit, Harmonie vor und ohne Erlösung'*]" (209).

19. "Between Ahab and the whale there plays out a drama that could be called metaphysical in a vague sense of the word, the same struggle that is played out between the Sirens and Ulysses. Each of these pairs wants to be everything, wants to be the absolute world, which makes coexistence with the other absolute world impossible; and yet each one has no greater desire than this very coexistence, this encounter" (Blanchot, *The Book to Come*, 8). *The Book to Come* (esp. 97–104) implicitly builds on Lukács's *Theory of the Novel* and Goethe's (or Gundolf's) idea of the demonic.

20. The idea of normative inversion, which I use here in an extended (perhaps stretched) sense, comes from Assmann's *Moses der Ägypter*. The idea of an inversion may help to explain Fehér's claim in "Am Scheideweg des romantischen Antikapitalismus": "'Luciferian' does not mean a repudiated or purely negative state in the vagaries of human history" (291, my translation).

21. Here one can note the differences between Benjamin's and Lukacs's conceptions. In the terms of Benjamin's "Elective Affinities," art could only be Luciferian if the interruption of *das Ausdruckslose* had never marked the borders of work and world.

22. On Lukács's idealization of Greek antiquity as the unity of perfect historical realization of culture and society, see Márkus, "Die Seele und das Leben" (118).

23. See the *Heidelberg Aesthetics*'s opening discussion of the heterogeneity of art and culture (15). Modern cultural forms are dependent and reproductive, which, in comparison to art, makes them less interesting. But if art is Luciferian, then a high valuation of art is symptomatic of cultural problems.

24. Nietzsche's *Birth of Tragedy* represents a conspicuous absence in Lukács's 1916–18 aesthetics, but it is a work he was certainly familiar with. Compare Lukács, *Briefwechsel*, 2 and 230. The *Theory of the Novel* also never names Nietzsche, but he is an easily discerned opponent of its opening section. Nietzsche "psychologizes" the Greeks and conceives "the perfection of form in an idiosyncratic and solipsistic way as a function of inner devastation [*als Funktion des inneren Zerstörtseins*]" (TdR 23).

25. According to Márkus, the *Heidelberger Ästhetik* represents "einen einzigen kritischen Kampf gegen den Geist der Hegelschen Philosophie" (*Die Seele und das Leben*, 227).

26. The idea of *Glanz* inverts a famous topos from *Faust II*: "in the colorful reflection [of the rainbow] we have life [*im farbigen Abglanz haben wir das Leben*]" (v. 4727; HA 149). This kind of reflection is not substantial enough for Lukács (HÄs 163), because colorful refractions are only broken light.

27. Especially in part 1, it is often uncertain which epics Lukács has in mind. Dante, Cervantes, and Goethe's *Wilhelm Meister* (TdR 45) in any case make the list, while part 2 introduces limit cases such as Pontoppidan's *Hans im Glück,* Flaubert's *Education sentimentale,* Tolstoy's *War and Peace*—and Dostoyevsky. Lukács never mentions Carlyle's *Sartor Resartus,* but its "theoretical" approach and connections to Goethe makes it an obvious precursor to Lukács's theory.

28. It is impossible to know to what degree Lukács may have had Goethe in mind in any given passage, but the following remark from the *Heidelberg Aesthetics* shows proficiency with Goethe's terms: "Das Zufällige ist hier im Sinne des Goethischen 'Tyche,' der produktiv-machenden Gelegenheit zu verstehen" (HÄs 205).

29. All of the *Urworte* are implicitly developed in part 2 of Lukács's theory. I read the more purely theoretical first half as a consequent execution of Goethe's paradigms of the demonic, whereas part 2 attempts to illustrate the theory's applicability, arguably to the point of excess, in formulations such as "der dämonische Charakter" (TdR 83), "die Dämonie der Verengung der Seele" vs. "die Dämonie des abstrakten Idealismus" (TdR 83), the "Verzaubertsein [der Wirklichkeit] von bösen Dämonen" (TdR 83), "dämonisches Besessensein" (TdR 85), "[die] vom Dämon nicht ergriffenen Gebieten der Seele" (TdR 86), "[der] Gott, . . . [der] in Wahrheit ein Dämon geworden [ist]" (TdR 89), "die [historische] Periode der freigelassenen Dämonie" (TdR 90), "[das] entweichen der aktiven Dämonen" (TdR 91), "reine Dämonie" (TdR 93), "das dämonisch Humorvolle" (TdR 94), "subjektiv-psychologische Dämonie" (TdR 94), "eine dämonische Gewalt" (TdR 97), "negative Dämonie" (TdR 97), "[das] wahnsinnig dämonische Gesichertsein" (TdR 116).

30. Lukács's enthusiasm for Dostoyevsky may have been partly inspired by the mania surrounding the Piper edition of his works (edited by the conservative revolutionary Arthur Moeller van den Bruck). According to Garstka's *Arthur Moeller van den Bruck,* German nationalists looked to Russia and Dostoyevsky for relief from Western-liberal ideas; they saw Russia as a land "of independent 'soulful' development" (*der eigenständigen 'seelischen' Entwicklung*), a "misinterpretation" that was "widespread among the German intelligentsia" of the first half of the twentieth century (18, my translation). Lukács's Dostoyevsky notes in fact refer to the Piper edition. One might further speculate that in the 1910s and 1920s, Dostoyevsky was read not only as a figure of national identity, but in the light of nostalgia for an *unreformed,* "orthodox" Christianity—Christianity without a "Protestant ethic" or an iron cage.

31. Volz's 1924 *Das Dämonische in Jahwe* argues (with Job in mind) that monotheism, in order to make its theodicy coherent, must assimilate demons into the concept of divinity. Gnosticisms and dualisms, on the other hand, undo this separation.

32. I borrow this term from Benjamin's *Trauerspielbuch,* in which it refers to baroque Christianity's and the baroque theater's tendency to overextend the difference between the desolation of the historical world and the perfection of salvation (GS 1.1:246).

33. This debate has been further reflected in two collections on the contemporary theoretical significance of the inheritances of Gnosticism: the first, from 1984, was edited by Taubes, *Religionstheorie und Politische Theologie, Bd. 2:*

Gnosis und Politik; and the second, from 1993, was edited by Sloterdijk and Macho, *Weltrevolution der Seele: Ein Lese- und Arbeitsbuch der Gnosis.* The main sources of the debate, from Eric Voegelin (214–15) to Blumenberg (228–34) and Odo Marquard (234–41), are excerpted in the later volume. The Taubes volume, in addition to an essay by the editor himself (9–15), again includes Marquard on the idea of a "gnostisches Rezidiv" (31–36) as well as a critique of this conception by Wolfgang Hübener (37–53). After Voegelin, the debate was reactivated by Blumenberg's arguments *against* a Gnostic relapse in *Die Legitimät der Neuzeit.* Schmitt's *Politische Theologie II* first brought Goethe (and *der ungeheuere Spruch*) into the equation, and Blumenberg devoted a chapter of *Work on Myth* to the refutation of this reading ("Lesarten des 'Ungeheueren Spruchs,'" AaM 567–604). The recently published Schmitt-Blumenberg *Briefwechsel* also includes selections of relevant texts (35–86). In the letters themselves, see especially Blumenberg's letter from August 7, 1975 (132–34). In the somewhat different context of "literary" Gnosticism, Bloom's "Lying Against Time: Gnosis, Poetry, Criticism" is also pertinent.

Chapter Seven

1. This conclusion roughly follows Kai Luehrs's *"Fledermausflügel im Bücherkasten"*; I am less convinced, however, that Lukács's theory is as epigonal as Luehrs imagines.

2. Doderer, *Die Dämonen,* 10; abbreviated DD.

3. See the entry on "Dämonen" from Henner Löffler's *Doderer-ABC* (94–104). Without claiming to have definitively identified every demon in the novel, Löffler offers helpful interpretive suggestions which generally equate the "demons" with the delusional "second realities" (*zweite Wirklichkeiten*) that plague the novel's protagonists.

4. Compare Honold, "Bernhards Dämonen": "Thomas Bernhard's grandfather was his good demon" (19, my translation). My work supports the connection between the demonic and the process of literary creation, but looking at it through Doderer highlights the implicit patricide in Bernhard's recourse to Dostoyevsky (his literary "grandfather").

5. Hoffmann, *Aus Gesprächen mit Thomas Bernhard,* 22.

6. See Liska, "Die Mortifikation der Kritik," who argues that the point of Benjamin's Goethe essay is to wrench some "congealed transcendence" out of the novel's "chaos of symbols"—a chaos which critics have often read as a sign of the work's aesthetic perfection (581). It makes a difference, in other words, whether the unresolvable meanings of the "total novel" are valued positively (as a kind of surplus) or negatively (as a deficiency characteristic of the modern, secular world).

7. The earliest genesis of the novel certainly lies before 1930. My findings show this, as does Kleinlercher's *Zwischen Wahrheit und Dichtung* (214–15).

8. The secondary literature on Doderer's novel, for good reasons, foregrounds the connection to Dostoyevsky. See especially Chevrel's "Die Dämonen: Doderer und der Fall Dostojewskij(s)." I do not deny Dostoyevsky's central importance, but he may also function as a decoy with respect to other sources. According to Doderer: "Criticism has been unable to establish an intensive connection between me and Dostoyevsky" (cited from Chevrel 142, my translation; see also Kleinlercher, *Zwischen Wahrheit und Dichtung,* 215).

9. Wundt's definitions are compatible with the absence of demons in Doderer's novel. According to Wundt, a demon is any incorporeal spirit, including dream images and everything which, from the subjective perspective, appears to be beyond "the usual course of events [*der gewöhnliche Verlauf des Geschehens*]"; demons manifest themselves in "metamorphoses that resist every rule [*jeder Regel widerstrebende Metamorphosen*]"; they exist "everywhere where unusual things happen [*überall, wo Ungewöhnliches geschieht*]" (*Völkerpsychologie*, 458, my translation).

10. The page numbers refer to points in Lukács's argument that support Doderer's epic conception of (1) the worldliness of the novel, (2) the importance of narration (and the figure of the narrator), (3) the problems of authorial-narrative perspective (*Gesinnung*) and meaning (*Sinn and Sinngebung*) and (4) the inadmissibility of direct communication between author and reader ("congealed transcendence"). After 1930, whenever Doderer cites Lukács in his diaries, he refers to at least one of the two passages noted in 1930 (TB 680, 684, 727, 898, 918, 1032, 1128, 1171–72, 1175); this continues into the '40s and '50s (*Tangenten*, 15–17, 25, 340–41, 351, 412, 455, 796, 826; *Commentarii I*, 174, 259).

11. In 1925, Doderer describes Kafka's *The Trial* as "one of the absolute best books of all of the ones I know" (TB 273). Of Rilke's *Malte*, he writes: "I admit that I had read the 'Notebooks of Malte Laurids Brigge' once before, but it is very evident that I did . . . not recognize what a work it is. Most powerful power that has given itself all of the attributes of power! [*Gewaltigste Kraft, die sich aller Attribute der Gewalt begeben hat!*]" (TB 286). In the same entry, Doderer mentions Rilke's "Stundenbuch," which he read as a prisoner of war in Siberia: "It was almost as if an angel—diving down and soaring up again—had lifted me up and drawn me out of all of the misery. This what a poet can do [*Solches vermag ein Dichter*]" (TB 286).

12. This is to my knowledge the only mention of Moeller in Doderer's writings. The mention of Moeller may add something to the existing accounts of the sources of Doderer's nationalism and anti-Semitism. Doderer was certainly influenced by the "conservative revolution" or "Germanic ideology," as Fritz Stern calls it in his *The Politics of Cultural Despair*. Stern claims: "No other modern writer save Nietzsche had as great an impact on German thought as Dostoyevsky, and the character of that impact was largely shaped by Moeller" (210).

13. See Kleinlercher, *Zwischen Wahrheit und Dichtung*, 214–15. In the 1940s, after the failure of *Die Dämonen*, Doderer's *Die Strudlhofstiege* emerged from his attempts to deepen his characters' earlier lives and their relation to their milieu. In the 1950s, after *Die Strudlhofstiege* was published to wide acclaim, Doderer revised *Die Dämonen* in ways that retained elements of the original conception while distancing himself from the political and anti-Semitic agenda that defined the novel in the 1930s.

14. Kleinlercher, *Zwischen Wahrheit und Dichtung*, 331.

15. Dostoyevsky, *Die Dämonen* (2008), 53.

16. Only two months before their final separation in November 1932, Gusti Hasterlik gave Doderer a copy of Dostoyevsky's *Die Dämonen* (see Kleinlercher, *Zwischen Wahrheit und Dichtung*, 215).

17. Compare TdR 38. The improvement of Doderer's Dostoyevsky reading can be seen in the entry of March 26, 1937. The figure of Schatoff is now

a representative of "the Russian ideology" (TB 984) and "what is monstrous about the whole thing [*das Ungeheuerliche an der ganzen Sache*] . . . is that Dostoyevsky here opens up one of his greatest perspectives on the philosophy of history [*eine seiner grössten geschichtsphilosophischen Perspektiven öffnet*] . . . without allowing this transcendence to congeal on him [*ohne dass ihm die Transcendenz gerinnt*]" (TB 985).

18. See Kleinlercher, *Zwischen Wahrheit und Dichtung*, 209–89. Though Kleinlercher's readings are perhaps not the last word in terms of literary nuance, she decisively shows how Doderer integrated an anti-Semitic program into the first version of *Die Dämonen* and how he came to distance himself from it in the published version.

19. See Sommer, "In die 'Sackgasse' und wieder hinaus."

20. Kleinlercher reads the figure of Zienhammer in Doderer's *Der Grenzwald* as a refusal of vilification. Doderer writes: "Zienhammer ist weitaus kein perfekter Schurke, wenn es so etwas überhaupt gibt" (Kleinlercher, *Zwischen Wahrheit und Dichtung*, 152).

21. See D. Weber's "'Welch ein gewaltiger Apperzipierer!' Zu einigen Goethe-Zitaten bei Heimito von Doderer." Weber portrays Doderer as a "lax" reader of Goethe who "cites from memory or second hand [*vom Hörensagen*]" (173, my translation). This may be accurate, but as a general characterization it may be inaccurate. Even if Doderer was often lax, this does not mean he was always lax. Weber also observes that Doderer's connection to Goethe was "extremely intensive" (*höchst intensiv*, 173).

22. Doderer, *Die Wiederkehr der Drachen*, 40; abbreviated WdD.

23. The German sentence reads: "Eine Beziehung, die durchaus im Innern zu entspringen schien, dennoch aber, seltsam genug, in manchen Augenblicken als ein Fremdes, Herantretendes erlebt ward" (WdD 42). This comes strikingly close to Goethe's Eros commentary: "der Mensch scheint nur sich zu gehorchen, sein eigenes Wollen walten zu lassen, seinem Triebe zu fröhnen, und doch sind es Zufälligkeiten die sich unterschieben, Fremdartiges was ihn von seinem Wege ablenkt" (UO 15).

24. Doderer is not consistent about the precise point of onset of the "adult world." The emphasis on language acquisition places it at the end of infancy—but he also often speaks of "childhood." The reticence of the newborn corresponds with Hofrat Gürtzner-Gontard's metaphor in *Die Dämonen* of the fetus covering its face: "The young human simply protests against entering into life on the conditions offered . . . [*Der junge Mensch wehrt sich einfach dagegen, unter den dargebotenen Bedingungen, ins Leben einzutretet . . .*]" (DD 487; see also 498).

25. Stefan Zweig's 1925 *Der Kampf mit dem Dämon* stands out among the numerous sources that could have inspired Doderer to connect the idea of the demonic to the "Typus" of the genius (11). Zweig's book is exemplary in the genre of "spiritual biography" of "heroic" geniuses (12) that was fashionable among conservative revolutionaries and the George circle. Zweig, implicitly in dialogue with Gundolf, justifies his focus on Hölderlin, Kleist, and Nietzsche as an anti-classical and anti-bourgeois—"tragic"—contrast to the model of Goethe.

26. The "Ouvertüre" to *Die Dämonen* from the 1930s is retained with minimal changes in the 1956 published version.

27. Sommer, ed., *Gassen und Landschaften,* 56.

28. Kleinlercher, *Zwischen Wahrheit und Dichtung,* also makes this point, with respect to the eventual collapse of Doderer's *Demons* project in 1940: "the fictional depiction of a social division of Jews and non-Jews . . . was already largely realized in reality" (330, my translation).

29. Important recent work has been devoted to these central and simultaneously marginal figures; see Petutschnig, *Ist er die Mitte?;* and Siegel, "The 'Dream Diary': Heimito von Doderer's Poetics of the Journal."

30. The idea of genius in latency is coined in *Die Strudlhofstiege* (510, 689, 706, 725); in *Die Dämonen* it can be observed in the contrast between Leonhard (whose genius emerges from latency) and the "struggling" main characters (who may not be geniuses at all); see my "Konjunktivisches Erzählen in Heimito von Doderers *Die Dämonen.*"

31. Another alter ego of the author, René von Stangeler, also has a split name: "René" (short for Renato?) echoes the name of the minor character Renata, who, as Siegel ("The 'Dream Diary' ") has emphasized, may be interpreted as a figure of "rebirth."

32. On the complexities of Quapp's development and the narration of it, see my "Konjunktivisches Erzählen in Heimito von Doderers *Die Dämonen.*"

33. Bastards especially need know-how in order to inherit. The contrast with an archetypal literary bastard, Edmund from Shakespeare's *King Lear,* shows the difference between Quapp's passivity and actively "knowing how to inherit."

34. The beginning of *Die Dämonen* finds Geyrenhoff, many years after the events of the novel, living—apparently having outlived his wife and her money—in a painter's atelier, which he had "more or less inherited" (*gewissermaßen beerbt*) from Schlaggenberg (DD 7). Schlaggenberg, a non-inheritor, is skilled at finding such quarters. The elapsed time between the novel's main plot and the narration of the "Overture"—and the uncertainty as to what happened in between—mutes the novel's happy endings.

35. For more on Quapp's *trema,* see my see my "Konjunktivisches Erzählen in Heimito von Doderers *Die Dämonen.*"

36. The *Dämon* as a traumatic inability to perform also appears in *Die Strudlhofstiege* in René's speech on "psychology . . . [as] disinfected demonology" (689).

37. This paradigm of the "seeking" protagonist (the "meaning" of whose life is supplied by the ironically reflecting figure of the narrator) fits precisely with Lukács's conception. It is also worth noting, however, that Doderer's most idealized figures (Kaps and Kakabsa) are no longer artists (or at least receive no recognition as such) and their development is not primarily defined by seeking, but by the development of a system for receiving and practicing internal inheritance. "Success" and a certain external recognition (as in Kakabsa's case) or the relative lack thereof (as in Kaps's case) is secondary in comparison to the narrator's recognition of these figures, which is crucial.

38. A far-fetched but related example is Bamford's *The Shadow Factory,* which chronicles the attempts of the National Security Agency to produce a total transcription of reality. Even given huge databases and a virtually limitless ability to collect and transcribe, the temporal factor may prove insurmountable even to a supercomputer devoted to "Total Information Awareness."

39. The chronicler who tries to write simultaneously with events—without the possibility of retrospective reductions—also parallels Pierre-Simon Laplace's famous "demon."

40. About two years later, on May 10, 1937, Doderer repeats the same point without direct reference to Lukács: "The narrator in his ideality has no other attitude [*Gesinnung*] than that of life where it really happens [*d[a]s Leben, wo es wirklich geschieht*]. He is the *advocatus vitae* against all congealed transcendence [*geronnene Transcendenz*]. . . . This means . . . that he never collects God in any kind of a verifiable way or into any single point but rather tries to distribute Him as such a fine emulsion through the entirety of all of the reported events [*als eine derart feine Emulsion durch das Ganze aller berichteten Begebenheiten*], that the writing hand itself . . . no longer knows what it is actually reporting about" (TB 980).

41. Because Doderer's *Die Strudlhofstiege* contains the kinds of caesuras that Benjamin finds in the *Elective Affinities*, it might be categorized as a traditional (not demonic) novel. The Strudlhof steps themselves fulfill this function, especially if Melzer's ascent (355, 895) is read in connection to what Benjamin calls "astral metaphorics." In *The Demons* "sick terrestrial stars" (*kranke Erden-sterne*) refer to the lights of the distant city and the astrological constellation of the fates of "our group" in this environment (DD 20, 285, 328, 388, 1093, 1118, 1125, 1141, 1146, 1152, 1162, 1343); this contrasts with *Die Strudlhofstiege*, in which the stars "rose, quietly twinkling, over his [Melzer's] inner as well as outer horizons . . . , an interpretable constellation [*ein deutbares Sternbild*] that became a figure [*die Figur annahm*], connected from star to star by fine silvery spider-threads [*von Stern zu Stern durch feine silberne Spinnenfäden verbunden*]" (894–95).

42. I rely implicitly on Petutschnig's *Is er die Mitte?*, which reads metaphors of wood and prosthetics as figurations of the problem of *zweite Wirklichkeit* (114–33). What emerges in light of the theory of the pure types is a conception of reality as essentially prosthetic, even and especially in the "success stories." Language is the ultimate prosthesis that must be integrated and subordinated to the free use of the individual, "a dead object which through exercise is intended to be immediately integrated into the body" (122, my translation).

43. This is comparable to Benjamin's criticism of the ambiguity of Goethe's concept of nature, which turns "the words of reason . . . [into] possessions of nature" (GS 1.1:148).

44. This conception, if one accepts it as fundamental to Doderer's thinking, would have deep implications for his theories of apperception. In *Der Fall Güter-sloh*, the "first reality," the first world, is the "distorted perspective" of the infant. The spontaneous force of apperception stands in relation to an act of deep memory that has nothing to do with the "objective" perception of a "real" world (whose conventional forms are pervasive and coercive). However, this theory of pure types contradicts the theory of second reality in Doderer's 1948 "Sexualität und der totale Staat," which also begins with a typological opposition that supposes a "true" "analogical" reality at the base of the "pseudological" second realities that individuals (in modern societies) create as defense mechanisms. The difference of argumentation between the two essays may reflect Doderer's commitment to a "realist" reading of his work (which became the most influential interpretation).

The reductions and misunderstandings that resulted from expectations of realism and their attribution to Doderer's intents are delineated in Rudolf Helmstetter's *Das Ornament der Grammatik* (esp. 116–19). Despite shifts and inconsistencies in Doderer's self-theorization, "the pure types" were not simply replaced by "second reality." As late as 1966, in "Meine neunzehn Lebensläufe," Doderer presented an autobiographical version of the theory of pure types; he characterizes his "development" as "the very belated attempt to make up for the prenatal advantage [*das sehr verspätete Nachholen jenes vorgeburtlichen Vorsprungs*]" of geniuses (WdD 493).

45. The German word *Frechheit*, which is also important for Doderer's next novel, *Die Merowinger*, is associated with demonic character; this is also the case in the Piper translation of Dostoyevsky's *Demons*. The word has no perfect English equivalent; in German it is a more fixed attribute without the implications of behavior expressed in English words like "audaciousness," "insolence," or "impertinence." Perhaps, following Benjamin's "Fate and Character," *Frechheit* may be seen as a morally neutral category because it does not pertain to freedom of action; it should also be noted, however, that *Frechheit* may have been a part of Doderer's vocabulary of anti-Semitic stereotyping.

46. The difference between "taking" and "receiving" is a crucial one throughout Doderer's works. It is characteristic of a certain (modern) psychology to want to "take" things that can only be "given" (*Dinge zu nehmen, die nur hinzugegeben werden können*). See, for example, *Die Strudlhofstiege*, 687.

47. Croix's name also reflects his demonic character. Doderer's "Grundlagen und Funktionen des Romans" points to a traditional connection between the "hybrid space" of the crossroads and the demonic (WdD 162). Geyrenhoff crosses paths with Croix (DD 840) at a moment when he is at an internal crossroads; the subsequent conversation is characterized as "a kind of central station" (*eine Art von Zentrale*, DD 844–45). In a June 5, 1959, diary entry, Doderer compares the demonic to a void at the base of life, like a plug pulled from a bathtub: "Das Dämonische—äußerste Intensität ohne Richtung, an Ort und Stelle kreisend—öffnet plötzlich ein Loch am Grunde unseres Lebens, als hätte man den Stöpsel einer Badewanne gezogen" (Commentarii I, 189).

48. On bad company and the demonic, Doderer wrote in his diary on March 2, 1962, that "all bad society has something demonic about it [*Alle schlechte Gesellschaft hat etwas Dämonisches*]": "Wir unterliegen in schlechter Gesellschaft keinem messenden Anspruche mehr, dürfen uns aber noch immer für was besseres halten. Keine Gesellschaft zieht so an sich wie die schlechteste" (*Commentarii I*, 322).

49. Doderer, *Repertorium*, 45; abbreviated R.

Conclusion

1. A comparison of Goethe's "Urworte" and Shakespeare's "The Seven Ages of Man" is illuminating: in Shakespeare, the universal moment is expressed mostly in the beginning ("all the world's a stage") and at the end ("mere oblivion," "sans everything"), whereas the intervening development is presented in historically and culturally specific images. Goethe, on the other hand, formulates his "ages" for maximum applicability.

2. See Schmitt's letter to Blumenberg from December 9, 1975 (*Briefwechsel*, 144).

3. A major force behind this shift was certainly Kierkegaard. See his *The Concept of Irony* (part 1, chapter 2.1), which introduces the demonic through Socrates: "the daimonian is a qualification of subjectivity . . . But subjectivity is not consummated in it; it still has something external" (165). As in Goethe's conception, in Kierkegaard it may be possible to find multiple conceptions of the demonic. For example, *The Concept of Anxiety* introduces the demonic under the heading of "Anxiety About the Good" (118). See Jaspers's summary of Kierkegaard's conception in *Psychologie der Weltanschauungen* (428–32). A telling difference with Goethe emerges in Jaspers's conception of *das Dämonische* as *der Dämonische*: "Der Dämonische existiert" (The demonic [person] exists, 429). Goebel's *Charis und Charisma* (79–94) also reflects a strong divergence between Goethe and Kierkegaard. The words "theological" and "psychological" may best capture the difference of emphasis. According to Goebel, Kierkegaard's theological decisionism attempts a systematic definition of what Goethe calls "demonic character" (87). Goethe's *Poetry and Truth*, though psychological in some aspects, is anti-theological insofar as it views the "private" theologies and psychologies of individuals as reactions to the uncontrollable contingency of a more impersonal-objective conception of the demonic as a force. Kierkegaard inverts this, turning the demonic into a pretext for its opposite, the leap of faith. Goebel argues that this famous leap is unable to be permanently stabilized, implying a reversion to Goethe's conception (94).

4. Doderer's de-substantialized and demystified approach sets his novel apart from Thomas Mann's *Doktor Faustus*. Doderer read Mann's novel at the end of the 1940s after the initial failure of his *Demons* project. Mann remains more obviously seduced by the idea of genius and its connection to a specifically German *Geistesgeschichte*, whereas Doderer's idea of "genius in latency" focuses less on the exceptional or demonic quality of geniuses than on the insurmountable obstacles to their development.

5. Blumenberg-Schmitt, *Briefwechsel*, 171.

Adorno, Theodor W. *Dialektik der Aufklärung.* In *Gesammelte Schriften* 3, edited by Rolf Tiedemann. Frankfurt am Main: Suhrkamp, 1944 and 1997.

———. "Spengler nach dem Untergang." In *Gesammelte Schriften* 10.1, 47–71. Edited by Rolf Tiedemann. Frankfurt am Main: Suhrkamp, 1980.

———. "Wird Spengler recht behalten?" In *Gesammelte Schriften* 20.1, 140–48. Edited by Rolf Tiedemann. Frankfurt am Main: Suhrkamp, 1986.

———. "Zur Schlußszene des Faust." In *Noten zur Literatur, Gesammelte Schriften* 11, 129–38. Edited by Rolf Tiedemann. Frankfurt am Main: Suhrkamp, 1997.

Agamben, Giorgio. "Walter Benjamin and the Demonic: Happiness and Historical Redemption." Translated by Daniel Heller-Roazen. In *Potentialities,* 138–59. Stanford, Calif.: Stanford University Press, 1999.

Anderegg, Johannes. *Transformationen: Über Himmlisches und Teuflisches in Goethes Faust.* Bielefeld: Aisthesis Verlag, 2011.

Assmann, Jan. *Moses der Ägypter: Entzifferung einer Gedächtnisspur.* Frankfurt am Main: Fischer, 1998 and 2011.

———. "Translating Gods: Religion as a Factor of Cultural (Un)Translatability." In *Religion: Beyond a Concept,* 139–49. Edited by Hent de Vries. New York: Fordham University Press, 2008.

Axer, Eva. "Alldeutig, zweideutig, undeutig: Walter Benjamins 'Bezwingung' dämonischer Zweideutigkeit im Essay zu Karl Kraus." In *Das Dämonische,* edited by Eva Geulen, Lars Friedrich, and Kirk Wetters. Munich: Fink Verlag, forthcoming 2014.

Bachofen, Johann Jakob. *Das Mutterrecht: Eine Untersuchung über die Gynaikokratie der atlen Welt nach ihrer religiösen und rechtlichen Natur.* Edited by Hans-Jürgen Heinrichs. Frankfurt am Main: Suhrkamp, 1975.

Bamford, James. *The Shadow Factory: The Ultra-Secret NSA from 9/11 to the Eavesdropping on America.* New York: Doubleday, 2008.

Benjamin, Walter. *Gesammelte Briefe.* Edited by the Theodor W. Adorno Archive. *Band VI: 1938–1950,* edited by Christoph Gödde and Henri Lonitz. Frankfurt am Main: Suhrkamp, 1998.

———. *Gesammelte Schriften.* Edited by Rolf Tiedemann. Frankfurt am Main: Suhrkamp, 1991.

Bernhard, Thomas. *Die Kälte: Eine Isolation.* Munich: DTV, 1984.

Bersier, Gabrielle. "Sinnliche Übermacht—übersinnliche Gegenmacht: Die dämonische Verwandlung des klassischen Eros in der Epoche der 'Wahlverwandtschaften.'" In *Verantwortung und Utopie: Zur Literatur der Goethezeit,* 404–18. Edited by Wolfgang Wittkowski. Tübingen: Niemeyer, 1988.

Blanchot, Maurice. *The Book to Come.* Translated by Charlotte Mandell. Stanford, Calif.: Stanford University Press, 2003.

Bloom, Harold. "Lying Against Time: Gnosis, Poetry, Criticism." In *The Rediscovery of Gnosticism (Proceedings of the International Conference on Gnosticism at Yale, New Haven, Connecticut, March 28–31, 1978). Vol. 1, The School of Valentinus*, 57–72. Edited by Bentley Layton. Leiden: E. J. Brill 1980.

Blumenberg, Hans. *Arbeit am Mythos*. Frankfurt am Main: Suhrkamp 1979.

———. "Ausblick auf eine Theorie der Unbegrifflichkeit." In *Schiffbruch mit Zuschauer: Paradigma einer Daseinmetapher*, 85–106. Frankfurt am Main: Suhrkamp, 1979 and 1997.

———. *Die Legitimät der Neuzeit*. Frankfurt am Main: Suhrkamp, 1966 and 1996.

———. *Theorie der Unbegrifflichkeit*. Edited by Anselm Haverkamp. Frankfurt am Main: Suhrkamp, 2007.

———. "Wirklichkeitsbegriff und Möglichkeit des Romans." In *Ästhetische und metaphorologische Schriften*, 47–73. Edited by Anselm Haverkamp. Frankfurt am Main: Suhrkamp, 2001.

Blumenberg, Hans, and Carl Schmitt. *Briefwechsel 1971–1978*. Edited by Alexander Schmitz and Marcel Lepper. Frankfurt am Main: Suhrkamp, 2007.

Borges, José Luis. "Pierre Menard." In *Collected Fictions*, 88–95. Translated by Andrew Hurley. New York: Penguin, 1998.

Brakke, David. *Demons and the Making of the Monk: Spiritual Combat in Early Christianity*. Cambridge, Mass.: Harvard University Press, 2006.

Breidbach, Olaf. *Goethes Metamorphosenlehre*. Munich: Fink, 2006.

Broch, Hermann. *Der Tod des Vergil (Kommentierte Werkausgabe Bd. 4.)* Edited by Paul Michael Lützeler. Frankfurt am Main: Suhrkamp, 1976.

Brodsky, Claudia. *In the Place of Language: Literature and the Architecture of the Referent*. New York: Fordham University Press, 2009.

Buck, Theo. "Dämonisches." In *Goethe Handbuch* 4.1, 179–81. Edited by Hans-Dietrich Dahnke and Regine Otto. Stuttgart: Metzler, 1998.

———. *Goethes "Urworte. Orphisch."* Frankfurt am Main: Peter Lang, 1996.

Bühler, Karl. *Die Krise der Psychologie*. 2nd edition. Jena: Fischer, 1929.

Campe, Rüdiger. "Goethes Mächtiges Überraschen." In *Babel: Festschrift für Werner Hamacher*, 92–101. Edited by Aris Fioretos. Solothurn, Switz.: Urs Engeler, 2008.

Carlyle, Thomas. *Sartor Resartus*. Edited by Kerry McSweeney and Peter Sabor. Oxford: Oxford University Press, 1987.

Cassirer, Ernst. "Bemerkungen zu Faustfragment und Faustdichtung." In *Kleinere Schriften zu Goethe und zur Geistesgeschichte 1925–1944*, 56–80. Edited by Barbara Naumann and Simon Zumsteg. Hamburg: Felix Meiner, 2006.

———. *Goethe und die geschichtliche Welt*. Hamburg: Felix Meiner, 1995.

———. *Philosophie der Aufklärung*. Hamburg: Felix Meiner, 1998.

Chevrel, Eric. "*Die Dämonen*: Doderer und der Fall Dostojewskij(s)." In *Gassen und Landschaften: Heimito von Doderers "Dämonen" vom Zentrum und vom Rande aus betrachtet*, 141–68. Edited by Gerald Sommer. Schriften der Heimito von Doderer-Gesellschaft, Band 3. Würzburg: Königshausen & Neumann, 2004.

Degner, Uta. *Bilder im Wechsel der Töne: Hölderlins Elegien und "Nachtgesänge."* Heidelberg: Winter, 2007.

De Man, Paul. *The Resistance to Theory*. Minneapolis: University of Minnesota Press, 1986.

Doderer, Heimito von. "Aide mémoire zu: 'Die Dämonen der Ostmark.'" Edited by Gerald Sommer. In *Gassen und Landschaften: Heimito von Doderers "Dämonen" vom Zentrum und vom Rande aus betrachtet*, 39–72. Edited by Gerald Sommer. Schriften der Heimito von Doderer-Gesellschaft, Band 3. Würzburg: Königshausen & Neumann, 2004.

———. *Commentarii 1951 bis 1956: Tagebücher aus dem Nachlaß (Erster Band)*. Edited by Wendelin Schmidt-Dengler. Munich: Biederstein, 1976.

———. *Commentarii 1957 bis 1966: Tagebücher aus dem Nachlaß (Zweiter Band)*. Edited by Wendelin Schmidt-Dengler. Munich: Biederstein, 1986.

———. *Das Letzte Abenteuer: Ein Ritter-Roman*. Edited by Wendelin Schmidt-Dengler. Stuttgart: Reclam, 1953 and 2002.

———. *Der Fall Gütersloh*. In *Die Wiederkehr der Drachen: Aufsätze, Traktate, Reden*, 39–109. Edited by Wendelin Schmidt-Dengler. Munich: Beck, 1996.

———. *Die Dämonen*. Munich: Biederstein, 1956.

———. *Die Merowinger oder Die totale Familie*. Munich: DTV, 1995 (Biederstein, 1962).

———. *Die Strudlhofstiege*. Munich: DTV, 1966 (Biederstein, 1951).

———. "Die Wiederkehr der Drachen." In *Die Wiederkehr der Drachen: Aufsätze, Traktate, Reden*, 15–35. Edited by Wendelin Schmidt-Dengler. Munich: Beck, 1996.

———. "Meine neunzehn Lebensläufe." In *Die Erzählungen*, 487–96. Edited by Wendelin Schmidt-Dengler. Munich, 1995.

———. *Repertorium: Ein Begreifbuch von höheren und niederen Lebens-Sachen*. Edited by Dietrich Weber. Munich: Beck, 1996.

———. "Sexualität und der Totale Staat." In *Die Wiederkehr der Drachen: Aufsätze, Traktate, Reden*, 275–98. Edited by Wendelin Schmidt-Dengler. Munich: Beck, 1996.

———. *Tagebücher 1920–1939*. Edited by Wendelin Schmidt-Dengler, Martin Loew-Cadonna, and Gerald Sommer. Munich: Beck, 1996.

———. *Tangenten*. Munich: Beck, 1964.

Dostojewski, Feodor. *Die Dämonen*. Translated by E. K. Rahsin (Less Kaerrick). Edited by Arthur Moeller van den Bruck. Munich: Piper, 1906 (3rd edition in two volumes, 1918).

———. *Die Dämonen*. Translated by E. K. Rahsin (Less Kaerrick). With an afterword by Aleksandar Flaker. Munich: Piper, 1985 (2008).

Eckermann, Johann Peter. *Gespräche mit Goethe*. Edited by Christoph Michel. Frankfurt am Main: Deutscher Klassiker Verlag, 1999.

Fehér, Ferenc. "Am Scheideweg des romantischen Antikapitalismus: Typologie und Beitrag zur deutschen Ideologiegeschichte gelegentlich des Briefwechsels zwischen Paul Ernst und Georg Lukács." In *Die Seele und das Leben: Studien zum frühen Lukács*, 241–327. Frankfurt am Main: Suhrkamp, 1977.

———. "Das Bündnis von Georg Lukács und Béla Balázs bis zur ungarischen Revolution 1918." In *Die Seele und das Leben: Studien zum frühen Lukács*, 131–76. Frankfurt am Main: Suhrkamp, 1977.

———. "Lukács und Benjamin: Affinitäten und Divergenzen." In *Georg Lukács: Jenseits der Polemiken: Beiträge zur Rekonstruktion seiner Philosophie*, 53–70. Edited by Rüdiger Dannemann. Frankfurt am Main: Sendler Verlag, 1986.

Fleischer, Wolfgang. *Das verleugnete Leben: Die Biographie des Heimito von Doderer.* Vienna: Kremayr & Scheriau, 1996.

Förster, Eckart. *Die 25 Jahre der Philosophie.* Frankfurt am Main: Klostermann, 2011.

———. "Goethe and the 'Auge des Geistes.'" *Deutsche Vierteljahrsschrift für Literaturwissenschaft und Geistesgeschichte* 75 (2001): 87–101.

Foucault, Michel. *The Order of Things.* New York: Vintage, 1994.

Freud, Sigmund. *Das Unbehagen in der Kultur.* Frankfurt am Main: Fischer 1994, 2010.

———. "Das Unheimliche." In *Studienausgabe,* vol. 4, 241–74. Edited by Alexander Mitscherlich, Angela Richards, and James Strachey. Frankfurt am Main: Fischer, 2000.

———. *Totem und Tabu: Einige Übereinstimmungen im Seelenleben der Wilden und der Neurotiker.* Frankfurt am Main: Fischer, 2000.

Fukuyama, Francis. *The End of History and the Last Man.* New York: Free Press (Macmillan), 1992.

Garstka, Christoph. *Arthur Moeller van den Bruck und die erste deutsche Gesamtausgabe der Werke Dostojewskijs im Piper-Verlag 1906–1919.* Frankfurt am Main: Peter Lang, 1998.

Geulen, Eva. "Metamorphosen der Metamorphose (Goethe, Cassirer, Blumenberg)." In *Intermedien: Zur kulturellen und artistischen Übertragung,* 203–17. Edited by Alexandra Kleihues, Barbara Naumann, and Edgar Pankow. Zurich: Chronos, 2010.

———. "Nachlese: Simmels Goethebuch und Benjamins Wahlverwandtschaftenaufsatz." (unpublished essay).

———. "Urpflanze (und Goethes Hefte zur Morphologie)." In *Urworte, Zur Geschichte und Funktion erstbegründender Begriffe,* 155–71. Edited by Michael Ott and Tobias Döring. Munich: Fink, 2012.

Gide, André. *The Counterfeiters.* Translated by Dorothy Bussy. New York: Vintage, 1973.

Goebel, Eckart. *Charis und Charisma: Grazie und Gewalt von Winckelmann bis Heidegger.* Berlin: Kadmos, 2006.

Goethe, Johann Wolfgang von. *Sämtliche Werke.* Vol. 24: *Schriften zur Morphologie.* Edited by Dorothea Kuhn. Frankfurt am Main: Deutscher Klassiker Verlag, 1987.

———. *Werke.* Edited by Karl Richter et al. Munich: Carl Hanser Verlag, 1985–1998.

———. *Werke.* Edited by Erich Trunz. Munich: DTV, 1998.

Goodwin, James. *Confronting Dostoyevsky's Demons: Anarchism and the Specter of Bakunin in Twentieth-Century Russia.* New York: Peter Lang, 2010.

Gundolf, Friedrich. *Goethe.* Berlin: Georg Bondi, 1916 and 1925.

Gütersloh, Albert Paris. *Bekenntnisse eines modernen Malers.* Vienna: Verlagsanstalt Dr. Zahn und Dr. Diamant, 1926.

Habermas, Jürgen. "Modernity: An Unfinished Project." In *Habermas and the Unfinished Project of Modernity: Critical Essays on The Philosophical Discourse of Modernity,* 38–55. Edited by Maurizio Passerin d'Entrèves and Seyla Benhabib. Cambridge, Mass.: MIT Press, 1997.

Hadot, Pierre. *N'oublie pas de vivre: Goethe et la tradition des exercices spirituels.* Paris: Albin Michel, 2008.

————. *Philosophy as a Way of Life: Spiritual Exercises from Socrates to Foucault.* Translated by Michael Chase. Malden, Mass.: Blackwell, 1995.

————. *Plotinus, or The Simplicity of Vision.* Translated by Michael Chase. Chicago: University of Chicago Press, 1993.

————. *The Veil of Isis: An Essay on the History of the Idea of Nature.* Translated by Michael Chase. Cambridge, Mass.: Harvard University Press, 2006.

Hamacher, Werner. "Afformativ, Streik." In *Was heißt "Darstellen"?,* 340–71. Edited by Christiaan L. Hart Nibbrig. Frankfurt am Main: Surhkamp, 1994.

————. "Guilt History: Walter Benjamin's Sketch 'Capitalism as Religion.' " Translated by Kirk Wetters. *Diacritics* 32, no. 3–4 (2002): 81–106.

Haverkamp, Anselm. *Figura Cryptica: Theorie der literarischen Latenz.* Frankfurt am Main: Suhrkamp, 2002.

Heidegger, Martin. "Brief über den 'Humanismus.' " In *Wegmarken,* 313–64. Frankfurt am Main: Vittorio Klostermann, 1976.

Helmstetter, Rudolf. *Das Ornament der Grammatik in der Eskalation der Zitate: "Die Strudlhofstiege": Doderers moderne Poetik des Romans und die Rezeptionsgeschichte.* Munich: Fink, 1995.

Herder, Johann Gottfried. "Über die Seelenwanderung." In *Werke in zwei Bänden,* 1:403–40. Edited by Karl-Gustav Gerold. Frankfurt am Main: Deutscher Klassiker Verlag, 1953.

Hoeschen, Andreas. *Das "Dostojewsky"-Projekt: Lukács' neukantianisches Frühwerk in seinem ideengeschichtlichen Kontext.* Tübingen: Niemeyer, 1999.

Hoffmann, Kurt. *Aus Gesprächen mit Thomas Bernhard.* Munich: DTV, 1991 and 2004.

Hofmann, Peter. *Goethes Theologie.* Paderborn: Schöningh, 2001.

Hohendahl, Peter Uwe. "Art Work and Modernity: The Legacy of Georg Lukács." *New German Critique* 42 (Autumn 1987): 33–49.

Hölderlin, Friedrich. *Sämtliche Werke und Briefe* 1. Edited by Jochen Schmidt. Frankfurt am Main: Deutscher Klassiker Verlag, 1992.

Honold, Alexander. "Bernhards Dämonen." In *Thomas Bernhard—eine Einschärfung,* 17–25. Edited by Joachim Hoell, Alexander Honold, and Kai Luehrs-Kaiser. Berlin: Vorwerk 8, 1988.

Janensch, Uwe. *Goethe und Nietzsche bei Spengler: Eine Untersuchung der strukturellen und konzeptionellen Grundlagen des Spenglerschen Systems.* Berlin: Wissenschaftlicher Verlag, 2006.

Jaspers, Karl. *Psychologie der Weltanschauungen.* 3rd edition. Berlin: Julius Springer, 1925.

Jonas, Hans. *Gnosis und Spätantiker Geist: Teil 1: Die Mythologische Gnosis.* Göttingen: Vandenhoeck & Ruprecht, 1934.

Kant, Immanuel. *Der Streit der Fakultäten.* In *Schriften zur Anthropologie, Geschichtsphilosophie, Politik und Pädagogik* 1 (*Werkausgabe* 11), 261–393. Edited by Wilhelm Weischedel. Frankfurt am Main: Suhrkamp, 1964 and 1977.

Kierkegaard, Søren. *The Concept of Anxiety.* Edited and translated by Howard V. Hong and Edna H. Hong. Princeton, N.J.: Princeton University Press, 1980.

———. *The Concept of Irony*. Edited and translated by Howard V. Hong and Edna H. Hong. Princeton, N.J.: Princeton University Press, 1989.

———. *Either/Or*. Edited and translated by Howard V. Hong and Edna H. Hong. Princeton, N.J.: Princeton University Press, 1987.

Kleinlercher, Alexandra. *Zwischen Wahrheit und Dichtung: Antisemitismus und Nationalsozialismus bei Heimito von Doderer*. Cologne: Boehlau, 2011.

Knobloch, Hans-Jörg, and Helmut Koopmann, eds. *Goethe: Neue Ansichten—Neue Einsichten*. Würzburg: Königshausen und Neumann, 2007.

Koktanek, Anton Mirko. "Zum Nachlass Oswald Spenglers." In *Der Aquädukt 1963: Im 200. Jahres ihres Bestehens herausgegeben von der C. H. Beck'schen Verlagsbuchhandlung*, 115–26. Munich: Beck, 1963.

Kraft, Werner. "Über Benjamin." In *Zur Aktualität Walter Benjamins: Aus Anlaß des 80. Geburtstags von Walter Benjamin*, 59–69. Edited by Siegfried Unseld. Frankfurt am Main: Suhrkamp, 1972.

Kreienbrock, Jörg. "Bilderfluchten: Zur Goetherezeption bei Hans Christoph Buch, Hans Blumenberg und Georg Simmel" (unpublished essay).

Krell, David Farrell. *Daimon Life: Heidegger and Life-Philosophy*. Bloomington: Indiana University Press, 1992.

Krois, John Michael. "Urworte: Cassirer als Goethe-Interpret." In *Kulturkritik nach Ernst Cassirer*, 297–324. Edited by Enno Rudolph and Bernd-Olaf Küppers. Hamburg: Felix Meiner, 1995.

Kuhnle, Till R. "Ekelhafte Stadtansichten." In *Die Andere Stadt*, 144–56. Edited by Albrecht Buschmann. Würzburg: Königshausen & Neumann, 2000.

Kunisch, Hermann. *Goethe-Studien*. Berlin: Duncker & Humblot, 1991.

Leacock, N. K. "Character, Silence, and the Novel: Walter Benjamin on Goethe's *Elective Affinities*." *Narrative* 10, no. 3 (October 2002): 277–306.

Liebs, Elke. "Eros des Unmöglichen oder Die Ontologie des Mangels: Goethe und Platon." In *Goethe: Neue Ansichten—Neue Einsichten*, 135–58. Edited by Hans-Jörg Knobloch and Helmut Koopmann. Würzburg: Königshausen & Neumann, 2007.

Lindner, Burkhard. "'Goethes Wahlverwandtschaften': Goethe im Gesamtwerk." In *Benjamin Handbuch: Leben—Werk—Wirkung*, 472–93. Edited by Burkhard Lindner. Stuttgart: Metzler, 2006.

Liska, Vivian. "Die Mortifikation der Kritik: Zum Nachleben von Walter Benjamins *Wahlverwandtschaften*-Essay." In *Spuren, Signaturen, Spiegelungen: Zur Goethe-Rezeption in Europa*, 581–99. Edited by Bernhard Beutler and Anke Bosse. Cologne: Böhlau, 2000.

Liu, Albert. "The Question Concerning Morphology: Language, Vision, History, 1918–1939." Ph.D. diss., Johns Hopkins University, 1996.

Loeffler, Henner. "Dämonen." In *Doderer-ABC: Ein Lexikon für Heimitisten*, 94–104. Munich: Beck, 2000.

Löwith, Karl. *Meaning in History*. Chicago: University of Chicago Press, 1949.

Löwy, Michael. "Der junge Lukács und Dostojewski." In *Georg Lukács: Jenseits der Polemiken: Beiträge zur Rekonstruktion seiner Philosophie*, 23–37. Edited by Rüdiger Dannemann. Frankfurt am Main: Senderl, 1986.

Lübbe, Hermann. "Historisch-politische Exaltationen: Spengler wiedergelesen." In *Spengler heute*, 1–24. Edited by Christian Ludz. Munich: Beck, 1980.

Luehrs, Kai. "Das ausgefallene Zentrum der *Dämonen:* Heimito von Doderers Studien I-III zu den *Dämonen der Ostmark.*" In *Literaturwissenschaftliches Jahrbuch (im Auftrage der Görres-Gesellschaft),* vol. 36, 243–76. Berlin: Duncker & Humblot, 1995.

———. "*Fledermausflügel im Bücherkasten:* Wirkungen Lukács' im Werk Heimito von Doderers." In "*Erst bricht man Fenster: Dann wird man selbst eines.*" *Zum 100. Geburtstag von Heimito von Doderer,* 107–20. Edited by Gerald Sommer and Wendelin Schmidt-Dengler. Riverside, Calif.: Ariadne, 1997.

Lukács, Georg. *Briefwechsel 1902–1917.* Stuttgart: Metzler, 1982.

———. *Die Theorie des Romans: Ein geschichtsphilosophischer Versuch über die Formen der großen Epik.* Neuwied: Luchterhand, 1971.

———. *Die Seele und die Formen: Essays.* Neuwied: Luchterhand, 1971.

———. *Dostojewski Notizen und Entwürfe.* Edited by J. C. Nyíri. Budapest: Akadémiai Kiadó: 1985.

———. *Heidelberger Ästhetik 1916–1918.* In *Werke* 17. Edited by György Márkus and Frank Benseler. Darmstadt: Luchterhand, 1974.

Mandelkow, Karl Robert. *Goethe in Deutschland: Rezeptionsgeschichte eines Klassikers (Band I 1773–1918).* Munich: Beck, 1989.

———. *Goethe in Deutschland: Rezeptionsgeschichte eines Klassikers (Band II 1919–1982).* Munich: Beck, 1980.

Márkus, György. "Die Seele und das Leben: Der junge Lukács und das Problem der 'Kultur.' " In *Die Seele und das Leben: Studien zum frühen Lukács,* 99–130. Frankfurt am Main: Suhrkamp, 1977.

———. "Lukács' erste Ästhetik: Zur Entwicklungsgeschichte der Philosophie des jungen Lukács." In *Die Seele und das Leben: Studien zum frühen Lukács,* 192–240. Frankfurt am Main: Suhrkamp, 1977.

Martínez, Matías. *Doppelte Welten: Struktur und Sinn zweideutigen Erzählens.* Göttingen: Vandenhoeck & Ruprecht, 1996.

Matala de Mazza, Ethel. "Goethe-Dämonologie: Anmerkungen zu Hans Blumenberg." In *Goethes Kritiker,* 154–71. Edited by Karl Eibl and Bernd Scheffer. Paderborn: Mentis, 2001.

Menasse, Robert. *Selige Zeiten, brüchige Welt.* Frankfurt am Main: Suhrkamp, 1991 and 1994.

Milder, Robert. "*Nemo Contra Deum. . .* : Melville and Goethe's 'Demonic.' " In *Ruined Eden of the Present: Hawthorne, Melville and Poe,* 205–44. Edited by G. R. Thompson and Virgil E. Lokke. West Lafayette, Ind.: Purdue University Press, 1981.

Misch, Manfred. " 'Glückliches Ereigniß'—Zur Beziehung zwischen Goethe und Schiller." In *Goethe: Neue Ansichten—Neue Einsichten,* 185–96. Edited by Hans-Jörg Knobloch and Helmut Koopmann. Würzburg: Königshausen & Neumann, 2007.

Mondon, Christine. "Die dämonischen Mächte im Werke Stefan Zweigs im Hinblick auf den Dostojewski-Essay." In *Stefan Zweig und das Dämonische,* 61–67. Edited by Matjaž Birk und Thomas Eicher. Würzburg: Königshausen & Neumann, 2008.

Moretti, Franco. *Modern Epic: The World System from Goethe to Garcia Márquez.* London: Verso, 1996.

Muschg, Walter. "Goethes Glaube an das Dämonische." *Deutsche Vierteljahrs-schrift für Literaturwissenschaft und Geistesgeschichte* 32, no. 3 (1958): 321–43.

Naumann, Barbara. "Talking Symbols: Ernst Cassirer's Repetition of Goethe." In *Kulturkritik nach Ernst Cassirer,* 353–72. Edited by Enno Rudolph and Bernd-Olaf Küppers. Hamburg: Felix Meiner, 1995.

Nicholls, Angus. *Goethe's Concept of the Daemonic: After the Ancients.* New York: Camden House, 2006.

Nicklas, Pascal. *Die Beständigkeit des Wandels: Metamorphosen in Literatur und Wissenschaft.* Hildesheim: Georg Olms, 2002.

Nietzsche, Friedrich. *The Birth of Tragedy out of the Spirit of Music.* Translated by Shaun Whiteside. Edited by Michael Tanner. London: Penguin, 1993.

Nisbet, H. B. "*Das Dämonische:* On the Logic of Goethe's Demonology." *Forum for Modern Studies* 7 (1971): 259–81.

Ophälders, Markus. "Dialektik eines Bildes des Abendlandes." In *Spengler—Ein Denker der Zeitenwende,* 243–50. Edited by Manfred Gangl et al. Frankfurt am Main: Peter Lang, 1996.

Osmancevic, Samir. *Oswald Spengler und das Ende der Geschichte.* Vienna: Turia & Kant, 2007.

Otto, Rudolf. *Das Heilige: Über das Irrationale in der Idee des Göttlichen und sein Verhältnis zum Rationalen.* Munich: Beck, 1963 (2004).

Padel, Ruth. *In and Out of the Mind: Greek Images of the Tragic Self.* Princeton, N.J.: Princeton University Press, 1992.

Petutschnig, Thomas Hans. *Ist er die Mitte? Anmerkungen zu Funktion und Bedeutung der Figur Leonhard Kakabsa in Heimito von Doderers Roman "Die Dämonen."* Vienna: Praesens, 2007.

Pörksen, Uwe. "'Alles ist Blatt': Über Reichweite und Grenzen der natur-wissenschaftlichen Sprache und Darstellungsmodelle Goethes." In *Wissenschaftssprache und Sprachkritik: Untersuchungen zu Geschichte und Gegenwart,* 109–30. Tübingen: Gunter Narr, 1994.

Puszkar, Norbert. "Dämonisches und Dämon: Zur Rolle des Schreibens in Goethes Wahlverwandtschaften." *German Quarterly* 59, no. 3 (Summer 1986): 414–30.

Richards, Robert J. *The Romantic Conception of Life: Science and Philosophy in the Age of Goethe.* Chicago: University of Chicago Press, 2002.

Rosen-Zvi, Ishay. *Demonic Desires: Yetzer Hara and the Problem of Evil in Late Antiquity.* Philadelphia: University of Pennsylvania Press, 2011.

Rothacker, Erich. *Philosophische Anthropologie.* 2nd edition. Bonn: Bouvier, 1966.

Sagnol, Marc. "Recht und Gerechtigkeit bei Walter Benjamin." In *Die Gegen-wart der Gerechtigkeit,* 57–65. Edited by Christoph Demmerling and Thomas Rentsch. Berlin: Akademie Verlag, 1995.

Sauder, Gerhard. "Goethes Ästhetik der Dämmerung." In *Goethe nach 1999: Positionen und Perspektiven,* 45–55. Edited by Matthias Luserke. Göttingen: Vandenhoeck & Ruprecht, 2001.

Schlüter, André. *Moeller van den Bruck: Leben und Werk.* Cologne: Böhlau, 2010.

Schmidt, Jochen. *Geschichte des Genie-Gedankens in der deutschen Literatur, Philosophie und Politik, 1750–1945*. Heidelberg: Winter, 2004.

——. *Goethes Altersgedicht Urworte. Orphisch: Grenzerfahrung und Entgrenzung*. Heidelberg: Winter, 2006.

Schmidt-Dengler, Wendeling. "Der erlösende Finalsatz—Überwindung des Fragmentarischen in Heimito von Doderers *Die Dämonen.*" In *Die Teile und das Ganze: Bausteine der literarischen Moderne in Österreich*, 232–41. Vienna: Zsolnay, 2003.

——. "Teuflisches bei Goethe." In *Goethe: Neue Ansichten—Neue Einsichten*, 59–71. Edited by Hans-Jörg Knobloch and Helmut Koopmann. Würzburg: Königshausen & Neumann, 2007.

Schmitt, Carl. *Politische Theologie II: Die Legende von der Erledigung jeder Politischen Theologie*. 4th edition. Berlin: Duncker & Humblot, 1996.

——. *Römischer Katholizismus und politische Form*. Stuttgart: Klett Cotta, 1954.

Schmitz, Hermann. "Das Ganz-Andere: Goethe und das Ungeheuerliche." In *Goethe und die Verzeitlichung der Natur*, 414–35. Edited by Peter Matussek. Munich: Beck, 1998.

Schrott, Ludwig. *Die Persönlichkeit Hans Pfitzners*. Zurich: Atlantis, 1959.

Seibt, Gustav. *Goethe und Napoleon: Eine historische Begegnung*. Munich: Beck, 2008.

Sewell, Elizabeth. *The Orphic Voice: Poetry and Natural History*. New Haven, Conn.: Yale University Press, 1960.

Siegel, Elke. "The 'Dream Diary': Heimito von Doderer's Poetics of the Journal." In *Schriften der Heimito von Doderer-Gesellschaft*. Würzburg: Königshausen & Neumann, forthcoming.

Simmel, Georg. *Goethe*. Leipzig: Klinkhardt & Biermann, 1913.

Simonis, Annette. *Gestalttheorie von Goethe bis Benjamin: Diskursgeschichte einer deutschen Denkfigur*. Cologne: Böhlau, 2001.

Sloterdijk, Peter, and Thomas Macho, eds. *Weltrevolution der Seele: Eine Lese- und Arbeitsbuch der Gnosis*. Zurich: Artemis & Winkler, 1993.

Sommer, Gerald. "In die 'Sackgasse' und wieder hinaus: Über den zur Romantendenz erhobenen Antisemitismus in Heimito von Doderers 'Aide mémoire.' " In *Gassen und Landschaften: Heimito von Doderers "Dämonen" vom Zentrum und vom Rande aus betrachtet*, 73–86. Edited by Gerald Sommer. Schriften der Heimito von Doderer-Gesellschaft, Band 3. Würzburg: Königshausen & Neumann, 2004.

Spengler, Oswald. *Der Untergang des Abendlandes: Umrisse einer Morphologie der Weltgeschichte*. Munich: DTV, 2006.

Staiger, Emil. *Goethe*. Vols. 1–3. Zurich: Atlantis, 1952, 1956, and 1959.

Steinhagen, Harald. "Die Metamorphose der Pflanzen: Zu Goethes naturwissenschaftlichem Denken." In *Goethe und Italien*, 329–39. Edited by Willi Hirdt and Birgit Tappert. Bonn: Bouvier, 2001.

Stern, Fritz. *The Politics of Cultural Despair: A Study in the Rise of the Germanic Ideology*. Berkeley: University of California Press, 1961.

Strong, Tracy, "Ontologie, Kritik und Enttäuschung." In *Spengler heute*, 74–99. Edited by Christian Ludz. Munich: Beck, 1980.

Suarez, Daniel. *Daemon*. London: Quercus, 2009.

————. *Freedom*™. London: Quercus, 2010.

Swales, Erika. "Johann Wolfgang von Goethe, 'Urworte. Orphisch.'" In *Landmarks in German Poetry*, 57–72. Edited by Peter Hutchinson. Oxford: Peter Lang, 2000.

Szondi, Peter. *Poetik und Geschichtsphilosophie* 1 and 2. *Studienausgabe der Vorlesungen* 2 and 3. Frankfurt am Main: Suhrkamp, 1974.

————. "Überwindung des Klassizismus." In *Schriften* 1:345–412. Frankfurt am Main: Suhrkamp, 1978.

Taubes, Jacob, ed. *Religionstheorie und Politische Theologie, Band. 2: Gnosis und Politik*. Munich: Fink, 1984.

Tillich, Paul. *Das Dämonische: Ein Beitrag zur Sinndeutung der Geschichte*. Tübingen: Mohr-Siebeck, 1926.

Van Dijk, Arjan. "Das Dämonische als moderne Rezeptionskategorie: Dargestellt an Goethes *Egmont* und *Torquato Tasso*." *Neophilologus* 83, 427–43. Dordrecht Netherlands: Kluwer, 1999.

Volz, Paul. *Das Dämonische in Jahwe*. Tübingen: Mohr-Siebeck, 1924.

Weber, Dietrich. "'Welch ein gewaltiger Apperzipierer!' Zu einigen Goethe-Zitaten bei Heimito von Doderer." In *Doderer-Miniaturen*, 170–76. Würzburg: Königshausen & Neumann, 2004.

Wellbery, David. *The Specular Moment: Goethe's Early Lyric and the Beginnings of Romanticism*. Stanford, Calif.: Stanford University Press, 1996.

Wetters, Kirk. "'Das Gefühl eines Ungeheuerlichen': Monster-Forms in Heimito von Doderer's *Die Dämonen*." Schriften der Heimito von Doderer-Gesellschaft. Würzburg: Königshausen & Neumann, forthcoming 2014.

————. "Konjunktivisches Erzählen in Heimito von Doderers *Die Dämonen*." *Zeitschrift für deutsche Philologie*, forthcoming.

————. *The Opinion System: Impasses of the Public Sphere from Hobbes to Habermas*. New York: Fordham University Press, 2008.

————. "Working Over Philosophy: Hans Blumenberg's Reformulations of the Absolute." *Telos* 158 (2012): 100–118.

Willer, Stefan. "Urwort: Zum Konzept und Verfahren der Etymologie." In *Urworte, Zur Geschichte und Funktion erstbegründender Begriffe*, 34–55. Edited by Michael Ott and Tobias Döring. Munich: Fink, 2012.

Wundt, Wilhelm. *Völkerpsychologie: Eine Untersuchung der Entwicklungsgesetze von Sprache, Mythus und Sitte. Vierter Band: Mythus und Religion*. Leipzig: Wilhelm Engelmann, 1910.

Zweig, Stefan. *Der Kampf mit dem Dämon*. Frankfurt am Main: Fischer, 2007.

INDEX

Adorno, Theodor, 96, 98, 111, 213n33, 221n10, 228n15
aesthetics, 13, 39, 57
Agamben, Giorgio, 15, 212n26, 223n1
Aichinger, Gerhard, 170–71, 172
Aristotle, 5, 6, 27, 101
Arnold, Gottfried, 51

Bachofen, Johann Jakob, 214n1, 215n11
Bamford, James, 234n38
Benjamin, Walter, 10, 13, 16, 73, 111–33, 161, 226nn25–28; on analogy and affinity, 118–20, 191; on character, 124; on criticism, 125–26, 128–29, 132, 133; on the demonic, xi, 10, 13, 56, 111–15, 122–26, 129, 133, 186, 194, 198; on equality, 113–14; on formulaic language, 116–18; Goethe and, 16, 18, 21, 74, 111, 113, 117, 120–22, 125–33; on law, 112–15, 123, 224n9, 225n12; on the mythic, 112–14, 121, 123–24, 125–26, 128–29, 132, 133, 150, 162, 167, 197; on the novel, 19, 132; on prehistory, 112, 114–15, 224n8; on sentimentalism, 120; on similitude, 118; Spengler and, 111–12, 115, 117, 119–20, 122, 223–24nn4–5; on tragedy and comedy, 123–24, 226n24
works: "Analogy and Affinity," 118–20; *Arcades Project*, 120, 121; "Critique of Violence," 112, 113–15; "Fate and Character," 113, 115–17, 122–25, 236n45; "Goethe's Elective Affinities," 16, 59–60, 111, 116–17, 122, 125–33, 167, 186, 226nn21–22, 226nn26–27, 229n21, 231n6, 235n41, 235n43; "Karl Kraus," 223n1, 226n22; "The Storyteller," 19, 111; *Trauerspielbuch*, 115, 120,

122, 125–26, 130–31, 133, 168, 226n24, 230n32. *See also under* fate; Gundolf, Friedrich; modernity; morphology
Benn, Gottfried, 211n18
Bernhard, Thomas, 165–67, 168, 231n4
Bildungstrieb, 221n17
Blanchot, Maurice, 140, 229n19
Blumenberg, Hans, 65, 104, 117, 228n16; on the demonic, xi, 3, 5, 6–9, 12–13, 66, 109, 159, 210n9, 210n11, 210nn13–15, 212n24; on form, 215n9; on myth, 7, 225n12; on political theology, 197; on prehistory, 215n5, 223n33; on Rothacker, 226n20; and Schmitt, 12, 158–59, 196, 197; self-assertion and, 53, 195
Boisserée, Sulpiz, 21, 22
Borges, Jorge Luis, 228n11
Brakke, David, 14–15
Broch, Hermann, 228n8
Brodsky, Claudia, 209n4
Buck, Theo, 23
Byron, George Gordon, Lord, 90

Caesar, Julius, 72, 73, 105, 109
Cagliostro, Alessandro di, 84
Carlyle, Thomas, xii, 10; *Sartor Resartus*, v, 211n20, 230n27
Cassirer, Ernst, 216n17, 219n12
Cervantes, Miguel de, 162, 169, 230n27
Creuzer, Friedrich, 21, 22, 24
Cuvier, Georges, 43, 103, 227n1

daemon (*daimon*), classical, 5, 6, 8, 12–15, 227n3
Dante Alighieri, 76, 148, 154, 167, 230n27
Darwin, Charles, 104
Degner, Uta, 221n17
Delph, Demoiselle, 77, 79